WEBSTER'S
FAMILY
ENCYCLOPEDIA

WEBSTER'S FAMILY ENCYCLOPEDIA

VOLUME 5

1995 Edition

Exclusively distributed by
Archer Worldwide, Inc.
Great Neck, New York, USA

Abbreviations Used in Webster's Family Encyclopedia

AD	After Christ	ht	height	N.M.	New Mexico
Adm.	Admiral	i.e.	that is	NNE	north-northeast
Ala.	Alabama	in	inches	NNW	north-northwest
Apr	April	Ind.	Indiana	Nov	November
AR	Autonomous	Ill.	Illinois	NW	northwest
	Republic	Jan	January	N.Y.	New York
at no	atomic number	K	Kelvin	OAS	Organization of
at wt	atomic weight	Kans.	Kansas		American States
Aug	August	kg	kilograms	Oct	October
b.	born	km	kilometers	Okla.	Oklahoma
BC	Before Christ	kph	kilometers per	OPEC	Organization of
bp	boiling point		hour		Petroleum Ex-
C	Celsius, Centi-	kW	kilowatts		porting Countries
	grade	lb	pounds	Pa.	Pennsylvania
c.	circa	Lt.	Lieutenant	PLO	Palestine Libera-
Calif.	California	Lt. Gen.	Lieutenant		tion Organization
Capt.	Captain		General	Pres.	President
CIS	Commonwealth	m	meters	R.I.	Rhode Island
	of Independent	M. Sgt.	Master Sergeant	S	south, southern
	States	Mar	March	S.C.	South Carolina
cm	centimeters	Mass.	Massachusetts	SE	southeast
Co.	Company	Md.	Maryland	Sen.	Senator
Col.	Colonel	mi	miles	Sept	September
Conn.	Connecticut	Mich.	Michigan	Sgt.	Sergeant
d.	died	Minn.	Minnesota	sq mi	square miles
Dec	December	Miss.	Mississippi	SSE	south-southeast
Del.	Delaware	mm	millimeters	SSW	south-southwest
E	east, eastern	Mo.	Missouri	SW	southwest
EC	European Com-	MP	Member of	Tenn.	Tennessee
	munity		Parliament	Tex.	Texas
e.g.	for example	mp	melting point	UN	United Nations
est	estimated	mph	miles per hour	US	United States
F	Fahrenheit	N	north, northern	USSR	Union of Soviet
Feb	February	NATO	North Atlantic		Socialist
Fl. Lt.	Flight Lieutenant		Treaty		Republics
Fla.	Florida		Organization	Va.	Virginia
ft	feet	NE	northeast	Vt.	Vermont
Ga.	Georgia	Neb.	Nebraska	W	west, western
Gen.	General	N.H.	New Hampshire	wt	weight
Gov.	Governor	N.J.	New Jersey		

Hafiz, Shams al-Din Muhammad (?1326–90) Persian lyric poet, born at Shiraz, where he lived and worked as a religious teacher and copyist of manuscripts. He subsequently became court poet. He is the acknowledged master of the *ghazal,* a short lyric poem on the traditional subjects of love and wine, which are often treated symbolically (the beloved, whether male or female, representing God, and wine symbolizing ecstasy). About 500 *ghazals* are attributed to him. They have been widely translated; Goethe's German versions are perhaps the best known.

hafnium (Hf) A dense ductile metal, first detected in zircon ($ZrSiO_4$) in 1923 and named for the Latin (Hafnia) for Copenhagen, where it was discovered. It is chemically similar to zirconium and the two elements are difficult to separate. The capacity of hafnium to absorb neutrons is used to control nuclear reactors, especially in submarines. Its compounds include the chloride ($HfCl_4$) and other halides, the oxide (HfO_2), the carbide (HfC), and the nitride (Hf_3N_4). At no 72; at wt 178.49; mp 3906°F (2150°C); bp 9762°F (5400°C).

Haganah (Hebrew: defense) The irregular organization of the early Jewish settlers in Palestine established in 1920 to counter the attacks of the Palestinian Arabs. After the partition of Palestine in 1947, the Haganah became the defense force of the Jewish state, coordinating opposition to the Palestinian and British forces, and in 1948 the national army of the state of Israel.

Hagen 51 22N 7 27E A city in NW Germany, in North Rhine-Westphalia in the *Ruhr. It has iron and steel, textile, and paper industries. Population (1991 est): 214,500.

Hagen, Walter Charles (1892–1969) US professional golfer, who did much to popularize the game with his exhibition matches and his extrovert personality. Between 1914 and 1929 he won four British and two US Open championships and five US Professional Golfers Association championships.

hagfish A fishlike vertebrate, 16–31 in (40–80 cm) long, sometimes called slime eel, belonging to a family (*Myxinidae*; about 20 species) of *cyclostomes. The eel-like body has 5–16 pairs of gill slits and a sucking mouth surrounded by several thick barbels. They occur on or near the sea bottom in cold regions and feed on dead or dying fish. Hagfishes are initially hermaphrodites but develop either male or female sex organs; fertilization is internal and the eggs hatch to produce young that resemble adults.

haggadah (*or* aggadah) **1.** Nonlegal portions of the Jewish *Midrash, as opposed to *halakhah. **2.** The liturgy recited in the Jewish home over the *Passover meal (*seder*). It contains a narrative of the Exodus from Egypt and various commentaries and hymns.

Haggai An Old Testament prophet. **The Book of Haggai** contains four addresses delivered after the *Babylonian exile (c. 520 BC). Their purpose is to encourage the completion of the Temple; the prophet rebukes the people's failure to complete the rebuilding of it, but prophesies a return of divine favor when it is rebuilt.

Haggard, Sir H(enry) Rider (1856–1925) British adventure novelist. His five years in government service in South Africa provided the background of his first and most popular novel, *King Solomon's Mines* (1885), notable for a sympathetic treatment of black Africans, reflecting his own liberal views. Of his many later romances, *She* (1887) is the best known.

haggis A traditional Scottish meat dish. Haggis is made from minced sheep's heart, liver, and lungs with onion, oatmeal, suet, seasonings, lemon juice, and stock. The ingredients are stuffed into a bag made from the sheep's stomach or a substitute and boiled for several hours.

Hague, The (Dutch name: 's Gravenhage *or* Den Haag) 52 05N 4 16E The seat of government of the Netherlands and capital of South Holland province. It developed as a settlement surrounding a 13th-century hunting lodge and became the seat of the States General of the seven United Provinces of the Netherlands in the 16th century. It is the residence of the court and the International Court of Justice is located here. Notable buildings include the 13th-century Binnenhof, in which the government is housed. It is chiefly a commercial and residential center with some light industry. Its port, Scheveningen, is a major herring-fishing center and the most popular Dutch seaside resort. Population (1977 est): 471,137.

THE HAGUE *The Peace Palace, home of the International Court of Justice, which was completed in 1913.*

Hague Peace Conferences (1899, 1907) Two international congresses on *disarmament, held at The Hague (Netherlands). The first conference, attended by representatives of 26 countries, codified some of the rules of war as recommended by the *Geneva Convention and instituted the permanent Court of Arbitration at The Hague. However, no agreement was reached on disarmament. The second conference, attended by 44 delegates, adopted further conventions on war (*see* neutrality) but again failed to limit armaments.

Hahn, Otto (1879–1968) German chemist and physicist. With Lise *Meitner he discovered protactinium in 1918. He continued to work with Meitner until she was forced to leave Germany in 1938. Together they discovered the process of nuclear fission. Hahn was unwilling to publish the results of this work, but Meitner did so from Sweden in 1939 and *Bohr took the information to the US. Although Hahn remained in Germany for the rest of his life, he did not work on Germany's unsuccessful attempt to make an atom bomb. In 1944 he was awarded the Nobel Prize in chemistry.

Hahnemann, Samuel Christian Friedrich (1755–1843) German physician and founder of *homeopathy. Hahnemann's methods aroused controversy among his contemporaries and he was forced to leave his practice in Leipzig, eventually settling in Paris.

hahnium (Ha) An artificial transuranic element, synthesized in the US in 1970 by bombarding californium-249 with nitrogen-15 in a particle accelerator and possibly also in the Soviet Union in 1967 by a different method. Named for Otto Hahn. At no 105; at wt 260.

Haifa 32 49N 34 59E A city in NE Israel, on the Mediterranean coast by Mount Carmel. It was the scene of fighting in the 1948–49 Arab-Israeli conflict and has since developed into a manufacturing town based on the deepwater port (opened 1933). Haifa University was founded in 1963. Population (1975 est): 227,200.

Haig, Alexander Meigs, Jr. (1924–   ) US Army officer and statesman; secretary of state (1981–82). A graduate of West Point (1947), he held positions ranging from aide to Gen. Douglas MacArthur and assistant to Robert McNamara, Henry Kissinger, and Richard Nixon to Army vice chief of staff (1973), chief of the White House staff (1973), and commander of NATO forces in Europe (1974–79); he retired as a full general. Appointed secretary of state by President *Reagan, he resigned over policy difference with the president. He recounted his experiences in *Caveat* (1984).

hail The approximately spherical ice pellets that fall from cumulonimbus clouds. These have been known to weigh almost 2.2 lb (1 kg). They originate as small ice particles around which alternate concentric layers of clear and opaque ice freeze as the ice pellets alternately fall or are uplifted within a cloud. Hailstorms occur most frequently in the continental interiors of temperate latitudes.

Haile Selassie I (1892–1975) Emperor of Ethiopia (1930–36, 1941–74). In 1936 Haile Selassie had to flee to England after the invasion by the Italians, against whom he personally fought, but was restored to the throne by the Allies in 1941. He did much to modernize Ethiopia and became a prominent figure in international affairs. However, his absolute rule provoked opposition and he was deposed by a military coup.

Hainan Island A Chinese island, the largest in the South China Sea, apart from Taiwan, and separated from the mainland by **Hainan Strait**. It is one of China's least developed regions. The aboriginal population has moved into the mountainous forested center and S as Chinese farmers have settled the N coastal plain. Rubber and timber are produced and iron ore and other minerals are mined. Area: 13,124 sq mi (33,991 sq km). Population (1990): 6,557,482. Capital: Haikou.

Hainaut (Flemish name: Henegouwen; French name: Hainault) A province in SW Belgium, bordering on France. It contains important coal fields, and industries include iron and steel processing. Area: 1466 sq mi (3997 sq km). Population (1975 est): 1,321,846. Capital: Mous.

Haiphong 20 50N 106 41E A city in N Vietnam, on the Red River delta. As Hanoi's port and an industrial center much developed after 1954 with Soviet and Chinese aid, it was severely bombed during the Vietnam War. Textiles, phosphates, and plastics are manufactured and minerals and rice exported. Population (1989): 456,000.

hair The threadlike structures forming the body covering of mammals. Each hair grows from the base of a sheath (hair follicle) embedded in the inner layer (dermis) of the *skin but only a few cells at its root are living. The rest consists of scaly dead cells made largely of *keratin and other proteins. Color is determined by the amount of *melanin pigment in hair. In most mammals hair forms an insulating and protective coat (the pelage), which reduces heat loss from the body and often provides camouflage. In humans hair is important only for personal adornment. Similar structures in lower animals (e.g. insects) often have a sensory function, and plants possess hairs on roots, stems, and leaves.

hairstreak A butterfly belonging to the family *Lycaenidae* and characterized by fine white streaks on the underwings and a small "tail" on each hindwing. Both Old and New World species show a great variety of coloration.

hairy frog A *frog, *Astylosternus robustus,* of the Cameroons. In the breeding season the skin on the sides and thighs of male frogs develops hairlike filaments, containing many blood vessels, that assist in breathing and compensate for its much reduced lungs. The females grow no hairs.

Haiti, Republic of A country in the Caribbean Sea, occupying the W third of the island of Hispaniola (the Dominican Republic occupies the E two thirds). Much of the country is mountainous and forested,with fertile plains lying between the three main mountain ranges. It is subject to hurricanes. The majority of the population is of African descent, with a minority of mulattoes. *Economy*: mainly agricultural, mostly organized in small farms. The main crops are coffee (the principal export), sugar, rice, bananas, and sisal. Mineral resources are largely unexploited although some bauxite and copper are mined. Hydroelectricity is an important source of power. Small industries are being encouraged, particularly manufactures for export. *History*: the island was discovered by Columbus in 1492 and became a Spanish colony. The Spanish virtually wiped out the native Indian population and large numbers of African slaves were imported. The E part was ceded to France in 1697, becoming the most prosperous of the French colonies, and the remainder was temporarily ceded between 1795 and 1809. The slave leader *Toussaint L'Ouverture briefly extended his rule over the whole island and in 1804, under General *Dessalines, Haiti gained its independence. A period of unrest was followed by union with the rest of the island (1822–44). For most of the time since it has been a republic; there was a brief period of occupation by the US (1915–34). After a series of coups Dr François *Duvalier ("Papa Doc") came to power in 1957 and was succeeded in 1971 by his son, Jean-Claude Duvalier ("Baby Doc"). Under Jean-Claude poor economic conditions caused many Haitians to flee to the US by boat, which led to refugee problems in Florida. Additionally, tourism in Haiti declined sharply in the 1980s because of the link between AIDS and Haitian immigrants in the US. The Duvalier regime was overthrown in 1986, but the country remained unsettled, and violence prevented the development of stable government. After Haiti's first free elections, Roman Catholic priest Jean-Bertrand Aristide succeeded to the presidency in 1991. He was ousted by the military eight months later. The US did not recognize the new government and suspended the economic aid that had begun with Aristide's presidency. Thousands of Haitians fled to the US, but many were turned back under a 1981 agreement. In the spring of 1992, negotiations to return Aristide to the presidency began but soon reached an impasse, despite international economic sanctions, designed to force Haiti's military to cooperate, that were imposed in 1993. Official language: French; Creole is widely spoken. Official religion: Roman Catholic. Area: 10,700 sq mi (27,750 sq km). Population (1990 est): 6,409,000. Capital and main port: Port-au-Prince.

hajj The pilgrimage to Mecca that every able Muslim is required to make, if means permit, at least once in his lifetime during the first half of the last month of the Islamic year. The pilgrimage includes circumambulations of the *Kaaba and visits to other holy places.

hake A food fish, of the genus *Merluccius,* that is related to *cod and occurs off European, African, and American coasts. Its elongated body, up to about 40 in (1 m) long, is dark gray above and lighter below, with two dorsal fins, the second running to the tail and matching the anal fin.

Hakka A Chinese ethnic minority group found in the provinces of Canton and Fujian and in Taiwan and Chinese settlements in East Asia. The Hakkas (guest people) migrated S from N China in the unrest of the 12th and 13th centuries and for several centuries were social outcasts, having brought with them the different dialect and customs that they still retain.

Hakluyt, Richard (c. 1553–1616) English geographer. As a clergyman he served in various posts, but his chief interest was in exploration, navigation, and the establishment of a colony in Virginia. His major work, *The Principal Navigations, Voyages, Traffics, and Discoveries of the English Nation* . . . (1 vol, 1589; 3 vols, 1598–1600), stimulated English overseas trade and colonization.

Hakodate 41 46N 140 44E A port in Japan, in SW Hokkaido on the Tsugaru Strait. It contains Japan's only Western-style fort (1855). Industries include fishing and ship building. Population (1990): 307,249.

halakhah Jewish law. The Hebrew word is used in different ways, either for the law as a whole or an individual regulation. The main halakhic sources are the *Torah, *Mishnah and *Talmuds, the gaonic responsa (*see* gaon), and the medieval codes (e.g. those of *Maimonides and Joseph *Caro). The halakhah embraces more than law: it governs every aspect of life and also embodies theological ideas. The authority of halakhah is one of the main points of disagreement between traditional and *Reform Judaism.

Halcyone In Greek legend, daughter of *Aeolus. She threw herself into the sea after her husband, Ceyx of Thrachis, drowned, and they were both transformed into kingfishers.

Hale, Nathan (1755–76) US patriot. A graduate of Yale University and a schoolteacher, he joined the Continental Army in 1775 and volunteered to spy on British Gen. William *Howe's activities on Long Island. He was captured (1776) and within a day hanged as a spy. The words "I only regret that I have but one life to lose for my country" are attributed to him while on the scaffold.

Haleakala National Park A national park on E Maui Island, E Hawaii. Established in 1961, the park has been a part of the larger Hawaii National Park since 1916. The volcano Haleakala, dormant since 1790, stands 10,023 ft (3055 m) high. Area: 34 sq mi (88 sq km).

Hale Observatories The group of observatories comprising the Palomar Observatory, Mount Wilson Observatory, Big Bear Solar Observatory, all in California, and Las Campanas Observatory, near La Serena, Chile. They are sponsored by the Californian Institute of Technology and the Carnegie Institution, Washington. The principal telescopes are the famous 200 in (5 m) reflector and a 48 in (1.2 m) *Schmidt telescope (Palomar), the oldest 100 in (2.5 m) reflector (Mount Wilson), and a new 100 in (2.5 m) reflector (Las Campanas). They are named for the US astronomer G. E. Hale (1868–1938), who founded the Mount Wilson Observatory.

Halévy, Jacques François (Fromental Elias Levy; 1799–1862) French composer of Jewish origin. A pupil of Cherubini at the Paris conservatory, he won the Prix de Rome in 1819. He composed ballets, incidental music, cantatas, and over 30 operas, including *La Juive* (1835).

Haley, Alex Palmer (1921–92) US author. He wrote *The Autobiography of Malcolm X* (1965) after retiring from the Coast Guard (1939–59) and then began researching his family lineage, which brought him back to Africa. From this research and from memories recounted by his grandmother in Henning, Tenn., evolved *Roots: The Saga of an American Family* (1976), which was serialized on television (1977).

half-life The time taken for half the atoms in a sample of a radioactive isotope to decay. It is therefore a measure of the activity of an isotope. A very active isotope may have a half-life of only a millionth of a second, whereas some more stable isotopes have half-lives of millions of years.

half-timber work A building technique used since ancient times. It involves constructing a wooden skeleton for a building, which is then filled out with either plasterwork or brick. Frequently the frame is left exposed. A quickly built and strong structure, it is best suited to temperate climates. The technique was frequently used in 15th- and 16th-century England.

halibut A *flatfish of the genus *Hippoglossus,* especially *H. hippoglossus*—a large food fish, up to about 7 ft (2 m) long, found in N Atlantic coastal waters. The eyed (right) side is brown or dark green with mottling. Family: *Pleuroncetidae.*

Other halibuts include the Greenland halibut and the California halibut, which belong to the family *Bothidae.*

Halicarnassus (modern name: Bodrum) An ancient city of *Caria on the SW coast of Asia Minor. Its rulers included *Artemisia and Mausolus, who made Halicarnassus his capital (c. 370 BC) and is remembered chiefly for his tomb, the *Mausoleum. Herodotus, the Greek historian, was born here.

Halifax 44 38N 63 35W A city and major port in E Canada, the capital of Nova Scotia on the Atlantic Ocean. Founded as a British naval base (1749), it dominates the cultural life, commerce, and industry of the *Maritime Provinces. Its industries include shipbuilding, oil refining, steel, and food processing. Population (1991): 114,455.

Halifax, Charles Montagu, 1st Earl of (1661–1715) English statesman. A Whig MP (1689–95), as a lord of the treasury (1692–94) he initiated the national debt and set up the *Bank of England (1694) and as chancellor of the exchequer (1694–95) he introduced a new coinage. In 1697 he became first lord of the treasury but in 1699 was forced by the Tories to resign; he again held the post in 1714–15. He was a patron of writers, including the playwright *Congreve.

halitosis Bad breath. Very foul-smelling breath may be caused by infection in the mouth, teeth, tonsils, or lungs and sometimes by stomach disease. The mild odor that many people have needs no treatment except regular cleaning of the teeth.

Halle 51 30N 11 59E A city in E central Germany, on the Saale River. The birthplace of Handel, Halle has many fine old buildings. Its diverse industries include sugar refining and coal mining. The university was founded in 1694. Population (1990 est): 310,000.

Halleck, Fitz-Greene (1790–1867) US poet. A bank employee in New York City, he was part of the Knickerbocker group of poets and coauthored the "Croaker Papers" (1819), satire published in the New York *Evening Post.* He also wrote "On the Death of Joseph Rodman Drake" (1820), "Marco Bozzarius" (1825), and "Young America" (1865).

Hall effect If a conductor carrying an electric current is placed in a magnetic field, so that the field and the current are at right angles to each other, an electric field appears across the material. The electric field is perpendicular to both the current and the magnetic field. The effect is due to the force experienced by all moving charges in a magnetic field: the charges flowing in the material are displaced to one side thus creating a potential difference. Named for Edwin H. Hall (1855–1938).

Haller, Albrecht von (1708–77) Swiss biologist, poet, and one of the founders of modern physiology. Haller showed how the stimulation of a nerve caused contraction of the muscle to which it was attached. He also studied the brain, heart, breathing mechanisms, and embryology; his works include *Elementa physiologiae corporis humani* (8 vols, 1757–66) and four large bibliographies of botany, anatomy, surgery, and medicine. His best-known poem is *Die Alpen.*

Halley, Edmund (1656–1742) British astronomer. He was the first to realize that *comets do not appear randomly but have periodic orbits. In 1705 he identified a particular comet, now known as **Halley's comet**, as having a period of 76 years. The years of its appearance in the 20th century are 1910 and 1986. He also discovered that stars have a proper motion of their own (1718). A friend of Sir Isaac Newton, he had earlier financed the publication of Newton's *Principia.*

hallmarks A set of marks stamped onto gold or silver objects manufactured in the UK, as a guarantee of purity. Each article has up to five marks: the mark of the assay office, an assay mark to indicate quality, a date mark, the sovereign's head (between 1784 and 1890), and the maker's mark. Gold articles also have a mark to indicate their purity in *karats.

Halloween Oct 31, the eve of All Saints' Day. The name is a contraction of All Hallows (hallowed or holy) Eve. In pre-Christian Britain, Oct 31 was the eve of New Year, when the souls of the dead were thought to revisit their homes. After it became a Christian festival supernatural associations continued, and Halloween customs include the shaping of a demon's face from a hollow pumpkin, in which a candle is then placed. Children, wearing disguises, go from door to door on Halloween demanding "treats" on penalty of "tricks."

Hallstatt The phase of the central European Iron Age (700–500 BC) preceding *La Tène. It is named for the site in the Salzkammergut in Austria, which is famous for its salt mines. Earlier Bronze Age (*see* Urnfield) people in the same area (1200–700 BC) are often included under the term. The wealth of Iron Age Hallstatt depended on extensive trade. Characteristic artifacts were iron swords and elaborate bronze vessels decorated with geometric patterns, solar symbols, or ducks. Wagon burial of chieftains was practiced, e.g. at Vix (France).

hallucination A vivid but false perception of something that is not really there. Any sense can be affected. It may be a result of mental illness, especially *psychosis, when the commonest forms are hearing voices and seeing frightening visions. It can also be caused by drugs, epilepsy, disease of the brain, and sensory deprivation. Transient hallucinations can be experienced by normal people, especially when they are falling asleep (hypnagogic hallucinations) or waking up (hypnopompic hallucinations) or if they have been bereaved (grief hallucinations, of the person who has been lost).

hallucinogens Drugs that produce hallucinations due to their stimulant action on the brain. Such drugs are also described as psychedelic. Hallucinogens, which include *cannabis and *LSD, tend to lead to some form of *drug dependence. The ability of any given hallucinogen to produce a hallucination depends very much on the personality of the individual. Some unlikely drugs (e.g. digitalis) may provoke hallucinations in susceptible individuals.

halogens The elements forming group VII of the *periodic table: fluorine, chlorine, bromine, iodine, and astatine. In chemical reactions they tend to form negative ions or covalent bonds and they have a valence of 1. All are reactive, particularly fluorine and chlorine. They produce salts on contact with metals ("halogen" means salt-yielding) and react with other nonmetals and many organic compounds.

Hals, Frans (c. 1581–1666) Dutch painter of portraits and scenes of everyday life. He was born in Antwerp but worked mainly in Haarlem. Apart from his *Laughing Cavalier* (1624), he is best known for his group portraits, such as those of the companies of archers and musketeers, which are characterized by lively expressions and gestures. Later works, such as *Lady-Governors of the Almshouse at Haarlem* (c. 1664), influenced by *Rembrandt, are more somber and show a greater sympathy for character.

Halsey, William Frederick (1882–1959) US naval officer. He graduated from the Naval Academy in 1904. After service aboard a destroyer in World War I and training as an aviator, he commanded the South Pacific area (1942–44) and the Third Fleet (1944–45) during World War II. His leadership contributed significantly to the American effort in the battles of *Guadalcanal and the Coral Sea (1942), *Leyte Gulf (1944), and Okinawa (1945), which marked the rise of aircraft as decisive weapons in naval warfare.

Hälsingborg (*or* Helsingborg) 56 05N 12 45E A seaport in S Sweden, on the Sound opposite Helsingør, Denmark. It changed hands several times between Denmark and Sweden before finally becoming Swedish in 1710. An industrial center, it has an important ship building industry. Population (1985 est): 105,500.

Hama 35 09N 36 44E A city in W Syria. It dates from Hittite times and still possesses the medieval water-wheels up to 89 ft (27 m) in diameter used for irrigation. It is mainly an agricultural and commercial center. Population (1990 est): 229,000.

Hamadan 34 46N 48 35E A city in W central Iran. Hamadan lies at a high altitude, and visitors are attracted by the cool summers; the winters, however, are severe. A university was founded there in 1973. Population (1986): 272,500.

hamadryas A small *baboon, *Papio hamadryas,* of NE Africa and Saudi Arabia; 40–55 in (100–140 cm) long including the tail (16–24 in [40–60 cm]), hamadryas baboons have a long silvery-brown mane, pinkish face, and red buttocks and live in groups with a complex social structure. They were sacred animals to the ancient Egyptians.

Hamamatsu 34 42N 137 42E A city in Japan, in S central Honshu. A commercial and industrial center, its manufactures include musical instruments, textiles, and motorcycles. Population (1990): 534,624.

Hamburg 53 33N 10 00E A city in N Germany, on the Elbe and Alster Rivers. A major port, it is also an important cultural center, with a university (1919), art galleries, and an opera house (1678). It is the birthplace of Mendelssohn and Brahms. Its many industries include ship building, engineering, and food processing. *History*: in 834 AD it was made the seat of a missionary archbishop. Its alliance with Lübeck (1241) became the basis of the Hanseatic League. It was a trading center from the Middle Ages and the first German stock exchange was established there (1558). It was severely bombed during World War II. Population (1991 est): 1,640,000.

Hamburg One of the constituent states in Germany, in the N, comprising the city of *Hamburg, its surrounding area, and two islands in the Elbe estuary. Area: 289 sq mi (748 sq km). Population (1990): 1,652,000.

Hamelin (German name: Hameln) 52 06N 9 21E A city in N Germany, in Lower Saxony on the Weser River. Its many Renaissance houses include the Ratcatcher's House (1602–03), associated with the legendary Pied Piper. Manufactures include carpets and chemicals. Population (1984): 56,300.

Hamersley Range A mountain range of N Western Australia. It extends W–E between the Fortesque and Ashburton Rivers, reaching 4024 ft (1227 m) at Mount Bruce, and contains large deposits of iron ore.

Hamhŭng (*or* Hamheung) 39 54N 127 35E A city in E central North Korea. Its industry was bombed during the Korean War (1950–53) but has been restored and developed. The principal manufactures are synthetic textiles, chemicals, and machinery. Its seaport, Hungnam, lies to the SE of the city. Population: Hamhŭng-Hungnam (1987 est): 700,000.

Hamilcar Barca (died c. 229 BC) Carthaginian general and Hannibal's father. Commander in Sicily during the first *Punic War, he negotiated peace in 241. After suppressing rebellious mercenaries in Carthage, he invaded Spain, accompanied by the young Hannibal. He was drowned after the siege of Helice.

Hamilton 43 15N 79 50W A city and port in central Canada, in S Ontario on Lake Ontario. Canada's main center of heavy industry, it is particularly important for iron and steel, motor vehicles, machinery, chemicals, and electrical goods. Hamilton is also a financial, agricultural, transportation, and educational center. McMaster University (1887) was moved here from Toronto in 1930. Population (1991): 318,499.

Hamilton 37 46S 175 18E A city in New Zealand, in N North Island on the Waikato River. It is the most imporant inland center and serves a pastoral and lumbering region. The University of Waikato was established in 1964. Population (1989 est): 104,000.

Hamilton, Alexander (1755–1804) American political leader. He joined the Continental Army at the outbreak of the *Revolutionary War and was appointed aide-de-camp to Gen. George *Washington in 1777. After the war, he served in the *Continental Congress (1782–83) and practiced law in New York City. Hamilton was an advocate of a strong federal government for the United States, and at the Annapolis Convention of 1786 he was instrumental in persuading the delegates to convene in Philadelphia for a *Constitutional Convention in the following year. He was chosen to be one of the New York delegates to that convention and he worked tirelessly for the ratification of the new *Constitution, collaborating with John *Jay and James *Madison in the publication of the *Federalist Papers.

After the Federalist victory in the elections of 1788, Hamilton was chosen to serve as secretary of the treasury in Washington's cabinet. In that position, he established the first national bank and structured the repayment program for the national debt. Even after his resignation from public office in 1795, Hamilton remained active in the *Federalist party. He was a bitter opponent of fellow New Yorker Aaron *Burr and his support for Jefferson in the 1800 elections resulted in Burr's defeat in his campaign for the presidency. In 1804, Hamilton opposed Burr's candidacy for governor of New York and Burr, outraged at Hamilton's continuing political enmity, killed him in a duel.

Hamilton, Lady Emma (c. 1761–1815) The mistress of Horatio *Nelson. Wife of Sir William Hamilton (1730–1803), envoy to the court of Naples (1764–1800), she met Nelson in Naples in 1793. They became lovers and in 1801 their daughter Horatia (d. 1881) was born. After Nelson's death (1805), Lady Emma squandered her inheritance and fled to Calais (1814), where she died.

Hamilton, Sir William Rowan (1805–65) Irish mathematician. A child prodigy, he had mastered 13 languages by the age of 13 and at 22 was appointed professor of astronomy at Trinity College, Dublin. His most important work was the discovery of quaternions, three-dimensional equivalents of *complex numbers. He also made important contributions to the mathematics of light rays and helped to establish the wave theory of light.

ALEXANDER HAMILTON *A Federalist who served as the first secretary of the treasury and established the Bank of the United States.*

Hamito-Semitic languages A language family spoken in N Africa and S Asia. It is more appropriately known as Afro-Asiatic, especially since the Hamitic section of the name describes no particular characteristics. It has five branches that descend from an ancestor language, Proto-Hamito-Semitic, which was spoken between the 6th and 8th millenniums BC. The five branches are Egyptian, Berber, Cushitic, Semitic, and Chadic. There is some doubt about the membership of the Chadic languages in this group.

Hamlin, Hannibal (1809–91) US politician; vice president (1861–65). He was a representative from Maine (1843–47) to the US Congress before becoming a senator (1848–57; 1869–81). In 1856 he switched allegiance from the Democratic to the Republican party and served briefly as governor of Maine in 1857. His one term as vice president under Pres. Abraham Lincoln was not renewed in 1864 because of his association with radical causes.

Hamm 51 40N 7 49E A city in NW Germany, in North Rhine-Westphalia. The rail center of the *Ruhr, it has the largest marshaling yards in the country. Its chief manufactures are wire, cable, and machinery. Population (1991 est): 180,000.

Hammarskjöld, Dag (Hjalmar Agne Carl) (1905–61) Swedish international civil servant; the son of Hjalmar Hammarskjöld (1862–1953), who was a prime minister of Sweden (1914–17). As deputy foreign minister (1951–53) he headed the Swedish delegation to the UN and in 1953 succeeded Trygve *Lie as secretary general of the UN. He dealt with the Suez crisis (1956) and the civil war arising from the grant of independence to the Congo (1960). He was killed in a plane crash and awarded the Nobel Peace Prize posthumously in 1961. His diary *Markings* was published in 1964.

hammerhead A dark-brown bird, *Scopus umbretta,* that is the only member of its family (*Scopidae*) and occurs in marshes and mangrove swamps of tropical Africa, Madagascar, and the Arabian Peninsula. It has a large bill and a long backward-pointing crest. Hammerheads feed on frogs, fish, and aquatic invertebrates and build a large domed nest of sticks cemented together with mud. Order: *Ciconiiformes* (herons, storks, etc.).

hammerhead shark A *shark of the family *Sphyrnidae,* found in warm and temperate salt waters. Up to 15 ft (4.5 m) long, the head is flattened and extended laterally into two hammer- or spade-shaped lobes, which bear the eyes and nostrils. They feed primarily on fish but may attack other animals, including man.

Hammerstein II, Oscar (1895–1960) US lyricist and librettist, who collaborated with several well-known musical comedy composers, including Jerome Kern, Sigmund Romberg, and Richard Rodgers. His works include *Show Boat* (1927), *Oklahoma!* (1943), *Carousel* (1945), *South Pacific* (1949), *The King and I* (1951), and *The Sound of Music* (1959).

hammer throw A field event for men in athletics. The hammer is an iron or brass sphere weighing 16 lb (7.26 kg) attached to a spring-steel wire handle and grip. It is thrown with both hands from within a circle 7 ft (2.13 m) in diameter. A competitor has six attempts in which to throw the hammer the farthest.

Hammer v. Dagenhart (1918) US Supreme Court decision that declared the Child Labor Act (1916) unconstitutional. The act prohibited interstate shipment of goods produced in factories that employed children under 14 or that imposed unreasonable working hours or conditions on children between 14 and 16. It was the belief of the court that the law violated the extent to which the federal government could regulate states. The decision was overruled by *United States* v. *Darby* (1941).

Hammett, (Samuel) Dashiell (1894–1961) US novelist. He worked as a Pinkerton detective for eight years before writing his first detective stories. His novels, the realistic and economical style of which influenced Raymond *Chandler and other detective-story writers, include *The Maltese Falcon* (1930), *The Glass Key* (1931), and *The Thin Man* (1932), all of which were made into successful movies. He was a close friend of Lillian *Hellman.

Hammurabi (d. 1750 BC) King of Babylon (1792–1750). After defeating the kingdoms of Eshunna, Elam, and Ashur, Hammurabi turned against his former allies, the kingdoms of Larsa and Mari. The Code of Hammurabi, a collection of Babylonian laws, has survived in the Akkadian language.

Hampton 37 02N 76 23W A port in SE Virginia, on Hampton Roads Harbor. Founded in 1610, it has large fish-packing and shipping industries. Several military installations are situated nearby. Population (1990): 133,793.

Hampton, Lionel (1913–   ) US jazz band leader and vibraphone player, who played with Benny Goodman before forming his own orchestra in 1940. Hampton was the first jazz musician to popularize the vibraphone; one of his biggest successes was the record *Flyin' Home* (1942).

Hampton Roads Conference (1865) US peace conference between the Union and the Confederate states at Hampton Roads in SE Virginia. The Union, represented by Pres. Abraham Lincoln and Secretary of State William Seward and Confederate representatives met to discuss peace terms; the conference foundered over the issue of restoration of the prewar Union versus independence for the southern states.

hamster A small *rodent of the family *Cricetidae*. The common hamster (*Cricetus cricetus*), native to Europe and W Asia, is solitary and aggressive and has a red-brown coat with white patches on the flanks, neck, and cheek. It feeds on seeds and grains, storing them in underground burrows. The golden hamster (*Mesocricetus auratus*) is a domestic pet and all are thought to have descended from a single family found at Aleppo, Syria, in 1930.

Hamsun, Knut (1859–1952) Norwegian novelist. His early novels, *Hunger* (1890), *Mysteries* (1892), and *Pan* (1894), reflected his interest in nature and the irrational. Much of his subsequent work was influenced by Nietzsche and Strindberg and revealed a distrust of society and civilization; it includes the novels *Vagabonds* (1927) and *Markens grøde* (*The Growth of the Soil*; 1917). He won the Nobel Prize in 1920. He was accused of pro-Nazi tendencies after World War II but was not tried; his own attitude toward the war is commented on in the autobiographical *På gjengrodde stier* (1949).

Han (206 BC–220 AD) A Chinese dynasty founded by the general Liu Bang (*or* Liu Pang; 256–195 BC), who overthrew the preceding Qin dynasty. The power of the Han was consolidated by the emperor, Wu Di (*or* Wu Ti; 157–87 BC; reigned 140–87), who completed the conquest of a vast empire. Confucianism was recognized as the state philosophy, Chinese export of silk increased, and a vast canal-building program was started. Paper was invented by the Han Chinese, who also produced early forms of porcelain and kept detailed historical records. The program of expansion led to financial difficulties that enabled *Wang Mang to usurp the throne in 8 AD. However, he was toppled in turn and the Han dynasty was restored for a second period, known as the Later Han (23–220 AD).

Hancock, John (1737–93) US patriot; president of the Continental Congress (1775–77). A prosperous Boston businessman, he led a group of patriots protesting the restrictions imposed by the British. His signature, the first on the Declaration of Independence (1776) has come to mean "signature." He served in the Continental Congress (1775–80; 1785; 1786) and as governor of Massachusetts (1780–85; 1789–93).

Hand, (Billings) Learned (1872–1961) US jurist and writer. He practiced law in New York and served on New York's District Court (1909–24) and on the US Circuit Court of Appeals, 2nd District (1924–51), of which he was chief judge from 1939. Known for his ability to think clearly, write concisely, and speak eloquently, his rulings were, at times, referred to in US Supreme Court cases. His works are collected in *The Spirit of Liberty* (1952) and *The Bill of Rights* (1958).

hand The terminal part of the arm. The human hand contains 27 bones. There are 8 carpal bones, which form the wrist and articulate with the forearm at a hinge joint; 5 metacarpals, in the palm of the hand; and 14 phalanges (the bones of the fingers and thumb). The thumb of man and other primates is unique in being opposable, i.e. it can be rotated to touch each of the other fingers, making possible a wide range of manual skills (including using tools and writing). This—combined with its sensitive skin—has produced a manipulative and exploratory organ that has contributed to the success of man as a species.

handball A court game related to *pelota and fives that probably originated in the Roman baths. It is played in a court against one, three, or four walls with a small rubber ball that is hit with the gloved hand.

Handel, George Frederick (1685–1759) German composer. He became famous as a harpsichordist and as a master of the Italianate style of composition. After visiting England in 1712, he received a court pension from Queen Anne. He became music master to the family of the Prince of Wales and director of the Royal Academy of Music upon its founding in 1720. His Italian operas were successfully produced in London. From 1739 he turned from opera to oratorio, producing such masterpieces as *Saul* (1739), *Israel in Egypt* (1739), and *Messiah* (1742), which maintained his public popularity. In 1751, however, he began to be afflicted with loss of sight and became completely blind, although he continued to compose until his death. His mastery of composition is reflected in the range of his works, which include the *Water Music* (1717), *Music for the Royal Fireworks* (1749), concerti grossi, sonatas, organ concertos, harpsichord suites, and anthems.

Handy, W(illiam) C(hristopher) (1873–1958) US jazz musician, remembered chiefly as the "The Father of the Blues." His best-known compositions are "Memphis Blues" (1912) and "St Louis Blues" (1914). In later life he became a music publisher, continuing to work until his death, even after becoming blind.

Han fei zi (d. 233 BC) Chinese diplomat and philosopher of law. Although an author of antiquity, he has been studied, along with the Taoists, in the modern period in China. He is best known for his conception of government by law and his advocacy of statecraft.

Hangchow. *See* Hangzhou.

hang-gliding Unpowered flight in a hang-glider, consisting of a large bat-shaped cloth wing on a light metal framework from which the pilot hangs in a harness, holding a horizontal control bar. In flight, the wing fills to form an aerofoil (*see* aeronautics). The first hang-glider was built by Otto *Lilienthal, but the prototype for modern design was the sail-wing invented by Frances Rogallo (1912–   ) as a means of recovering space vehicles. Hang-gliding became popular in the late 1960s, acquiring a reputation as a dangerous sport largely because hang-gliders are relatively easy to attempt to fly without instruction.

hanging. *See* capital punishment.

Hanging Gardens of Babylon Ancient gardens in the palace of Nebuchadnezzar II (604–562 BC) on the E side of Babylon. One of the Seven Wonders of the World, they were built on top of stone arches 75 ft (23 m) above ground and watered from the Euphrates by a complicated mechanical system.

Hangzhou (Hang-chou *or* Hangchow) 30 18N 120 07E A city in E China, the capital of Zhejiang province on Hangzhou Bay, an inlet of the East China Sea. It was the capital (1132–1276) of the Southern *Song dynasty. A picturesque tourist center, it is the site of three universities. Its varied industries include silk production. Population (1991 est): 1,100,000.

haniwa Japanese terra-cotta sculptures, originally cylindrical in shape, placed on the outside of tomb mounds between about 330 and 552 AD. By the 5th century modeled houses and later horses and human figures were placed on top of the cylinders.

Hankou (*or* Hankow). *See* Wuhan.

Hanks, Tom (Thomas J., 1956–   ) US actor, noted for his low-key humor. Trained as a stage actor, he appeared on television before reaching stardom in *Splash* (1984) and *Big* (1988), in which he portrayed a boy in a man's body. He subsequently played a variety of roles, achieving great success in *Bonfire of the Vanities* (1990); *A League of Their Own* (1992), in which he was the manager of a women's professional baseball team; *Sleepless in Seattle* (1993); and *Philadelphia* (1994), in which he played an AIDS patient.

Hanna, Mark (Marcus Alonso H.; 1837–1904) US politician and businessman. A successful businessman in Cleveland, he engineered the political career of William McKinley through the governorship of Ohio (1891–93) to the presidency (1897–1901) and served as Republican national chairman (1896). He was a senator from 1897 until his death in 1904.

Hannibal (247–c. 183 BC) Carthaginian general. Appointed commander in Spain in 221, he deliberately provoked the second *Punic War with Rome. Advancing swiftly, in 218 he crossed the Alps in winter, reaching N Italy after a heroic trek in which he lost about 10,000 of his 35,000 men. For two years he devastated Italy but, after disastrous Roman defeats at Trasimene and *Cannae, Hannibal lost ground in the face of *Fabius's guerrilla tactics. Recalled to defend Carthage after *Scipio Africanus's invasion of Africa, Hannibal was defeated at Zama (202). Domestic politics occupied him until, suspected of rebellion, he was forced to flee Roman retribution. He committed suicide to avoid capture.

Hannibal 39 42N 91 22W A city in NE Missouri, on the Mississippi River. Mark Twain lived there as a boy in the mid-1800s and it is from his life here that many of his stories came. His family's home and memorabilia draw many visitors to the city. Other industries include fertilizers, building materials, machinery, and printing. Population (1990): 18,004.

Hanoi 20 57N 105 55E The capital of Vietnam, situated in the NE of the country on the Red River. The capital of the Vietnamese empire from the 11th until the 17th centuries, it was occupied by the French in 1873 and became the capital of French Indochina. Following the Japanese occupation in World War II, it became the capital of the Democratic Republic of Vietnam. Despite the frequent bombing by the US during the Vietnam War, many ancient buildings in the Vietnamese quarter remain, together with several imposing buildings in the European quarter built by the French. Its university was established in 1956. Population (1989): 1,088,862.

Hanover (German name: Hannover) 52 23N 9 44E An industrial city in N Germany, the capital of Lower Saxony on the Leine River. It is a transshipment port and a commercial and industrial center, where an important industrial fair is held annually. After the destruction of World War II it was largely rebuilt and some buildings, such as the old town hall (1435–80), were reconstructed. The Leine Palace (founded 1636) is now the *Land* Parliament building. Hanover's manufactures include machinery, rubber, textiles, and motor vehicles. *History*: in 1638 Hanover became the capital of an area of Brunswick that was later the electorate and then the kingdom of Hanover. In 1714, Elector George Louis became George I of Great Britain, (*see* Settlement, Act of). The kings of Great Britain were electors (later kings) of Hanover until 1837. Population (1991 est): 513,000.

Hanoverian A breed of horse developed in Hanover and originally used for hauling. During the 19th and 20th centuries crosses with English Thoroughbreds produced the strong but elegant modern Hanoverian, which is popular for showjumping and hunting. Height: 16–17 hands (1.63–1.73 m).

Han River A river in E central China, rising in S Shenxi province and flowing SE to join the Yangtze River at Wuhan. Length: about 900 mi (1450 km).

Hansberry, Lorraine (1930–65) US dramatist. She wrote *Raisin in the Sun* (1959), which became the first play by an African American to be produced on Broadway. It was also awarded the New York Drama Critics' Circle Award in 1959 and was made into a musical and a movie. She also wrote *The Sign in Sidney Brustein's Window* (1964) and was honored posthumously by a dramatic adaptation of her writings in *To Be Young, Gifted and Black* (1969).

Hanseatic League An association of N European trading towns (the Hanse) formed in the 13th century to protect their economic interests overseas. By the mid-14th century, the League, comprising some hundred towns, had become a powerful corporate body and was able to establish trading monopolies in much of NE Europe. It faced considerable opposition from Denmark and England, with which it conducted a number of trade wars. The rise of the non-German Baltic states during the 15th and 16th centuries, as well as changing trade routes, contributed to the League's declining influence. It was finally dissolved in 1669.

hansom cab. *See* cab.

Hanukkah A Jewish festival, commemorating the revolt of the *Maccabees. It falls in midwinter and is celebrated by lighting lamps or candles.

Hanuman In Hindu mythology, a monkey god and one of the principal characters in the *Ramayana*, in which he helps Rama to recover his wife Sita from the demon Ravana. There are numerous temples dedicated to him in both India and Japan.

Hanyang. *See* Wuhan.

Hapsburgs (*or* Habsburgs) The most prominent European royal dynasty from the 15th to 20th centuries. The family originated in Switzerland in the 10th century. In 1273 *Rudolf I was elected Holy Roman Emperor and consolidated through marriage and conquest his family's possession of Austria, Carniola, and Styria. After Rudolf's death (1291) the Hapsburgs lost the imperial title until 1438 but thereafter kept it until 1740, holding it again from 1745 to 1806. In 1516 *Charles V inherited the Spanish crown, adding Spain with its European and American possessions to the Hapsburg domains. When he abdicated in 1556 he left the Spanish crown to his son, *Philip II, and his Austrian possessions to his brother, *Ferdinand I. The Spanish branch ruled until 1700, when it died out and was replaced by the Bourbons. The Austrian Hapsburgs continued to rule, becoming emperors of Austria in 1804 and of *Austria-Hungary in 1848, which they ruled until the end of World War I.

hara-kiri The honorable way of death for Japanese *samurai who wished to avoid shame or demonstrate sincerity. In its strict form it involved ceremoniously cutting one's stomach open with a dagger before one's head was struck off by the single blow of another samurai's sword. In later times, however, there was often only a token gesture of disembowelment before decapitation. It is still sometimes practiced by Japanese suicides, although it is now illegal.

Harappa The site in the Punjab in Pakistan of a great city of the *Indus Valley civilization. Its cemeteries and brick buildings (excavated 1920s, 1946) equal *Mohenjo-Daro in importance.

Harar (*or* Harer) 9 20N 42 10E A city in E Ethiopia, the capital of Harar province. Situated at 6000 ft (1800 m), it is Ethiopia's only walled city. Its capture by British forces (1941) led to the eventual collapse of Mussolini's African colonial empire. Trade is based on coffee and grain. Population (1984): 62,200.

Harare (formerly, Salisbury) 17 50S 31 02E The capital of Zimbabwe, on a plateau in the NE. Founded in 1890 as Salisbury, it was the capital of the Federation of Rhodesia and Nyasaland (1953–63). The University of Zimbabwe (formerly Rhodesia) was founded there in 1970 and there are Anglican and Roman Catholic cathedrals. The center of a tobacco-growing area, it has an important trade and industry in tobacco. Other industries include textiles and engineering. Population (1987 est): 863,000.

Harbin. *See* Ha-er-bin.

harbor seal The common *seal, *Phoca vitulina,* of coastal Pacific and Atlantic waters. Up to 6 ft (1.8 m) long, with a blotchy gray coat, harbor seals inhabit sandbanks and river estuaries, feeding on fish. Family: *Phocidae.* □mammal.

Hardanger Fjord A fjord in SW Norway, S of Bergen, penetrating inland from the North Sea for 68 mi (110 km). It is edged by spectacular mountains and many waterfalls.

Hardecanute (*or* Harthacanute; c. 1019–42) The last Danish king of England (1040–42), succeeding his illegitimate half-brother Harold I Harefoot, and king of Denmark (1035–42). As the legitimate son of Canute, he ordered Harold's corpse to be disinterred and thrown into the Thames as a revenge for Harold's seizure of the throne after Canute's death. He razed Worcester following a riot there against his tax collectors. He died of a seizure at a marriage feast.

Hardenberg, Karl (August), Fürst von (1750–1822) Prussian statesman. He was foreign minister under Frederick William III from 1804 to 1806 and prime minister in 1807, when Prussia was subject to Napoleonic rule. Again prime minister from 1810 until his death, he introduced administrative and economic reforms that strengthened Prussia and enabled it to break away from French control in 1813. However, monarchist opposition to his progressive policies resulted in his declining influence after 1815.

Harding, Warren G(amaliel) (1865–1923) US statesman; Republican president (1921–23). He built up and ran a successful newspaper, the *Marion Star,* in Ohio before becoming a state senator (1898–1902) and lieutenant governor (1902–04). In 1912 he gave the nomination speech for William Howard Taft at the Republican national convention. He became a US senator (1915–21) and, in 1920, emerged as the dark-horse candidate on the Republican ticket for president. His campaign theme of a "return to normalcy" after World War I helped him win the election as the 29th president of the US. He, urged by others, called the Washington Disarmament Conference (1921–22); he established the Bureau of the Budget. His administration was characterized by complacency and scandal. Under Attorney General Harry M. Daugherty and Secretary of the Interior Albert B. Fall, corruption blossomed, resulting in many scandals, among them the *Teapot Dome incident. He died while on a trip across the country, after receiving news of the scandals and impending congressional investigation.

Hardouin-Mansart, Jules (1646–1708) French *baroque architect, who succeeded Le Vau as court architect to Louis XIV. He built Les Invalides, Paris (1680–91), but is most famous for his huge extensions to *Versailles, begun in 1678. These include the Galérie des Glaces (Gallery of Mirrors) and the orangery. He was also a town planner, his most notable design being the Place Vendôme (1699) in Paris.

Hardwar 29 58N 78 09E A city in N India, in Uttar Pradesh. One of the most sacred Hindu pilgrimage centers, its bathing ghat (or steps) along the Ganges River is believed to contain the footprint of the god Vishnu. Population (1991): 148,882.

Hardy, Thomas (1840–1928) British novelist and poet. The son of a mason, he went to London in 1862 to study architecture. His major novels, which include *The Return of the Native* (1878), *The Mayor of Casterbridge* (1886), and

Tess of the D'Urbervilles (1891), are tragic tales set in his native Dorset (called "Wessex" in the novels). After the public outrage caused by the alleged immorality of *Jude the Obscure* (1895) he published only verse, beginning with *Wessex Poems* (1898), and an epic drama, *The Dynasts* (1903–08).

hare A mammal belonging to the widely distributed family *Leporidae* (which also includes the *rabbits). Hares are typically larger than rabbits (the European hare (*Lepus europaeus*) weighs up to 9 lb [4 kg]) and have long black-tipped ears. They live and breed in the open (rather than in burrows) and are mainly nocturnal, feeding on grass and bark. The young are born fully furred with open eyes. Chief genus: *Lepus* (about 26 species); order: *Lagomorpha*.

harebell A herbaceous perennial plant, *Campanula rotundifolia,* of N temperate regions, growing to a height of 24 in (60 cm). It has rounded leaves and blue nodding bell-shaped flowers on slender stems. Harebell grows in a variety of open habitats. Family: *Campanulaceae.*

Hare Krishna movement (Sanskrit: hail Krishna) An international religious community, the International Society for Krishna Consciousness (ISKCON), founded in New York in 1966 on Hindu principles by an Indian, Swami Prabhupada. Members live according to a strict vegetarian regime that also prohibits gambling, extramarital sex, and the use of drugs. They dress in saffron linen robes and the men have shaved heads. Daily worship includes the chanting of the Hare Krishna mantra and dancing in the streets. The movement is financed by begging, the sale of literature and incense, and donations.

HARE KRISHNA MOVEMENT *The distinctive chant of the saffron-robed members of the society was heard in many cities in the 1970s.*

harelip A defect, present at birth, in which there is a cleft in the upper lip. There is often a simultaneous defect in the roof of the mouth (*see* cleft palate). Both defects interfere with speaking and feeding but they can be repaired surgically.

Hargeisa 9 20N 43 57E A city in N Somalia, near the Ethiopian border. It was the summer capital of former British Somaliland (1941–60). It is a watering and trading place for nomadic herdsmen. Population (1981 est): 70,000.

haricot bean A variety of *French bean (*Phaseolus vulgaris*) grown in warm climates. The seeds, which are dried for storage and soaked before use, are either brown or light-colored and are used for making baked beans.

Harishchandra (1850–85) Hindi poet, dramatist, and essayist, also known as Bharatendu. He founded two literary Hindi magazines and through his writings and patronage of other writers he contributed to the literary development of Hindi, which eventually became the official language of India. In *Bharat durdasa* (1880) and other plays he attributed the decline of Indian civilization to Muslim and Western influences.

Harlan, John Marshall (1833–1911) US jurist. Educated in law at Transylvania University, Harlan served as judge of Franklin County, Ky., in 1858 and later as Kentucky attorney general (1863–67). After two unsuccessful campaigns for governor, he was appointed by Pres. Rutherford B. *Hayes in 1877 to become an associate justice of the US Supreme Court. He remained on the bench until his death and became noted for his dissenting opinions, often in support of minorities. In the case of *Plessy* v. *Ferguson* (1896), he vigorously opposed the Supreme Court's decision upholding the constitutionality of racial segregation in public schools.

Harlem 40 49N 73 57W A residential district of New York City, in Manhattan. It is a political and social focus for African Americans. The poets Langston Hughes (1902–67) and Countee *Cullen (1903–46) were part of the Harlem Renaissance of the 1920s.

Harlem Globetrotters An African-American American professional basketball team formed by Abraham Saperstein (1903–66) in 1926. They traveled in the midwest, becoming known for their skill as well as for their clowning and tricky maneuvers. Today they travel all over the world playing in exhibition games. Among their best players have been Reese "Goose" Tatum and George "Meadowlark" Lemon.

Harlem Renaissance A movement in the 1920s, centered in the Harlem section of New York City, that brought African-American culture into its own—away from the southern dialect and imitation of the white world. Many new works by its African-American writers and poets, who included James Weldon *Johnson, Claude McKay (1890–1948), Countee *Cullen, and Langston *Hughes, emerged from this movement.

harlequin duck A short-billed *diving duck, *Histrionicus histrionicus,* occurring in coastal waters of Iceland and Greenland. The female is brown with white patches around the eyes; the male is gray-blue with black-edged white markings on the head, neck, breast, and wings and chestnut flanks.

Harley, Robert, 1st Earl of Oxford (1661–1724) English statesman under Queen Anne. An MP from 1688, he was a Tory but allied with the Whigs, becoming Speaker of the House of Commons (1701) and then secretary of state (1704). Intriguing against his Whig colleagues *Godolphin and *Marlborough, he was dismissed in 1708 and rejoined the Tories. After the fall of the Whigs, he became Anne's chief minister as chancellor of the exchequer (1710–11) and Lord Treasurer (1711–14). The machinations of his rival *Bolingbroke brought his dismissal and after the accession of George I he was imprisoned (1714–17) for his Tory (and, by implication, *Jacobite) views.

Harlow 51 47N 0 08E A city in SE England, in Essex. It is a new town, developed since 1947 as a satellite town of London with light industries (surgical and scientific instruments, electronics, engineering, furniture, glass). Population: 79,160.

Harlow, Jean (Harlean Carpentier; 1911–37) US film actress. Her well-publicized sex appeal and her talent for comedy won great popularity during the 1930s. After such movies as *Platinum Blond* (1931) and *Bombshell* (1933), she became known as the "blonde bombshell." She died from kidney failure while making *Saratoga* (1937).

harmonica 1. The mouth organ: the smallest member of the reed-organ family; its invention is attributed to Sir Charles *Wheatstone in 1829. Notes and chords are obtained by blowing or sucking rows of parallel reeds. It is used mainly in light music. **2.** The glass harmonica: an obsolete instrument consisting of tuned glasses rubbed with a damp finger.

harmonic analysis A procedure, developed in 1822 by Joseph *Fourier, by which complicated periodic functions, such as sound waves, can be written as the sum of a number of simple wave functions known as a Fourier series. One wave function, called the fundamental, has the same frequency as the original function. Those that have frequencies that are integral multiples of the fundamental are called harmonics.

harmonium A keyboard instrument of the reed organ family, patented in 1848 by Alexandre Debain (1809–77) in Paris. It is a free *reed instrument, the air being blown by a bellows activated by foot pedals. It may have several stops (*see* organ).

harmony In music, the combining of notes into chords, so that they are heard simultaneously. Harmony can be defined as the "vertical" aspect of music in contrast to melody, its "horizontal" aspect; it has greater importance in Western music than in any other musical tradition. Before about 1650 composers made use of *polyphony, in which the combination of a number of melodic lines based on *modes was of prime importance. Between about 1650 and about 1900 (the **harmonic period**) a system of harmony evolved based on diatonic chords (*see* scale). Such chords consist of three notes sounded simultaneously; a note of the scale of the *tonality of the composition and the notes a third and a fifth above it. The constituent notes of any chord can be rearranged to provide variety. A **harmonic progression** consists of a particular sequence of chords, especially one leading (*or* modulating) into another tonality. When chords are subject to increasing *chromaticism the harmony becomes more complex and the tonality of the music becomes ambiguous. During the last half of the 19th century the music of Wagner, Liszt, and Richard Strauss became increasingly chromatic. In the early years of the 20th century Schoenberg first adopted *atonality and later invented *serialism as a substitute for traditional harmony. Debussy developed novel harmonic practices, such as harmonizing melodies with chords from unrelated tonalities and chords derived from whole-tone and pentatonic scales. Composers of the 20th century have made use of a wide range of harmonic styles, some following Schoenberg, some deliberately cultivating dissonance, and others modifying traditional harmonic practice in various ways.

Harnack, Adolf von (1851–1930) German Protestant theologian. A professor at the Universities of Leipzig, Marburg, and Berlin, Harnack was considered the greatest scholar of his day on the early Church Fathers. His influential *History of Dogma* (1886–90), which traced the history of Christian doctrine down to the Reformation, was strongly criticized by conservative theologians.

harness racing A form of horse racing in which each horse pulls a light two-wheeled *sulky with a single driver. The races are of two sorts, according to the pace that the horses are trained to use: trotting (a two-beat gait with legs moving in diagonal pairs) or pacing (a two-beat gait with legs moving in lateral pairs). Races are usually run over 1 mi (1.6 km) on oval dirt tracks. The sport is particularly popular in the US and Australia.

Harold I Harefoot (d. 1040) Danish king of England (1037–40). The illegitimate son of Canute, he became king while Hardecanute, Canute's legitimate son, was preoccupied in Denmark. Before Hardecanute could oust him, Harold died.

Harold II (c. 1022–66) The last Anglo-Saxon king of England (1066), reputedly designated heir by the dying Edward the Confessor. He was the son of Earl *Godwin. After becoming king, he crushed the forces of his brother *Tostig and *Harold III Hardraade of Norway, who claimed the throne, at Stamford Bridge (1066). Harold was killed in the battle of *Hastings by the army of another, successful, claimant to the throne, *William the Conqueror.

Harold III Hardraade (1015–66) King of Norway (1047–66). His nickname means Hard Ruler. Until 1045 he served in the Byzantine army, his exploits in which became the subject of Norse sagas. After his return to Norway he briefly shared the throne with Magnus I (d. 1047); when he became sole ruler, he tried unsuccessfully to conquer Denmark. In 1066 he invaded England in support of *Tostig against Harold II and died at Stamford Bridge.

harp A plucked stringed instrument of ancient origin, consisting of an open frame with strings of varying length and tension. The modern orchestral harp is triangular in shape with about 45 strings stretched between the long soundbox, which rests against the player's body, and the curved neck, which takes the tuning pegs. The pillar, which completes the triangle, contains a mechanism invented in 1810 by Sébastien Érard (1752–1831). This enables the player to raise each string by one or two semitones by means of pedals at the base. It gives the harp a full chromatic range of six and a half octaves from the B below the bass stave. □musical instruments.

Harpers Ferry Raid (1859) The capture of the federal arsenal at Harpers Ferry, West Va., by John *Brown. An abolitionist (*see* Abolition Movement), Brown seized the arsenal as a base for a slave insurrection. Robert E. *Lee, in command of federal troops, assaulted and captured Brown's position. Brown was hanged, a martyr to the abolitionist cause. The town, at the confluence of the Potomac and Shenandoah Rivers, was the site of several engagements during the Civil War.

Harpies In Greek mythology, malicious spirits, originally conceived as winds, who carried off their victims to their deaths. They were later portrayed as rapacious birds with ugly women's faces.

harpsichord A keyboard instrument with strings plucked by quills, rather than hit by hammers (*see* spinet; virginals; *compare* clavichord; piano). In the 16th, 17th, and 18th centuries it was an instrument of great importance and it has been successfully revived in the 20th century. It lacks the sustaining power and dynamic variation of the piano; the tone can be changed by the addition of stops, which sound strings an octave below or above the note depressed. A muted effect can be obtained by use of the lute stop.

harpy eagle A tropical South American *eagle, *Harpia harpyja*, that lives in rain forests. It is the largest of the eagles, 40 in (100 cm) long, and has a huge hooked bill and extremely powerful feet for gripping its prey, which includes monkeys, sloths, opossums, and parrots. Mottled gray with a dark-banded tail, it has a large erectile crest.

harquebus (*or* arquebus). *See* musket.

harrier (bird) A slender long-legged *hawk belonging to a widely distributed genus (*Circus*). Harriers are about 20 in (50 cm) long and are usually brown (in some species the males are gray), with a small bill and a long tail. They fly low over fields and marshes, searching for frogs, mice, snakes, and insects. *See also* marsh harrier.

harrier (dog) A breed of hound used for hunting hares. It is similar to the *foxhound but smaller. The short smooth coat is usually black, tan, and white but may be mottled blue-gray. Height: 18–22 in (46–56 cm).

Harriman, Edward Henry (1848–1909) US stockbroker and businessman. As a broker on the New York Stock Exchange he specialized in bankrupt railroads and by 1903 was president of the Union Pacific Railroad, a line he had completely reorganized and rebuilt. He speculated in other railroad stock and his desire to gain control of the Northern Pacific Railroad and ultimately the Chicago, Burlington & Quincy Railroad caused the Panic of 1901.

Harriman, W(illiam) Averell (1891–1986) US diplomat. Entering government service in 1934, he served as ambassador to the Soviet Union (1943–46), to Great Britain (1946), and as secretary of commerce (1946–48). He was governor of New York (1955–58) and then helped to negotiate the *Nuclear Test-Ban Treaty (1963). He was ambassador to the Paris peace talks on Vietnam (1968–69).

Harris, Joel Chandler (1848–1908) US local-color novelist and short-story writer. His Uncle Remus stories, drawing on his knowledge of African-American folklore gained from his work as a journalist and on plantations, were published in several volumes, beginning with *Uncle Remus, His Songs and His Sayings* (1880).

Harris, Roy (1898–1979) US composer. He studied with Nadia Boulanger in Paris and held various university teaching posts. His compositions, which include 11 symphonies, concertos, chamber music, and choral music, show the influence of Gregorian chant and folk music. Among his best works are *When Johnny Comes Marching Home* (1934), *Third Symphony* (performed 1937), and *Piano Quintet* (1936).

Harris, Townsend (1804–78) US diplomat. While president of New York City's board of education (1846–47) he was instrumental in the founding of the College of the City of New York (1847). After conducting a trading business in the Orient he was appointed consul general to Japan (1855–60), shortly after Japan was opened to Western trade, and negotiated a complete trade and diplomatic representative treaty in 1858.

Harrisburg 40 17N 76 54W The capital city of Pennsylvania, on the Susquehanna River. An important rail center, its manufactures include bricks, steel, and clothing. In March 1979, a failure in the cooling system at the nuclear power plant at nearby Three Mile Island caused widespread concern. Population (1990): 52,376.

Harrison, Benjamin (1833–1901) US statesman; Republican president (1889–93) and grandson of William Henry *Harrison. A lawyer in Indiana, he commanded a regiment during the Civil War. Elected to the US Senate (1881–87), he spoke out in favor of civil rights, reform of the civil service system, and the protection of US industry. Although he was not reelected to the Senate by a Democratic legislature in Indiana, he was nominated to run as the Republican candidate for president in 1888. During his administration the first Pan American Conference (1889) was held, the US participated in the Berlin Conference (1889) that prevented war between Britain and Germany, and international disputes were settled. At home, the *Sherman Anti-Trust Act (1890), the McKinley

Tariff Act (1890), and the *Sherman Silver Purchase Act (1890) were passed. Defeated for reelection by Grover *Cleveland, he returned to his law practice, taking time out (1898–99) to negotiate Venezuela's boundary dispute with Great Britain.

Harrison, George (1943–) British rock musician, formerly a member of the *Beatles. When the group disbanded, Harrison embarked on a solo career and made four albums influenced by his interest in eastern mysticism, notably *All Things Must Pass* (1970) and *Extra Texture* (1975).

Harrison, William Henry (1773–1841) US military and political leader; 9th president of the United States (1841). After beginning medical studies at the University of Pennsylvania, Harrison left school to embark on a military career in the *Northwest Territory, gaining distinction in the Battle of *Fallen Timbers (1794). In 1801 he was appointed governor of the newly established Indiana territory by Pres. John Adams. In that post, Harrison led US army forces against the Shawnee Indians of the territory, defeating their leader Tecumseh at the Battle of Tippicanoe (1811). After service in the *War of 1812, Harrison settled in Ohio, where he was elected congressman (1816–19), state senator (1819–21), and US senator (1825–28). He resigned the latter position to become US minister to Colombia. Active in the Whig party, Harrison unsuccessfully campaigned for the presidency in 1836. In 1840 he was again the Whig nominee and, with vice presidential nominee John *Tyler, ran with the famous campaign slogan "Tippicanoe and Tyler Too." Although Harrison was elected, he died less than a month after taking office.

Harrogate 54 00N 1 33W A residential city and spa in N England, in North Yorkshire. It is a holiday resort, noted for its parks and open spaces. Harrogate has also become an important center for conferences and trade fairs. Population: 64,620.

Harsa (*or* Harsha; c. 590–c. 647 AD) King of N India (c. 606–47). He ruled an extensive empire from his capital of Kanauj. In later life he became a devout Buddhist and combined his successful rule with the pursuit of poetry and the arts. His life and reign were well documented by the author *Bana.

Hart, Moss (1904–61) US dramatist. He collaborated with George S. *Kaufman on a great number of successful Broadway comedies, including *You Can't Take It With You* (1936) and *The Man Who Came to Dinner* (1939). He also wrote librettos for musicals by Irving *Berlin and Kurt *Weill, notably *Lady in the Dark* (1941). His autobiography, *Act One,* was published in 1959.

Harte, (Francis) Bret(t) (1836–1902) US local-color writer. He gained international fame with stories about the miners, gamblers, and prostitutes of California, collected in *The Luck of the Roaring Camp and Other Sketches* (1870). He collaborated with Mark Twain on the play *Ah Sin* (1877). After publishing a series of articles in *Atlantic Monthly,* he spent his last years in Europe.

hartebeest A long-faced antelope, *Alcephalus busephalus,* of African plains. About 47 in (120 cm) high at the shoulder, hartebeests are slender fast-running animals. There are several races, ranging in color from dark chestnut to fawn; their horns are united at the base and are generally lyre-shaped. Hartebeests live in small herds, grazing by day.

Hartford 41 45N 72 42W The capital city of Connecticut. Founded in 1633, it has many notable buildings. Trinity College (1823) and the law and insurance schools of the University of Connecticut are situated here. A commercial, industrial, and financial center, Hartford is one of the leading insurance centers in the world. Population (1990): 139,739.

Hartford Convention (1814–15) A meeting in Hartford, Conn., of Federalist delegates from Connecticut, Massachusetts, Rhode Island, Vermont, and New Hampshire to protest against Pres. James Madison's policies and conduct of the War of 1812. They proposed a strong states' rights program and came out against the military draft and embargos on trade. The end of the War of 1812 (1815) overshadowed their demands.

Hartmann, (Karl Robert) Eduard von (1842–1906) German philosopher. He wrote a massive and eclectic work, *Philosophy of the Unconscious* (1869), which sought to reconcile all previous systems and all sciences by means of the hypothesis of the unconscious mind.

Hartmann, Nicolai (1882–1950) Russian-born German philosopher. He was troubled by the problem of cultural relativism pervading all branches of philosophy. Ideas, and even the concepts of logic, were historically conditioned, so that no thinker could begin without preconceptions. Systematic metaphysics, as presented by 19th-century idealists, was impossible, and the task of the philosopher was to draw the boundary between the rational and the irrational.

Harun ar-Rashid (?766–809 AD) The fifth caliph (786–809) of the 'Abbasid dynasty of Islam. He relied greatly on the support of the powerful Barmecide family until it fell from power in 803. His reign was troubled by revolts in subject territories and saw the beginning of Tunisian independence. Harun sent expeditions against the Byzantines and forced them to accept a humiliating treaty in 806. He has become an almost legendary figure because of the references to him in *The Arabian Nights*. Muslim sources, however, say nothing of his alleged close relations with Charlemagne.

Harvard classification system A system, introduced in the 1890s by astronomers at the Harvard College Observatory, by which stars are classified according to features in their spectra. Stellar spectral differences arise mainly from differing surface and atmospheric temperatures, and the stars are grouped accordingly into seven major spectral types: O, B, A, F, G, K, and M, in order of decreasing temperature. These types range in color from blue (O and B) through white, yellow, and orange, to red (M). There are 10 subdivisions for each spectral type, indicated by a digit (0–9) placed after the letter. Stars of one spectral type can be further classified into supergiants, giants, etc., according to their *luminosity. See also* Hertzsprung-Russell diagram.

Harvard University The oldest university in the US. It was founded in 1636 by a grant from the Massachusetts Bay Colony and located at Cambridge, Mass. It is named for a clergyman, John Harvard (1607–38), who bequeathed his books to the college. Today the library is one of the country's best. The associated women's college, Radcliffe College, dates from 1879.

harvestman An *arachnid, also called harvest spider, belonging to the order *Opiliones* (or *Phalangida*; 2200 species), found in tropical and temperate regions. It has an undivided body, 0.04–0.86 in (1–22 mm) long, and very long delicate legs. It is found in fields, woods, and buildings, feeding on insects and plant materials, and is particularly common in late summer in temperate regions.

harvest mite A *mite, also called chigger and scrub mite, belonging to the genus *Trombicula*. Its larvae are parasitic on vertebrates, including man, feeding on skin to cause intense itching and inflammation. Certain species transmit diseases, including scrub typhus.

harvest mouse A tiny *mouse, *Micromys minutus,* of Europe and Asia. Light red-brown with white underparts, harvest mice are about 1.6 in (4 cm) long with a prehensile tail of the same length. They weave a nest of grass among the stems of plants in cornfields and reedbeds, but are becoming rarer as a result of mechanical farming methods.

HARVEST MOUSE *These rodents are small enough to be able to climb cornstalks, with the aid of their prehensile tails, and feed on the grain.*

Harvey, William (1578–1657) English physician and anatomist, who discovered the circulation of the blood. Harvey studied under the great anatomist *Fabricius ab Aquapendente and later became physician to James I and Charles I. From his numerous dissections and experiments on animals, Harvey concluded that blood flowed from the heart to the lungs, returned to the heart, and was pumped out via the arteries to the limbs and viscera, returning to the heart through the veins. His findings, published in *On the Motion of the Heart and Blood in Animals* (1628), aroused controversy, but by his death the circulation of blood was generally accepted. Harvey also made valuable studies of the development of chick embryos.

Haryana A state in N India, mostly in the fertile Upper Ganges plain. Predominantly rural, it produces wheat, other grains, cotton, sugar cane, and oil-seeds. There is some light industry, including textiles, agricultural implements, and sugar refining. *History*: an important center of Hinduism, Haryana lies on the migration route into India. Britain merged it with the Punjab, but it was separated in 1966. Area: 17,070 sq mi (44,222 sq km). Population (1991): 16,317,715. Capital: Chandigarh.

Harz Mountains A mountain range in Germany, extending about 56 mi (90 km) W of Halle. They are the northernmost range of the European mountain system. The highest peak is the *Brocken.

Hasan al-Basri, al- (d. 728) Muslim ascetic and religious thinker. He was active in Basra in Iraq and is important in the development of Muslim theology, although little is known about him. He is said to have supported the idea of human free will against that of divine predetermination.

Hasdrubal (Barca) (d. 207 BC) Carthaginian general; the son of *Hamilcar Barca and the brother of *Hannibal. Hasdrubal commanded the Carthaginian army in Spain following Hannibal's departure to campaign in Italy but was recalled to Africa after being defeated by the Romans in 217. He returned to Spain in 212, campaigning successfully before following Hannibal across the Alps in 207. He was defeated at Metaurus and died in battle.

Hašek, Jaroslav (1883–1923) Czech novelist, who established an early reputation as a satirist and anarchist. During World War I he was captured by the Russians, joined the Czech liberation army, and became a communist. His unfinished novel sequence *The Good Soldier Schweik* (1920–23) is a bawdy and irreverent satire upon bureaucracy and bourgeois values.

Haselrig, Sir Arthur. *See* Hesilrige, Sir Arthur.

Hashemites The Arab descendants of the prophet Mohammed, including the fourth caliph *Ali and the line of hereditary emirs of Mecca. King Hussein of Jordan is a modern representative of the line.

hashish. *See* cannabis.

Hasidism A Jewish religious movement, founded by the *Ba'al Shem Tov. Essentially a blend of *kabbalah and popular pietism, Hasidism spread, against strong opposition, throughout the Jewish communities of E Europe in the 18th and 19th centuries. Led by charismatic teachers (*zaddikim*), the Hasidim stressed simple piety and ecstatic prayer and denounced what they saw as the arid scholasticism of the talmudic academies. A more intellectual approach was adopted by the Habad Hasidim, whose leader is the Lubavitch Rabbi, now based in New York. Most of the Hasidic communities in Europe were wiped out during the *holocaust, but Hasidism still thrives in North America and Israel.

Haskalah (Hebrew: enlightenment) The intellectual movement for spreading modern European culture among the Jews. It began in Germany in the 18th century, largely under the influence of Moses *Mendelssohn, and spread to Russia in the 19th century. Linked to the movement for the political emancipation of the Jews, it attempted to provide them with a modern Hebrew culture of their own and rejected the previous alternatives of the medieval ghetto culture or total assimilation. In its day it exercised an enormous influence, giving birth to modern *Judaism, *Zionism, and the modern Hebrew language and literature. In the West it succumbed to linguistic and cultural assimilation; in Russia, after enjoying a period of government support, it yielded, in the face of the growing *anti-Semitism of the 1880s, to attempts to find a political solution to the Jewish problem.

Hassan II (1929–   ) King of Morocco (1961–   ). Educated in France, Hassan maintains autocratic rule in Morocco. He introduced some reforms in 1971 following an attempted coup and oversaw the occupation of Western Sahara from 1976.

Hasselt 50 56N 5 20E A city in NE Belgium. It was the site of a Dutch victory over the Belgians in 1831. Industries include brewing and distilling.

Hastings 50 51N 0 36E A city on the S coast of England, in East Sussex. Formerly a port (chief of the Cinque Ports), it is now a resort and residential town with a ruined castle built by William the Conqueror, who landed at nearby Pevensey in 1066 (*see* Hastings, Battle of). Population (1981): 77,000.

Hastings, Battle of (Oct 14, 1066) The battle between the Normans and the English at Senlac Hill, near Hastings, in which William, duke of Normandy, claiming the English throne, defeated Harold II of England. The battle was dominated by the Norman use of archery supported by cavalry to break through the defensive ranks of infantry, which alone made up the English army. Both sides suffered heavy losses but the death of Harold allowed William to conquer England (*see* Norman conquest) and become its king.

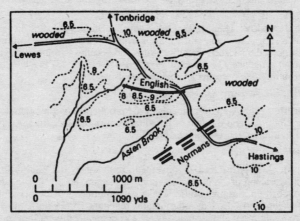

BATTLE OF HASTINGS *The three lines of Norman troops were led by archers, including crossbowmen (making their first recorded appearance in battle), who were able to undermine the advantage of the English position on a ridge above.*

Hastings, Warren (1732–1818) British colonial administrator; the first governor general of India (1774–85). He first went to India in 1750 in the employ of the East India Company. After several promotions he became, in 1771, governor of Bengal, and then governor general of India. His outstanding administration consolidated British control of India and introduced administrative, legal, and financial reforms that provided the basis of subsequent British government there. Hastings failed, however, to maintain good relations with his colleagues, especially Sir Philip *Francis, with whom he fought a duel in 1779. On his return to England he was impeached for corruption. The trial before the House of Lords, which lasted until 1795, ended in his acquittal.

hatchetfish A carnivorous hatchet-shaped fish, up to 4 in (10 cm) long, belonging to one of two unrelated groups. Deepsea hatchetfish (family *Sternoptychidae*; 15 species) are related to *salmon and occur in warm and temperate waters down to about 3280 ft (1000 m). The freshwater or flying hatchetfish (family *Gasteropelecidae*; about 9 species) of South America are related to *carp. They swim near the surface and are able to leap out of the water and "fly" short distances by flapping their large pectoral fins. □oceans.

Hathaway, Anne (c. 1556–1623) The wife of William *Shakespeare. She was born at Shottery, near Stratford. She married Shakespeare in 1582 and bore him three children. Her cottage may still be seen in Stratford.

Hathor An Egyptian sky goddess, worshiped as goddess of fertility and of love, happiness, and beauty. She was usually portrayed as a cow or with a cow's horns and is sometimes identified with *Isis.

Hatshepsut Queen of Egypt (c. 1490–1468 BC) of the 18th dynasty. The half-sister and widow of *Thutmose II, she overshadowed the young *Thutmose III, and assumed the status of pharaoh. During her reign direct communications with Punt (now S Eritrea) were reopened. Illustrated accounts of her expedition there and of the transport of her obelisks from Aswan are carved on her funerary temple at Dayr al-Bahri. After her death Thutmose III attempted to obliterate her memory by defacing her monuments.

Hatteras, Cape 35 14N 75 31W A low sandy promontory in North Carolina, on Hatteras Island. Its shallows are a danger to navigation.

Hattusas The ancient capital of the *Hittite empire (c. 1700–1230 BC) situated at Boğazköy (*or* Boğazkale) in central Turkey. The massive fortifications still visible date from the reign of *Suppiluliumas (c. 1375–c. 1335 BC). Thousands of tablets, forming part of the royal archives, have been found here and provide invaluable evidence for diplomatic and commercial activity in the period.

Hauptmann, Gerhart (1862–1946) German dramatist. After studying sculpture he turned to writing plays, establishing his reputation with *Before Dawn* (1889). His early work was influenced by *naturalism in its use of dialect and in its social themes, as in *The Weavers* (1892). This element later alternated with a mystical and *Symbolist strain, as in *The Assumption of Hannele* (1893). He also wrote novels (*The Fool in Christ,* 1910), novellas (*Flagman Thiel,* 1888), and poetry (*Der grosse Traum,* 1942). He was awarded a Nobel Prize in 1912.

Hauraki Gulf A large inlet of the South Pacific Ocean, in New Zealand on the E coast of North Island. Waitemata Harbour, on which stands Auckland, is situated in the SW. Area: about 884 sq mi (2290 sq km).

Hausa A people of NW Nigeria and S Niger, numbering about nine million. Their language belongs to the Chadic subgroup of the *Hamito-Semitic family, but has absorbed many Arabic words and influences. It is an official language of Nigeria and a second language in much of West Africa. The Hausa are mainly Muslim. There were once several Hausa states ruled on feudal lines by emirs and titled office holders who held villages as fiefs. This hierarchical system emphasized elaborate etiquette. Slavery was practiced but slaves could attain high office. The economy is based on the cultivation of maize, millet, sorghum, and other crops. Crafts are highly developed and trade is extensive. Cities, such as *Kano, date from precolonial times but most Hausa live in small rural settlements.

Haussmann, Georges-Eugène, Baron (1809–91) French town planner, responsible for extensive rebuilding in Paris under *Napoleon III. Haussmann's long avenues and dramatic vistas, for example the avenues radiating from the *Arc de Triomphe, form much of the city's present-day character. His schemes, while improving sanitation and public utilities, destroyed many remnants of the medieval town.

Havana (Spanish name: La Habana) 23 00N 82 30W The capital of Cuba, a port in the NW. It exports sugar, cotton, and tobacco. The city has been considerably modernized during the Castro regime but much of the Spanish-colonial element remains, including the cathedral. The university was founded in 1728. *History:*

the original settlement was on the S coast, but the inhabitants moved to the city's present site in 1519. It became the capital of Cuba in the late 16th century. Because of its excellent natural harbor, Havana has long been of strategic and commercial importance and during the early 19th century it was among the wealthiest commercial centers in the New World. Population (1989 est): 2,078,000.

Havana cat A breed of short-haired cat, formerly known as Chestnut Brown Foreign. The Havana has a lithe slender body with a long tail, a long head, and large ears. The coat is chestnut-brown and the eyes are green and slanting.

Hawaii (former name: Sandwich Islands) Fiftieth US state, one of the 2 states (the other being Alaska) lying outside the coterminous 48 US states, in the central Pacific Ocean 2100 mi (3360 km) SW of San Francisco. Occupying a chain of over 20 volcanic islands, Hawaii consists of 5 major islands and numerous smaller ones. The main islands include Hawaii (the largest), Maui, Oahu, Kauai, and Molokai. Its population, concentrated mainly on Oahu, is more ethnically diverse than that of any other US state, the largest groups being white Americans and Japanese. Its industry relies heavily on imported raw materials; manufactures include oil and chemical products, steel, textiles, and food. Agriculture is important, the main crops being sugar and pineapples. The principal industry, however, is tourism. There is some lumbering and fishing. Hawaii's strategic position for the defense of the US means that there are a large number of military bases. Hawaii's cultural and scientific institutions reflect both Western and Pacific cultures. *History*: the Polynesians who first settled the islands are thought to have occupied Hawaii around the 8th century. In 1788, Captain James Cook became the first European to discover the islands. In 1810 the islands were united under King Kamehameha. Prosperity prevailed until the arrival of European and American traders who introduced infectious diseases previously unknown to the islanders; the population was greatly reduced as a consequence. In the late 1820s, US missionaries and planters established sugar plantations and quickly came to dominate the island's economy. The Japanese attack on Pearl Harbor in 1941 precipitated the US entry into World War II. Hawaii became a state in 1959. Following statehood, the state's economy and population boomed, primarily through tourism and related industries. Area: 6425 sq mi (16,641 sq km). Population (1990): 1,108,229. Capital: Honolulu.

Hawaiian goose A rare *goose, *Branta sandvicensis,* native to Hawaii and Maui, where it is called néné. It has a gray-brown plumage barred with white and an orange neck. Its numbers are now increasing by breeding programs.

Hawaiian guitar (*or* steel guitar) A type of guitar held flat on the player's lap. The strings are stopped by a sliding steel bar, which produces a characteristic glissando.

Hawaii Volcanoes National Park A national park on SE Hawaii Island, Hawaii. Within the park are two active volcanoes, Mauna Loa (13,680 ft; 4170 m) and Kilauea (4000 ft; 1220 m). Tourists may drive around the rim of Kilauea's crater and are able to watch its eruptions safely. Area: 344 sq mi (891 sq km).

hawfinch A large *finch, *Coccothraustes cocothraustes,* of Eurasia and N Africa; 7 in (18 cm) long, it has a reddish-brown plumage with paler underparts, a black bib, and black-and-white wings. Its massive bill is used to crack open the stones of cherries, sloes, and damsons to extract the seeds.

Haw-Haw, Lord. *See* Joyce, William.

hawk A bird of prey belonging to a widely distributed family (*Accipitridae*; 205 species) that includes buzzards, eagles, harriers, kites, and vultures. Hawks range in size from small *sparrowhawks to the *harpy eagle and have down-curved pointed bills, powerful gripping feet, and highly developed eyesight.

Hawks typically fly fast in pursuit of live prey, using their strong claws for killing, and have broad rounded wings; they usually nest in trees or crags. Order: *Falconiformes. Compare* falcon. *See also falconry.*

Hawke, Robert James Lee (1929–) Australian political leader; prime minister (1983–91). A Rhodes scholar (1952–55), he joined the Australian Council of Trade Unions (1958) as a researcher and negotiator and eventually served as its president (1970–80). He became president of the Australian Labor Party (ALP) in 1974 and in 1980 was elected to the House of Representatives. In 1983 he defeated Malcolm Fraser by a wide margin to become prime minister. Conservative in nature, he attempted to slow down Australia's economy and to curb its ambitions internationally. He was succeeded by Paul Keating.

Hawke Bay An inlet of the SW Pacific Ocean, in New Zealand in E North Island. The surrounding land area of Hawke's Bay is important for sheep rearing. Length: 50 mi (80 km).

Hawkesbury River A river in SE Australia, rising in the Great Dividing Range in New South Wales and flowing generally NE to enter the Tasman Sea at Broken Bay. Length: 293 mi (472 km).

Hawkins, Sir John (1532–95) English navigator. In 1562 he became the first English slave trader, transporting slaves from West Africa to the Spanish West Indies. His third expedition (1567–69), in which Drake participated, met with the Spaniards on its way home and only the ships of Drake and Hawkins escaped. In 1577 he became treasurer of the navy, instituting reforms that greatly contributed to England's victory against the Spanish *Armada (1588), and died at Puerto Rico on a new expedition with Drake.

hawk moth A moth belonging to the widespread family *Sphingidae* (about 1000 species), also called sphinx moth or hummingbird moth. They have large bodies with relatively small wings (spanning 2–8 in [5–20 cm]), which they beat rapidly, hovering over flowers and sipping nectar through their long proboscis. The leaf-eating greenish larvae pupate in soil or litter.

hawk owl An *owl, *Surnia ulula,* that occurs in northern coniferous forests of Eurasia and North America. It is 16 in (40 cm) long and has a long tail, a small head, and short pointed wings, which give a hawklike silhouette in flight. It hunts by day.

Hawks, Howard (1896–1977) US film director. He started as a writer but from 1938 produced and directed numerous movies, the best known of which were comedies like *Bringing Up Baby* (1938), fast-paced action dramas such as *To Have and Have Not* (1944), *The Big Sleep* (1946), a Western, *Red River* (1948), and a musical, *Gentlemen Prefer Blondes* (1953).

hawksbill turtle A small sea turtle, *Eretmochelys imbricata,* found in warm waters worldwide. It has hooked jaws, feeds on algae, fish, and invertebrates, and is usually 16–22 in (40–55 cm) long. The polished translucent mottled brown shell is the tortoiseshell used to make ornamental combs, spectacle frames, etc.

hawkweed A perennial herb of the genus *Hieraceum* (about 1000 species), of temperate regions and tropical mountains. It grows to a height of about 24 in (60 cm) and usually has yellow flower heads. The name derives from the old belief that hawks ate these plants to improve their eyesight. Family: *Compositae.*

Hawley-Smoot Tariff (1930) A US law that imposed high taxes on imported goods in an attempt to protect domestic products. Other countries, in retaliation, imposed the same taxes on US goods coming into their countries, and foreign trade as a whole took a sharp drop.

HAWK OWL *Unlike many owls, this species is active by day, preying on a wide variety of mammals and birds. Its swooping flight and long tail resemble those of a hawk.*

Haworth, Sir Walter Norman (1883–1950) British biochemist, who first synthesized artificial vitamin C (ascorbic acid), thus enabling its cheap production for medical use. He shared a Nobel Prize (1937) with the Swiss chemist Paul Karrer (1889–1971).

hawthorn A thorny shrub or tree of the N temperate genus *Crataegus* (about 200 species). Hawthorns have lobed leaves, usually about 1.6 in (4 cm) long, white spring-blooming flowers, and yellow, black, or red fruits. The common hawthorn, or may (*C. monogyna*), is found in hedgerows and thickets in Europe and the Mediterranean. Up to 33 ft (10 m) high, it has red fruits (haws). There are many horticultural forms, including pink and double-flowered varieties. Family: *Rosaceae*.

Hawthorne, Nathaniel (1804–64) US novelist and short-story writer. His two best-known novels, *The Scarlet Letter* (1850) and *The House of the Seven Gables* (1851), concern the psychological effects of Puritanism in New England. He was a friend of Herman *Melville, who visited him in England after his appointment as consul at Liverpool in 1853. In 1857 he traveled in Italy, the setting of *The Marble Faun* (1860).

Hay, John Milton (1838–1905) US statesman, politician, and writer. He served as a private secretary to Pres. Abraham Lincoln (1861–65) and in various European diplomatic posts, including ambassador to Britain (1897–98). Appointed secretary of state by Pres. William McKinley in 1898, he openly advocated the *Open Door Policy and was instrumental in retaining US influence in the Philippines, China, and Panama. He remained secretary of state until 1905, also serving under Pres. Theodore Roosevelt. He is best known for his 10-volume history of Lincoln (1890).

Haya de la Torre, Victor Raúl (1895–1979) Peruvian politician. In exile following an attempt at revolution in 1923, he founded the radical Alianza Popular

Revolucionaria Americana (APRA). He ran for the presidency in 1931 and, successfully, in 1962, only to have the result cancelled by a military coup.

Haydn, Franz Joseph (1732–1809) Austrian composer, born in Rohrau. He became a cathedral chorister in Vienna at the age of eight and subsequently worked as a freelance musician and music teacher, studying the works of C. P. E. Bach to learn the art of composition. He subsequently studied with the Italian composer Nicola Porpora (1686–1768) and in 1760 made an unfortunate marriage. In 1761 he became kapellmeister to the Esterházy family, a post he held for the rest of his life. In 1791 and 1794 he visited London and wrote his last 12 symphonies, which include the *Oxford* and *London* symphonies. Haydn's numerous compositions include piano sonatas, piano trios, string quartets, masses, concertos, 104 symphonies, operas, and the oratorios *The Creation* (1798) and *The Seasons* (1801).

Hayes, Helen (Helen Hayes Brown; 1900–93) US actress. At home on the stage from the age of five, she appeared in *Dear Brutus* (1918), *Caesar and Cleopatra* (1925), *What Every Woman Knows* (1926), *Mary of Scotland* (1933), *Victoria Regina* (1935–39), *Harriet* (1944), *The Glass Menagerie* (1948), *Time Remembered* (1958), and *Harvey* (1970). Her movie credits include *The Sin of Madelon Claudet* (1931) and *Airport* (1969) for which she won Academy Awards. She was married (1928) to playwright Charles MacArthur (1895–1956). Her life and experiences are recounted in *A Gift of Joy* (1965).

Hayes, Rutherford B(irchard) (1822–93) US statesman; 19th president of the United States (1877–81). A graduate of Kenyon College (1842) and Harvard Law School (1845), Hayes began his political career in Cincinnati, Ohio, where he served as city solicitor (1858–61). During the Civil War, he was active in the *Republican party and was elected to the US House of Representatives in 1864. Hayes served three terms as governor of Ohio (1868–72, 1876–77) and won the Republican presidential nomination in 1876. Although he received fewer popular votes than his Democratic opponent, Samuel Tilden, he was declared the winner by the *Electoral College. Hayes's administration marked the end of the *Reconstruction period and federal troops were withdrawn from the South. Among Hayes's other achievements was a courageous but unpopular proposal to reform the civil service system. Opposition to this measure within the Republican party prevented Hayes from gaining renomination in 1880.

hay fever An *allergy to pollen, which leads to sneezing, a streaming nose, and inflamed eyes. If the sufferer is allergic to only one kind of pollen it may be possible to desensitize him (*see* desensitization); otherwise treatment is with *antihistamines or, in severe cases, steroids.

Haymarket Massacre (1886) A riot during a labor union protest rally in Haymarket Square, Chicago, that resulted in the deaths of seven policemen. Anarchists, who organized the meeting to protest against police brutality at a strike site the day before, bombed police attempting to disperse the crowd. The police retaliated with gunfire; rioting and panic ensued. The anarchist leaders were arrested, charged, and convicted of murder; four were hanged (1887), one took his own life, and three were pardoned (1893).

Hays, Arthur Garfield (1885–1954) US civil liberties lawyer. As a defense attorney with Clarence *Darrow, he participated in the Scopes evolution trial (1925). Other well-known cases in which he was the defense lawyer included the Sacco-Vanzetti case (1927) and the murder trial of the Scottsboro Nine (1931). He also defended Pennsylvania and Kentucky coal miners' attempts to unionize and championed civil rights in Puerto Rico. He wrote *Let Freedom Ring* (1928), *Trial by Prejudice* (1933), and *Democracy Works* (1939).

Haywood, William Dudley (1869–1928) US labor leader. Active in the unionization of miners in the West, he was instrumental in the founding of the Industrial Workers of the World (IWW) in 1905. Also in 1905 he was tried for being involved in the murder of former Idaho governor Frank R. Steunenberg, who opposed unions. Acquitted, Haywood went on to head the IWW and advocated violence to achieve labor's aims. He denounced World War I in 1917, was arrested, convicted of sedition, and given a 20-year prison sentence. He escaped while on bail and fled to the Soviet Union.

hazard A dice game of great antiquity, played in Europe since the Middle Ages and popular among gamblers since the 17th and 18th centuries. Two dice are used. The person throwing the dice calls a number between 5 and 9; to win he must throw either this number or a 12 if he has called 6 or 8, or an 11 if he has called 7. An ace loses him the throw, as does an 11 if he has called 5, 6, 8, or 9, or a 12 if he has called 5, 7, or 9. He continues to throw until he either wins or loses. *See also* craps.

hazel A hardy shrub or tree of the N temperate genus *Corylus* (15 species), cultivated since ancient times for its edible nuts, also called cobnuts. Flowers appear in early spring, before the leaves (which are rounded and toothed). The male flowers are attractive yellow catkins; each female flower, which consists only of two bright-red stigmas, develops into a nut partly enclosed in a green fringed husk. The best-known species is the European hazel (*C. avellana*), up to 39 ft (12 m) high. Family: *Betulaceae* (birch family) or, according to some authorities, *Corylaceae*.

Hazlitt, William (1778–1830) British critic and essayist. He studied art and philosophy before becoming a journalist on various dailies and periodicals, including the *Edinburgh Review*. A friend of Wordsworth and Coleridge, Hazlitt held independent opinions in politics and literary matters and expressed them in a style notable for its brilliant invective. His best-known collections of essays and lectures are *Characters of Shakespeare's Plays* (1818–19), *Lectures on the English Poets* (1818) and *The Spirit of the Age* (1825).

Health and Human Services, Department of (HHS) A US cabinet-level executive branch department that deals with human concerns. Headed by the secretary of Health and Human Services, the department includes the Office of Human Development Services; the Public Health Service, which includes Centers for Disease Control; Medicare and Medicaid programs; the Food and Drug Administration; the National Institutes of Health; and the Social Security Administration. Created as the Department of *Health, Education, and Welfare (1953), it assumed its current duties and was renamed in 1979.

Health, Education, and Welfare, Department of US cabinet-level executive branch department (1953–79). It was divided into the Department of *Education and the Department of *Health and Human Services.

health physics The study of the problems that arise from the use of radiation of various kinds, especially those emitted by radioactive substances. Particular areas of study include *radioactive waste disposal, the maximum levels of radiation to which workers may reasonably be exposed, and the causes and effects of *radiation sickness. Health physics is a multidisciplinary subject involving physics, medicine, mathematics, chemistry, biology, and hygiene.

Heard and MacDonald Islands A group of uninhabited subantarctic islands in the S Indian Ocean, under Australian control since 1947. Heard Island is mountainous and chiefly ice covered; its elephant seals and penguins were hunted in the 19th century. The MacDonald Islands consist of a group of rocky islets.

hearing aid A device used by the partially deaf to increase the loudness of sounds. A simple form of hearing aid is the ear trumpet, which by its conical shape increases the sound pressure at the ear. Modern hearing aids are electronic and, since the advent of microcircuitry, can be made sufficiently small to be unobtrusive. An electronic hearing aid consists of a microphone to convert the sound into electrical signals, which are passed into an amplifier. The amplified signal is then fed into an earphone to convert the signal back into a sound wave of increased intensity.

Hearst, William Randolph (1863–1951) US newspaper publisher. Beginning with the *San Francisco Examiner,* which he took over from his father, and the New York *Morning Journal,* which he bought, he built up a vast newspaper empire whose commercial success was based on popular sensationalism, known as "yellow journalism." His career inspired Orson *Welles's movie *Citizen Kane* (1941).

heart A four-chambered muscular organ that pumps blood around the body. Two chambers—the left and right atria—dilate to receive oxygen-rich blood from the lungs and oxygen-depleted blood from the rest of the body, respectively (this is called diastole). Contraction of the heart (called systole) starts in the atria, forcing blood into the two ventricles. The left ventricle then contracts to force blood into a large artery—the aorta, which leads from the heart and feeds all the other arteries. The right ventricle pumps blood into the pulmonary artery and to the lungs, where it receives oxygen. Valves between the atria and ventricles and at the arterial exits of the heart prevent the backflow of blood. The rhythm of the heartbeat is maintained by the electrical activity of a group of specialized cells within the heart (*see* pacemaker). The muscle of the heart is supplied with blood by the coronary arteries. *Atherosclerosis of these arteries is the most common form of heart disease in industrial societies: it may lead to a heart attack (*see* coronary heart disease; myocardial infarction). Other disorders affecting the heart include disease of the valves (which may result from rheumatic fever) and congenital heart disease—defects in the heart present at birth. *See also* circulation of the blood.

heartburn A burning pain felt behind the breastbone. It is usually due to regurgitation of the contents of the stomach into the gullet and may be associated with inflammation of the gullet. It is relieved by antacids (drugs that neutralize stomach acids).

heart-lung machine An apparatus that temporarily replaces the functions of the heart and the lungs during heart surgery. Blood from two main veins is drained from the body through tubes to an apparatus that bubbles oxygen through it. The oxygenated blood is then returned to a large artery in the body by a mechanical pump.

heartsease. *See* pansy.

heart urchin A marine invertebrate animal belonging to an order (*Spatangoida*) of *echinoderms. It typically has a rigid heart-shaped body, covered with short fine spines used for locomotion and defense. It lives in burrows lined with mucus and uses long tentacles (modified tube feet) to pick up particles of food from the surrounding sand. Class: *Echinoidea.*

heat The form of energy that is transferred from one body or region to another at a lower temperature. The amount of heat gained or lost by a body is equal to the product of its *heat capacity and the temperature through which it rises or falls. Heat is transferred by conduction, convection, or radiation (*see* heat transfer). The heat contained by a body is equal to the *total* *kinetic energy of its component atoms and molecules; its temperature is the *average* of their kinetic energies. Heat is measured in joules, but older units, such as calories and British thermal units, are still sometimes used.

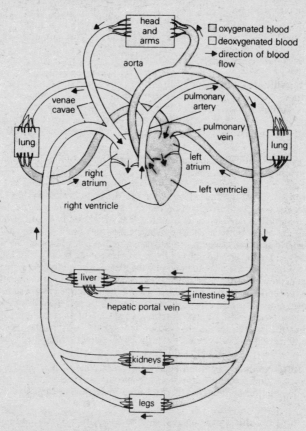

HEART *In man and other mammals the right and left chambers of the heart are completely separate from each other. This ensures that oxygenated and deoxygenated blood do not mix and enables oxygen-depleted blood to receive a fresh supply of oxygen from the lungs before circulating to the rest of the body.*

heat capacity The amount of heat needed to raise the temperature of a body through one degree Celsius (symbol: *C*). It is measured in joules per kelvin. For a gas, the heat capacity may be measured under conditions of either constant pressure or constant volume. *See also* specific heat capacity.

heat death of universe A hypothetical final state of the universe in which its *entropy is at a maximum and no heat is available to do work. In any closed system the total entropy can never decrease during any process. Thus the entropy of the universe will eventually reach a maximum value and when that happens all matter will be totally disordered and at a uniform temperature. This assumes that the universe can be treated as a closed system.

heat engine A device that converts heat energy into work. Examples are gasoline and diesel engines, gas turbines, and steam engines. In terms of *thermodynamics, the heat engine converts a quantity of heat q_1 at temperature T_1 into work w; but the conversion can never be complete, some of the heat q_2 will be wasted and can be regarded as being discharged into a heat sink at a temperature T_2. The efficiency of the engine is defined as the work output divided by the heat input (w/q_1). As the work, w, is equal to $q_1 - q_2$ (according to the first law of thermodynamics), the efficiency is $1 - q_2/q_1$, or $1 - T_2/T_1$. It is therefore important to make T_1 as high as possible and T_2 as low as possible. *See also* Carnot cycle; internal-combustion engine.

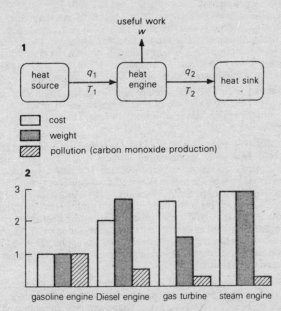

HEAT ENGINE *The efficiency of a heat engine depends on the temperature* T_1 *at which heat is fed to it and the temperature* T_2 *at which waste heat is discharged* (1). *A comparison of cost, weight, and pollution for various types of heat engine is shown at* (2).

heath An evergreen shrub or tree of the genus *Erica* (about 500 species) of Europe and Africa (about 470 species are native to South Africa). Heaths have small whorled often needlelike leaves and spikes of bell-shaped or tubular flowers, white, pink, purple, or yellow in color. Dwarf heaths, such as the European species *E. tetralix* (bog heather) and *E. cinerea* (bell heather), are abundant on acid peaty soils, such as moorlands. There are many cultivated varieties, which are popular in rock gardens. Some tree heaths grow to a height of 20 ft (6 m). Family: *Ericaceae*.

Heath, Edward (Richard George) (1916–   ) British statesman; Conservative prime minister (1970–74), who took the UK into the EEC (1973). He entered Parliament in 1950 and held several cabinet posts. In 1965 he succeeded Douglas-Home as leader of the Conservative party. His government faced economic difficulties and union strife. Defeated in 1975 he relinquished the party leadership to Margaret Thatcher.

heather (*or* ling) An evergreen shrub, *Calluna vulgaris,* up to 24 in (60 cm) high, with scaly leaves and clusters of pale-purple bell-shaped flowers. It grows—often with *heath—on acid soils of heaths, moors, and bogs throughout Europe and in parts of N Africa and North America (where it was probably introduced). Family: *Ericaceae.*

Heathrow (or London Airport) 51 28N 0 27W The chief airport for the UK, in the Greater London borough of Hounslow.

heat pump A device that extracts heat from one substance at a low temperature and supplies it to another substance at a higher temperature. Such a process would violate the second law of *thermodynamics if it occurred spontaneously; therefore the heat pump necessarily consumes energy in the process. Heat pumps are used to extract the low temperature heat from rivers that flow through towns and to convert it to a higher temperature so that use can be made of it, for example in space- and water-heating units. *See also* refrigeration.

heatstroke A rise in body temperature associated with *dehydration and exhaustion, caused by overexposure to high temperatures. The emergency treatment is to cool the patient down with water or fans, but medical treatment may be needed in addition.

heat transfer The transference of energy between two bodies or regions by virtue of the difference in temperatures between them. The three methods of transference are: *convection, *conduction, and *radiation. In convection the heat is transferred by a hotter region flowing into a colder region, either as a result of density differences (natural convection) or by using a fan (forced convection). In conduction, on the other hand, the heat is transferred by direct contact without any apparent relative motion. In radiation the heat is transferred by means of either *infrared radiation or *microwave radiation. Radiation is the only method of transferring heat through a vacuum. The *Dewar (Thermos) flask is designed to minimize heat transfer, whereas the heat exchanger or radiator is designed to maximize it.

heat treatment The process of heating a metal to a temperature below its melting point and then cooling it in order to change its physical properties. Metals are made up of tiny crystals (grains). Their hardness, strength, and ductility is determined by the concentration and distribution of irregularities (dislocations) in the crystal lattice. In response to stress the dislocations move and change the shape and orientation of the grains. Heating creates and redistributes dislocations, relieving any internal stresses that have built up. This makes the metal softer and more ductile; a process known as annealing. Dislocation movement is restricted by the boundaries between grains and by the presence of impurities, which "pin" the dislocations making the metal harder and less ductile. Because both the impurity distribution and the grain structure are affected by heating and the rate of cooling, so also is the metal's strength. In steel manufacture, rapid cooling (quenching) by immersion in water or oil hardens the steel, leaving it brittle. Slow cooling makes it soft and ductile. The process of heating steel to around 900°C and quenching it, followed by warming to about 300°, is known as hardening and tempering. This results in a tough springy steel. *See also* case hardening; work hardening.

heaven In Christian belief, the abode of God and the angels, in which the souls of the virtuous will be rewarded with everlasting life. The iconography of heaven is based upon the account in the Book of Revelation. The peace, light, and harmony of heaven are generally interpreted as metaphors for the bliss enjoyed by beings in the uninterrupted praise and contemplation of God (*compare* hell). Analogous concepts exist in other major religions.

Heaviside, Oliver (1850–1925) British physicist, who pioneered the mathematical study of electric circuits and helped to develop vector analysis. Independently of *Kennelly, he predicted and then discovered a charged layer of the upper atmosphere that was capable of reflecting radio waves. This region, now known as the E-region of the *ionosphere, was formerly called the Heaviside layer or Heaviside-Kennelly layer.

heavy water Deuterium oxide (D_2O), the form of water containing the isotope of hydrogen with mass number 2. It is chemically less reactive than normal water and has a relative density of 1.1; its boiling point is 215°F (101.42°C). It is present to an extent of 1 part in 5000 in natural water and it is used as a moderator and coolant in some nuclear reactors.

Hebe In Greek mythology, the personification of youth. She was the daughter of Zeus and Hera and is described by Homer as cupbearer to the gods and the wife of Heracles.

Hebei (Ho-pei *or* Hopeh) A province in NE China, on the Yellow Sea. Its fertile S plain is one of the earliest areas of civilization. Chief products are cereals, cotton, coal, and iron. Area: 79,053 sq mi (202,700 sq km). Population (1968 est): 43,000,000. Capital: Shijiazhuang.

Hébert, Jacques-René (1757–94) French journalist and revolutionary. With his newspaper *Le Père Duchesne* he attained a wide following among the Parisian working class (*see* sans-culottes), becoming their leading demagogue. In 1792 he helped engineer the overthrow of the monarchy and became the procurator general of the Paris Commune. His unsuccessful attempt to incite a popular uprising against the Committee of *Public Safety resulted in his execution.

Hebrew A Semitic language. It is written from right to left in an alphabet of 22 letters, all consonants, with vowels indicated by subscript and superscript diacritical marks. The oldest and best-known works of Hebrew literature are those preserved in the *Bible (Old Testament). Mishnaic Hebrew is a somewhat different language, spoken in Palestine until the 2nd century AD. It is the language of the *Mishna and the oldest extant Jewish prayers. Hebrew continued to be a literary language throughout the Middle Ages, with a particularly rich poetic tradition, besides prose writing. The study of Hebrew grammar was developed by the *Masoretes, and by the *gaon Saadya and later grammarians. In more modern times the *Haskala movement led to a renaissance in Hebrew writing, and from the late 19th century Hebrew was revived as a spoken language, particularly in Russia and Palestine. The *Ashkenazim and *Sephardim differ in their pronunciation of Hebrew. In 1948 it became an official language of Israel.

Hebrew literature A body of literature originating as early as 1200 BC in Old Testament writings and still flourishing in the modern secular idiom of Israel. Not synonymous with Jewish literature (which was frequently composed in other languages, e.g. Arabic or Yiddish), Hebrew literature reflects the vicissitudes of the Hebrew language, being confined after about 200 AD to religious and legal texts and commentaries (*see* Mishna; Talmud). Medieval Spain produced some original talents, including the poets *Judah ha-Levi and *Ibn Gabirol and the philosopher *Maimonides. The 18th-century Haskala (enlightenment) in E Europe initiated the renaissance of secular literature, and the rise of Zionism encouraged the novelist *Agnon and the poet *Bialik, among others, to mold Hebrew into a modern literary language.

Hebrews, Epistle to the A New Testament book by an unknown author (formerly believed to be Paul), probably written between 62 and 69 AD. The book asserts that Christ is the high priest and greater than any of the *Levites and that his work fulfills and renders obsolete the old *covenant between God and Israel. The book is obviously addressed to readers who had a thorough knowledge of Judaism and is intended to confirm such converts in their new faith.

Hebrides, the A group of about 500 islands off the W coast of Scotland. The islands are subdivided into the Inner and Outer Hebrides, separated by the Minch. The chief islands of the Outer Hebrides include Lewis with Harris and the Uists; those of the Inner Hebrides include Skye, Mull, Islay, and Jura. The main occupations are stock rearing, fishing, and crofting (producing fodder crops, potatoes, and vegetables). Harris tweed is produced, especially in the Uists.

Hebron (Arabic name: Al Khalil) 31 32N 35 06E A city in the S of the *West Bank of the Jordan River. It is one of the oldest continuously inhabited cities in the world and is revered by both Jews and Muslims as the burial place of Abraham. Population: 43,000.

Hecate A primitive Greek fertility goddess and a ruler of the underworld. She was associated with witchcraft and magic and was worshiped at crossroads. She witnessed the abduction of *Persephone and accompanied *Demeter in her search for her daughter.

Hecht, Ben (1894–1964) US dramatist and writer. A newspaperman in Chicago from 1910, he coauthored, with fellow newspaperman Charles MacArthur, *The Front Page* (1928). His novels include *Erik Dorn* (1921), *Gargoyles* (1922), *The Florentine Dagger* (1923), *Count Bruga* (1926), and *A Jew in Love* (1930). He wrote and produced screenplays, including *Scarface* (1932), *Design for Living* (1933), *Notorious* (1946), and *The Scoundrel* (1935), which received an Academy Award.

hectare (ha) A unit of area in the *metric system equal to 100 ares or 10,000 square meters; 1 ha = 2.471 acres.

Hector In Greek legend, the eldest son of Priam, king of Troy, and the chief Trojan warrior. He was the husband of Andromache. He fought Ajax in single combat, killed *Patroclus, and was killed in revenge by *Achilles. Priam pleaded for the return of his body, which was buried with great ceremony.

Hecuba In Greek legend, the wife of Priam, king of Troy, and mother of *Hector. She was captured by the Greeks after the fall of Troy, but in revenge for the death of her son Polydorus, she blinded King Polymestor of Thrace and killed his sons.

hedgehog A nocturnal prickly-coated insectivorous mammal belonging to the subfamily *Erinaceinae* (15 species), of Africa, Europe, and Asia. The European hedgehog (*Erinaceus europaeus*) grows up to 12 in (30 cm) long and has brown and cream spines and soft gray-brown underfur. It feeds on worms, beetles, slugs, and snails, hunting mainly by scent and hearing along ditches and hedgerows. Hedgehogs hibernate in colder climates. Family: *Erinaceidae*. □mammal.

hedgehog cactus A cactus of the North American genus *Echinocactus* (10 species), some species of which are cultivated as pot plants. They have round or cylindrical strongly ribbed woolly stems bearing many spines and—at the top— mainly yellow flowers.

hedge sparrow. *See* dunnock.

hedging A commercial operation enabling a trader or speculator to protect himself against unpredictable changes in price. In *commodity markets, trading in futures (goods for delivery in the future) provides a hedging facility. For example, a manufacturer may wish to purchase a year's supply of a commodity for regular deliveries throughout the year but may expect the price to fall over the period. In this case he could hedge his purchase by selling short (i.e. selling without buying) on a futures market so that he could cover (buy back) the sales at a lower price if there was a fall in prices.

hedonism The ethical theory holding that pleasure is the greatest good. Varying definitions of pleasure distinguished the classical hedonistic schools but all considered individual rather than communal happiness. *Utilitarianism, the most important modern form of hedonism, uses a social criterion: "The greatest good of the greatest number." *Compare* Epicureanism.

Hefei (*or* Hofei) 31 55N 117 18E A city in E China, capital of Anhui province. The capital of a 10th-century kingdom, it is now a fast-growing industrial center with an industrial university and a scientific university. Population (1990): 733,278.

Hegel, Georg Wilhelm Friedrich (1770–1831) German philosopher, one of the greatest and most influential thinkers of the 19th century. He followed *Kant, *Fichte, and *Schelling but exceeded them all in the scale and erudition of his work. He developed his ideas slowly and steadily; his first major work, *The Phenomenology of Mind,* was published in 1807, the *Encyclopedia of the Philosophical Sciences* in 1817, and *The Philosophy of Right* in 1821. Besides these major works, he left voluminous lecture notes on history, religion, and aesthetics. He became an eminent and respected figure, collecting disciples, appointments, and decorations before dying, in Berlin, of cholera. *See also* Hegelianism.

Hegelianism The idealist school of thought based on the philosophy of *Hegel. His followers built on his idea that philosophy is the highest available form of knowledge and that all other forms (scientific, religious, etc.) must be referred to it. Ambiguity in Hegel's own thought has encouraged considerable diversity in interpreters of Hegelianism. The so-called Old Hegelians thought religion could be brought into harmony with philosophy, while the Young Hegelians saw philosophy as essentially critical of religion. *Marx was influenced by the Young Hegelians, especially *Feuerbach.

Hegira (Arabic *hijrah*: migration) The usual English name for the Muslim era. Based on lunar months, it is reckoned from 622 AD (or 1 AH, from Latin *anno hegirae*), the date of Mohammed's migration from Mecca to Medina. Most Muslim countries now use both the Hegira calendar and the Christian or Common Era calendar.

Heidegger, Martin (1889–1976) German philosopher. His main philosophical work was *Sein und Zeit* (*Being and Time*; 1927). As rector of Freiburg University (1933–34) he supported Hitler and this association, together with logical flaws in his work, has damaged his reputation. Although his preoccupation with *Angst* (dread) as a fundamental part of human consciousness is typical of *existentialism, Heidegger himself denied that he was an existentialist.

Heidelberg 49 25N 08 42E A city in SW Germany, in the state of Baden-Württemberg on the Neckar River. A tourist center, it has a ruined castle (mainly 16th–17th centuries) and the oldest university in Germany (1386), famed for its student prison. Its varied manufactures include printing presses, cigars, and electrical appliances. *History*: the capital of the Palatinate until 1685, it was devastated during the Thirty Years' War and later by the French. During the 19th century it was the student center of Germany. In 1952 it became the European headquarters of the US army. Population (1991 est): 136,800.

Heifetz, Jascha (1901–87) US violinist; born in Russia. A child prodigy, he was performing internationally by 1912. He made his American debut in 1917 at Carnegie Hall, New York City, moved to California, and became an American citizen. He toured extensively, often playing with Gregor Piatigorsky, cellist, and William Primrose, violist.

Heilbronn 49 08N 9 14E A city in SW Germany, in Baden-Württemberg on the Neckar River. Many historic buildings, including the town hall (1540), were reconstructed after World War II. It is a transshipment point and a center for electrical engineering. Population (1991 est): 115,800.

Heilongjiang (Hei-lung-chiang *or* Heilungkiang) A province in NE China, bordering on Russia, comprising N Manchuria. The Da Hinggan Ling (mountains) provide valuable timber, while wheat is grown on the S plain. Oil, coal, and gold are produced. Area: 179,000 sq mi (464,000 sq km). Population (1990): 35,214,873. Capital: Ha-er-bin.

Heimdall The Norse god of light and dawn, who guarded the Bifrost bridge between *Asgard (the home of the gods) and *Midgard (the earth). He possessed miraculously sharp sight and hearing.

Heine, Heinrich (1797–1856) German-Jewish poet and writer. Before establishing himself as a writer, he worked in banking and studied law. His early works include *Buch der Lieder* (1827), a collection of poetry, and his prose *Reisebilder* (1826–31), in which accounts of his travels are mixed with satirical comment. Sympathetic to revolutionary politics, he moved to Paris in 1831 and remained there until his death. In this period he wrote essays on French and German culture and some satirical poetry, notably *Atta Troll: Ein Sommernachtstraum* (1847).

Heinlein, Robert Anson (1907–88) US science-fiction writer. A pioneer in science fiction, he wrote *The Green Hills of Earth* (1951), *Double Star* (1956), *Door into Summer* (1957), *Stranger in a Strange Land* (1961), *I Will Fear No Evil* (1970), and *Friday* (1982). His books for children include *Rocket Ship Galileo* (1947) and *The Star Beast* (1954).

Heisenberg, Werner Karl (1901–76) German physicist, who, with *Schrödinger, was the main architect of quantum mechanics. In 1927 Heisenberg created a mathematical system, known as matrix mechanics, to explain the structure of the hydrogen atom. *Dirac soon showed that matrix mechanics and Schrödinger's wave mechanics were equivalent. In the same year he put forward the theory known as the *Heisenberg uncertainty principle, which has had a profound effect on both physics and philosophy. For this discovery he was awarded the Nobel Prize in 1932. Heisenberg was one of the few major physicists to remain in Germany during the Nazi period; during World War II he was in charge of Germany's unsuccessful attempts to make an atom bomb at the Max Planck Institute in Berlin. After the war he became director of the Max Planck Institute for Physics in Göttingen.

Heisenberg uncertainty principle If a simultaneous measurement is made of the position and momentum of a particle then, no matter how accurate the measurements, there is always an uncertainty in the values obtained. The product of the uncertainties is of the same order as *Planck's constant. A similar uncertainty exists with the simultaneous measurement of energy and time. The uncertainty arises because the act of observing the system interferes with it in an unpredictable way. Uncertainty is only important at the atomic and subatomic levels and at this level throws the principle of causality into doubt. Named for Werner *Heisenberg.

Hejaz A historic province in Saudi Arabia, bordering on the Red Sea. Hilly inland, its coastal plain supports some agriculture; significant income is also derived from light industry and from pilgrims to the holy Muslim cities of Mecca and Medina. The largest town is Jidda. Hejaz, formerly independent, joined *Najd in a dual kingdom in 1926, and both became part of Saudi Arabia in 1932. Area: about 135,107 sq mi (350,000 sq km).

Hel In Norse mythology, the underworld; also called Nifleheim. It was covered with ice and guarded by the dog Garm. It is also the name of the goddess of death and ruler of the underworld, who was the daughter of the giant *Loki.

Helder, Den. *See* Den Helder.

Helen In Greek legend, the daughter of Zeus and *Leda, famed for her supreme beauty. She married Menelaus, king of Sparta, but later fled to Troy with *Paris, thus precipitating the *Trojan War. After the fall of Troy she was reunited with Menelaus.

Helena 46 35N 112 00W The capital city of Montana. It is the commercial center for an agricultural and mining region. Population (1990): 24,569.

Helena, St (c. 248–c. 328 AD) Roman empress, mother of Constantine the Great. A Christian from 313, she made a pilgrimage to the Holy Land (c. 326), where she founded several churches and, according to tradition, rediscovered the cross used at the crucifixion. Feast day: Aug 18. Emblem: the cross.

Helgoland (*or* Heligoland) 54 09N 7 52E A German island in the North Sea, in the North Frisian group. Ceded to Britain in 1814, it was transferred to Germany in exchange for Zanzibar (1890) and was a major German naval base during both World Wars. With the end of World War II its fortifications were destroyed. Area: about .6 sq mi (1.5 sq km).

Heliconia A genus of perennial herbaceous plants (about 120 species), native to tropical America and cultivated for ornament in the tropics. They have stout or reedlike stems and the leaves are often coppery with an ivory and pink midrib. The small flowers are contained within brightly colored pointed bracts: *H. psittacorum* has green-yellow black-spotted flowers and red bracts. Family: *Heliconiaceae*.

helicopter An aircraft that obtains both its lift and its thrust from rotors rotating about a vertical axis (*compare* autogiro). The principle was known to Leonardo da Vinci, but the first successful helicopter was made in the US in 1939 by Igor *Sikorsky (his 1909 model, made in Russia, failed to lift a man). A helicopter using a single rotor requires an antitorque tail propeller and some models also use a vertical propeller for forward thrust. Helicopters can rise and drop vertically, hover, and move backward, forward, and sideways by control of the pitch of the rotors. First used in World War II, helicopters were widely employed for military purposes in the Korean and Vietnam wars. They have since been developed for rescue services, police and traffic observation, and urban passenger services.

heliocentric system Any model of the solar system in which the planets move around the sun. The geocentric *Ptolemaic system was accepted for centuries until the heliocentric system of *Copernicus was published in 1543 and, after much religious and scientific controversy, shown to be true.

Heliopolis An ancient Egyptian city near present-day Cairo dedicated to the cult of the sun god Re. *Cleopatra's Needles came from there.

Helios The Greek sun god, usually represented as a charioteer driving the sun across the sky each day. In later legends he was identified with Hyperion or Apollo. Because he was all-seeing he was called to witness oaths and promises.

heliotrope A herb or shrub of the genus *Heliotropium* (220 species), found in tropical and temperate regions and having heads of blue or white flowers. Many will withstand cold, but none will survive frost. Many horticultural varieties of the cherry-pie plant (*H. peruvianum*) and *H. corymbosa* are used as bedding plants in cooler climates. Family: *Boraginaceae*.

helium (He) The lightest noble gas, first detected in 1868 by Janssen (1838–1904) as an unexpected line in the spectrum of the sun. The term is derived from Greek *helios,* sun. Helium was discovered in 1895 in the uranium mineral, clevite, as a radioactive decay product (*see* radioactivity). Because of its low density and chemical inertness, it is extensively used for filling balloons. It is also used as a gas shield in arc welding, and to replace nitrogen in the breathing mixture used by divers. Helium has the lowest melting point of any element. At no 2; at wt 4.0026; mp −458°F (−272.2°C); bp −452°F (−268.9°C).

helium dating A method of dating materials that utilizes the production of helium in the form of *alpha particles during the radioactive decay of uranium-235, uranium-238, or thorium-232. The amount of helium trapped in the sample may be used to measure its age, after correction to allow for diffusion. The method is used mainly for rocks, minerals, and fossils.

hell In Christian belief, the place in which the fallen *angels under *Lucifer and the souls of the wicked are imprisoned in everlasting torment. The concept of hell as a dark and fiery pit derives from the Book of Revelation and opinions have differed widely regarding its nature. Some Christians insist upon the physical reality of hellfire; others consider it a metaphor for the misery of a soul deprived forever of the vision of God (*compare* heaven). According to the doctrine often condemned as a heresy and known as apocatastasis, hell is not everlasting but will eventually be destroyed and all creatures, even the fallen angels, will be restored to God's grace. *Compare* purgatory.

hellbender The largest North American *salamander, *Cryptobranchus alleganiensis.* Growing to over 24 in (60 cm), it is dark olive-green with a wrinkled shiny skin. Hellbenders inhabit fast-moving oxygen-rich water, emerging from under rocks to feed at night on small animals and carrion. Family: *Cryptobranchidae*.

hellebore A poisonous perennial herb of the genus *Helleborus* (20 species), of Europe and W Asia. The stinking hellebore (*H. foetidus*) grows to a height of 12–20 in (30–50 cm) and bears clusters of cup-shaped purple-edged green flowers. Family: *Ranunculaceae*. *See also* Christmas rose.

helleborine A terrestrial *orchid of either of the genera *Cephalanthera* (about 14 species) or *Epipactis* (about 24 species), native to N temperate regions. They have tall thin stems, crinkled leaves, and clusters of flowers, which are either small, stalked, and drooping (*Epipactis*) or larger, stalkless, and held erect (*Cephalanthera*). The white helleborine (*C. damasonium*) and the marsh helleborine (*E. palustris*) are two Eurasian species.

Hellen In Greek mythology, the grandson of Prometheus and eponymous ancestor of the Greeks, who called themselves the Hellenes and their country Hellas. The four subgroups of the Hellenes, the Aeolians, Dorians, Ionians, and Achaeans, were named for his sons and grandsons.

Hellenistic age The period, between the death of Alexander the Great of Macedon (323 BC) and the accession of the Roman emperor Augustus (27 BC), when Greek culture spread throughout the Mediterranean. Alexander's conquests took Greek ideas to the East and in the political confusion that followed his death city-states became cosmopolitan and Greek colonists, following in

Alexander's footsteps, implanted Greek ideas in their new environments. In the Hellenistic period Alexandria in Egypt was the major commercial city and center of intellectual life, including scholarly literature and grandiose art, *Epicureanism, *Neoplatonism, Stoic philosophy, *gnosticism, and Christianity. The Koine, common Greek, was the universal language.

Heller, Joseph (1923–   ) US novelist. He served in the Air Force during World War II and subsequently worked in advertising. His best-known novel, *Catch-22* (1961), is a satirical portrayal of the horrors of modern warfare and bureaucracy. He has also written three other novels, *Something Happened* (1974), *Good as Gold* (1979), and *God Knows* (1984), and a play, *We Bombed in New Haven* (1968). In 1994 a sequel to *Catch-22*, *Closing Time*, was published.

Hellespont. *See* Dardanelles.

Hellman, Lillian (1905–84) US dramatist. Her plays, often concerning political themes, include *The Children's Hour* (1934), *The Little Foxes* (1939), *Watch on the Rhine* (1941), *The Searching Wind* (1944), and *Another Part of the Forest* (1946). She was a close friend of Dashiell *Hammett and published volumes of memoirs, including *An Unfinished Woman* (1969), *Pentimento* (1973), and *Scoundrel Time* (1976).

Helmand River (Helmund *or* Hilmand) The longest river in Afghanistan. Rising in the E of the country, it flows generally SW then N to enter the marshy lake of Helmand on the Afghan-Iranian border. Length: 870 mi (1400 km).

helmet shell A *gastropod mollusk belonging to the family *Cassidae* (about 60 species), also called bonnet shell. Found in shallow tropical seas and measuring 0.8–10 in (2–25 cm) long, they feed mainly on sea urchins. ☐shells.

Helmholtz, Hermann Ludwig Ferdinand von (1821–94) German physicist and physiologist, who made contributions to many fields of science. In physiology his main interest was the sense organs, discovering the function of the cochlea in the inner ear and developing T. *Young's theory of color vision (now known as the Young-Helmholtz theory). This work was published in his *Physiological Optics* (1856). His study of muscle action led him to formulate a much more accurate theory concerning the conservation of energy than that earlier proposed by Julius *Mayer and James *Joule. He played a considerable part in the development of thermodynamics, especially in formulating the concept of free energy.

Helmont, Jan Baptist van (1580–1644) Belgian alchemist and physician, who discovered the gas now called *carbon dioxide. Although Helmont was an alchemist he was a skilled and careful experimenter and helped to transform alchemy into chemistry.

Heloise. *See* Abelard, Peter.

helots Indigenous Peloponnesian Greeks who lost their lands and freedom under the repressive state control of Sparta. They formed the farming communities of Messenia and Laconia.

Helsingborg. *See* Hälsingborg.

Helsingfors. *See* Helsinki.

Helsingør (*or* Elsinore) 56 03N 12 38E A seaport in Denmark, in NE Sjælland situated on the *Sound opposite Hälsingborg in Sweden. It contains the fortress of Kronborg (1580), famous as the scene of Shakespeare's play *Hamlet*. Its industries include shipbuilding, brewing, and food processing. Population: 55,404.

Helsinki (Swedish name: Helsingfors) 60 13N 24 55E The capital of Finland, a port in the S on the Gulf of Finland. It is the country's commercial and administrative center; industries include metals, textiles, food processing, and paper. Among its fine pale granite buildings are the 18th-century cathedral and the old senate house. The city is well laid out and spacious in appearance and is renowned for its 20th-century architecture. The university was moved there from Turku in 1828. *History*: founded by Gustavus I Vasa of Sweden in 1550 it was largely rebuilt following a fire in 1808. It replaced Turku as capital of Finland (then under Russian rule) in 1812. It was badly bombed in World War II. Population (1992 est): 496,300.

Helvetia. *See* Switzerland, Confederation of.

Helvetii A Celtic tribe that settled about 200 BC in what is now Switzerland. Defeated by Caesar as they migrated southward, they nevertheless retained their former territory, which was a buffer state between Rome and the Germans for over 400 years.

Helvétius, Claude Adrien (1715–71) French philosopher. He followed Hume in holding that self-interest was the only motive of human action. His principle of the artificial identity of interests (i.e. interests manipulated by government) influenced *Bentham. De l'esprit* (1758), expounding these views, was furiously denounced and burned by the public hangman.

hematite The principal ore of iron, ferric oxide, varying in color from red to gray to black. It contains over 70% iron. It occurs either in crystalline form (specular iron ore) or in massive form. Most ore deposits are derived from altered iron carbonates and silicates in sedimentary rocks.

hematology The study of blood and its diseases. This medical specialty is concerned particularly with treating *leukemias, *hemophilia, and rare kinds of anemia.

Hemel Hempstead 51 46N 0 28W A city in SE England, in Hertfordshire. Designated a new town in 1946, the principal industries include light engineering (aircraft components, scientific, electronic, and photographic equipment), paper, and pyrotechnics. Population: 78,000.

Hemichordata A phylum of marine invertebrate animals (about 100 species), found in coastal sand or mud and on the sea bed. The gill slits and nervous system show similarities with those of chordates—hence their name. The group comprises the *acornworms and the pterobranchs (class *Pterobranchia*). These are up to 0.28 in (7 mm) long and have tentacle-bearing arms. They often form colonies and reproduce both sexually and by budding.

Hemingway, Ernest (1899–1961) US novelist. After serving in the Red Cross during World War I he joined the American expatriate community in Paris. His first successful novel was *The Sun Also Rises* (1926). He was a keen sportsman and adventurer, and in his short stories and his later novels, including *For Whom the Bell Tolls* (1940), about the Spanish Civil War, and *The Old Man and the Sea* (1952), he celebrated the virtues of courage and stoicism in a forceful economical style. His other works include the novels *A Farewell to Arms* (1929), *To Have and Have Not* (1937), *A Moveable Feast* (1964), and *Islands in the Stream* (1970). Among his many memorable short stories were "The Snows of Kilimanjaro" (1936) and "The Short Happy Life of Francis Macomber" (1936). He won the Nobel Prize in 1954. Subject to severe depressions after leaving his home in Cuba in 1960, he committed suicide.

hemiplegia. *See* paralysis.

ERNEST HEMINGWAY *Noted for his short stories and novels emphasizing courage, Hemingway was awarded the Nobel Prize (1954).*

Hemiptera An order of insects (about 50,000 species)—the true bugs—having piercing mouthparts for sucking the juices from plants or animals. The suborder *Heteroptera* includes plant and animal feeders (*see* plant bug; water bug). The forewings of these insects have both a leathery and a membranous region and are held flat over the body at rest. The suborder *Homoptera,* including the *froghoppers, *aphids, *cicadas, and *scale insects, are all plant feeders and have uniform front wings, held roof-wise over the body at rest.

hemlock 1. A poisonous biennial plant, *Conium maculatum,* native to Europe, W Asia, and N Africa. It grows in damp places to a height of 7 ft (2 m) and has branching purple-spotted stems that bear much-divided leaves and clusters of tiny white flowers. The plant is notorious as the means by which Socrates died. Family: *Umbelliferae.* **2.** A coniferous tree of the genus *Tsuga* (15 species), native to S and E Asia and North America. The narrow bladelike leaves, up to 0.8 in (2 cm) long, are grouped in two rows along the stems and the brown egg-shaped cones are 0.8–1.2 in (2–3 cm) long. The western hemlock (*T. heterophylla*), of W North America, can reach a height of 197 ft (60 m); it is grown both for its strong timber and for ornament. Family: *Pinaceae.*

hemoglobin The substance, contained within the red blood cells (*see* erythrocyte), that is responsible for the color of blood. In humans hemoglobin consists of a protein (globin) combined with an iron-containing pigment (hem). Hem combines with oxygen, which is absorbed into the blood at the lungs, to form oxyhemoglobin, which gives arterial blood its bright-red color and is the means by which oxygen is transported around the body. Oxygen is released at the tissues and the pigment acquires a bluish tinge, responsible for the bluish-red color of venous blood.

hemophilia A hereditary disease in which the blood does not clot properly due to absence of one of the clotting factors. Some of the children of both Queen Victoria and Tsar Nicholas II had this disease, which is almost entirely restricted to boys but is transmitted through the mother. If an affected person (a hemophiliac) cuts himself seriously he may bleed to death without appropriate plasma transfusions. Hemophiliacs also bleed easily into their joints and other parts of the body and must therefore restrict their activities.

hemorrhage Bleeding. Large amounts of blood may be lost in severe injuries, from bleeding peptic ulcers, during operations, in childbirth, or if the patient has a clotting disorder (such as *hemophilia). In these circumstances it may be necessary to give a blood transfusion to avoid *shock and death. If hemorrhage occurs in a confined space, such as the brain or the eye, damage results from destruction of normal tissue.

hemorrhoids (*or* piles) Swollen (varicose) veins in the anal canal, which may enlarge sufficiently to hang down outside the anus. They are very common, usually resulting from chronic constipation, and tend to run in families. Piles may cause bleeding from the anus and itchiness, but rarely severe pain. In severe cases they may need to be surgically removed or injected with a sclerosing agent, which makes them shrivel up. External hemorrhoids are painful swellings at the side of the anus, caused by rupture of an anal vein.

hemp An annual herb, *Cannabis sativa,* native to central Asia and widely cultivated. It grows to a height of 16 ft (5 m) and bears lobed leaves and small yellow flowers. Hemp is cultivated in many temperate regions (e.g. Italy) for its fiber, obtained from the inner stem bark and used for ropes, sacking, and sailcloth. The flowers, bark, twigs, and leaves contain a narcotic resin (*see* cannabis)—source of marijuana and related drugs—for which the plant is widely grown, especially in the tropics. Family: *Moraceae. See also* Indian hemp.

Henan (*or* Honan) A province in E central China. The Yellow and the Huai Rivers irrigate the E fertile plain. Densely populated, it has been a center of Chinese culture since about 2000 BC. Chief products are cereals, cotton, silk, and coal. Area: 65,000 sq mi (167,000 sq km). Population (1990): 85,509,535. Capital: Zhengzhou.

henbane A strong-smelling poisonous annual or biennial herb, *Hyoscyamus niger,* native to Europe and N Africa. Up to 31 in (80 cm) high, it has funnel-shaped yellow flowers, veined with purple, and grows in sandy places. It contains the alkaloid hyoscyamine, used medicinally. Family: *Solanaceae.*

Henderson, Arthur (1863–1935) British Labour politician. He entered Parliament in 1903 and later led the parliamentary Labour party (1908–1910, 1914–1917). As foreign secretary (1929–31), he ardently supported the League of Nations and the Disarmament Conference, of which he became chairman in 1932. In 1934 he won the Nobel Peace Prize.

Hendricks, Thomas Andrews (1819–85) US politician; vice president (1885). A Democrat, he served in the Indiana state legislature before going to Congress as a representative (1851–55) and senator (1863–69). He was governor of Indiana (1873–77). He attained the vice presidency under Pres. Grover Cleveland, only to die in office nine months later.

Hendrix, Jimi (James Marshall H.; 1942–70) US rock singer and guitarist. With his group, the Jimi Hendrix Experience, Hendrix recorded such hits as "Purple Haze" and "Foxey Lady" and became famous for his virtuoso electric-guitar playing. He died as a result of a drug overdose.

henequen A perennial herbaceous plant, *Agave fourcroydes,* native to Mexico and cultivated for its leaf fibers called Yucatan, or Cuban, sisal. The plant stems grow to an average height of 35 in (90 cm) in cultivation and the lance-shaped leaves form a dense rosette. Each plant yields 25 leaves annually from 5 to 16 years after planting. The fibers, which have an average length of 4 ft (1.3 m), are made into twines used in agriculture, shipping, and rope. Family: *Agavaceae.*

Hengist and Horsa Legendary leaders of the first Anglo-Saxon settlers in Britain. According to the Anglo-Saxon Chronicle (late 9th century AD) Horsa was killed in 455 AD and his brother Hengist ruled over Kent from 455 to 488.

Hengyang 26 58N 112 31E A city in S China, in Hunan province on the Xiang (*or* Siang) River. A long-established communications, commercial, and cultural center, many historic buildings survive. Chemicals and machinery are manufactured. Population (1990): 487,148.

henna A shrub, *Lawsonia inermis,* occurring in Egypt, India, and the Middle East. Up to 7 ft (2 m) high, it has fragrant white-and-yellow flowers. The leaves are powdered and used for tinting the hair and nails a reddish color. It also has medicinal uses. Family: *Lythraceae.*

henry (H) The *SI unit of inductance equal to the inductance of a closed circuit such that a rate of change of current of one ampere per second produces an induced e.m.f of one volt. Named for Joseph *Henry.

Henry (I) the Fowler (c. 876–936) Duke of Saxony (912–36) and German king (919–36), founder of the Saxon dynasty (918–1024). In 925 he recovered Lotharingia for Germany, in 933 he defeated the Hungarians, and in 934, after invading Denmark, he won Schleswig for Germany.

Henry I (1069–1135) King of England (1100–35); the youngest son of *William (I) the Conqueror. Henry became king on the death of his brother William Rufus. In England his reign is notable for important legal and administrative reforms, and for the final resolution of the *investiture controversy. Abroad, Henry waged several campaigns in order to consolidate and expand his continental possessions.

Henry (II) the Saint (973–1024) German king and Holy Roman Emperor (1002–24; crowned 1014). After a protracted conflict with Poland he was forced to cede Lusatia but in Italy he successfully defended the papacy against the Greeks and Lombards. He sponsored Church reform, founding monasteries and schools. He was canonized in 1145.

Henry II (1133–89) King of England (1154–89); the son of Matilda and Geoffrey of Anjou and the grandson of Henry I. Henry succeeded Stephen. Married (1152) to *Eleanor of Aquitaine, he ruled an empire that stretched from the River Tweed to the Pyrenees (*see* Angevins). In spite of frequent hostilities with the French king, his own family, and rebellious barons (culminating in the great revolt of 1173–74) and his quarrel with Thomas *Becket, Henry maintained control over his possessions until shortly before his death. His judicial and administrative reforms, which greatly increased royal control and influence at the expense of the barons, were of great constitutional importance.

Henry II (1519–59) King of France (1547–59); the husband from 1533 of *Catherine de' Medici. He concluded war against the Emperor *Charles V at

Cateau-Cambrésis (1559), after winning the bishoprics of Metz, Toul, and Verdun. An ardent Roman Catholic, he began the systematic persecution of Huguenots, which ultimately led to the *Wars of Religion. He died of blood poisoning following injury in a tournament.

Henry III (1017–56) German king and Holy Roman Emperor (1039–56; crowned 1046), who greatly enhanced the power of the Empire. He became interested in Church reform under the influence of his second wife, Agnes, and at the synod of Constance (1043) announced his desire to reform the Church. His suppression of heresy, however, was unpopular and toward the end of his reign he faced rebellions in Germany, Hungary, and S Italy.

Henry III (1207–72) King of England (1216–72), succeeding his father John. A minor when he took the throne, Henry did not take the reins of government himself until 1234. Baronial discontent simmered, boiling over in 1258, when Henry, facing financial disaster, attempted to raise large sums from his magnates. Reforms were agreed upon but then renounced by Henry. Simon de *Montfort led a rebellion against the king (see Barons' Wars), which was defeated after initial success. Thereafter, the aged Henry ceded much power to his son, the future Edward I.

Henry III (1551–89) King of France (1574–89) during the *Wars of Religion. Elected king of Poland in 1573, he abandoned that country on succeeding to the French throne. In France he was caught between the Huguenot and Roman Catholic parties and after fleeing Paris following an uprising (1588) allied with the Huguenot Henry of Navarre (the future *Henry IV). He was assassinated while besieging Paris.

Henry IV (1056–1106) German king (1056–84) and Holy Roman Emperor (1056–1106; crowned 1084), famous as the opponent of Pope Gregory VII in the *investiture controversy. The conflict over Henry's right to appoint bishops led him in 1076 to depose Gregory, who proceeded to excommunicate Henry. In 1077, however, Henry did penance at Canossa but was then dethroned by the German princes (1078–80). Again excommunicated, in 1084 he entered Rome, deposed Gregory, and nominated the antipope Clement III (d. 1100) by whom he was crowned emperor. He subsequently faced a further rebellion of the German princes and his sons Conrad and the future Emperor Henry V.

Henry IV (1366–1413) King of England (1399–1413); the eldest son of *John of Gaunt. As Henry Bolingbroke, he seized the throne from Richard II. In the early years of his reign Henry faced considerable opposition from Richard's supporters, led by the Earl of Northumberland and his son Hotspur (see Percy, Sir Henry), and from the Welsh under *Glendower. Successful in defeating his enemies, the costs of these wars and resultant taxation led to protracted struggles between king and Parliament for control of royal expenditure. Increasingly incapacitated by illness, Henry's last years were marked by bitter factional struggles within his council.

Henry IV (1553–1610) The first Bourbon king of France (1589–1610), who restored peace and prosperity following the *Wars of Religion. A Protestant, he succeeded his mother to the throne of Navarre in 1572. Shortly afterward he married Charles IX's sister *Margaret of Valois and was forced to renounce his religion and confine himself to court. In 1576 he escaped and became a *Huguenot (Protestant) leader in the Wars of Religion. His succession to the throne was only secured in 1594, when he became a Roman Catholic, and civil war continued until he granted the Huguenots freedom of worship by the Edict of *Nantes (1598). Thereafter he sponsored the efforts of his minister *Sully to restore France's shattered economy. Henry died at the hands of an assassin.

Henry V (1081–1125) German king (1089–1125) and Holy Roman Emperor (1106–25; crowned 1111); son of Emperor *Henry IV and first husband of Matilda of England. His reign saw the settlement of the *investiture controversy with the papacy by the Concordat of Worms (1122), which brought him control of the German Church but antagonized his bishops.

Henry V (1387–1422) King of England (1413–22); the eldest son of Henry IV. He vigorously resumed the *Hundred Years' War, partly as a distraction from domestic tensions. His first campaign culminated in the battle of *Agincourt (1415) and by 1420, in alliance with Burgundy, he controlled much of N France. He married Catherine of Valois and gained recognition (1420) as the heir of her father *Charles VI (1420). He was noted by contemporaries as much for his personal piety and love of justice as for military prowess.

Henry VI (1165–97) German king (1169–97) and Holy Roman Emperor (1190–97). Son of *Frederick Barbarossa, he acquired Sicily through his marriage (1189) to Constance of Sicily (1152–98). His reign was dominated by his attempts to secure Sicily and to subdue *Henry the Lion. In 1193 he imprisoned the English king, Richard the Lionheart, and received a large ransom in return for his release.

Henry VI (1421–71) King of England (1422–61, 1470–71), succeeding his father Henry V. He married (1445), and was dominated by, *Margaret of Anjou. His inability to govern led to bitter struggles that culminated in the Wars of the *Roses. Deposed and imprisoned by the Yorkists (1461), he was briefly restored to power (1470–71), only to be again defeated and probably murdered. He was a notable patron of learning and religion: he founded Eton College (1440) and King's College, Cambridge (1447).

Henry VII (c. 1275–1313) Holy Roman Emperor (1309–1313; crowned 1312) and, as Henry VI, Count of Luxembourg (1288–1313). He became king of the Lombards in 1313 but had to contend with *Guelf (anti-imperial) opposition in Italy. He arranged a brilliant match between his son John, the future count of Luxembourg, and Elizabeth of Bohemia.

Henry VII (1457–1509) King of England (1485–1509). As Henry Tudor, earl of Richmond, he defeated Richard III at *Bosworth (1485) and his marriage (1486) to Richard's niece Elizabeth of York (1465–1503) united the Houses of *Lancaster and *York, effectively ending the Wars of the *Roses. Until 1499, however, he faced Yorkist plots, such as those of *Simnel and *Warbeck. His domestic rule was noted for its harsh financial exactions, efficient royal administration, and growing prosperity. His foreign policy temporarily put an end to war with France (on favorable terms, 1492), while treaties with Burgundy and the Holy Roman Empire resulted in a new pattern of European alliances.

Henry VIII (1491–1547) King of England (1509–47), who initiated the English *Reformation. In 1512 he joined a European alliance against France, which he defeated at the battle of the *Spurs (1513), gaining Tournai, and in the same year his army thwarted a Scottish invasion at *Flodden. His desire to make England a notable European power was pursued from 1515 by his Lord Chancellor, Cardinal *Wolsey, who arranged the meeting between Henry and *Francis I of France at the *Field of the Cloth of Gold, near Calais (1520). From 1527 Henry was preoccupied by his wish to divorce *Catherine of Aragon, who had been the widow of his elder brother Arthur (d. 1502). He blamed her failure to produce a son (she had given birth to the future Mary I in 1516) on the canonical prohibition against marrying one's brother's widow, a conviction that was enforced by his love affair with Anne *Boleyn. Wolsey's failure to gain a papal annulment of Henry's marriage brought about the cardinal's fall in 1529 but only in 1533, after Thomas *Cromwell had initiated the legislation that made the English Church, under Henry's supreme headship, independent of Rome, could the king marry Anne. In the same year she gave birth to the future Elizabeth I. In 1535 Thomas *More was executed for refusing to acknowledge royal supremacy over the Church and in the following year Anne met the same fate for adultery. Henry then married Jane *Seymour, who died shortly after giving birth to the future Edward VI (1537). His next marriage, arranged by Cromwell, to *Anne of Cleves was short-lived, ending in divorce and the execution of Cromwell (1540). Shortly afterward Henry married Catherine *Howard, who was executed in 1542, and finally, in 1543, Catherine *Parr, who outlived him. Henry's last years were dominated by war with France and Scotland, consequent economic problems, and his attempts to hold back the forces of Protestantism, which "the King's great matter" had unleashed.

HENRY VIII *The imposing figure of Henry, in an engraving after a painting derived from a cartoon by Holbein, symbolizes the strength of the Tudor monarchy.*

Henry, Joseph (1797–1878) US physicist, who made important contributions to the investigation of electromagnetism. He built the largest electromagnet then known, which could lift over 660 lbs (300 kg); he also discovered electromagnetic induction independently of *Faraday. Henry invented an early form of the telegraph and the electrical relay. In 1846 he was appointed secretary of the

Smithsonian Institution and he was one of the founders of the National Academy of Sciences. The unit of inductance (*see* henry) is named for him.

Henry, O. (William Sidney Porter; 1862–1910) US short-story writer. He adopted his pseudonym while serving a prison sentence for embezzlement. He subsequently worked in New York, where he published *Cabbages and Kings* (1904), the first of many volumes of short stories characterized by the use of coincidence and unexpected endings. Other collections include *The Four Million* (1906), *Heart of the West* (1907), and *Strictly Business* (1910).

Henry, Patrick (1736–99) American Revolutionary orator; first governor of Virginia (1776–79). As a lawyer and member of the Virginia assembly (the House of Burgesses), Henry defended colonial rights against British rule. The mobilization of a Virginia militia on the eve of the American Revolution was ensured by Henry's famous speech ending "give me liberty or give me death." He was again governor of Virginia from 1784 to 1786.

PATRICK HENRY *Patriot and orator whose "give me liberty or give me death" speech inspired the Virginia militia against Britain.*

Henry the Lion (?1129–95) Duke of Saxony (1142–81), whose wealth and power brought him into conflict with the Holy Roman Emperors. He gave support to *Frederick Barbarossa in return for regaining Bavaria (1154) but when he broke with Frederick in 1176 most of his lands were confiscated and he was exiled. In 1194, after further conflict, he was reconciled with Frederick's son and successor Emperor *Henry VI.

Henry the Navigator (1394–1460) Portuguese patron of explorers; the fourth son of John I. He won a military reputation at the capture of Ceuta (1415) in N Africa, which kindled his interest in the exploration of the continent. Becoming governor of the Algarve (1419) he set up a school of navigation at Sagres and inspired and sponsored explorers. Under his auspices Madeira, the Azores, and the

Cape Verde Islands were colonized, the W coast of Africa was explored, probably as far as Sierra Leone, and many trading stations were established.

Henze, Hans Werner (1926–) German composer, a pupil of Wolfgang Fortner. His piano concerto won the Schumann Prize in 1951 and he settled in Italy in 1953. He has organized an annual festival at Montepulciano since 1977. Henze has made use of a number of different styles of composition, including serialism and neoromanticism. His Marxist sympathies are evident in such works as the oratorio *The Raft of the Medusa* (1968), for which he wrote both text and music. He has composed symphonies; concertos for piano, violin, viola, and double bass; ballet music; and the operas *Elegy for Young Lovers* (1961) and *The Bassarids* (1966).

heparin An *anticoagulant that occurs naturally in the tissues and is also used in medicine. Heparin is a complex carbohydrate produced and secreted by special cells (mast cells) in connective tissues, especially in the lungs. It inhibits the enzymes responsible for blood clotting.

hepatitis Inflammation of the liver, most commonly caused by viruses. The two main types are infectious hepatitis, usually contracted by ingesting the virus from food or drink, and serum hepatitis, contracted mainly from dirty hypodermic needles or blood products. Some chemicals (e.g. alcohol) can also cause hepatitis. The patient usually has a fever, loses his appetite, and later becomes jaundiced. Hepatitis usually resolves without specific treatment, but sometimes chronic disease develops.

Hepburn, Katharine (1909–) US actress. Her performances in both films and the theater are distinguished by her intelligence and versatility. Among the many movies she made with Spencer *Tracy are *Woman of the Year* (1942), *Adam's Rib* (1949), and *Pat and Mike* (1952). Her other movies include *The Philadelphia Story* (1940), *The African Queen* (1952), and *Summertime* (1955). She won Academy Awards for *Guess Who's Coming to Dinner* (1967), *The Lion in Winter* (1968), and *On Golden Pond* (1981).

Hepburn Act (1906) A US law that increased the powers of the Interstate Commerce Commission over railroads. Regulation of rates, routes, and taxes were strengthened, and the act prohibited railroads from transporting those products in which it had a financial interest.

Hephaestus The Greek god of fire and crafts, the son of Zeus and Hera. According to Hesiod he created *Pandora, the first woman. He is identified with the Roman *Vulcan.

Hepplewhite, George (d. 1786) British furniture designer and cabinetmaker, who established a business in London. His neoclassical furniture is a simplified and more functional version of the designs of Robert *Adam, with whom he sometimes collaborated. Usually in inlaid mahogany or satinwood, it is characterized by straight tapering legs and heart- or oval-shaped chairbacks filled with openwork designs.

heptane (C_7H_{16}) A colorless flammable liquid *alkane. It is obtained from *oil and is used as a solvent and to make other chemicals. Heptane is also a standard in determining the *octane rating of gasoline.

Hepworth, Dame Barbara (1903–75) British sculptor. She studied in Leeds and at the Royal College of Art. A friend of Henry *Moore, she was also influenced by *Brancusi and *Arp. Her abstract carving in wood and stone developed after *Pierced Form* (1931), creating massive shapes broken by holes with wires stretched across their openings.

Hera In Greek mythology, the daughter of Cronus and Rhea and the sister and wife of Zeus. She was jealous of Zeus's many mistresses and cruel to their children but gave loyal support to *Jason and *Achilles. She was worshiped as a goddess of women and marriage. She is identified with the Roman *Juno.

Heracles (*or* Hercules) A Greek legendary hero, famed for his strength and courage. He was the son of Zeus and Alcmene (*see* Amphitryon). After killing his wife and children in a fit of madness inflicted by Hera, he went to the court of King Eurystheus of Tiryns, where he performed the Twelve Labors in expiation: he killed the Nemean lion and the *Hydra of Lerna, captured the Hind of Ceryneia and the Boar of Erymanthus, cleaned the Augean stables, chased away the Stymphalian birds, captured the Cretan bull and the horses of Diomedes, stole the girdle of Hippolyte, captured the oxen of Geryon, stole the apples of the *Hesperides, and finally captured and bound *Cerberus in Hades. The last Labor was taken to represent the conquest of Death itself.

Heraclitus (c. 535–c. 475 BC) Greek philosopher of *Ephesus. His treatise *On Nature* postulates that fire is the universe's basic constituent. Rejecting *Parmenides' doctrine of a unitary static reality, Heraclitus maintained that reality is transitory and every object "a harmony of opposite tensions." Everything was always changing ("you cannot step into the same river twice") and wisdom consisted in seeking to understand this eternal dynamic principle (*see* logos), which unified the diversity of nature.

Heraclius (c. 575–641 AD) Byzantine emperor. Between 613 and 628 he faced the aggression of the Persians, who took Syria, Palestine, and Egypt and besieged Constantinople (626). Finally victorious following a campaign in 626–28, Heraclius restored the Holy Cross to Jerusalem (629), a deed that was immortalized in medieval legend. His success was short-lived for in 634 the Arabs attacked the empire, defeating the Byzantines at Yarmuk (636) and taking Palestine, Syria, and Egypt. He divided Anatolia into military units, from which peasants were enlisted for military service in return for land.

Herakleion. *See* Iráklion.

heraldry A system of pictorial devices on shields originally used to identify individuals when wearing armor. Personal devices on shields are of great antiquity but in the early 12th century armorial devices became hereditary in Europe. They were also used as *seals. Coats of arms are also granted to institutions. Coats of arms comprise the shield, a helmet surmounted by a crest, a mantling (stylized drapery behind the shield), a wreath, and a motto. The shield bears the heraldic signs (charges), which have ancient fixed meanings. From these heralds can determine the genealogy and status of the bearer.

Herat (*or* Harat) 34 20N 62 10E A city in W Afghanistan. Near the site of several ancient cities, including one built by Alexander the Great, Herat developed as a scientific and cultural center under the rule of the Turkish conqueror Timur, who seized the city in 1393. An agricultural and commercial center, Herat's industries include flour milling and textiles. Population (1988 est): 177,000.

herbaceous plant A plant that lacks woody stems and the aerial parts of which die each winter. Many herbaceous plants are *annuals but some are *perennials, surviving the winter in the form of underground bulbs, corms, rhizomes, etc.

Herbart, Johann Friedrich (1776–1841) German educational theorist, who pioneered the application of psychology to teaching. Rejecting *Fichte's philosophy with its emphasis on freedom, he preferred *Kant's pluralism, believing that beyond the phenomenal world there existed many real "things-in-themselves," which are inaccessible to the mind. Herbart, like Kant, sought to

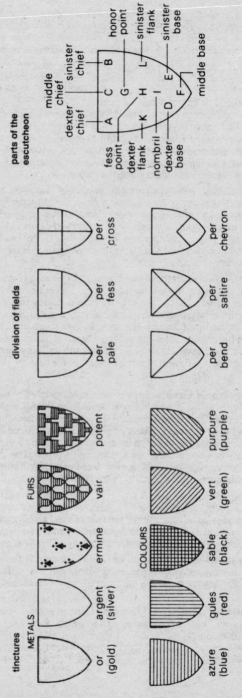

HERALDRY *The terminology of heraldry, of which a few terms are illustrated, reveals the science's French origins.*

make psychology a mathematical science and wasted time developing fruitless systems that had no experimental foundation.

herbicide (*or* weed killer) A chemical used to kill unwanted plants (*see* weed). Selective weed killers kill the target without harming the plants among which it is growing. Some of these act by interfering with the growth of the weed and are often based on plant hormones. An example is 2,4-D, a synthetic *auxin, which is used to control broadleaved weeds in cereal crops. Herbicides used to clear waste ground are nonselective and kill every plant with which they come into contact. An example is Paraquat.

herb Paris A perennial herbaceous plant, *Paris quadrifolia,* native to woodlands of Europe and Asia. Up to 12 in (30 cm) high, it has a whorl of usually four leaves and a solitary flower with prominent sepals and narrow yellow petals. The fruit is a fleshy capsule. Family: *Trilliaceae.*

herb Robert An annual or biennial herb, *Geranium robertianum,* growing up to 20 in (50 cm) high and found in woods and hedgerows throughout temperate Eurasia and introduced to North and South America. The small flowers are pink or red. Family: *Geraniaceae.*

herbs and spices The fresh or dried parts of aromatic or pungent plants used in food, drink, medicine, and perfumery. Herbs are generally the leaves of plants and are best used fresh. They grow in temperate zones. Common culinary herbs are *basil, *bay leaves, *marjoram, *mint, *parsley, and *thyme. Spices generally grow in hot countries. They were formerly a valuable trade commodity; the Roman Empire's spice trade extended to Indochina and Zanzibar and the quest for spice routes motivated 15th-century European exploration of the East and the Americas. Spices are usually dried and may be obtained from the root (e.g. *ginger), bark (e.g. *cinnamon), flower (e.g. *clove), seed pod (e.g. *chili), or, most commonly, from the seed itself (e.g. *coriander, *cumin, *pepper).

Hercegovina. *See* Bosnia and Hercegovina.

Herculaneum An ancient Italian city near *Naples in Italy. It was destroyed by the same eruption as *Pompeii (79 AD). It was smaller, better planned, and wealthier than Pompeii. Entombment beneath solidified volcanic mud makes excavation there very difficult and much remains buried.

Hercules. *See* Heracles.

hercules beetle A giant green and black beetle, *Dynastes herculeus,* occurring in Central and South America. The male may reach a length of 6 in (15 cm), nearly two-thirds of which is taken up by an enormous pair of horns, extending from the thorax and head. Family: *Scarabeidae* (*see* scarab beetle).

hercules moth A large Australian *saturniid moth, *Coscinoscera hercules.* The adult has broad dark-brown wings, spanning about 11 in (28 cm), with a wing area that is possibly the largest of any insect.

Herder, Johann Gottfried (1744–1803) German philosopher and poet. At first a disciple and later a critic of *Kant, he developed a form of religious humanism based on his readings of Shakespeare, Homer, and the Bible. His works include *A Treatise upon the Origin of Language* (1772) and *Outline of a Philosophy of the History of Man* (1784–91).

Hereford cattle A breed of beef cattle originating from Herefordshire and surrounding areas in W England. They are large and stocky with red coats and white faces. Hardy and maturing quickly, Herefords are often mated with dairy breeds to produce a white-faced beef cross.

Herero A group of Bantu-speaking peoples of SW Africa, Botswana, and Angola. They are traditionally cattle, sheep, and goat herders but some adopted agriculture after European contact. Their social organization is based on the common principle of counting descent in the male line for some purposes and in the female line for others.

hermaphrodite (*or* bisexual) A plant or animal possessing both male and female reproductive organs. Such organisms may show cross- or self-*fertilization: the latter method is particularly common when the opportunity of finding a mate is remote, for example in parasitic invertebrates and deepsea fish. True hermaphroditism rarely occurs in humans. More common is **pseudohermaphroditism**, in which an individual develops secondary characteristics appropriate to the opposite sex (e.g. enlarged external genitals in a woman or breasts in a man), due to hormone imbalance.

Hermes In Greek mythology, the messenger and herald of the gods and the guide of travelers. He was regarded as the god of riches and good luck, the protector of merchants and thieves, and the god of dreams. He was usually portrayed as an athletic youth wearing a cap and winged sandals and carrying a golden staff. He was the son of Zeus and Maia. He conducted the souls of the dead to Hades and is credited with the invention of the lyre, which he gave to Apollo. He is identified with the Roman *Mercury.

Hermes Trismegistos (Greek: Hermes the thrice great) The name applied by Greek Neoplatonists to the Egyptian god *Thoth. It is also the name given, after the third century AD, to the author of certain Neoplatonic writings.

Hermeticism An Italian literary movement of the early 20th century. Its leading writers were the poets Ungaretti, Quasimodo, and Montale, whose early poetry was influenced by the theories of the French *Symbolists and characterized by verbal experiment and esoteric symbolism. After World War II all three poets developed more accessible styles.

hermit crab A *crab with a soft unprotected abdomen, belonging to the worldwide families *Paguridae* and *Coenobitidae*. It lives in portable hollow objects, such as snail shells, for protection and changes these for successively larger ones as it grows. Hermit crabs are found in sandy or muddy-bottomed waters and occasionally on land and in trees. Tribe: *Anomura*.

Hermite, Charles (1822–1901) French mathematician, who (in 1873), discovered the first transcendental number: e, the base of natural *logarithms. Such numbers cannot be expressed as a root of a polynomial equation, i.e. an equation of the form $a_0 + a_1x + \ldots + a_nx^n = 0$, where n and the a's are integers. *Liouville had already shown that such numbers exist but could not identify any.

Hermon, Mount 33 24N 35 50E A mountain on the Syrian-Lebanese border, at the S end of the Anti-Lebanon Mountains. It is the highest point near the E coast of the Mediterranean Sea. Height: 9232 ft (2814 m).

Hermosillo 29 15N 110 59W A city in NW Mexico. It is an important commercial center for the surrounding agricultural areas and has a university (1938). Population (1980): 297,175.

Herne 51 32N 7 12E A city in NW Germany, in North Rhine-Westphalia on the Rhine-Herne Canal. It is a coal mining and industrial center. Population (1991 est): 178,000.

hernia The protrusion of an organ or tissue through a weak spot in the wall that normally contains it. The most common types are the inguinal hernia (popularly called a rupture), which is a swelling in the groin caused by the protrusion of the abdominal contents, and the hiatus hernia, in which part of the stomach protrudes into the chest cavity. Other common hernias are femoral (also in the groin) and umbilical (at the navel). Hernias should usually be surgically repaired or they may become painful and cut off from their blood supply (strangulated).

Hero and Leander Legendary lovers whose story was recounted by the Greek poet Musaeus (4th or 5th century AD). Hero was a priestess of Aphrodite at Sestos and Leander swam to her each night across the Hellespont from Abydos. After a stormy night Hero found her lover's drowned body and in despair drowned herself.

Herod (I) the Great (c. 73–4 BC) King of Judaea (37–4); the son of *Antipater. Supported by Mark Antony, he became the Romans' king in Judaea. A Jew of Arab origins, he was regarded as a usurper by nationalists, who resented his encouragement of Greek culture; he retained power by control of the religious establishment and rigorous suppression of opposition. His jealousy and cruelty were exacerbated by feuds among his 10 wives and their sons. Shortly before his death he ordered the massacre of the infants of Bethlehem.

Herod Agrippa I (c. 10 BC–44 AD) King of Judaea (41–44); the grandson of *Herod the Great. An impecunious adventurer, he was educated at the Roman imperial court after the execution of his father by Herod the Great. He intrigued in imperial family politics and helped Emperor *Claudius to power, for which he was made king of Judaea. He was a popular ruler but persecuted Christians, executing St James, the son of Zebedee, and imprisoning St Peter.

Herod Agrippa II (died c. 100 AD) King of Chalcis (50–c. 100) in S Lebanon; the son of *Herod Agrippa I. In 60 he heard the case of the arrested St Paul and found him innocent. He attempted to prevent the Jewish rebellion of 66, during which his troops fought on the Roman side, and helped to take Jerusalem in 70.

Herod Antipas (21 BC–39 AD) Tetrarch (governor) of Galilee (4–39 AD) after the partition of the realm of his father *Herod the Great. He divorced his wife to marry his niece Herodias, for which he was censured by John the Baptist. Herodias persuaded her daughter Salome to ask for John's head in return for dancing at Antipas's birthday celebration and John was executed. Jesus Christ, as a Galilean, was brought before Antipas after his arrest, but Antipas returned him to Pontius Pilate of Judaea without passing judgment. After the death of Antipas's friend Emperor *Tiberius, religious riots gave *Caligula an excuse to exile Antipas.

Herodotus (c. 484–c. 425 BC) Greek historian. Born at Halicarnassus, he was exiled for political reasons and moved to Samos. He subsequently moved to Athens and then to the Athenian colony of Thurii in S Italy, where he died. Called "the father of history" by Cicero, he was the first historian to subject his material to critical evaluation and research. His narrative account of the wars between Greece and Perisa in nine books contained much incidental anthropological and geographical information gathered on his travels in the Mediterranean countries, Egypt, and Asia, and was written in a lively dramatic style.

heroin (or diamorphine) A pain-killing drug with a stronger action and fewer side effects than *morphine, from which it is made. Heroin is used in some countries to alleviate the suffering of terminal illness. Because the regular use of heroin readily leads to physical dependence its use in medicine has been restricted. *See* drug dependence.

heron A wading bird belonging to a subfamily (*Ardeinae*; 60 species) occurring on lakes and rivers worldwide, especially in the tropics; 30–59 in (75–150 cm) long, herons have a slim body, longish legs, long toes, broad wings, a short tail, and a loose plumage colored gray, blue, greenish, white, purple, or reddish.

Herons hunt by standing at the water's edge and seizing fish and insects with the long pointed bill. In the breeding season herons may develop ornamental plumes and perform elaborate courtship displays. Family: *Ardeidae* (herons and bitterns). *See also* egret; night heron.

Hero of Alexandria (mid-1st century AD) Greek engineer and mathematician, best known for his invention of the aeolipile, the earliest known steam engine. It consisted of a sphere containing water with two bent tubes extending from it. When heated, steam issued from the tubes, causing the sphere to rotate. However, the device was only used for trivial purposes, such as controlling doors and causing statues to move. He also discovered the well-known formula for calculating the area of a triangle from the lengths of its sides.

Herophilus (c. 335–c. 280 BC) Greek physician, who founded one of the earliest medical schools in Alexandria. Herophilus performed public dissections of human cadavers, distinguished between sensory and motor nerve trunks, and described parts of the brain, duodenum, and several other organs.

herpes A virus that causes *chickenpox, *shingles, and cold sores. Herpes zoster causes chickenpox in children and shingles in adults. Herpes simplex (type 1 or oral type) causes cold sores. The genital type (type 2) is sexually transmitted. The virus is usually dormant, but when active it causes painful sores, during which the disease is highly contagious. No cure is known; however, the drug acyclovir is active against the virus in its active stage.

Herrera, Juan de (1530–97) Spanish architect. After having studied in Italy, Herrera designed a palace in Aranjuez (1569) and the Exchange in Seville (1582) in an Italianate style that had great influence on Spanish architecture. He is best known for his completion of the *Escorial.

Herrera the Younger, Francisco de (1622–85) Spanish baroque painter and architect, born in Seville, the son and pupil of the painter and engraver **Francisco de Herrera the Elder** (1576–1656). After leaving his father's tutelage, he studied in Italy. On his return to Seville, he introduced the dramatic style of Italian baroque in such religious works as *Triumph of St Hermengild* (Prado). He later worked in Madrid, where he designed the high altar of the church of Montserrat.

Herrick, Robert (1591–1674) English poet. A friend of Jonson and other members of London literary society, he was ordained (1623) and served as rector of Dean Prior, Devonshire, from 1630 to 1646 and again after the Restoration. The majority of his secular and religious peoms, collected in *Hesperides* (1648), are short lyrics influenced by classical models.

herring An important food fish, *Clupea harengus,* found mainly in cold waters of the N Atlantic and the North Sea. It has a slender silvery blue-green body, up to about 16 in (40 cm) long, with a single short dorsal fin and swims in large shoals, feeding on plankton. A related species (*C. pallasi*) occurs in the N Pacific. Many other small silvery fish of the family *Clupeidae* are called herring. Herrings have long been fished in N Europe, where they are eaten fresh, pickled, and smoked. In the UK, smoked herring are known as kippers, and are produced mainly in Scotland. Overfishing and pollution have greatly reduced catches of herring in European waters in recent years. Order: *Clupeiformes. See also* whitebait.

herring gull A large gray and white *gull, *Larus argentatus,* occurring around coasts in the N hemisphere. It is omnivorous and is commonly seen scavenging at refuse heaps. Adults are 22 in (57 cm) long and have pink legs and a yellow bill with a red spot on the lower mandible.

Herriot, Édouard (1872–1957) French statesman and writer; prime minister of a Radical-Socialist coalition (1924–25, 1926 (for two days), 1932). During World War II, he opposed the Vichy Government and spent the years 1942–45 in prison. From 1947 to 1953 he served as president of the national assembly.

Herschel, Sir William (1738–1822) British astronomer, born in Germany. Working with his sister **Caroline Herschel** (1750–1848), he became expert in grinding lenses and built the largest telescopes then known. In 1781 Herschel discovered the planet *Uranus, the first such discovery since prehistoric times. His other discoveries include binary stars, two new satellites of Saturn, and *infrared rays from the sun (1800).

Hersey, John (Richard) (1914–93) US writer; born in China. He was a foreign news correspondent (1937–46) and wrote his first novel, *A Bell for Adano* (1944; Pulitzer Prize; film, 1945), about the Allied campaign in Italy during World War II. His other works include *Men on Bataan* (1942); *Hiroshima* (1946), about the first atomic bomb; *The Wall* (1950), about the revolt in the Warsaw ghetto; *The Algiers Motel Incident* (1968); *My Petition for More Space* (1974); *The President* (1975); *The Walnut Door* (1977); and *Aspects of the Presidency* (1980).

Hertogenbosch, 's. *See* 's Hertogenbosch.

hertz (Hz) The *SI unit of frequency equal to one cycle per second. Named for Heinrich *Hertz.

Hertz, Heinrich Rudolf (1857–94) German physicist, who first produced and detected *radio waves (1888). *Maxwell's equations had predicted the existence of *electromagnetic radiation over a wide spectrum of frequencies but, until Hertz's discovery, radio-frequency radiation was unknown. The unit of frequency is named for him.

Hertzog, James Barry Munnik (1866–1942) South African statesman; prime minister of the Union of South Africa (1924–39). In the second *Boer War he led the Orange Free State forces. He formed the Afrikaner Nationalist party in 1914, becoming prime minister in 1924. In 1933 he formed a coalition government with *Smuts but resigned in 1939, when his motion against entering World War II was defeated. With *Malan he then revived the Nationalist party but retired from politics in 1940.

Hertzsprung-Russell diagram A graphic representation of the classification of stars according to spectral type (*see* Harvard classification system) and brightness—usually absolute *magnitude. The stars are not uniformly distributed. Most, including the sun, lie on a diagonal band, the main sequence, the brightest stars of which are spectral types O and B and the faintest are M stars. Main-sequence stars are often called dwarf stars. The somewhat brighter *giant stars, the even brighter *supergiants, and the faint *white dwarfs fall into their own distinct groupings. The diagram was originally produced, independently, in 1911 by E. Hertzsprung (1873–1967) and in 1913 by H. N. Russell (1897–1957).

Herzl, Theodor (1860–1904) Hungarian-born journalist and playwright, who founded the movement to establish a Jewish nation (*see* Zionism). Living mostly in Vienna, he published the pamphlet *The Jewish State* (1896), calling for a world council to discuss the problem of finding a Jewish homeland. At a world congress of Zionists in Basle (1897) the World Zionist Organization was established, Herzl becoming the first president.

Herzog, Chaim (1918–   ) Israeli soldier and statesman; president (1983–   ); born in Ireland. Educated in Israel and England, he served in the British Army during World War II. He was in Israeli military intelligence (director, 1948–54) and became military commander of the Jerusalem district (1954–59) and again director of military intelligence (1959–62). He was thrust into the limelight during the Six Days War (1967), when he broadcast war reports, and later was ambassador to the UN (1975–78). As the Labor party's candidate, he succeeded Yitzhak Navon as president.

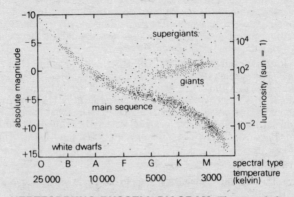

HERTZSPRUNG-RUSSELL DIAGRAM *This graph for bright stars is important in studies of stellar evolution and in determining distance.*

Hesiod (8th century BC) Greek poet, the earliest known after Homer. He was a farmer near Mount Helicon in Boeotia in central Greece and was involved in a long dispute with his brother Perses concerning their inheritance. His two major works are the *Theogony,* concerning the gods and their myths, and *Works and Days,* a realistic and personal account of farming life.

Hesperides (Greek: daughters of evening) In Greek mythology, three nymphs who guarded the sacred golden apples of Hera in a garden in the far west. The apples were stolen by *Heracles as one of his Twelve Labors.

Hesperornis A genus of extinct flightless seabirds whose fossils date from the Cretaceous period (125–60 million years ago). It was 7 ft (2 m) long and adapted for swimming and catching fish in shallow seas, having large powerful feet and legs, a long slender neck, a small head, and a long bill (possibly with teeth), but only tiny wing bones and reduced flight muscles.

Hess, Rudolf (1894–1987) German Nazi politician. Hess joined the Nazi party in 1920, becoming Hitler's close friend and deputy party leader (1933). However, his declining influence in the late 1930s led to his unsuccessful secret mission to Scotland to negotiate a separate peace with Britain in 1941. There, he was imprisoned until 1946, when he was convicted at the Nuremberg war trials and sent to Spandau prison in Berlin. In later years his release from Spandau, where he was the only prisoner, was urged, but he died there.

Hess, Victor Francis (1883–1964) US physicist, born in Austria. Using a balloon to investigate atmospheric background radiation, he discovered that the radiation increased with altitude. This was contrary to expectation, because background radiation was then believed to emanate from rocks. This work led to the discovery of *cosmic rays, for which he shared a Nobel Prize in 1936 with Carl *Anderson.

Hesse (German name: Hessen) A *Land* in central Germany. Formed in 1945, it consists of the former duchies of Hesse-Darmstadt and Nassau. Hilly and forested, it is chiefly agricultural, producing potatoes, sugar beet, and wheat. Industry, concentrated in the S, includes publishing and the manufacture of machinery and chemicals. Iron ore, salt, and coal are mined. Area: 8150 sq mi (21,112 sq km). Population (1991 est): 5,763,000. Capital: Wiesbaden.

Hesse, Hermann (1877–1962) German novelist and poet. He rejected traditional schooling and worked as a bookseller until publication of his first novel, *Peter Camenzind* (1904). His early themes of art and self-knowledge were later extended by his interest in Indian mysticism and Jungian psychology, reflected in *Siddharta* (1922). His other major novels are *Steppenwolf* (1927) and *Narziss und Goldmund* (1930). After publication of his last novel, *The Glass Bead Game* (1943), he was awarded a Nobel Prize (1946). From 1911 until his death he lived in Switzerland. He was a conscientious objector and an opponent of Hitler.

Hestia The Greek goddess of the hearth, daughter of Cronus and Rhea and the oldest of the Olympian deities. She vowed to remain a virgin, rejecting both Apollo and Poseidon as consorts. She is identified with the Roman *Vesta.

Hevesy, George Charles von (1885–1966) Hungarian-born chemist, who worked in Denmark and Sweden. He discovered the use of *radioactive tracers to follow the course of compounds in a system, for which he received the 1943 Nobel Prize. He also discovered the element *hafnium in 1923, by analyzing zirconium ores.

Heyerdahl, Thor (1914–   ) Norwegian ethnologist, who led the *Kon-Tiki* expedition (1947). The *Kon-Tiki* was a balsawood raft that Heyerdahl built and sailed with five companions from the Pacific coast of South America to Polynesia to show that the pre-Incan inhabitants of Peru might thus have migrated to Polynesia. In 1969–70 he attempted to cross the Atlantic Ocean from Morocco to South America in a papyrus boat—the *Ra*; he reached Barbados, showing the possibility of Egyptian influence on the pre-Columbian civilization of America. Heyerdahl wrote accounts of both expeditions. In 1978, on his way from Iraq to India, he burned his reed boat, the *Tigris,* in protest against the war in the Horn of Africa.

Heysham. *See* Morecambe.

Heywood, Thomas (c. 1574–1641) English dramatist. An actor as well as a prolific and versatile writer, he wrote numerous comedies, chronicle plays, and scripts for pageants and masques. His best-known work is the domestic tragedy *A Woman Killed with Kindness* (1607).

Hezekiah King of Judah (c. 715–c. 686 BC), noted as a religious reformer. Allied with Egypt, he rebelled against *Sennacherib of Assyria, against Isaiah's advice, and was defeated and forced to pay huge indemnities.

Hialeah 25 49N 80 17W A city in SE Floria, NW of Miami, on the Miami Canal. One of its main attractions is winter horse racing. Industries include the manufacture of metal, chemical, and clothing products. Population (1990): 188,004.

Hiawatha The legendary chief of the Onondaga tribe of American Indians, who was said to have formed the *Iroquois League. His story is the subject of Longfellow's *Song of Hiawatha* (1855).

hibernation A state of *dormancy in winter experienced by many fish, amphibians, reptiles, and mammals of temperate and Arctic regions: it is an adaption to avoid death by heat loss, freezing, or food scarcity. True hibernation is seasonal and not simply a reaction to a drop in temperature. It occurs in a few mammals, including bats and hedgehogs, and some birds. Hibernation involves a period of sleep during which the body temperature drops almost to that of the surroundings, the body processes are slowed, and the hibernator lives on a reserve of body fat until it awakens in the spring.

Hibiscus A genus of tropical and subtropical herbs, shrubs, and trees (about 150 species). Several species are cultivated for their showy five-petaled flowers; two popular shrubs, up to 10 ft (3 m) high, are the Chinese *H. rosa-sinensis* (rose of China), which has red, pink, or yellow flowers with prominent stigmas, and the Syrian *H. syriacus* (rose of Sharon), which has pink, blue, or white hollyhock-like flowers. Both can be grown as pot plants. The genus also includes plants cultivated for their food value (*see* okra; roselle) and for their fiber (*see* kenaf). Family: *Malvaceae.*

hiccup (*or* hiccough) A sudden involuntary intake of breath interrupted by closure of the glottis (in the larynx), producing a characteristic sound. Hiccups are commonly due to indigestion or eating too quickly, but they may be associated with kidney disease or alcoholism.

Hickok, James Butler (1837–76) US lawman, known as Wild Bill Hickok. He was celebrated for his skill and speed as a gunman. After Union army service in the Civil War and against the Indians he was a marshal in several Kansas towns (1866–71) and toured with Buffalo Bill. He was shot dead from behind while playing poker in a saloon.

hickory A tree of the genus *Carya* (20 species), native to E North America and Asia and cultivated for timber, nuts, and ornament. They grow to a height of about 100 ft (30 m) and have compound leaves consisting of paired leaflets. Commercially important species are the shagbark (*C. ovata*), which yields hard durable timber, and the pecan (*C. illinoensis*), which produces thin-shelled nuts resembling walnuts. Both species are North American. Family: *Juglandaceae.*

hide A unit of land measurement in Anglo-Saxon England based on the approximate area of land needed to support a peasant household. Tax assessments were often calculated on the basis of the number of hides comprising an estate. The size of the hide varied, ranging in different areas from 40 to 120 acres.

Hideyoshi (1536–98) Japanese military ruler, who brought feudal Japan under his dominance. Of humble birth, Hideyoshi became by sheer ability a leading commander of *Oda Nobunaga, aiding him to become master of central Japan. Succeeding to Oda's power in 1582, he achieved national hegemony by 1590 but then wasted his energy on an unsuccessful invasion of Korea.

hieroglyphics Originally, an Egyptian system of picture writing in use from about 3000 BC to 300 AD; the term now denotes any *pictographic or *ideographic writing system. The Egyptians used hieroglyphics largely for monumental inscriptions. The characters are careful reproductions of people, animals, and objects and may be interpreted as representing either the objects they portray or the sounds that are featured in the pronunciation of the referent. Hieroglyphic records are coextensive with hieratic, a more cursive stylized form appropriate to brush and ink and the smooth surfaces of papyrus and wood.

hi-fi. *See* high-fidelity sound systems.

high-fidelity sound systems (*or* hi-fi) Systems of recording and reproducing sound in which the quality of the reproduced sound is as close as possible to that of the original source. A typical reproducing system consists of a record player or *cassette player, a stereophonic amplifier, and two loudspeakers. To achieve high fidelity, total distortion in such a system must be less than 2%, the frequency response must be constant between 20 and 20,000 hertz, and the system must be able to reproduce stereophonic or quadraphonic recordings. While two frontal stereophonic speakers can reproduce the spatial pattern of the sound source, reproduction of the reverberation characteristics of the place at which the recording was made can be reproduced more fully by a quadraphonic system with two additional rear speakers.

The term high fidelity is commonly applied to a wide range of domestic record- and tape-reproducing systems, many of which do not fulfil the requirements of true high fidelity. Stereophonic and quadraphonic radio broadcasts can also be used as sound sources in many hi-fi systems.

eye   to fly   old age

HIEROGLYPHICS *A picture was used to represent objects, related ideas, and sounds.*

high jump A field event in athletics in which jumpers compete to clear a horizontal bar. A competitor is allowed three attempts at a height and is eliminated if he fails to clear it. The height is increased until there is only one jumper left.

Highland Games Scottish athletics meetings, usually professional, held in the Highlands. As amateur competitions they are popular in the US and Canada among those of Scottish descent. Events include standard track and field events as well as such Scottish sports as *caber tossing, and there are also competitions in highland dancing and playing the bagpipes. The modern games date from the early 19th century but they originated far earlier in clan assemblies. The most famous meeting, the Braemar Games, can be traced back to the 8th century AD.

high priest The chief official of the ancient Jerusalem *Temple. The office was hereditary in the family of Aaron. The Hasmonean rulers (*see* Maccabees) claimed the title themselves, and in the last century of the temple the high priests were appointed by political rulers. With the destruction of the temple (70 AD) the office ceased to exist.

Hilary of Poitiers, St (c. 315–c. 367 AD) French churchman; bishop and Doctor of the Church. A leading opponent of *Arianism, he was converted to Christianity from Neoplatonism and became Bishop of Poitiers in about 353. His works include *De trinitate* and *De synodis*. Feast day: Jan 14.

Hilbert, David (1862–1943) German mathematician, who gave geometry a mathematically rigorous foundation. In a book entitled *Foundations of Geometry* (1899), he defined such concepts as the point, the line, and the parallel relationship, which *Euclid in his *Elements* had assumed to be intuitively obvious. Hilbert then developed geometry from a much more rigorous set of axioms than those of Euclid. He also studies the properties of infinite-dimensional space, known as Hilbert space, which is used in the mathematics of quantum theory.

Hildebrand. *See* Gregory VII, St.

Hildesheim 52 09N 9 58E A city in N Germany, in Lower Saxony. The romanesque 11th-century cathedral escaped the destruction of World War II. A notable collection of Roman silver was found nearby in 1868. Its manufactures include machinery, textiles, and carpets. Population (1988): 101,000.

Hill, Ambrose Powell (1825–65) US Confederate general. A career Army officer who had served in the *Mexican War, he resigned to join the Confederate Army in 1861. By 1862 he was a general and participated in both battles at *Bull Run, at Williamsburg (1862), *Antietam, *Fredericksburg, and *Chancellorsville. He was killed at Petersburg (1865).

Hill, Archibald Vivian (1886–1977) British physiologist, noted for his work on muscle contraction. Hill found that oxygen was needed not for the contraction of a muscle but for its recovery, which provided a clue to the underlying biochemistry involved. Hill shared the 1922 Nobel Prize with Otto *Meyerhoff.

Hill, Graham (1929–75) British automobile racer, who was world champion in 1962 and 1968 and was runner-up from 1963 to 1965. Despite breaking both legs in an accident (1969) he continued to race. He was killed in a flying accident.

Hill, James Jerome (1838–1916) US businessman; born in Canada. He began by acquiring the bankrupt St Paul and Pacific Railroad, reorganizing and extending it, and eventually bringing it and other lines under one parent company, the Great Northern Railway Company (1890). His Northern Securities Company, which oversaw all of his properties, was ruled in violation of antitrust laws in 1904 and ordered dissolved by the US Supreme Court. Other business ventures included banking and mining.

Hillary, Sir Edmund (Percival) (1919–   ) New Zealand mountaineer and explorer. In 1953 he and *Tenzing Norgay were the first to reach the summit of Mount Everest, for which achievement he was knighted. In 1958–59 he participated in an Antarctic expedition, preparing the way for *Fuchs's crossing of Antarctica.

Hillel (1st century BC) Jewish teacher, lawyer, and biblical scholar. Many of his teachings subsequently became authoritative in rabbinic Judaism. His tolerant character and views are often contrasted with those of his contemporary Shammai.

Hilliard, Nicholas (1547–1619) English portrait miniaturist. He became court painter to Elizabeth I and James I. His high reputation among his contemporaries led many prominent Elizabethans to have their portraits done by him. In his *Treatise on the Art of Limning* (c. 1600), he describes his style and technique of painting miniatures. The elegance and symbolism of his *Unknown Man Against a Background of Flames* is typical of his best work.

hill mynah A glossy black songbird, *Graculus religiosa,* native to India and the East Indies; 10–15 in (25–37 cm) long, it has a yellow bill and yellow wattles on the neck and beneath the eyes. It is a popular cagebird with a remarkable ability to mimic human speech. Family: *Sturnidae* (starlings). *See also* mynah.

Hilo 19 43N 155 05W A city in Hawaii on E Hawaii Island. The tourist industry is important; from the city visitors travel to Hawaii Volcanoes National Park to the SW. The city services and ships the fruits and flowers grown on the island. Population (1990): 37,808.

Hilton, James (1900–54) British novelist. His two most popular novels are *Lost Horizon* (1933), set in the Tibetan monastery of Shangri-La, and *Goodbye, Mr Chips* (1934). From 1935 he worked as a scriptwriter in Hollywood, where he died.

Hilversum 52 14N 5 10E A city in the central Netherlands, in North Holland province. It is a summer resort and commuter town for Amsterdam and is the country's main radio and television broadcasting center. Population (1988 est): 85,200.

Himachal Pradesh A state in NW India, in the W Himalayas beside Tibet's border. Long part of the *Punjab, it was formed by the combination of various hill states (1948). Most of the inhabitants are Pahari-speaking Hindus who farm grains, potatoes, maize, and livestock. The forests yield timber and bamboo. Himachal Pradesh has enormous hydroelectric potential, as yet undeveloped. Area: 21,490 sq mi (55,673 sq km). Population (1991): 5,111,079. Capital: Simla.

Himalayas A vast mountain system, the highest in the world, structurally the S edge of the great plateau of central Asia. They extend about 1550 mi (2400 km) along the N Indian border in a W–E arc, 125–250 mi (200–400 km) wide, reaching 29,028 ft (8848 m) at Mount *Everest.

Himeji 34 50N 134 40E A city in Japan, in SW Honshu. It developed around its famous 16th-century castle, one of the few remaining castles in Japan. Its industries include textiles and steel. Population (1990): 454,360.

Himmler, Heinrich (1900–45) German Nazi politician, infamous for his direction of the *SS. He joined the Nazi party in 1925 and became head of the SS in 1929. From 1936 he also directed the Gestapo and supervised the extermination of Jews in E Europe. After the Nazi collapse he was captured by the Allies and committed suicide.

Hims. *See* Homs.

Hincmar of Reims (c. 806–82) French theologian, archbishop of Reims (845–82). He came into conflict with the emperor Lothair I and successive popes over the extent of his jurisdiction. He also engaged in controversy with the Benedictine monk Gottschalk (d. 868) over the doctrine of predestination.

Hindemith, Paul (1895–1963) German composer and viola player. From the age of 11 he supported himself by playing in dance halls and later studied in Frankfurt am Main, where he led the opera orchestra (1915–23). He also played the viola in the Amar Quartet. In 1927 he began teaching in Berlin. His music was banned by the Nazis in 1933; he moved to Turkey and in 1939 went to the US, becoming an American citizen. His early works were highly dissonant; he later evolved his own system of tonal harmony. Many of his compositions are neoclassical in character (*see* neoclassicism); they include the operas *Cardillac* (1926) and *Mathis der Maler* (1938), the ballet *Nobilissima Visione* (1938), many concertos, instrumental sonatas, and much *Gebrauchsmusik* (German: utility music).

Hindenburg, Paul von Beneckendorff und von (1847–1934) German general, who was recalled from retirement at the outbreak of World War I and with *Ludendorff controlled Germany after the great victory at *Tannenberg (1914). In 1916 Hindenburg became commander in chief and directed the German retreat to the **Hindenburg line** (fortified defense on the Western Front). After Germany's defeat he again retired but became president in 1925. Reelected in 1932, he was forced to appoint Hitler as chancellor early in 1933.

Hindi The national language of India and the most widely spoken, having approximately 134 million speakers. It is an *Indo-Aryan language, showing strong *Sanskrit influence in its written form but with a much simpler grammar. The standard form, written in Devanagari script, is based on the Khari Boli dialect of Delhi. This belongs to the western dialect division from which *Urdu also developed.

Hinduism The religious beliefs and institutions of about 400 million inhabitants of India and parts of neighboring countries. Hinduism is not a religion with a formal creed, but the complex result of about 5000 years of continuous cultural development. It includes a number of extremely diverse traditional beliefs and practices and over the centuries it has influenced and been influenced by younger religions, including Buddhism, Jainism, Christianity, Islam, and Sikhism. One of its central concepts is that the necessary result of one's actions in life leads to *reincarnation at a higher or lower level of life (*see* karma), a belief that has given rise both to the system of *castes and to a deep respect for all forms of life (*see* ahimsa). The goal of the religion is to find a release from the cycle of rebirth and to return to the ultimate unchanging reality, *Brahman. Release may be sought through good works, devotion to a particular god, such as the popular deity *Krishna, or through various types of meditation and asceticism (*see* samadhi; yoga). The principle gods are Brahma, Vishnu, and Shiva, together known as the *Trimurti; the last two are especially venerated by the two major sects, the Vaishnavas and the Shaivas. These and all the innumerable lesser gods and spirits are seen by many Hindus as manifestations of one reality (Brahman). Popular devotion consists mainly of temple worship and the celebration of numerous festivals. Hinduism originated in early *animism and *totemism (before 2750 BC) and developed a sacrificial worship of a pantheon of nature gods, such as *Indra, during the period of the *Vedas (c. 1500–500 BC). *Brahmanism was the dominant form of Hinduism in the 6th century BC, when Buddhism and Jainism were established in reaction to it. The great Hindu texts, the *Mahabharata* and the *Ramayana,* were composed at this time. Vishnu and Shiva became the prominent deities in the medieval period (after 800 AD). New schools have continued to emerge in recent times, most of them concerned with universalizing Hindu thought. *See also* Arya samaj; Brahmo samaj; Ramakrishna; Vedanta; Vivekananda.

Hindu Kush A mountain range in central Asia, extending about 500 mi (800 km) W from the Pamirs to the Koh-i-Baba Mountains of central Afghanistan. Its highest peak is Tirich Mir, at 25,236 ft (7692 m).

Hindustani An *Indo-Aryan language that originated in the dialect of the Delhi district. The Moguls and the British promoted its use as a lingua franca throughout India. *Urdu and *Hindi are the literary forms developed from it.

Hines, Earl (Fatha) (1905–83) US jazz pianist and songwriter, who trained as a concert pianist but formed his own jazz band in 1928. He worked with Louis Armstrong from 1948–51 and became well known for his complex and virtuosic piano playing. He wrote the songs "The Earl" and "I Got It Bad."

hinny The sterile offspring of a female ass and a male horse. Smaller than a *mule, hinnies are used as pack animals, especially in hot climates, but are less common than mules.

Hinshelwood, Sir Cyril Norman (1897–1967) British chemist, who became professor at Oxford University in 1937. He pioneered the investigation of reaction kinetics and discovered several chain reaction mechanisms. He shared the Nobel Prize with N. N. Semyonov in 1956. He was knighted in 1948.

hip The part of the body where the legs are joined to the trunk. The skeleton of the hip consists of the *pelvis and the part of the spine (the sacrum) to which it is attached. The hip joint—the articulation between the pelvis and femur (thigh bone)—is a common site for arthritis: in severe cases the whole joint may be replaced by an artificial one or pins or other devices may be inserted into the damaged parts.

Hipparchus (c. 190–c. 120 BC) Greek astronomer, born in Nicaea. He produced the first accurate map of over 1000 stars, indicating their positions by means of latitude and longitude. He also discovered the precession of the equinoxes and accurately measured the distance to the moon by parallax. In mathematics he invented trigonometry by constructing a table of the ratios of the sides of right-angle triangles.

Hipparion An extinct *horse that lived in the Pliocene epoch (about seven million years ago). It was slender and fast-running, about the size of a modern pony, and lived on open plains. Its foot had a distinct hoof, the remaining toes being small and not touching the ground. *See also* eohippus.

Hippeastrum A genus of herbaceous plants (60 species), native to tropical and subtropical America and cultivated as ornamental garden and pot plants. They have large bulbs (about 10 cm in diameter), broad straight-sided leaves, and a stout flower stem terminating in a cluster of white, pink, or red flowers, each 10 cm across. The genus includes the Barbados lily (*H. equestre*), with scarlet flowers. Family: *Amaryllidaceae.*

Hippocrates (c. 460–c. 377 BC) Greek physician and founder of the Hippocratic school of medicine, which greatly influenced medical science until the 18th century. Hippocrates seems to have been a prominent physician, who traveled widely in Greece and Asia Minor. His followers believed that health was governed by the balance of four body fluids, or humors: phlegm, blood, black bile, and yellow bile. The Hippocratic Collection of 60 or so medical works is ascribed to various authors and the Hippocratic Oath, taken by medical students, was probably not written by Hippocrates.

Hippolytus In Greek legend, the bastard son of *Theseus and Hippolyta, queen of the Amazons. A devotee of *Artemis, his dedication to chastity led him to reject the advances of Theseus's wife *Phaedra, and he was destroyed by a bull from the sea sent by Poseidon.

hippopotamus A large hoofed mammal, *Hippopotamus amphibius,* of tropical Africa. About 59 in (150 cm) high at the shoulder and weighing around 3.5 tons, hippos have virtually naked dark-brown skin and continuously growing tusks up to 24 in (60 cm) long. They spend the day in rivers or waterholes, emerging at night to graze on surrounding pasture. Herds usually number 10–15 individuals. Hippos are highly territorial, marking the boundaries of their grazing ground with piles of dung. Family: *Hippopotamidae. See also* pygmy hippopotamus.

Hirabayashi v. United States (1943) US Supreme Court decision that upheld temporary restrictions placed on all persons of Japanese descent living in the US during World War II. The suit, brought by an American of Japanese ancestry, claimed the restrictions and curfews violated the 5th Amendment.

Hirohito (1901–89) Emperor of Japan (1926–89), having previously been regent for five years after his father Yoshihito (1879–1926) had been declared insane. He married (1924) Princess Nagako Kuai. Ruling as divine emperor until Japan's defeat in World War II, he became no more than a constitutional monarch under the 1946 constitution (introduced under US pressure). The author of several books on marine biology, he is believed to have played a reluctant role in Japan's expansionist aspirations. He was succeeded by his son Akihito.

Hiroshige (Ando Tokitaro; 1797–1858) Japanese color-print artist of the □ukiyo-e movement. Trained under another ukiyo-e master, Toyohiro (1774–1829), Hiroshige first specialized in prints of women. From about 1830 he turned to landscapes, which he often depicted in snow, rain, or moonlight. His best-known print series is *Fifty-Three Stages of the Tokaido Highway* (1833).

Hiroshima 34 23N 132 27E A city in Japan, in SW Honshu on the delta of the Ota River. A former military base and important seaport, it was largely destroyed (Aug 6, 1945) by the first atomic bomb to be used in warfare; over 130,000 people were killed or injured. Many leading architects helped design the rapid rebuilding of the city and it is now a major industrial center. An international conference is held here annually to oppose nuclear weapons. Its university was established in 1949. Population (1990): 1,090,048.

Hispaniola The second largest West Indian island, in the Greater Antilles. It is politically divided between the *Dominican Republic and the Republic of *Haiti. Area: 29,418 sq mi (18,703 sq km).

histamine An amine, derived from the amino acid histidine, that is released from body tissues after injury or in an allergic reaction, such as asthma or hay fever. It dilates blood vessels, producing inflammation; contracts smooth muscle, which in the lungs leads to breathing difficulties; and stimulates the secretion of gastric juice. Its effects can be counteracted with *antihistamine drugs.

histology The study of *tissues. Originally histology was limited to the study of tissues by light microscopy, but the development of such techniques as electron microscopy, immunofluorescence, and autoradiography has enabled the details of subcellular structure to be revealed. *See also* cytology.

history The story of the past. The student of history discovers, examines, and interprets the records of past human societies. Records of events are found in the inscriptions of the ancient Egyptians but history as a literary activity is generally regarded as beginning with the ancient Greeks, among whom *Herodotus, *Thucydides, and *Xenophon were outstanding. The desire of ancient historians for accuracy was sometimes subordinated to their purely literary ambitions and the Romans (notably *Sallust, *Cicero, *Livy, and *Tacitus) were also concerned to glorify Rome. Early Christian history writing (historiography) was influenced by Jewish historians, such as *Josephus, and Christian preconceptions and subject matter continued to influence the writing of history throughout the Middle Ages. Medieval historiography consisted largely of chronicles, such as those of *Bede, Matthew *Paris, and Jean *Froissart. The later Middle Ages were influenced by Byzantine historians, including *Anna Comnena, and by such Arabs as *Ibn Khaldun and al-*Tabari. The classical interests of early Renaissance scholars (*see* humanism) led to a new concern for textual criticism, which led to the outstanding work of *Machiavelli and *Guicciardini in the early 16th century. Their critical approach to sources was continued by 17th-century historians but the 18th-century Enlightenment enlarged the interests of historians to include a more fundamental study of the pattern of change in human societies. This concern is reflected in the work of the 18th-century British historian Edward Gibbon, who tried to show that the history of mankind is one of continuous progress. In the 19th century, under the influence of the German school of historians, which included von *Ranke and *Mommsen, history was established as an academic discipline in the universities. The scope of historiography has greatly widened in the 20th century under the influence of sociology, anthropology, and psychiatry, and new techniques, such as the use of computers to analyze statistics, have been introduced.

Hitachi 36 35N 140 40E A city in Japan, in E Honshu on the Pacific Ocean. Copper has been mined here since 1591 and the city is Japan's leading producer of electrical equipment. Population (1990): 202,465.

Hitchcock, Sir Alfred (1899–1980) British movie director. He worked almost exclusively in Hollywood from 1940. He specialized in sophisticated thrillers, using calculated cinematic effects to create an atmosphere of tension and suspense. His technique was appreciated by and influenced directors of the *New Wave. His movies include *The Thirty-Nine Steps* (1935), *Rebecca* (1940), *Notorious* (1946), *Strangers on a Train* (1951), *To Catch a Thief* (1953), *Dial M for Murder* (1954), *Rear Window* (1954), *The Man Who Knew Too Much* (1956), *Psycho* (1960), and *The Birds* (1963).

ALFRED HITCHCOCK

Hitler, Adolf (1889–1945) German dictator. Born in Austria, the son of a customs officer, he fought in World War I, rising to the rank of lance corporal and winning the Iron Cross. After several years of poverty in Vienna and Munich, often working as a housepainter, he joined (1919) the German Workers' party, which was renamed the National Socialist (abbreviated to *Nazi) party in 1920. He became its president in 1921 and two years later staged an abortive coup—the Munich Putsch—against the Bavarian government. During a brief imprisonment he wrote most of *Mein Kampf* (*My Struggle*), setting out his political philosophy, based on a notion of the innate superiority of the Aryan race, the culpability of the Jews for Germany's defeat in World War I, and a violent anticommunism. In the economic crisis of the late 1920s and early 1930s Hitler's extraordinary powers of oratory and his propaganda machine (headed by *Goebbels) brought the Nazis increasing support, especially from German industrialists, and in 1932 they won a majority of the seats in the Reichstag. In 1933, aided by the machinations of von *Papen, Hitler was offered the chancellorship by *Hindenburg, the German president. The *Reichstag fire enabled him to discredit the opposition and to acquire the far-reaching dictatorial powers he sought; following Hindenburg's death in 1934 he assumed the title of Führer (leader). He proceeded to crush his opponents, institute his fanatical persecution of the Jews by the establishment of *concentration camps, and launch a massive rearmament program in preparation for the wars of conquest that he planned for the Third Reich. He lent his support to Mussolini in Italy and Franco in Spain, precipitating *World War II by invading Austria (1938) and then Czechoslovakia and Poland (1939). Military reverses in 1943 led to Stauffenberg's unsuccessful attempt (1944) to assassinate Hitler, but as the Third Reich collapsed in the face of Allied victory the Führer committed suicide with Eva *Braun (whom he had married shortly before) in the bunker of the chancellory in Berlin. How Hitler was able, unchecked for over a decade, to implement policies of an unparalleled atrociousness is a question that continues to plague mankind.

Hittites An *Indo-European people who appeared in Anatolia around the beginning of the second millennium BC. By 1340 BC they had emerged as a major power, with their capital at *Hattusas (or Boğazköy) from which they conquered much of Anatolia and also Syria (see Carchemish). In their polytheistic religion, their king was believed to be the representative of god on earth and became a god himself on death. The society was feudal in organization and also upheld the institution of slavery. Their language is extinct, but is known from cuneiform tablets and inscriptions (see Indo-Hittite languages).

hives. See urticaria.

Hoare-Laval Pact. See Laval, Pierre.

hoatzin A primitive bird, *Opisthocomus hoazin,* that occurs in tropical South American swamps. It is 25.5 in (65 cm) long and has a small head with wispy crest and a long tail. Its plumage is streaked brown with yellowish underparts and it feeds chiefly on flowers and fruit. It is the only member of its family (*Opisthocomidae*). Order: *Galliformes* (pheasants, turkeys, etc.).

Hobart 42 54S 147 18E A city in Australia, the capital and chief port of Tasmania on the Derwent River estuary. It has an excellent natural harbor with small tidal changes. Industries include zinc refining and food processing; the chief exports are apples, wool, timber, and dairy products. The University of Tasmania was established there in 1890. Population (1990): 183,500.

Hobbema, Meindert (1638–1709) Dutch landscape painter, born in Amsterdam. He often sketched with *Ruisdael but, unlike him, Hobbema specialized in peaceful woodland and rural scenes with watermills. Through his marriage (1668) he gained a minor post in the local excise department but continued with his painting, producing in this period perhaps his best work, *The Avenue, Middelharnis* (1689; National Gallery, London).

Hobbes, Thomas (1588–1679) English political philosopher. Hobbes was a vigorous proponent of scientific *materialism, particularly with regard to human nature. His interests lay in mathematics, geography, and the classics until the breakdown of English political and social order in the 1640s inspired him to devise his own political theory. *Leviathan* (1651) argues that because people are inherently selfish they need to be ruled by an absolute sovereign, whose function is to enforce public order. Contemporary theories of natural rights, and the civil rights thought to derive from them, were anathema to him. His theories made him a loyalist both to the English monarchy and, during the Interregnum, to its parliamentary opponents.

hobby A *falcon, *Falco subbuteo,* occurring in open regions of Eurasia and NW Africa. It is 13 in (33 cm) long and has a dark-gray back, whitish underparts streaked with black, and red "trousers." It feeds on large insects and small birds caught in flight.

Hochhuth, Rolf (1933–   ) Left-wing Swiss dramatist, who writes in German. His controversial documentary plays include *The Representative* (1962), criticizing the attitude of Pius XII to the Nazi persecution of the Jews, and *The Soldiers* (1966), accusing Winston *Churchill of complicity in the death of the Polish general Sikorski. His novel *German Love Story* (1980) analyzes the extent of the involvement of the German people in Nazi atrocities.

Ho Chi Minh (Nguyen That Thanh; 1890–1969) Vietnamese statesman, who led Vietnam in its struggle for independence from the French. As a young man he lived in England (1915–17) and then in France (1917–23), where in 1920 he joined the French Communist party. In 1924 he went to communist-controlled Canton, where he formed the Association of Young Vietnamese Revolutionaries (Thanh Nien), the forerunner of the Indochinese Communist party (1930). Returning to Vietnam in 1941, following the French defeat by the Germans in World War II, he formed the *Viet Minh, which waged the long and ultimately victorious colonial war against the French (1945–54; *see* Indochina). According to the Geneva Accords, which Ho Chi Minh attended, Vietnam was divided on either side of the 17th parallel into North Vietnam, of which Ho became president, and South Vietnam. In 1959 he extended support to the *Viet Cong guerrilla movement in the South (*see also* Vietnam War) with the aim of Vietnamese unification, which was achieved after his death.

Ho Chi Minh City (name until 1976: Saigon) 10 46N 106 43E A city in S Vietnam, on the Saigon River. The University of Saigon (now Ho Chi Minh City) was established in 1917. It is the major commercial and industrial center of the S, with shipbuilding, metalworking, textile, and chemical industries. *History*: an ancient Khmer town, it was the capital of *Cochinchina and then of French Indochina (1887–1902). During the *Vietnam War, as the capital of South Vietnam, US presence brought an economic boom but left problems of prostitution, crime, and drug addiction. Population (1989): 3,169,135.

Hockney, David (1937–   ) British painter. After studying at the Royal College of Art (1959–62), he traveled widely in the US, where he developed his realistic but witty style, his favorite subjects being figure studies and aquatic themes. He has also designed stage sets and illustrated books.

Hodeida (*or* Hudaydah) 14 50N 42 58E A city in Yemen, on the Red Sea coast. It is the country's principal port, exporting cotton and mocha coffee. Population (1986): 155,110.

Hodgkin, Alan Lloyd (1914–   ) British physiologist, who discovered the chemical changes associated with the propagation of a nerve impulse (*see* action potential) along a nerve fiber. He wrote *Conduction of the Nervous Impulse* (1964) and shared a Nobel Prize (1963) with A. F. Huxley (his colleague) and Sir John Eccles.

Hodgkin, Dorothy Mary Crowfoot (1910–   ) British biochemist, who determined the structure of several complex molecules by means of *X-ray diffraction. She helped to determine the structure of penicillin (in the 1940s) and of vitamin B_{12} (in the early 1950s). She was awarded the Nobel Prize in 1964.

Hodgkin, Thomas (1798–1866) British physician, who described the disease of the lymphatic system now known as **Hodgkin's disease** (*see* lymphoma). Hodgkin made a considerable contribution to the pathology of diseases.

Hofei. *See* Hefei.

Hoffa, James Riddle (1913–75?) US labor leader. He headed a local Teamsters union in the Midwest during the union movement of the 1930s and by 1952 was vice president of the International Teamsters. He served as president

(1957–71) during which time he served almost 5 years in prison (1967–71) for jury and pension fund tampering. He disappeared in 1975, presumed murdered because of his attempts to regain the Teamsters' presidency.

Hoffman, Dustin (1937–   ) US movie actor. He made his reputation in the movies *The Graduate* (1967) and *Midnight Cowboy* (1969). He was awarded Oscars for his performance as a divorced man bringing up his son in *Kramer vs Kramer* (1980), and for *Rain Man* (1988), in which he portrayed an autistic man. Other movies include *Lenny* (1974), in which he played comedian Lenny Bruce, *Tootsie* (1982), in which he impersonated a woman, and *Hook* (1991). He performed in *Death of a Salesman* on Broadway (1984) and on television (1985).

Hofmann, Joseph Casimir (1876–1957) Polish-born pianist. A performer from the age of six, he was a pupil of Anton Rubinstein. He also composed under the name "Michael Dvorsky." He toured extensively and became a US citizen in 1926.

Hofmannsthal, Hugo von (1874–1929) Austrian poet and dramatist. In 1901, after studying law and philology, he devoted himself to writing. His influential essay "The Letter of Lord Chandos" (1902), expressing his loss of confidence in language, divides the lyrical aestheticism of his short early plays from the social concern of his later ones, such as *Der Turm* (1925). He was librettist for several Richard *Strauss operas, including *Der Rosenkavalier* (1911) and *Ariadne auf Naxos* (1912). He was a cofounder of the Salzburg Festival in 1920.

Hofmeister, Wilhelm Friedrich Benedict (1824–77) German botanist, who pioneered the science of comparative plant morphology. His major work established the relationship between the cryptogams (algae, mosses, ferns, etc.), the gymnosperms (e.g. conifers), and the angiosperms (flowering plants). Hofmeister also discovered that regular alternation between sexual and asexual generations occurs in mosses, ferns, and seed plants.

Hogan, Ben (William Benjamin H.; 1912–   ) US professional golfer, most of whose major successes, including winning the Masters Tournament in 1951 and 1953, came after a car accident that was expected to cripple him (1949).

Hogarth, William (1697–1764) British painter and engraver. He studied under a silverplate engraver before establishing his reputation with the paintings and engravings of *A Harlot's Progress* (1731–32). He excelled in moralizing social satires in such narrative series as *A Rake's Progress, Industry and Idleness, Gin Lane,* and the paintings of *Marriage à la Mode*. As a portraitist the naturalism and vivacity of *Captain Coram* and *Hogarth's Servants* were influential, although unpopular with his contemporaries. His artistic theories are expressed in his treatise *The Analysis of Beauty* (1753).

hogfish A beautifully colored tropical marine fish belonging to a genus (*Bodianus*) of *wrasses. They change color while growing and are very popular in aquaria.

Hoggar Mountains. *See* Ahaggar Mountains.

hogweed A biennial herb, *Heracleum sphondylium,* also called cow parsnip, native to Eurasia and N Africa and introduced to North America. Up to 7 ft (2 m) high, it has hollow ridged stems, divided leaves, and umbrella-like clusters of white or pinkish flowers. The giant hogweed (*H. mantegazzianum*) may reach a height of 11 ft (3.5 m) and is grown as an ornamental. Family: *Umbelliferae.*

Hohenlinden, Battle of (Dec 3, 1800) The battle in the Napoleonic Wars in which the French under Jean Victor *Moreau defeated the Austrians. It was fought 16 mi (31 km) E of Munich. The French victory brought the collapse of the second coalition against Napoleon. *See* Revolutionary and Napoleonic Wars.

WILLIAM HOGARTH *The British painter and engraver's* Self-Portrait with His Pug.

Hohenlohe-Schillingsfürst, Chlodwig Karl Viktor, Fürst zu (1819–1901) German statesman; chancellor (1894–1900). He came to prominence during the 1860s as a vigorous supporter of Bismarck's policy of German unification. He served as ambassador to Paris (1874–78) and as governor of Alsace-Lorraine (1885–94) before becoming chancellor, when he attempted to exercise a moderating influence on William II. He was succeeded by his protégé Bernhard von Bülow.

Hohenstaufen A German dynasty, founded by Frederick, duke of Swabia (d. 1105), that ruled the Holy Roman Empire from 1138 to 1254. *Conrad III was the first Hohenstaufen emperor and, of his successors, the most important were *Frederick (I) Barbarossa and *Frederick II. Frequently in conflict with Italian city states and the papacy, the dynasty was destroyed by its defeat at Tagliacozzo by a papal alliance (1268).

Hohenzollern A dynasty, originating in Swabia, that ruled *Brandenburg, then *Prussia, and later Germany. First prominent in the late 12th century, the Hohenzollerns became Electors of Brandenburg in the 15th century. During the

next 300 years they acquired other territories, including Prussia, of which
*Frederick I became king in 1701. From 1871 they ruled the German Empire
until its collapse in 1918.

Hohhot (*or* Huhehot) 40 49N 111 37E A city in NE China, the capital of Inner
Mongolia. An old frontier trading town, its industry was developed after 1949.
The university was established in 1957. Population (1990): 652,534.

Hojo Hereditary holders of the regency for the military overlordship (*see*
shogun) of Japan between 1204 and 1333. Hojo Tokimasa (1138–1215) became
the first regent in 1204 although he had held actual power from the death
(1199) of his son-in-law, the first shogun *Minamoto Yoritomo. The Hojo regents were notable for their codification of feudal law, their encouragement of
Zen Buddhism, and their repulse of the Mongols (1274, 1281). Their power
was destroyed in 1333 by a combination of other feudal lords and the emperor
*Daigo II.

Hokan languages An American Indian language group spoken mainly in the
NW of the US and in California. Some Hokan languages are found in Mexico,
including the most widely spoken, Tlapanecan and Tquistlatecan. The Yuman
subdivision found in Colorado and California also has a comparatively large
number of speakers. The Mohave language is a member of this subgroup.

Hokkaido (former name: Yezo) The second largest and northernmost of the
four main islands of Japan, separated from Honshu by the Tsugaru Strait and
from the Russian island of Sakhalin by La Perouse Strait. Mountainous, volcanic, and forested, with a relatively cool climate, it is popular for winter sports.
It has a sizable aboriginal population and the N is largely uninhabited. Main industries are coal mining, agriculture, and fishing. *History*: the Japanese began to
settle on the island in the 16th century but did not develop it seriously until after
1868. It became administratively autonomous in 1885. Area: 30,077 sq mi
(78,200 sq km). Population (1990): 5,647,500. Capital: Sapporo.

Hokusai (Katsushika H.; 1760–1849) Japanese painter and book illustrator,
the most famous *ukiyo-e designer of color prints. He began as a wood engraver, becoming in 1778 a pupil of the painter and printmaker Shunsho
(1726–92). From the 1790s he illustrated historical novels, verse anthologies,
etc., and designed greeting and announcement cards. His early prints were
chiefly of women and actors but he is best known for his later landscapes, which
deeply influenced the impressionists and postimpressionists. His most famous
works include his *Views of Mount Fuji* (1835) and his collection of sketchbooks,
the *Hokusai Manga*, published from 1814 onward.

Holbein the Younger, Hans (c. 1497–1543) German painter, born in Augs-
burg. In 1515 he settled in Basle, where he designed woodcuts of the *Dance of
Death*. Through his friend Erasmus he obtained the patronage of Sir Thomas
More in England (1526–28). Settling in England in 1532, he painted portraits of
merchants before becoming court painter and designer to Henry VIII (1536).
His portrait of Henry VIII in a wall painting (destroyed) for Whitehall Palace
became the prototype for other paintings of the king. He was also commissioned
to paint Henry's prospective wives, *Christina, Duchess of Milan* (National
Gallery, London) and *Anne of Cleves* (Louvre) and established a thriving
portrait-painting business, e.g. *The Ambassadors* (National Gallery, London).
Many of the preparatory drawings for his English portraits are in the Royal Col-
lection, Windsor. Holbein died of the plague. His father **Hans Holbein the
Elder** (c. 1465–1524) was also a painter, whose major work is the *S Sebastian
Altar* (Alte Pinakothek, Munich).

Hölderlin, (Johann Christian) Friedrich (1770–1843) German poet. Trained as a Lutheran minister, he found Christianity incompatible with his enthusiasm for Greek mythology. While working as a private tutor, he fell in love with his employer's wife, who is portrayed in his novel *Hyperion* (1797–99). After her death in 1802 his life was dominated by his schizophrenia, from which he never recovered. His great lyrical talent was unrecognized until the 20th century, when a comprehensive edition of his poetry was published.

hole. *See* semiconductors.

Holguín 20 54N 76 15W A city in E Cuba. It is an important commercial center; the chief exports through its port Gilbara (to the NE) are sugar and tobacco. Population (1989 est): 222,800.

Holiday, Billie (Eleanor Gough McKay; 1915–59) US jazz singer, known as "Lady Day." She was discovered in Harlem by Benny Goodman and made her first recording in 1933. She subsequently sang with the bands of Count Basie and Artie Shaw. She was best known for singing torch songs, such as "My Man," "Lover Man," and "Mean to Me." Addiction to heroin caused her death.

BILLIE HOLIDAY

Holland The low-lying NW region of the Netherlands, now comprising the provinces of *North Holland and *South Holland. A county of the Holy Roman Empire from the 12th century, Holland came under Burgundy in the 15th century and then (1500) under the Hapsburgs. Prominent in the 16th-century *Revolt of the Netherlands against Spanish Hapsburg rule, Holland became the chief province of the independent United Provinces of the Netherlands. When the kingdom of the *Netherlands was established in 1814, Holland became an administrative province, and its importance diminished. Nevertheless the whole country is still commonly called Holland.

Holland, Sir Sidney (George) (1893–1961) New Zealand statesman; National party prime minister (1949–57). His government was repressive in industrial disputes and unable to control inflation. His party was defeated shortly after his retirement in 1957.

holly A tree or shrub of the widely distributed genus *Ilex* (300 species). The evergreen English holly (*I. aquifolium*) grows to a height of 50 ft (15 m) and has spiny lustrous dark-green leaves and small white male and female flowers growing on separate trees: the female flowers develop into red berries. It is widely cultivated for hedging and used for Christmas decorations. Family: *Aquifoliaceae. See also* maté.

hollyhock A perennial herb, *Althaea rosea,* native to China but widely cultivated as a garden flower (garden hollyhocks are usually treated as biennials). It grows to a height of 10 ft (3 m) and bears tall spikes of large white, yellow, or red flowers. Family: *Malvaceae.*

holly oak. *See* holm oak.

Hollywood 34 04N 118 15W A NW suburb of Los Angeles, in California. Founded in the 1880s, it has been the center of the US film industry since 1911.

Hollywood 26 00N 80 09W A city in SE Florida, N of Miami, on the Atlantic Ocean. Developed as a winter resort in the 1920s, it has building materials, electronic equipment, and furniture industries. Population (1990): 121,697.

Holmes, Oliver Wendell (1809–94) US essayist and poet. Trained as a physician, Holmes became dean of the Harvard Medical School and wrote several important medical works. In addition to the acclaim he received for his scientific writings, Holmes was recognized for his literary talents. Among his best-known poems are "Old Ironsides" (1830) and "The Chambered Nautilus" (1858). He also published several collections of conversational essays, including *The Autocrat of the Breakfast Table* (1857) and *Over the Teacups* (1891). His son **Oliver Wendell Holmes Jr.** (1841–1935) was a prominent jurist who became professor of law at Harvard in 1882. In 1902, after service as chief justice of the Massachusetts Supreme Court, the younger Holmes was nominated by Pres. Theodore *Roosevelt to become an associate justice of the US Supreme Court. In that position Holmes distinguished himself as a defender of individual rights, often dissenting from the majority opinions of his colleagues. In particular, he opposed the use of the 14th Amendment to the *Constitution by the federal government to prohibit state wage and hour standards as in the case of *Lochner* v. *NY* (1905). Holmes resigned from the Supreme Court in 1932.

holmium (Ho) A metallic lanthanide element, discovered in 1879 by P. T. Cleve (1840–1905) and named for his native city, Stockholm. Holmium occurs in rare-earth minerals, such as monazite ($CePO_4$). It forms an oxide (Ho_2O_3) and halides (HoX_3), but has few uses. At no 67; at wt 164.9304; mp 2688°F (1474°C); bp 4888°F (2695°C).

holm oak An evergreen *oak tree, *Quercus ilex,* also called holly oak, native to S Europe and cultivated for ornament and for its durable wood. Growing to a height of 100 ft (30 m), it has a broad dense crown and the leaves of young trees resemble holly leaves.

holocaust The extermination of European *Jews by the Nazis (1939–45). Some six million Jews from many countries, approximately two-thirds of European Jewry, were killed in Auschwitz and other *concentration camps. The holocaust has raised serious theological problems and questions about the nature of European civilization.

Holocene epoch The present, or Recent, epoch in *geological time, including the last 10,000 years from the end of the Pleistocene. Since it follows all the main glacial episodes it is sometimes called the Postglacial, although some authorities consider it to be only an interglacial phase of the Pleistocene. At the beginning of the Holocene the general rise in sea level resulting from the melting of the ice isolated Britain from the rest of the Continent of Europe.

OLIVER WENDELL HOLMES, JR. *Supreme Court justice, "The Great Dissenter," who championed civil rights.*

holography A method of producing a stereoscopic image without using a camera. A monochromatic beam of *coherent radiation from a laser is split into two using a semitransparent mirror; one beam falls directly onto a photographic film or plate and the other is reflected by the subject onto the film. The two beams form *interference patterns on the film, which is called a hologram. To reconstruct the image, light of the same wavelength from a laser is shone onto the hologram. The interference pattern on the hologram diffracts the beam and splits it into two parts. One part gives a real two-dimensional image and the other a virtual three-dimensional image. The theory of holography was suggested by Denis *Gabor in 1947 but could not be put into practice until the laser was invented 16 years later.

Holst, Gustav (Theodore) (1874–1934) British composer. His interest in oriental philosophy inspired the chamber opera *Savitri* (1908) and other works. Among his most famous compositions are the choral work *The Hymn of Jesus* (1917), the tone poem *Egdon Heath* (1927), and the orchestral suite *The Planets* (1914–16).

Holt, Harold (Edward) (1908–67) Australian statesman; Liberal prime minister from 1966 until his death, apparently by drowning. His administration relaxed immigration and citizenship laws and supported involvement in the Vietnam War.

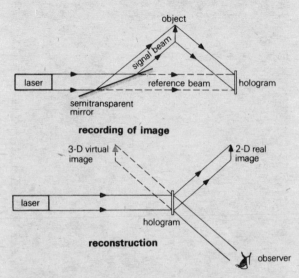

HOLOGRAPHY *A three-dimensional image formed by two beams of light is recorded as an interference pattern on a single plate. The two images, giving a 3-D effect, are reconstructed by shining two similar beams through the hologram.*

Holy Grail In medieval legend and romance, a vessel or dish having supernatural power. Originally the grail may have had some significance in pre-Christian Celtic mythology; but by the 12th century, in romances by *Chrétien de Troyes and Robert de Boron's *Joseph d'Arimathie,* it was associated with the chalice used by Christ at the Last Supper and later given to *Joseph of Arimathea, who received the blood of Christ in it at the crucifixion. Chrétien had combined the grail legend with the *Arthurian legend, and the knightly quest for the Holy Grail, undertaken by Percival, Galahad, and other Knights of the Round Table, is a dominant theme in many Arthurian romances. According to a passage in William of Malmesbury, Joseph brought the Holy Grail to Glastonbury, where he also allegedly built the first church in England.

Holy Island (*or* Lindisfarne) 55 41N 1 48W An island, in NE England off the NE coast of Northumberland. Its monastery was founded by St Aidan (635 AD); St Cuthbert was a bishop here (685–87).

Holy Lance The lance said to have pierced Christ's side at the crucifixion. This relic was discovered (1098) after a visionary revelation to a peasant, Peter Bartholomew, at the siege of Antioch during the first *Crusade. Accepted as genuine by most, but not all, of the Crusaders, its discovery raised morale and inspired the capture of Antioch from the Muslims.

Holy League Any of several alliances formed in the 15th, 16th, and 17th centuries usually for the furtherance of papal or Roman Catholic interests. The best known are those formed against the French invasion of Italy (1494) and against the Huguenots in the French *Wars of Religion (1576).

Holyoake, Sir Keith Jacka (1904–83) New Zealand statesman; National party prime minister (1957, 1960–72). He entered Parliament in 1932, became deputy leader of the National party in 1947, and was deputy prime minister and minister for agriculture from 1949 until Sir Sidney Holland's resignation in 1957. He was governor general of New Zealand (1977–80).

Holy of Holies The central shrine of the Jewish *tabernacle (Exodus 25–31, 35–40) and later of the *Temple of Jerusalem. Originally it contained the Ark of the Covenant (the receptacle of the two tablets of the law) and other cultic objects. In the second Temple it was apparently empty. The *high priest entered it once a year, on *Yom Kippur, to make atonement for the people.

holy orders In Christian Churches, specifically those accepting *episcopacy, the ranks of bishop, priest, etc., conferred by a bishop. They are traditionally divided into major and minor orders, the former being the ranks of bishop, priest, deacon, and (in the Roman Church) subdeacon. In the Roman Catholic Church, there are four minor orders: porters (or doorkeepers), lectors (or readers), exorcists, and acolytes. Holy orders are considered a *sacrament by the Orthodox and Roman Catholic Churches; they are also held to impose an "indelible character" on the recipient, so that they remain valid after the most serious sin and can be conferred only once.

Holy Roman Empire The successor to the western *Roman Empire of antiquity. The name itself was not employed until the mid-13th century but the institution dates from 800, when *Charlemagne was crowned emperor of the West by Pope Leo III. Its territory came to comprise much of W and central Europe, being centered on Germany and Austria and including areas of E France and N Italy. After the failure of Charlemagne's *Carolingian dynasty the imperial title, which was nominally elective (*see* electors), passed (962) to the German kings, who retained it until the Empire's abolition in 1806; from the 13th century the emperors were almost always *Hapsburgs. Between the 11th and 13th centuries the emperors (especially those of the *Hohenstaufen dynasty) vied with the popes for dominance in Europe (*see* investiture controversy; Guelfs and Ghibellines), a conflict from which the Empire emerged much weakened. It was further undermined by the Protestant *Reformation in the 16th century, the *Thirty Years' War in the 17th century, and the rise of Prussia and was finally broken by Napoleon's conquest of imperial territories in the early 19th century.

Holy Spirit (*or* Holy Ghost) In Christian theology, the third person of the Trinity, coequal and of one substance with the Father and the Son. Old Testament references to the spirit of God are given a more specific application in the New Testament Gospels; in St John's Gospel the Holy Spirit is seen as the "Paraclete" or Comforter, sent to inspire Christ's followers after the *Ascension. In Acts, the descent of the Holy Spirit upon the Apostles is described, an event commemorated at the Feast of Pentecost (the 50th day after Easter). In art, the Holy Spirit is usually symbolized by a dove.

homeomorphism In mathematics, a one-to-one correspondence. In *set theory it is a property of two sets in which every member of one set is capable of being paired with one member of the other set and vice versa. In *topology, two shapes are homeomorphic if one can be transformed into the other by a continuous deformation, without being cut; for example, the surfaces of a sphere and a cube are homeomorphic.

homeopathy The system of treating illness developed by Samuel *Hahnemann at the end of the 18th century and based on the principle of "like cures like." To treat a particular disease homeopathists prescribe small doses of a drug that in larger quantities would cause the symptoms of the disease in a healthy person.

homeostasis The self-regulating process by which living organisms tend to maintain their bodies in a constant physiological state regardless of environmental extremes. The extent to which this independence is achieved by a particular group is a measure of its success: protozoans, for instance, are affected by many external factors, whereas man is relatively independent. In man, reflex activity of the nervous system and the action of hormones are important means of achieving homeostatic control. Claude *Bernard was one of the first to recognize the importance of this kind of regulation.

Homer (8th century BC) Greek epic poet, presumed author of the *Iliad* and *Odyssey*. He is believed to have lived in Ionia in Asia Minor and according to legend was blind. Working within a primitive oral tradition, his achievement lay in ordering a wealth of traditional material into a monumental and unified poetic structure. The *Iliad* concerns the Trojan War, and its basic tragic theme is enlivened by the variety and human sympathy of its individual episodes. The *Odyssey* relates the various adventures of *Odysseus during his voyage home from the Trojan War to his kingdom of Ithaca. Both poems were revered by the ancient Greeks for their moral as well as their literary value and have had a profound influence on Western culture.

Homer, Winslow (1836–1910) US painter of everyday life, landscapes, and seascapes. In his native Boston he trained under a lithographer. In New York he worked as an illustrator and as an artist-correspondent of the Civil War, achieving prominence with his painting *Prisoners from the Front* (1866). Many of his paintings depict typically American scenes, such as the rural game in *Crack the Whip* (1872). After a visit to England (1881–83), he settled in the Maine fishing village of Prouts Neck, where he painted a number of watercolors of fishermen and the sea, often in dramatic conflict, as in *The Northeaster* (1895) and *The Gulf Stream* (1899).

Home Rule An Irish political movement to repeal the Act of *Union with Britain and give Ireland a legislature responsible for domestic affairs. Founded by Isaac Butt (1813–79) in 1870, the Home Rule movement achieved parliamentary prominence under the leadership of *Parnell from 1880. *Gladstone's conversion to Home Rule produced the Home Rule bills of 1886 and 1893 but both were defeated. In 1914 the third Home Rule bill was passed but suspended for the duration of World War I. A modified act, passed in 1920, was accepted by the north but rejected by the south, which in 1922 gained dominion status as the Irish Free State.

Homestead Act (1862) An act to encourage settlement of the West. Anyone at least 21 years old, and willing to farm for five years, was given 160 acres (65 hectares) in the West. After this initial period the land was theirs. The act was instrumental in opening up the West, and about one out of every three farmers was successful.

Homestead Massacre (1892) A clash between strikers and security forces during a steel strike in Homestead, in SW Pennsylvania. The Carnegie Steel Company, in an effort to discourage pickets, hired about 300 Pinkerton detectives to disrupt the pickets. Violence erupted, ten people were killed, and the national guard was posted there for three months. The power of the union remained weak until 1937 when the steel industry was unionized.

homing instinct. *See* migration, animal.

hominid A member of the *Hominidae* family of primates, to which man belongs. Besides man, there are no surviving hominids: the others are known only from fossil remains. The *Hominidae* include the genera **Ramapithecus, *Australopithecus,* and **Homo.* The hominids appeared between five and one million years ago in Africa and Asia. The first to appear in Europe date from between 600,000 and 800,000 years ago.

Homo A genus of *hominids characterized by a large cranial capacity, erect posture, bipedal gait, a thumb capable of a precision grip, and the ability to make and use tools. The genus includes the species *Homo erectus* (*see* Pithecanthropus), which may have been ancestral to modern man. This species, which first appeared more than one million years ago during the middle *Pleistocene, includes specimens from Java, Peking, Heidelberg, and elsewhere. *Neanderthal man also belongs to the genus *Homo,* as does *Cro-Magnon man, who was probably an early form of the species *Homo sapiens* (modern man). *See also* Australopithecus.

homoiothermy The condition of being warm-blooded, i.e. of maintaining a fairly constant body temperature by physiological mechanisms. Birds and mammals are warm-blooded: in cold climates body heat is conserved and also produced by muscle activity, such as shivering, while in hot weather body heat is lost by sweating and panting. *Compare* poikilothermy.

homosexuality Sexual attraction or relations between persons of the same sex. It is known as lesbianism when the persons involved are females. Homosexuality is an ancient and widespread phenomenon that can involve moral stigma and even punishment, as in the Judeo-Christian tradition, but just as often is regarded as neither abnormal nor immoral, as in ancient Greece. Related phenomena are bisexuality (when an individual is attracted by people of both sexes) and transsexuality (*see* transvestism). Many countries have in recent years liberalized their laws concerning homosexuality. Contemporary movements, such as Gay Liberation, seek to alleviate any residual social problems that may persist for homosexuals in a predominantly heterosexual society.

Homs (Arabic name: Hims) 34 44N 36 43E A city in Syria, on the Orontes River close to the border with N Lebanon. There is a large Crusader fortress here, and Homs is an important trading and industrial town. Population (1977 est): 292,280.

Honan. *See* Henan.

Honduras, Republic of A country in Central America, with a N coastline on the Caribbean Sea and a short S one on the Pacific Ocean. Narrow coastal plains rise to mountainous country, dissected by river valleys. The majority of the population is of mixed Indian and Spanish descent. *Economy*: mainly agricultural, the chief crops are bananas and coffee (the principal exports). Almost half the land is forested, with valuable hardwoods in the NE and pine in the interior. Fishing is important, especially shrimps for export. The considerable mineral resources, some as yet unexploited, include gold, silver, lead, tin and zinc, and mercury. Hydroelectricity is being developed. *History*: the area was a center of Mayan culture from the 4th to the 9th centuries AD and was later occupied by the Lenca Indians. Discovered by Columbus in 1502, it became part of the Spanish captaincy general of Guatemala. It gained independence from Spain in 1821 and then formed part of the Central American Federation (1823–38). Honduras has suffered much internal unrest as well as a long conflict with Guatemala and, more recently, with El Salvador: in 1969 war broke out following El Salvador's defeat of Honduras in a World Cup soccer match. In 1972 a former (1966–71) president, Gen. Oswaldo López, seized power in a bloodless coup but he in turn

evolution of Homo sapiens *The picture of human evolution is constantly changing as new fossil evidence comes to light. The fossil Propliopithecus represents the apparent divergence of the gibbons (Hylobatidae), great apes (Pongidae), and humans (Hominidae) from the monkeys, but paleontologists are still debating many of the other classifications and relationships shown on this chart. What, for instance, is the connection between Zinjanthropus and the older but more highly developed Homo habilis, found on the same site?*

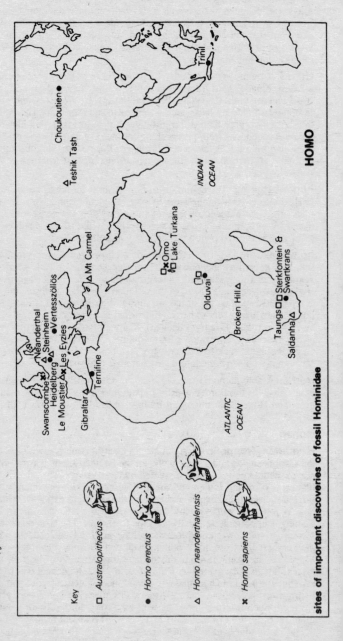

sites of important discoveries of fossil Hominidae

HOMO

Key

□ *Australopithecus*

● *Homo erectus*

△ *Homo neanderthalensis*

✕ *Homo sapiens*

Choukoutien ●

△ Teshik Tash

INDIAN OCEAN

Neanderthal
△ Steinheim
● Vertesszöllös
× Swanscombe
Heidelberg △ Les Eyzies
△ Le Moustier △ Mt Carmel
Gibraltar △
△ Ternifine

× Omo
□ □ Lake Turkana
□ □ Olduvai
Broken Hill △
Taungs □ □ Sterkfontein &
△ Saldanha ● Swartkrans

ATLANTIC OCEAN

Trinil ●

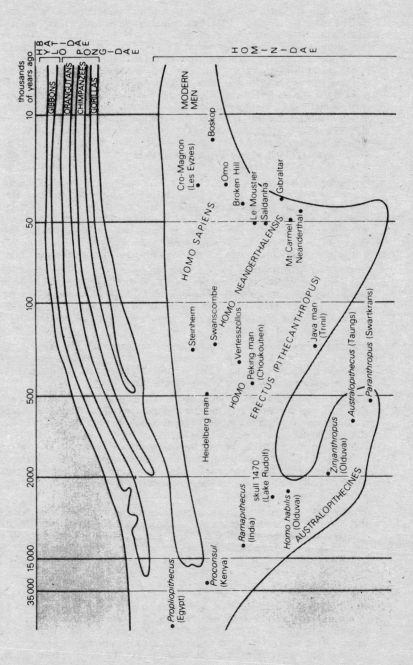

HOMO

GIBBONS
ORANGUTANS
CHIMPANZEES
GORILLAS

HYLOBATIDAE
PONGIDAE

HOMINIDAE

thousands
of years ago

MODERN MEN

Boskop

Cro-Magnon
(Les Eyzies)

Omo

Broken Hill

Le Moustier

Saldanha

Gibraltar

HOMO SAPIENS

HOMO NEANDERTHALENSIS

Mt Carmel

Neanderthal

Steinheim

Swanscombe

Vertesszöllos

HOMO

Peking man
(Choukoutien)

Java man
(Trinil)

Australopithecus (Taungs)

Paranthropus (Swartkrans)

HOMO ERECTUS (PITHECANTHROPUS)

Heidelberg man

Zinjanthropus
(Olduvai)

Ramapithecus
(India)

skull 1470
(Lake Rudolf)

Homo habilis
(Olduvai)

AUSTRALOPITHECINES

Propliopithecus
(Egypt)

Proconsul
(Kenya)

10

50

100

500

2000

15 000

35 000

was overthrown in 1975. Military rule continued under Col. Juan Melgar Castro, until he was in turn deposed (1978) by a military junta headed by Gen. Paz García. Honduras's growing involvement in the Central American conflict and its escalating struggle against the Sandinista government in Nicaragua created worldwide concern. The US strengthened its ties with Honduras, its closest ally in Central America, by supplying military and economic assistance. Honduras was used also as a base for the contra guerrillas fighting the Nicaraguan government. Rafael Leonardo Callejas, who became president in 1989, faced a devastated economy and labor unrest. By 1992, he had instituted many of the austerity measures required for foreign aid, but the economy had hardly improved. Honduras is a member of the OAS and the Organization of Central American States. Official language: Spanish. Official currency: lempira of 100 centavos. Area: 43,227 sq mi (112,088 sq km). Population (1989 est): 5,106,000. Capital: Tegucigalpa. Main ports: Amapala on the Pacific and La Ceiba on the Atlantic.

Honecker, Erich (1912–) East German statesman; first secretary of the Socialist Unity party (1971–90). After his release from Nazi imprisonment, Honecker led a German youth group (1946–1955). From 1958 to 1971 he was responsible for security matters. In 1990, he was indicted for the murders of over 200 people, killed while trying to cross the Berlin Wall to West Germany. Honecker fled to the Soviet Union, was returned to Germany in 1992, and in 1993 was judged too sick to continue his trial and allowed to join his family in Chile.

Honegger, Arthur (1892–1955) French composer, born in Switzerland. He was a pupil of Widor and d'Indy and one of Les *Six. He developed his own polyphonic and dissonant style. His compositions include five symphonies, the stage works *King David* (1921) and *Joan of Arc at the Stake* (1934–35), an orchestral depiction of a large steam locomotive entitled *Pacific 231* (1923), chamber music, and piano music.

honesty A herbaceous plant of the European genus *Lunaria* (3 species). Up to 40 in (1 m) high, it is often grown in gardens for its decorative disc-shaped papery seed heads. *L. annua* has white to purple flowers while *L. variegata* has crimson flowers and variegated foliage. Family: *Cruciferae*.

honey A sweet thick yellow syrup collected from the honeycomb of bee hives. Bees suck nectar from flowers and empty it into the cells of their hives, where they convert the sugar it contains from sucrose into dextrose and fructose. Honey from heather is golden and that from white clover is greenish-white. It is commercially extracted by heating the honeycomb. Honey consists of about 70% sugars, 18% water, and small amounts of minerals, pollen, and wax. Honey was used for embalming in ancient Egypt and was a favorite food of the ancient Greeks. Mildly antiseptic on account of its acidity, it has also been used medicinally for a variety of purposes.

honey ant An *ant belonging to subfamilies (*Camponotinae* or *Dolichoderine*) occurring in North America, Africa, Australia, and New Guinea. Certain members of the colony, called repletes, gorge themselves with honeydew (mainly from aphids and scale insects) gathered by other workers. They then hang from the ceiling of their underground chamber and regurgitate this food store when stimulated by the other ants.

honey badger. *See* ratel.

honeybee A social *bee, *Apis mellifera,* also called hive bee. Native to SE Asia, it is reared worldwide for its *honey and *beeswax. Honeybees have large colonies with 50,000–80,000 workers during the summer and a well-defined caste system. Workers attend to nest building, food gathering, and brood care; they use dances to communicate the location of food sources to other colony members. The queen lays her eggs in wax chambers (cells). Developing drones and workers are fed on protein-rich "royal jelly" for a few days and then changed to a diet of pollen and honey. Larvae hatching from fertilized eggs and fed on royal jelly throughout their development become queens, rather than workers. New colonies are formed by a swarm of workers led by the old queen (*compare* bumblebee); a young queen continues the established colony. Family: *Apidae.*

honeycreeper A songbird belonging to a family (*Drepanididae;* 22 species) restricted to the Hawaiian Islands, where they appear to have evolved from a single species. Honeycreepers are of two types: nectar feeders with colorful plumage and long slender curved bills and drab-green seed eaters with short bills. Some honeycreepers face extinction due to man's destruction of their specialized habitats.

honeyeater An arboreal songbird belonging to a family (*Meliphagidae;* 160 species) occurring chiefly in SE Asia and Australasia. They are 4–14 in (10–35 cm) long and have a drab plumage with wattles or naked patches on the face. The slender bill is down-curved and the long extensible tongue has a central trough, through which nectar is drunk, and a brushlike tip for collection pollen and small insects.

honey fungus A fungus, *Armillaria mellea,* also called bootlace fungus, that forms clusters of toadstools on or near old trees or stumps, to which it is attached by thick black rootlike structures resembling bootlaces. These may be found beneath the bark of an infected tree. The toadstool is 1.2–4 in (3–10 cm) in diameter and may be yellowish, green, brown, gray, or pink. Honey fungus is a serious pest of trees. Family: *Tricholomataceae;* class: **Basidiomycetes.*

honey guide An arboreal bird belonging to a tropical Old World family (*Indicatoridae;* 12 species). Honey guides are 4.5–8 in (11.5–20 cm) long and dullbrown, gray, or greenish in color. They feed mainly on bees and wasps and certain species are known to guide honey badgers or men to bees' nests by chattering and flying in the direction of the nest; the mammal robs the nest and the bird feeds on the remains. Order: *Piciformes* (woodpeckers, etc.).

honey locust A tree of the genus *Gleditschia* (11 species), occurring in warm parts of America, Africa, and Asia. The American species *G. triacanthos* is planted for ornament in Europe. It has stout thorns, compound leaves with paired leaflets, and small green flowers producing long pods. Family: **Leguminosae.*

honey mouse A small marsupial, *Tarsipes spenserae,* of SW Australia, also called honey possum or phalanger. It has a gray-brown body (2.75–3 in [70–85 mm] long) with three dark stripes along the back; a long snout; and a very long prehensile tail 3–4 in (88–100 mm). The honey mouse climbs shrubs to feed on nectar, using its long bristly tongue to reach inside the flowers. Family: *Phalangeridae.*

honeysuckle A shrub or twining plant of the genus *Lonicera* (100 species), of the N hemisphere. The common European honeysuckle (*L. pericylmenum*), also called woodbine, is a trailing shrub, up to 20 ft (6 m) long, and bears clusters of elongated tubular yellowish flowers. A number of species are cultivated as ornamentals, including the fragrant climbing honeysuckle (*L. japonica*). Family: *Caprifoliaceae.*

Hong Kong A British crown colony lying off the S coast of China. It consists of the island of Hong Kong, the mainland peninsula of Jiulong, the New Territories, and Stonecutters Island. Much of the land is steep and barren. The majority of the population is Chinese. *Economy*: owing to its strategic position and fine natural harbor, it is an important entrepôt port and banking center.

Much of China's foreign trade passes through Hong Kong. The export of manufactured goods has become increasingly important following the rapid industrial expansion since World War II and the textile and clothing industry (developed by immigrants from Shanghai) accounts for over half the total domestic exports. Electronics and plastics are also important and there is some heavy industry, such as ship building and repair and iron and steel manufacture. There is a certain amount of cultivation, although agricultural land is scarce and the reclamation of land from the sea has long been important in the colony's history. Tourism is also a major source of revenue. *History*: the island was ceded to Britain by China at the end of the first Opium War (1842) and Kowloon was added in 1860. In 1898 the New Territories were granted on a 99-year lease from China. Hong Kong was occupied by the Japanese during World War II. Britain's lease on the New Territories (which constitutes most of the colony), scheduled to expire in 1997, caused concern over the future of the colony in the early 1980s. China was firm in its insistence that Hong Kong revert to Chinese control. Pessimism was reflected in a depressed economy, with few new internal investments and a sharp increase in investment outside the colony. In 1984, China and Britain signed an agreement covering the status of Hong Kong after 1997. Under the agreement Hong Kong would be a special administrative region of China, with considerable autonomy, its own legal system, and the right to maintain its capitalist system. Official language: English; Cantonese is widely spoken. Official currency: Hong Kong dollar of 100 cents. Area: 398 sq mi (1031 sq km). Population (1990 est): 5,841,000. Capital and main port: Victoria.

Hong-wu (*or* Hung-wu; 1328–98) The title of Chu Yuan-zhang (*or* Chu Yüanchang), who became the first emperor (1368–98) of the Ming dynasty. A monk, he became a rebel leader and outstanding military tactician, ousting the Yuan dynasty and declaring himself emperor. He made Nanjing his capital and by 1382 he had united China.

Hong Xiu Quan (*or* Hung Hsiu-ch'uan; 1814–64) Chinese religious leader and revolutionary. After failing to get a place in the civil service, he espoused a strongly political Protestant Christianity, declaring himself God's second son and savior of China. He led the *Taiping Rebellion, but eventually ceased to take part in politics and committed suicide in Nanjing shortly before it fell.

Honolulu 21 19N 157 50W The capital city of Hawaii, on SE Oahu. Famed for its beauty, it is the economic center of the islands and a transpacific route stop. It is the site of three universities and of Iolani Palace, the former royal residence. *Pearl Harbor is still an important naval base. Population (1990): 365,272.

Honorius II (Lamberto Scannabecchi; d. 1130) Pope (1124–30). An architect of the Concordat of Worms, which ended the *investiture controversy (1122), he reestablished relations between the papacy and Empire, supporting the claims of Lothair II against Conrad III. Fearing the growing strength of the Normans under Roger II in Sicily, he led an army against him and was defeated and forced to accept Roger as Duke of Apulia.

Honshu The largest of the four main islands of Japan, situated between the Pacific Ocean and the Sea of Japan. It is mountainous, volcanic, and prone to earthquakes, with a great difference in climate between the subtropical S and the cooler N. The historic center of Japan, it has been the site of its capital since earliest times. Most of Japan's major ports and cities are here, although agriculture is also very important; rice, fruit, cotton, and tea are grown. Mineral wealth includes oil, zinc, and copper. The traditional industry is silk but the many modern industries include ship building, iron and steel, chemicals, and textiles. Area:

88,976 sq mi (230,448 sq km). Population (1990): 99,254,194. Chief city: Tokyo.

Honthorst, Gerrit von (1590–1656) Dutch painter. Working in Rome (c. 1610–1620), Utrecht, London (1628), and The Hague, he painted biblical, mythological, and everyday scenes, which were influenced by *Caravaggio in their use of candlelight. His portraits include one of Charles I and Henrietta Maria (Hampton Court).

Hooch, Pieter de (1629–c. 1684) Dutch painter, born in Rotterdam. Working in Delft, Leiden, and Amsterdam, he excelled in small paintings, such as *The Pantry* (Rijksmuseum, Amsterdam), depicting household tasks in courtyards or dark interiors that open into sunlit rooms.

Hood, John Bell (1831–79) US Confederate general. After serving in the Indian wars in the West, he resigned (1861) to join the Confederate Army and command the Texas Brigade. He fought at *Bull Run (1862) and, promoted to general, at *Antietam, Gettysburg, and Chickamauga. Although he had lost a leg, he was put in command of the Confederate Army (1864) at Atlanta, where he was defeated. After a crushing defeat at Nashville, he resigned.

hooded crow A crow, *Corvus corone cornix,* identical to the *carrion crow except for its gray back and underparts. It is found in N and E Europe, where the carrion crow does not occur, but in the narrow zone where the two races overlap they hybridize, producing birds of mixed coloration.

hooded seal A *seal, *Cystophora cristata,* of deep Arctic waters, also called bladdernose, or crested seal. About 10 ft (3 m) long, pale gray with dark blotches, hooded seals have a red inflatable bladder on top of the nose. In males the inflated bladder may be used to frighten enemies. Hooded seals are solitary except when breeding. Family: *Phocidae.*

Hooft, Pieter Corneliszoon (1581–1647) Dutch poet and historian, who traveled in France and Italy, where he was influenced by Renaissance art and literature. He gathered a circle of writers, artists, and musicians at the castle at Muiden, of which he was made steward in 1609. Hooft expressed his humanistic and pacifist philosophy in the pastoral play *Granida* (1605), while his love poetry echoed that of Petrarch. His history of the Dutch revolt against Spain, *Nederlandsche Historien* (1628–47), remained a model of Dutch prose for over 200 years.

Hooghly River (Hoogli R *or* Hugli R) A river in India, rising in West Bengal. The W stream of the Ganges delta, it flows S through Calcutta to the Bay of Bengal. Length: 145 mi (233 km).

Hooke, Robert (1635–1703) British physicist and instrument maker. In 1660 he discovered *Hooke's law. His work on springs led him into horology and he claimed to have invented the hair spring (also claimed by *Huygens). He was one of the first scientists to examine vegetable matter with a microscope, in 1667 discovering the existence of cells in cork. Many of his microscope studies were published in *Micrographia* (1665).

Hooker, Joseph (1814–79) US Union general. A West Point graduate who had been out of active service since 1853, he joined the Union Army (1861), was made a general, and fought in the major battles of the *Peninsular Campaign. Chosen to lead the Army of the Potomac in 1863, he suffered a crushing defeat at Chancellorsville and was relieved of his command.

Hooker, Thomas (1586–1647) US colonist and minister; born in England. As a Puritan he had gone to Holland in 1630 to escape religious persecution and then emigrated to Massachusetts (1633). Dissatisfied with conditions in Cambridge, the site of his first pastorate, he brought his Congregationalist followers to Connecticut where he was instrumental in the founding of Hartford (1636). He helped to draft the Fundamental Orders of Connecticut (1639) and to found the New England Confederation (1643).

Hooke's law For an elastic body, the *stress is directly proportional to the *strain. For example, if a heavy mass is hung from a wire, the fractional extension is directly proportional to the mass. The law applies only up to the elastic limit (*see* elasticity). Named for its discoverer Sir Robert *Hooke, who stated it in the form *ut tensio, sic vis.*

Hook of Holland (Dutch name: Hoek van Holland) 51 59 N 4 07E A port in the SW Netherlands, in South Holland province at the North Sea end of the Nieuwe Waterweg (New Waterway). A ferry service operates from here to Harwich, England.

hookworm A parasitic *nematode worm inhabiting the intestine of animals and man. About 0.4 in (1 cm) long, hookworms attach themselves to the gut lining and feed by sucking blood and body fluids. The two main species infecting man are *Necator americanus,* of the southern US and Africa, and the Eurasian *Ancylostoma duodenale.* Both cause lowered resistance to disease, anemia, and malnutrition. The larvae enter the body through the skin, usually the feet, and migrate to the intestine. Infection can be prevented by wearing shoes and improving sanitation.

hoopoe A bird, *Upupa epops,* of S Eurasia and Africa; 11 in (28 cm) long, it has a pink-brown plumage with black and white barred wings, a long tail, and a long black-tipped crest. It feeds on insects and larvae with its long downcurved bill. It is the only member of its family (*Upupidae*). Order: *Coraciformes* (hornbills, kingfishers, etc.).

Hoover, Herbert Clark (1874–1964) US statesman; 31st president of the United States (1929–33). Beginning his career as an international mining engineer, Hoover was appointed chairman of American relief committees in Great Britain and Belgium and US Food Administrator after *World War I. He later served as secretary of commerce in the administrations of Presidents Warren *Harding and Calvin *Coolidge. As the nominee of the *Republican party, Hoover was elected president in 1928. Soon after taking office, he faced a severe economic crisis with the collapse of the US stock market and the beginning of the *Depression. As a fiscal conservative, however, Hoover was unwilling to initiate massive federal programs to restore the economy and he came under increasing criticism. Defeated for reelection in 1932 by Franklin *Roosevelt, Hoover later headed the Commissions on Organization of the Executive Branch of the Federal Government (known as the Hoover Commissions, 1947–49, 1953–55). His three-volume autobiography, *Memoirs,* was published in 1952.

Hoover, J(ohn) Edgar (1895–1972) US lawyer, director of the Federal Bureau of Investigation (FBI) from 1924 to 1972. He fought the gangsters of the 1930s with his reformed FBI and established the first fingerprint file and crime-detection laboratory. In his later years he was criticized for the power that he had amassed and for his autocratic methods.

hop A perennial climbing herb, *Humulus lupus.* Native to Eurasia, where it grows to a length of 10–20 ft (3–6 m) in hedges and thickets, it is widely cultivated for its pale yellow-green female flowers ("cones"), which are used in brewing to flavor beer. The male flowers are smaller. The young shoots have been eaten as a vegetable. Family: *Cannabiaceae.*

Hope, Anthony (Sir Anthony Hope Hawkins; 1863–1933) British novelist. He gave up careers in law and politics after the immediate popular success of

The Prisoner of Zenda (1894), a tale of adventure set in the imaginary country of Ruritania. He wrote many other successful romances of this kind.

HERBERT HOOVER *President (1929–33) whose adminis-tration was criticized for its handling of the effects of the Depression, leading to his election defeat in 1932.*

Hope, Bob (Leslie Townes Hope; 1903–   ) US comedian, born in Britain. He starred in a number of popular movies during the 1940s, including *Road to Zanzibar* (1941) and other "Road" movies with Bing *Crosby and Dorothy Lamour. He gave many performances for US troops in World War II, Korea, and Vietnam, as well as in peacetime. He has starred in radio, television, and vaude-ville in addition to film.

Hopeh. *See* Hebei.

hop-hornbeam A tree of the N temperate genus *Ostrya* (7 species). Related to hornbeams, they have hard wood, furrowed bark, flowers in catkins, and conelike fruits resembling those of the hop. The European hop-hornbeam (*O. carpinifolia*) may grow to a height of over 65 ft (20 m). Family: *Corylaceae*. *See also* ironwood.

HOP *Ripe female flowers ("cones"), which have a bitter flavor and are dried in an oast house before being added to the wort during beer making.*

Hopi North American Indians of NE Arizona whose language belongs to the Uto-Aztecan family (*see* Aztec-Tanoan languages). They live in stone and adobe houses forming small towns built on rocky plateaus (mesas). They are peaceful cultivators and sheep farmers, much given to religious practice and ceremony. There are about 6000 now living but they are rapidly losing their traditional culture. *See also* Pueblo Indians.

Hopkins, Sir Frederick Gowland (1861–1947) British biochemist, who discovered that certain substances—now known as *vitamins—are essential in the diet in trace amounts. He also showed that some amino acids (called essential amino acids) cannot be manufactured by certain animals. He shared a Nobel Prize (1929) with Christian *Eijkman and served as president of the Royal Society (1930–35).

Hopkins, Gerard Manley (1844–89) British poet. He was converted to Roman Catholicism in 1866 and ordained as a Jesuit priest in 1877. In verse of daring originality he rejected conventional meters in favor of a flexible "sprung rhythm." "The Wreck of the Deutschland" and "The Windhover" are among his best-known poems, which were published posthumously in 1918 and were highly influential on poets writing in the 1920s and 1930s.

Hopkins, Harry (Lloyd) (1890–1946) US government administrator. His longstanding interest in social welfare projects culminated in his administration of *New Deal relief programs during the Depression. As aide to President Roosevelt during World War II he negotiated with Churchill and Stalin and headed the US lend-lease program (*see* Lend Lease Act).

Hopper, Edward (1882–1967) US artist. Although initially an illustrator, he studied (1901–06) under Robert Henri and was greatly influenced by the *Ashcan School of painting. His urban scenes are starkly realistic and geometrically exact, depicting loneliness and anonymity. His works include *Model Reading* (1925), *Early Sunday Morning* (1930), *Room in Brooklyn* (1932), *Nighthawks* (1942), *Sunlight in a Cafeteria* (1958), and *Second-Story Sunlight* (1960).

Horace (Quintus Horatius Flaccus; 65–8 BC) Roman poet. He was the son of a freed slave. Although he was reduced to poverty after fighting for Brutus in the Civil War, he became a leading poet under the emperor Augustus and acquired a farm near Rome, celebrated in his poetry. His *Odes* and his more informal *Satires* and verse *Epistles* vividly portray contemporary Roman society and express his own humane and tolerant personality.

Horae Greek goddesses of the seasons. They were originally three in number, the daughters of Zeus and Themis, and associated with the concepts of order, justice, and peace. They later became the four seasons, daughters of Helios and Selene (the sun and moon).

Horatii and Curiatii In Roman legend, two sets of three brothers who fought on opposing sides in the war between Rome and Alba in the reign of Tullus Hostilius, legendary king of Rome. The single survivor, Horatius, killed his grief-stricken sister on finding she had been engaged to one of the Curiatii, but was acquitted after appealing to the people of Rome.

horehound (*or* hoarhound) Either of two Eurasian perennial herbs growing in dry waste places and waysides. White horehound (*Marrubium vulgare*) reaches a height of 10 ft (3 m) and has whorls of white flowers while black horehound (*Balleta nigra*) has whorls of purple flowers and a disagreeable odor. Both have been used medicinally. Family: *Labiatae.*

hormone A substance that is secreted into the blood in small quantities to cause a response in a specific target organ or tissue of the body. Hormones are produced and secreted by *endocrine glands and by specialized nerve cells (*see* neurohormone) under the control of the nervous system or in response to changes in the chemical composition of the blood. Hormones regulate short-term physiological processes, such as digestion, and long-term changes, such as those associated with growth and reproduction; they also help to maintain a constant internal environment in the body (*see* homeostasis). The first demonstration of hormone activity was made in 1905, by *Bayliss and Starling, working with the digestive hormone secretin. The following are some of the more important hormones now known in man: *ACTH, *gonadotrophin, *growth hormone, and *prolactin (secreted by the pituitary); *corticosteroids, *aldosterone, and *adrenaline (from the adrenal glands); *androgens and *estrogens (from the sex glands); thyroid hormone (from the *thyroid gland); *insulin and *glucagon (from the pancreas). Chemically, most hormones are proteins or steroids. The study of hormones—and the diseases caused by their under- or over-production—is called endocrinology. Substances that regulate plant growth, e.g. *auxins, *gibberellins, and *kinins, are sometimes known as plant hormones.

Horn, Filips van Montmorency, Graaf van (*or* Hoorne; ?1524–68) Flemish statesman and admiral, who played a leading part in the resistance to Philip II's religious and domestic policies in the Netherlands. He served his Spanish rulers in military, naval, and administrative capacities, becoming stadtholder (chief magistrate) of Gelder and Zutphen in 1555. However, he joined *Egmont and William the Silent in resigning from the state council (1565) and demanding the abolition of the Inquisition. He was executed for treason and heresy by the Duke of *Alba. *See also* Revolt of the Netherlands.

hornbeam A tree of the genus *Carpinus* (26 species), of N temperate regions. The common Eurasian hornbeam (*C. betulus*) grows to a height of 100 ft (30 m) in the wild (cultivated trees are up to 60 ft [19 m] tall); it has smooth gray bark, oval pointed leaves with prominent veins, and small nuts with conspicuous winged bracts. It is planted for ornament and for its hard fine-grained timber. Family: *Corylaceae.*

hornbill A bird belonging to a family (*Bucerotidae;* 45 species) occurring in Old World tropical regions; 15–59 in (38–150 cm) long, hornbills are characterized by a huge bill, often bearing a large bony "helmet," and feed on fruit and berries. Most hornbills nest in treeholes in which the female imprisons herself by plastering the entrance with mud, leaving only a small hole through which the male feeds her, until the young hatch. Order: *Coraciiformes* (kingfishers, etc.).

hornblende A mineral of the *amphibole group, which occurs widely in igneous and metamorphic rocks. It consists mainly of silicates of sodium, calcium, magnesium, and iron. It is black or greenish black and occurs in crystalline or massive form. Hornblende schist is a rock consisting mainly of orientated hornblende crystals.

horned lizard. *See* horned toad.

horned poppy One of two herbs belonging to the *poppy family and having slender hornlike seed pods. The perennial or biennial yellow horned poppy (*Glaucium flavum*) of Eurasia grows to a height of 35 in (90 cm) and is found mainly on seashores. The red horned poppy (*G. corniculatus*) is an annual of the Mediterranean region.

horned toad A desert-dwelling lizard, also called horned lizard, belonging to the genus *Phrynosoma,* occurring in North and Central America and characterized by hornlike spines on its head; 3–5 in (8–13 cm) long, they have a flattened oval body with a fringe of scales along the sides and hide by wriggling sideways until buried in sand. In defense, they may squirt blood from their eyes. Family: *Iguanidae.*

horned viper A mildly venomous desert *viper, *Cerastes cornutus,* that occurs in Africa and the Middle East and has a hornlike scale over each eye. Up to 24 in (60 cm) long, it has a broad head and is pale with dark spots and bars.

hornet A social *wasp, *Vespa crabro,* that is common throughout Europe and has spread to North America and elsewhere; 1 in (35 mm) long, it is tawny-yellow with brown markings and nests in hollow trees. It feeds chiefly on insects, nectar, and fruit juices and its painful sting can be dangerous to man.

Members of the genera *Dolichorespula, Paravespula,* and *Vespula* may also be known as hornets.

hornpipe A traditional British dance, originally accompanied by a wooden pipe. It retains its popularity with sailors as it requires no partners and little space. Like the jigs and reels to which it is related, it was often danced in clogs. Handel composed a hornpipe for his *Water Music.*

horntail A *wasp, also called wood wasp, belonging to the family *Siricidae* (about 60 species), having a hornlike projection on its abdomen. Horntails are usually brown, blue, or black with yellow bands and can be up to 1.4 in (37.5 mm) long. The females have strong ovipositors to insert their eggs into hardwood trees, particularly elm, beech, and maple, in which the larvae develop.

hornwort 1. A plant of the widely distributed genus *Cetarophyllum* (3 species), which grows submerged in ponds and streams. *C. demersum* is rootless, with a stem 8–40 in (20–100 cm) long and simple forked leaves, 0.4–8 in (1–2 cm) long. The small flowers produce a three-spined nutlike fruit. Family: *Ceratophyllaceae.* **2.** A thallose *liverwort of the order *Anthocerotales,* also called horned liverwort and often classified as a separate class of bryophytes—the *Anthocerotae.* Distributed worldwide, they consist of a flat leaflike gamete-producing plant from which arises a long-lived spikelike spore-producing structure, 0.8–2 in (2–5 cm) long.

horoscope. *See* astrology.

Horowitz, Vladimir (1904–89) US pianist, born in Russia. He settled in the US in 1940. Horowitz excelled in the music of Chopin, Schumann, and Liszt and in his own transcriptions. He twice made a triumphant return to the concert platform after periods of illness during 1936–39 and 1953–65 and in 1986 returned to Moscow to perform.

horse A hoofed mammal, *Equus caballus,* domesticated worldwide for pack and draft work, riding, and sport (*see* equestrianism). The earliest horse is believed to have been *eohippus, which is thought to have originated in North America and spread to Asia. Successive larger forms evolved, in which the central toe became enlarged as the hoof and the remaining toes became smaller and fewer (*see* Hipparion). These horses developed from forest browers to become grazing animals of the plains with well-developed senses to detect predators.

The many breeds of modern horse—thought to have evolved from several different Asian and European forms, including *Przewalski's horse and the *tarpan—are commonly grouped into ponies, light horses, and draft horses. They range in size from the tiny *Falabella to the massive *Shire horse and are measured in hands (1 hand = 4 in = 10.16 cm) to the top of the shoulders (withers). According to breed, horses mature at 3.5–5 years of age and the lifespan is usually 20–35 years. Mares have a gestation period of 11 months, producing usually a single foal. Except for breeding stallions, males are usually castrated, being called geldings. Horses belong to the family *Equidae,* which also includes *asses and *zebras.

horse chestnut A broad spreading □tree, *Aesculus hippocastanum,* native to SE Europe and widely planted as an ornamental. It grows to a height of 80 ft (25 m), producing large compound leaves and erect clusters of white flowers; the green spiny fruits ripen to release large brown shiny seeds (conkers). The red horse chestnut (*A.* × *catnea*) is similar but has red flowers. It is a hybrid between the horse chestnut and *A. pavia.* Family: *Hippocastanaceae.*

horsefly A stout-bodied fly of the genus *Tabanus* (the term is also used loosely for the other genera—*Chrysops* [deerflies] and *Haematopota* [cleg flies]—of the family *Tabanidae*; 2500 species). Male horseflies feed on nectar but the females are bloodsuckers and inflict painful bites on man, horses, cattle, etc. A few species may also transmit diseases, such as tularemia and anthrax. The carnivorous larvae live mainly in damp soil and mud.

horsehair worm A long thin hairlike aquatic invertebrate of the phylum *Nematomorpha* (about 80 species), found mostly in fresh water. They range in length from 0.4–40 in (1–100 cm), with a diameter of only 0.01–0.08 in (0.3–2 mm) Their larvae are parasitic in beetles, crickets, and grasshoppers.

horsepower (hp) A unit of power equal to 550 foot-pounds per second. It was devised by James *Watt, who found that a strong horse could raise a weight of 150 pounds 4 feet in 1 second. *See also* watt.

1226

HORSE

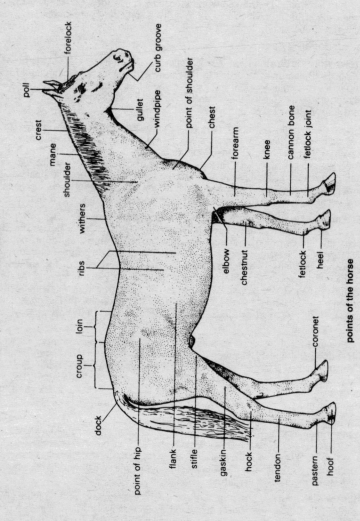

points of the horse

Thoroughbred

Tennessee Walking Horse

Arab Horse

Lipizzaner

Parcheron

Exmoor
Pony

horse racing A form of contest in which horses are ridden or driven. Its three main forms are *flat racing, *steeplechase and hurdling, and *harness racing.

horseradish A perennial herb, *Amoracia rusticana,* probably native to SE Europe and W Asia and widely cultivated. Growing to a height of 50 in (125 cm), it has thick fleshy pungent roots from which horseradish sauce is made and it bears small white flowers. Family: *Cruciferae.*

horseshoe bat An insect-eating *bat belonging to the genus *Rhinolophus* (74 species), found in temperate and tropical regions of the Old World. Horseshoe bats are named for the fleshy structure surrounding the nostrils, which focuses the ultrasonic signals that the bat emits when navigating. They also have large ears for receiving the echoes. Family: *Rhinolophidae.*

horseshoe crab A large nocturnal marine *arthropod (up to 20 in [50 cm] long), also called king crab, belonging to the subclass *Xiphosura,* most members of which are now extinct. The two living genera, *Limulus* and *Tachypleus,* are found in shallow waters on the E coasts of North America and Asia respectively. They have a hinged body covered by a brown horseshoe-shaped carapace and a long tail spine. They can swim but usually borrow in sand, feeding on worms and thin-shelled mollusks. Class: *Meristomata.*

horsetail A rushlike perennial *pteridophyte plant, also called scouring rush, belonging to the only living genus (*Equisetum;* about 30 species) of the class *Sphenopsida* (which includes many giant extinct forms, such as *Calamites). Horsetails grow in moist rich soils everywhere except Australasia. Their creeping rhizomes give rise to aerial jointed stems of two kinds—green sterile stems, often branched in whorls, and pale fertile stems, bearing cone-shaped clusters of spore capsules. The leaves are reduced to sheaths encircling each stem joint. Tropical horsetails may grow to a height of 20 ft (6 m), but temperate species are much smaller. They are used as abrasives and in folk medicine.

horse trials Contests to test a horse's abilities and the rider's skill in horsemanship. The three-day event is an Olympic sport involving, on successive days: *dressage; speed, endurance, and jumping tests on *steeplechase and cross-country courses; and *showjumping. The one-day event is a reduced version.

horst. *See* fault.

Horta, Victor (1861–1947) Belgian architect, a proponent of *Art Nouveau. His early work, particularly the Hôtel Tassel (1892) and the Maison du Peuple (1896) in Brussels, are fine examples of this style. He later abandoned Art Nouveau for classicism.

Horthy de Nagybánya, Miklós (1868–1957) Hungarian admiral and statesman. After the collapse of *Austria-Hungary (1919), he organized an army against Béla *Kun's communist government. Elected regent of Hungary in 1920, he preserved an independent constitutional system, despite alliance with Nazi Germany. When he attempted to negotiate a surrender to Russia (1944) the Germans deposed him.

horticulture The cultivation of vegetables (also known as market gardening) and fruit for food and of trees, shrubs, and other plants for ornament. Traditionally practiced in small gardens and orchards, horticulture is now both a popular domestic pastime and an important commercial activity using large field and greenhouse acreages. The introduction of new higher-yielding and more disease-resistant plant varieties, increased mechanization of planting and harvesting, the use of new cultivation techniques, such as *hydroponics, and the application of fertilizers and pesticides have all contributed to improved productivity and quality. Also, modern refrigeration, storage, and transport mean that many crops are now available throughout the year.

Horus The Egyptian sun-god, usually portrayed as a falcon or with a falcon's head. He was the son of *Osiris and *Isis and avenged his father's death by killing *Set. The pharaohs were conceived as the incarnations of Horus as earthly ruler and added the god's name to their titles.

Hosea (8th century BC) An Old Testament prophet of Israel. In the **Book of Hosea** the unfaithfulness of Israel to God is presented in terms of a spiritual adultery, comparable to the infidelity that the author has experienced in his own life. This familial analogy was later developed in the Christian concepts of the Fatherhood of God and of the Church as the bride of Christ.

Hosokawa, Morihiro (1938–) Japanese political leader and prime minister (1993–). From a distinguished noble family whose members included a former prime minister, he worked as a journalist before entering the Diet, Japan's legislature, in 1971 as a representative of the ruling Liberal Democratic party (LDP). He left the Diet in 1983 to become governor of his home region of Kumamoto and was successful in improving its economy. In 1992, after failing to convince the LDP to adopt reforms, he formed the Japan New party, promising a more liberal and less corrupt approach to politics than the LDP. When the LDP failed to hold its majority in the 1993 elections, Hosokawa was selected as prime minister by a multiparty coalition.

hospital An institution providing diagnostic and therapeutic services for the sick on a residential (in-patient) or nonresidential (out-patient) basis. In the ancient world such medical services as existed were provided by religious organizations (e.g. the Temple of Aesculapius at Epidauros in Greece). In Europe in the Middle Ages many institutions for the care of the sick were founded by monastic orders and later, during the Crusades, by orders of knighthood. St Bartholomew's (1123) and St Thomas's (1207) in London date back to this period. During the 18th and 19th centuries, new voluntary hospitals were founded by philanthropists and staffed by doctors who gave their services free. Municipal hospitals arose alongside the voluntary hospitals; they had paid medical staff. Modern hospitals have a variety of administrative structures and have become increasingly specialized, often concentrating on the treatment of particular diseases (e.g. cancer).

Hospitallers (Order of the Hospital of St John of Jerusalem) A religious order of knighthood that began as a hospital for pilgrims to Jerusalem (c. 1070) and during the *Crusades took on a military function. Immensely wealthy, the Hospitallers were the great rivals of the *Templars. After the fall of Acre (1291) they established themselves in Cyprus, Rhodes, and finally Malta.

Hosta A genus of perennial herbaceous plants (10 species), native to China and Japan and widely planted in gardens. They are grown chiefly for their foliage—the leaves are large (5–10 in [12–25 cm] long), oval, and pointed and come in a variety of colors, often variegated—but they also produce attractive spikes of purplish or white funnel-shaped flowers. Family: *Liliaceae*.

hot spring A spring from which hot water flows continuously from deep within the earth's crusts. Like *geysers, hot springs normally occur in areas that are (or have recently been) volcanically active. A distinction is sometimes made between hot springs (at a temperature above that of the human body) and *thermal springs* (above the mean annual temperature of the place where they emerge). The water is charged with minerals, and deposits of travertine or sinter usually build up.

Hot Springs 34 30N 93 03W A health resort city in W central Arkansas, in the Ouachita Mountains. It surrounds Hot Springs National Park, and its economy derives from the therapeutic benefits of the park's hot spring water, which is piped to bathhouses in the city and bottled for national distribution. Several medical facilities are housed here. Population (1990): 32,462.

Hot Springs National Park A national park in W central Arkansas, in the Ouachita Mountains. Forty-seven hot springs (143°F; 62°C) are here, as well as mountains for hiking and lakes for swimming. A government-designated health resort since 1832, it was established as a national park in 1921. Area: 5.5 sq mi (15 sq km).

Hotspur. *See* Percy, Sir Henry.

Hottentot fig A perennial herb, *Carpobrotus edulis,* native to South Africa but naturalized in many warm temperate regions. It has creeping woody stems, fleshy leaves, showy magenta or yellow flowers, and edible fruits. Family: *Aizoaceae.*

HARRY HOUDINI *Posing with a submersible canister from which he would escape under water.*

Houdini, Harry (Erich Weiss; 1874–1926) US magician. Becoming a professional magician in 1897, he was able to escape from handcuffs, straitjackets, and locked containers, even when under water, which gained him an international reputation. He wrote articles and books on magic and was deeply interested in spiritualism and frequently exposed fraud. His books include *The Unmasking of Robert Houdin* (1908) and *A Magician Among the Spirits* (1924).

Houdon, Jean Antoine (1741–1828) French sculptor. Houdon's highly successful career began in Rome (1764–68) with his *St Bruno* (1767; Sta Maria degli Angeli, Rome). Although he made many religious and mythological sculptures, he was most popular as a portrait sculptor; famous sitters included Voltaire, Benjamin Franklin, Catherine the Great, and Napoleon. He visited the US (1785) to make a statue of George Washington.

Houphouët-Boigny, Félix (1905–93) Ivory Coast statesman; president (1960–93). In 1946 he founded the Ivory Coast branch of the Rassemblement démocratique africain and was a member of the French Constituent Assembly (1945–46) and National Assembly (1946–59). In 1959 he became prime minister and, on independence in 1960, president. In 1990, he was reelected to his seventh term as president.

housecarl A member of the household bodyguard of the Danish kings of England (1016–51). Originally warriors from the Scandinavian army, the housecarls performed strictly organized military and administrative services for which they were rewarded with gifts of money and land.

House, Edward M(andell) (1858–1938) US diplomat and presidential adviser. Nicknamed Colonel House in his native Texas, he actively campaigned for US Pres. Woodrow Wilson in 1912 and became his confidential adviser. He served on many World War I commissions and represented Wilson at the preliminary peace meetings and at Versailles where he helped to frame Wilson's Fourteen Points (1918) and the Treaty of Versailles (1919).

housefly A dull-gray fly, *Musca domestica,* that is a worldwide household pest. The adult is 0.20–0.28 in (5–7 mm) long, with mouthparts used for sucking up organic liquids of all kinds. Through the contamination of food it spreads many serious diseases, such as typhoid, tuberculosis, and dysentery. The scavenging larvae grow quickly on practically any decaying organic matter, especially dung. Family: *Muscidae.*

houseleek A European perennial herb, *Sempervivum tectorum*, that has a basal rosette of fleshy leaves and bears heads of dull-red flowers on stems up to 24 in (60 cm) long. Growing on walls and roofs, it was formerly believed to guard against fire, sorcery, and death and had many medicinal uses. Family: *Crassulaceae.*

House of Representatives The larger chamber of the US Congress, composed of representatives from each state. The number of representatives (or congressmen) from each state is determined by state population; regardless of population each state is entitled to at least one representative. Each representative represents a congressional district within the state and is elected by those people within the district. Membership is limited to 435, with additional, but nonvoting, members from Puerto Rico, the District of Columbia, the Virgin Islands, and Guam. Each representative serves a 2-year term, must be at least 25 years old, and must be a resident of the state and a US citizen for at least 7 years. Constitutionally delegated powers of the House are origination of revenue bills, initiation of impeachment proceedings, and authorization to elect the president when a tie or lack of majority exists in the electoral college. The House first met in 1789 with 59 members.

house sparrow A Eurasian *sparrow, *Passer domesticus,* that originated in Africa and spread north with Neolithic man: it is now also found in the New World. The male has a black-streaked brown plumage with gray underparts and a black bib and eye stripe; the female has a paler drabber plumage.

Housing and Urban Development, Department of (HUD) US cabinet-level executive branch department. It is concerned with housing needs, fair housing opportunities, and improving and developing communities. It administers mortgage insurance and rental subsidy programs, antidiscrimination in housing activities, neighborhood rehabilitation, and urban preservation. Directed by the secretary of Housing and Urban Development, it was established in 1965.

Housman, A(lfred) E(dward) (1859–1936) British poet and scholar. Although he failed to earn his degree at Oxford, he continued his classical studies. He was eventually rewarded with professorships. His volumes of lyrics, *A Shropshire Lad* (1896), *Last Poems* (1922), and *More Poems* (1936) are concerned with themes of human vanity and transience and are imbued with an atmosphere of romantic pessimism. He also published editions of the Roman poets Juvenal and Manilius.

Houston, Sam(uel) (1793–1863) US soldier, frontier leader, and statesman. He served in the War of 1812 and then as an Indian agent in Tennessee and Arkansas. From 1819 he had a law practice in Nashville and was elected to Congress (1823–27) and then as governor of Tennessee (1827–29). Following marital problems he resigned the governorship and lived with the Cherokee Indians in Oklahoma. In 1832 he was sent to Texas to negotiate Indian treaties. During the Mexico-Texas border disputes in 1835 the Texas settlers were led into battle by Sam Houston. After he and his troops defeated Gen. *Santa Anna at San Jacinto, Texas became independent and Houston its first president (1836–38; 1841–44). After Texas became a state (1845), he was a US senator (1846–59) and governor (1859–61).

Houston 29 45N 95 25W A city, the main port in Texas. Founded in 1836, it is named for the Texan leader Sam *Houston (1793–1863). It expanded rapidly following the building of a canal (1912–14), linking it to the Gulf of Mexico, and the development of coastal oil fields. Today it is one of the world's major oil and petrochemical centers; other industries include shipbuilding and the manufacture of steel. Among its many educational institutions is the Texas medical center, and the Lyndon B. Johnson Space Center is nearby. Population (1990): 1,630,553.

Hovercraft (*or* air-cushion vehicle) A shiplike vehicle equipped with powerful horizontal blowers capable of lifting it off a surface so that it rides on a cushion of air, which is contained within a rubber skirt. It can navigate on almost any kind of surface (water, swamp, or land) and is moved forward at high speed by vertical propellers. Hovercraft are used as ferries between England and France, Hong Kong and Macao, between ports in Scandinavia, and elsewhere.

hoverfly A fly, also called a flowerfly or syrphid fly, belonging to the family *Syrphidae* (about 4000 species). Many species are black and yellow, resembling bees and wasps, but they do not sting. The larvae of many hoverflies are scavengers in decaying organic matter or in the nests of ants, termites, or bees. Others are predators of aphids and plant lice, while a few are plant pests. *See also* maggot. □insect.

Howard, Catherine (c. 1520–42) The fifth wife (1540–42) of Henry VIII of England. She was beheaded for treason when Henry learned of her premarital love affairs.

Howard, Leslie (Leslie Howard Stainer; 1890–1943) British actor of Hungarian descent. He became famous for his performances as the romantic leading man in both British and US films, including *The Scarlet Pimpernel* (1935), *Pygmalion* (1938), and *Gone with the Wind* (1939).

Howard, Oliver Otis (1830–1909) US Union general. In 1861 he took command of a brigade from Maine in the Civil War, and saw extensive action, losing his right arm at Fair Oaks. In 1864 he was appointed commander of the Army of the Tennessee. After the war he headed the Freedman's Bureau, was a cofounder

(1867) and president (1869–73) of Howard University, named for him. Returning to the military in 1874, he fought in various Indian campaigns.

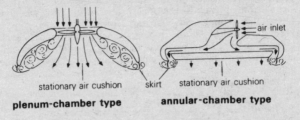

plenum-chamber type   **annular-chamber type**

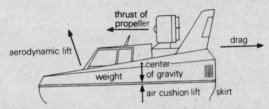

HOVERCRAFT *In the plenum chamber the air cushion is produced by a horizontal fan; the cushion in the center is almost at rest and is surrounded by a fast-moving ring of turbulent air. In the annular chamber the cushion is formed within an annular ring of jets, the nozzles of which are sloped inwards. The lower figures shows the forces acting on a Hovercraft.*

Howard, Trevor (1916–88) British actor. After working in the theater in the 1930s he concentrated on films from the 1940s, often appearing in leading romantic roles. His films include *Brief Encounter* (1946), *The Third Man* (1949), *Mutiny on the Bounty* (1962), *Ryan's Daughter* (1970), and *Conduct Unbecoming* (1975).

Howard of Effingham, Charles, 2nd Baron (1536–1624) English lord high admiral (1585–1618), who commanded the English victory against the Spanish *Armada (1588). He was a commander of the expedition that sacked Cádiz (1596), for which he was created 1st earl of Nottingham.

Howe, Elias (1819–67) US inventor, who invented a lockstitch sewing machine, patented in 1846. It was not at first well received but by the 1850s large numbers were being manufactured in infringement of Howe's patent rights. Successful in a series of legal suits, he subsequently earned a fortune from royalties.

Howe, Gordie (1928–   ) Canadian ice hockey player. He played for the National Hockey League's (NHL) Detroit Red Wings (1946–71) and scored 1850 career points. He came out of retirement to play for the World Hockey League's Houston Aeros and New England Whalers (1973–77) and the NHL's Hartford Whalers (1977–79).

Howe, Julia Ward (1819–1910) US reformer and writer. She and her husband, Samuel Gridley Howe, were active in the abolition movement. She wrote "The Battle Hymn of the Republic" (1862), a poem that, set to music, became associated with the Union cause during the Civil War. Always concerned with women's rights, she was active in many women's suffrage groups.

Howe, Richard, Earl (1726–99) British admiral. In the Seven Years' War (1756–63) he fought with distinction off the N French coast. In 1776 he became commander of the British fleet in the American Revolution. He is best known for the victory in the French Revolutionary Wars of the Glorious First of June (1793). His brother **William, 5th Viscount Howe** (1729–1814) gained fame in the army. He fought under *Wolfe in North America during the French and Indian War and in the American Revolution commanded at *Bunker Hill (1775), after which he became commander in chief in America. Although he scored successes, notably at *Brandywine (1777), his career ended in anticlimax after the failure at *Valley Forge (1778).

Howells, William Dean (1837–1920) US editor, critic, and author. He worked for the *Atlantic Monthly* from 1866 and was its editor (1871–81), during which time he was instrumental in publishing Mark *Twain, Bret *Harte, and Henry *James. After 1882 he devoted his time to his own works. His nonfiction criticized the *Haymarket Massacre trial, took issue with various wars, and promoted the cause of African Americans. His realistic novels include *Their Wedding Journey* (1872), *The Lady of the Aroostook* (1879), *The Rise of Silas Lapham* (1885), *A Traveler from Altruria* (1894), and *Through the Eye of the Needle* (1907). He also wrote for the "Editor's Study" (1886–92) and "Easy Chair" (1900–20), columns of *Harper's Magazine*.

howitzer A low-velocity *artillery firearm with a shorter barrel and a larger bore than a *gun but a smaller bore and longer barrel than a *mortar. They are often mounted on carriages that enable them to fire either flat gun-type trajectories or arched mortar-type trajectories. They were widely used in World War I but the distinction between a gun and a howitzer in modern practice is now much reduced. The word comes from the Dutch *houwitzer,* catapult.

howler monkey A large monkey belonging to the genus *Alouatta* (6 species), of Central and South American forests. Howlers are 45–71 in (115–180 cm) long including the tail (24–36 in; 58–91 cm) and are named for their loud voices. They have beards over their enlarged throats, prehensile tails, and live in groups of up to 40 individuals. Family: *Cebidae.*

Howrah 22 35N 88 20E A city and port in India, in West Bengal situated on the Hooghly River opposite Calcutta. The focal point of rail and road routes, its industries include ship building, jute milling, engineering, and chemicals. Population (1991): 946,732.

Hoxha, Enver (1908–85) Albanian leader (1946–85). In World War II Hoxha led Albania's struggle against Italy and founded the country's Communist party (1941), becoming (1943) its general secretary. He was prime minister (1946–54) and then first secretary (1954–85) of the newly named Party of Labor. After the Sino-Soviet disagreement in 1961, Hoxha supported China until 1978.

Hoyle, Edmond (1672–1769) British authority on card games. His book *A Short Treatise on the Game of Whist* (1742) was highly successful and his revised rules of 1760 governed whist until 1864. The idiom "according to Hoyle" (meaning according to the rules) is an allusion to this book.

Hoyle, Sir Fred (1915–) British astronomer, who with H. *Bondi and T. *Gold proposed the *steady-state theory of the universe. His other theoretical studies have mainly been concerned with stellar evolution. He is also one of the foremost of today's science writers, his *Galaxies, Nuclei and Quasars* (1965) being a standard work, and a notable science-fiction writer.

Hsia Kuei. *See* Xia Gui.

Hsiang-t'an. *See* Xiangtan.

Hsi Chiang. *See* Xi Jiang.

Hsin dynasty. *See* Wang Mang.

Hsi-ning. *See* Xining.

Hsiung-nu. *See* Xiong Nu.

Hsuan-tsang. *See* Xuan Cang.

Hua Guo Feng (*or* Hua Kuo-feng; 1921–   ) Chinese communist statesman; chairman of the Chinese Community party (1976–81). A communist from boyhood, he became party secretary in Hunan, which he made one of the most efficiently run provinces in China. He survived a *Red Guard attack during the Cultural Revolution to succeed Chou En-lai as prime minister and then Mao Tse-tung as chairman, the victor of a power struggle with the radicals led by Mao's widow, *Jiang Qing. The pragmatic policies pursued by China under Hau are regarded as being in part the result of the influence of *Deng Xiao Ping.

Huainan 32 41N 117 06E A city in E China, in Anhui province. Situated on a rich coal field, it has been developed during the 20th century. Industries include iron and steel and chemicals. Population (1990): 703,934.

Huambo (name until 1973: Nova Lisboa) 12 47S 15 44E A city in W Angola. It is a commercial center with a trade in agricultural produce and has important railroad industries. Population (1983 est): 203,000.

Huancayo 12 05S 75 12W A city in W Peru, the chief commercial center of the central Andes. It has a cathedral and a university (1962). Population (1972): 126,754.

Huang Hai. *See* Yellow Sea.

Huang Ho. *See* Yellow River.

Huari An ancient city in the central Peruvian Andes that was briefly the center of an empire (c. 600–800 AD). Huari itself remained prosperous until abandoned about 1000 and the influence of its pottery styles prevailed over most of its central Peruvian neighbors until the rise of the *Chimú.

Huascar (c. 1495–1532) Ruler of the Incas, who lost his throne and was murdered after being defeated in civil war by his half-brother *Atahuallpa in 1532. Their conflict helped *Pizarro to conquer the Incas.

Huascarán (*or* Nevado Huascarán) 9 08S 77 36W The highest mountain in Peru, in the Andes. In 1962 an avalanche buried the village of Raurahirca, killing about 3500 people. Height: 22,205 ft (6768 m).

Hubble, Edwin Powell (1889–1953) US astronomer, who used the 100-inch telescope at Mount Wilson Observatory to measure the speed of recession of the galaxies. He discovered that the speed of recession of the galaxies is proportional to their distance from the earth, which led to the evaluation of the *Hubble constant.

Hubble constant (H_o) The rate at which the velocity of expansion of the universe changes with distance. It relates the recessional velocity, V, of a distant galaxy to its distance, D. **Hubble's law**, proposed in 1929 by Edwin *Hubble, states that recessional velocity and distance are directly proportional: $V = H_o D$. A widely accepted value for H_o is 55 km s^{-1} megaparsec^{-1}, although higher values are and have been used.

Hubei (*or* Hupei) A province in E central China. Its fertile E plain has many lakes and rivers, including the Yangtze River. It was devastated during the Taiping Rebellion (1851–64) and the 1911 revolution began there. Products include wheat, rice, cotton, fish, and steel. Area: 72,394 sq mi (187,500 sq km). Population (1990): 53,969,210. Capital: Wuhan.

Hubli 15 20N 75 14E A city in India, in Karnataka. Together with Dharwar, it forms one of the state's most populous areas. Industries include cotton and newspapers. Population (1991): 647,640.

hubris (*or* hybris) The ancient Greek concept of human pride or arrogance that results in the transgression of the natural order and subsequent retribution by the gods. The concept is important in Greek tragedies, the protagonists of which, being talented and powerful, were especially prone to this fault.

Huddersfield 58 39N 1 47W A city in N England, at the confluence of the Rivers Colne and Holme. One of the major wool textile towns of West Yorkshire, Huddersfield produces various fabrics and has important engineering (tractors, textile machinery) and metalworking industries. Population (1981): 148,544.

Hudson, Henry (d. 1611) English navigator. In 1607, in a small ship with 10 sailors, he sailed in search of the *Northeast Passage to China, reaching Spitzbergen. He tried again, unsuccessfully, in 1608. On a third voyage, under the auspices of the Dutch East India Company, he sailed some 150 mi (240 km) down what came to be called the Hudson River, establishing Dutch claims to the area. His fourth voyage (1610–11), in the *Discovery*, took him to what is now Hudson Bay (NE Canada), where his men mutinied and cast him adrift. Nothing more was heard of him.

Hudson Bay A huge shallow oceanic bay in N central Canada, linked to the Atlantic Ocean by Hudson Strait and to the Arctic Ocean by Foxe Channel. Frozen during winter, in summer it carries grain ships from W Canada to Europe.

Hudson River A river in New York, flowing from the Adirondack Mountains to New York Bay, where it forms part of New York Harbor. An important commercial waterway, it is linked by canals with the *Great Lakes and the *St Lawrence Seaway. Length: 306 mi (492 km).

Hudson River School (1825–75) Group of US landscape artists, whose paintings depicted the unspoiled beauty of the Catskill Mountains and Hudson River. Its members, the first school of painting to originate in the US, included such artists as Thomas *Cole, Thomas Doughty (1793–1856), Asher Brown *Durand, Martin Johnson Heade (1819–1904), Frederick Edwin Church (1826–1900), and John Frederick Kensett (1818–72). Cole's four-canvas work, *The Voyage of Life*, Doughty's *In Nature's Wonderland*, Durand's *Summer Woods*, and Kensett's *Lake George* are among the paintings typical of this school.

Hudson's Bay Company A fur-trading company, formed in 1670, that was given settlement and trading rights in Canada; its first governor was Prince *Rupert (*see also* Rupert's Land). The company engaged in bitter rivalry with the *Northwest Company from the 1780s until 1821, when they were united under the name of the Hudson's Bay Company. It maintained a monopoly of the fur trade in Rupert's Land until 1859. In 1870 it sold its territories to Canada but remained a major fur-trading agency with headquarters in London.

Hue 16 28N 107 35E An ancient city in central Vietnam, on the Huong estuary. The University of Hue was established in 1957. A commercial center, Hue has textile, timber, and cement industries. *History*: a Chinese military stronghold from about 200 BC, Hue later fell to Champa and after 1635 was the capital of *Annam and after 1802 of the short-lived Vietnamese empire. It suffered heavily during the Vietnam War, in which it was a part of South Vietnam, and lost many of the historic buildings and treasures of the imperial citadel. Its population was also increased sixfold by refugees. Population (1989): 211,085.

Huelva 37 15N 6 56W A port in SW Spain, in Andalusia on the Odiel estuary. It ships copper from the Ríotinto mines and also iron, manganese, and wine. Population (1991): 141,041.

Huesca 42 08N 0 25W A city in NE Spain, in Aragon. Quintus Sertorius (c. 123–72 BC) founded his school here in 77 BC. It has a cathedral (13th–16th centuries). Population (1982): 41,000.

Huggins, Sir William (1824–1910) British astronomer, who pioneered the application of spectroscopy to astronomy, using the technique to discover that stars consist of the same elements as those found on the earth. He also discovered the *red shift in the lines of a star's spectrum. He was knighted in 1897.

Hugh Capet (c. 940–96 AD) The first *Capetian king of France (987–96). Son of the count of Paris, Hugh seized the throne after the failure of the *Carolingian line.

Hughes, Charles Evans (1862–1948) US lawyer and jurist; US Supreme Court chief justice (1930–41). He began practicing law in New York in 1884 and served on state legislature investigating committees. He was governor of New York (1907–10) before being appointed to the Supreme Court by President *Taft in 1910. Known as a liberal associate justice he served until 1916,when he accepted the Republican presidential nomination; he lost to Woodrow Wilson. Hughes was secretary of state (1921–25) under Presidents Warren Harding and Calvin Coolidge and organized the Washington Armament Conference (1921–22). Appointed US Supreme Court chief justice by Pres. Herbert Hoover in 1930, he was a moderate conversative who presided over a court generally opposed to Pres. Franklin D. Roosevelt's New Deal legislation. When Roosevelt attempted to "pack the court" by increasing the number of justices, Hughes helped to defeat the proposal.

Hughes, Howard (Robard) (1905–76) US aviator, film producer, and entrepreneur. His investments came to include Las Vegas hotels, airlines, and motion picture studios. After founding the Hughes Aircraft Company he broke the air speed record in 1935, reaching a speed of 352 mph (566 km per hr) in a craft of his own design. His films include *Hell's Angels* (1930), *Scarface* (1932), and *The Outlaw* (1944), the last of which he also directed. A billionaire at his death, he left no valid will. From 1950 until his death he lived in seclusion.

Hughes, (James Mercer) Langston (1902–67) US writer and poet; part of the *Harlem Renaissance. His writings portrayed growing up and living as an African American in the US. His works include the poem collections *The Weary Blues* (1926), *Fine Clothes to the Jew* (1927), and *Scottsboro Limited* (1932); stage plays and musicals *Simply Heavenly* (1957), *Tambourines to Glory* (1959), *Black Nativity* (1961), and *The Prodigal Son* (1964); and the short-story collection *The Ways of White Folks* (1934). His newspaper columns introduced his character Jesse B. ("Simple") Semple, who typified the urban African American; the columns were collected in *Simple Speaks His Mind* (1950) and *Simple Stakes a Claim* (1957).

Hughes, Richard (1900–76) British novelist. His best-known novel is *A High Wind in Jamaica* (1929), concerning a family of children captured by pirates. *The Fox in the Attic* (1961) and *The Wooden Shepherdess* (1973) are the first two parts of an unfinished work concerning British and German society during the interwar years.

Hughes, Ted (1930–   ) British poet and poet laureate (1984–   ). His first volume, *The Hawk in the Rain* (1957), contained many poems concerned with the natural world written in a forceful energetic style. The poems in *Crow* (1970) and subsequent volumes, such as *River* (1983), are characterized by increased violence of language and subject matter. He married Sylvia *Plath in 1956.

Hughes, Thomas (1822–96) British writer. *Tom Brown's Schooldays* (1857), his best-known novel, is a celebration of the boarding-school ethos formulated by Thomas *Arnold. He was a Christian Socialist and a Liberal member of Parliament from 1865 to 1874.

Hughes, William M(orris) (1864–1952) Australian statesman, born in London; prime minister (1915–23) as leader of the Labor party (1915–16) and then of the newly founded Nationalist party. An advocate of Australian federation in the 1890s, he was attorney general (1908–09, 1910–13, 1914–21, 1939–41). As prime minister he attended the Paris Peace Conference (1919) after World War I.

Hugh of Saint-Victor (1096–1141) French theologian. He joined the abbey of St Victor in Paris as a canon regular and, under his direction, its school became a major center of learning. His best-known book is *The Sacraments of the Christian Faith.*

Hugo, Victor (Marie) (1802–85) French poet, dramatist, and novelist. After several early novels and volumes of poetry, his leadership of the Romantic movement was confirmed by the success of his drama *Hernani* (1831). During the 1840s he became increasingly involved in politics as a champion of republican ideals and, after the coup d'état by the future Napoleon III in 1851, he went into exile in the Channel Islands until 1870. His later major works included *Les Contemplations* (1856), a volume of poems, and the novel *Les Misérables* (1862). The greatest French poet of the 19th century, during his last years he was honored as a national literary figure. He died in Paris and was buried in the Panthéon.

Huguenots French Protestants. Their name is derived from the Swiss-German *Eidgenoss,* confederate. The Huguenots, chiefly followers of John Calvin, were soon an influential national minority. The rivalry of their leaders, especially the *Condé, with the prominent Roman Catholic *Guise family gave rise to the *Wars of Religion (1562–94). The Edict of Nantes (1598) guaranteed the Huguenots freedom of worship but in Louis XIV's reign they were increasingly persecuted and after the revocation of the Edict (1685) over 250,000 Huguenots emigrated. Persecution continued until the French Revolution.

Huhehot. *See* Hohhot.

Hui Chinese Muslims of NW China, mainly in the provinces of Hebei, Xinjiang, Gansu, and Qinghai. Numbering about 3.5 million, they are descended from Chinese who were converted as a result of contact and intermarriage with *Turkic peoples during the 14th and 15th centuries. They are also known as Dungan (*or* T'ung-kan).

huia An extinct New Zealand songbird, *Heteralocha acutirostris,* 18 in (45 cm) long, that had a glossy black plumage with a white-tipped tail and orange wattles at the base of the bill. The bill of the male was strong and straight; that of the female was long, slender, and curved. Huias were hunted for the feathers by Maoris but their extinction was caused by the destruction of their habitat and excessive collection of specimens as curios by European settlers. Family: *Callaeidae* (wattlebirds).

Huitzilopochtli The Aztec sun- and war-god. He was portrayed as a hummingbird, or with armor of hummingbird feathers, and dead warriors were believed to be reincarnated as this bird. His temple at Tenochtitlan, founded in 1325 in the Valley of Mexico, was the principal Aztec religious structure. He was identified with the sun as a warrior who defeated the night stars, was reborn each day, and depended for nourishment on the blood of human sacrificial victims.

Huizinga, Johan (1872–1945) Dutch historian. Huizinga was professor of history, first at Groningen and then at Leyden University. His best-known book, *The Waning of the Middle Ages* (1919), was a study of life, thought, and art in late medieval France and the Netherlands. He also wrote *Erasmus* (1924), *In the Shadow of Tomorrow* (1935), an analysis of the malaise of contemporary Western society, and *Homo Ludens* (1938).

Hull (official name: Kingston-upon-Hull) 53 45N 0 20W A city and port in NE England, situated on the Humber estuary. An important fishing port, Hull has vast docks and serves as a port for much of the North and Midlands. Its industries include vegetable-oil extraction, sawmills, flour milling, paints, chemicals, and engineering, as well as fish-related industries. Its university was established in 1927. Population (1981): 325,485.

Hull 45 26N 75 45W A city in E Canada, in SW Quebec on the Ottawa River opposite Ottawa. One of North America's main pulp-and-paper and timber centers, it has acquired many federal government offices in recent years. Population (1991): 60,707.

Hull, Cordell (1871–1955) US Democratic politician; secretary of state (1933–44) under Franklin D. Roosevelt. He did much to foster good relations with Latin America (*see* Good Neighbor Policy), attending the important Montevideo Conference in 1933, and supported China against Japanese ambitions in East Asia. He was instrumental in the foundation of the UN, for which he won the Nobel Peace Prize in 1945.

humanism 1. The intellectual movement that formed the inspiration and the basis of Renaissance culture. Humanist scholars based their program upon the rediscovery and study of classical Greek and Roman authors, which had been initiated in Italy by such men as *Petrarch and *Boccaccio. They turned away from the exclusively theological bias of their medieval forerunners and concentrated instead upon human achievements in the arts and sciences. *Erasmus was the greatest N European humanist. For him and the other Renaissance thinkers humanism by no means implied rejection of Christianity. **2.** A 20th-century philosophical viewpoint that is based on a policy of *atheism, holding religion to be an outmoded superstition unworthy of serious consideration.

human rights Privileges claimed or enjoyed by a human being simply by virtue of being human. The concept developed from Roman ideas of "natural law" entailing "natural rights," via *Locke, *Paine, and the American Declaration of Independence (1776), to 20th-century liberal acceptance of the idea that human beings should have certain equal civil, political, and economic rights. Since the horrors of World War II, moves have been made to ensure international enforcement of human-rights agreements as embodied in the UN Charter. The UN Universal Declaration of Human Rights (1948), itself not a legally binding code, has spawned various subsequent agreements, such as the Covenants on Civil and Political Rights and on Economic, Social, and Cultural Rights (1966), which have been accepted as binding by 35 nations.

Humber An estuary in N England, flowing from the confluence of the Rivers Ouse and Trent to the North Sea past the ports of Hull, Immingham, and Grimsby. It is crossed by the world's largest single-span suspension bridge. Length: 40 mi (64 km).

Humboldt, (Karl) Wilhelm von (1767–1835) German scholar and states-man; friend of Schiller and Goethe. As minister of education he founded Berlin University (1809) and was subsequently employed as a diplomat. His writings on language are especially profound: he saw language as a generative process rather than a lifeless structure. He perceived that language and thought are in-separable and identified various kinds of structures by which languages may be differentiated. His brother (**Friedrich Wilhelm Karl Heinrich**) **Alexander von Humboldt** (1769–1859) was a scientist and explorer. In 1799 he set off with Aimé Bonpland (1773–1858) to explore Central and South America and in the following five years the two men collected a large number of samples and much data relating to earth sciences. He subsequently explored central Asia, again col-lecting scientific material of great importance. In his great work *Kosmos* (5 vols, 1845–62) he set out his views on the whole universe. The *Humboldt Current and Glacier were named for him.

Humboldt Current (*or* Peru Current) An ocean current constituting part of the South Pacific oceanic circulation system. It flows N off the Peruvian coast of South America. Because of its Antarctic origins and the upwelling of cold water along the W coast of South America, it is a cold current rich in plankton and the fish that feed on them, giving rise to Peru's prosperous fishing industry.

Humboldt Glacier The largest known glacier in the N hemisphere, in NW Greenland. At its end in Kane Basin it is 60 mi (100 km) wide and 300 ft (91 m) high.

Hume, David (1711–76) Scottish philosopher and historian. He spent three years in France (1734–37) but for the rest of his life lived in either London or Ed-inburgh. In *A Treatise of Human Nature* (1739–40) he developed his influential distinction between impression and ideas, claiming that impressions have more force than ideas. We receive impressions from an unknown source and ideas de-rive from them through the operations of memory and imagination. For Hume al-most nothing about existence was demonstrable; regarding the existence of God, his position throughout his numerous works is an incisive *agnosticism. Al-though an empiricist like *Locke and *Berkeley, Hume modified problematic as-pects of their philosophies in favor of psychological explanations. Another aspect of Hume's thought that is influential among 20th-century philosophers is his analysis of cause and effect as no more than "constant conjunction": we can *ob-serve* that one thing follows another but we can never *know* that it must follow, because of the limitations in the nature and scope of human understanding. Hume's *History of England* (1754–62) was a best-seller for many years.

humerus. *See* arm.

humidity A measure of the amount of water vapor in the atmosphere. Absolute humidity is the mass of water vapor in unit volume of air, measured in kilograms per cubic meter. Relative humidity is the ratio of the absolute humidity at a given temperature to the maximum humidity without precipitation at the same temperature, usually expressed as a percentage.

Hummel, Johann Nepomuk (1778–1837) Hungarian pianist and composer. He numbered Mozart and Haydn among his teachers. He toured Europe as a concert pianist and was famous as an improviser. His compositions include con-certos and many piano solos.

hummingbird A brightly colored bird belonging to a New World family (*Trochilidae;* 320 species). Hummingbirds are 2–8 in (5.5–20 cm) long and have a slender often downcurved bill and a brush-tipped tongue for feeding on nectar and small insects. Hummingbirds can hover, fly backward, and produce a humming noise by the rapid vibration of their wings during flight. Order: *Apodiformes* (swifts, etc.).

HUMMINGBIRD *Gould's long-tailed sylph hummingbird* (Aglaiocercus kingi) *extracting nectar while hovering by a flower. This species is found in the Andes and from Venezuela to Peru and Bolivia.*

humpback whale A *rorqual whale, *Megaptera novaeangliae,* found in coastal waters throughout the world. It is 49 ft (15 m) long with long flippers and a large dorsal fin with lobes down to the tail. It is an acrobatic swimmer and lives in communities, feeding on crustaceans and small fish. □oceans.

Humperdinck, Engelbert (1854–1921) German composer. He assisted Wagner with the score of *Parsifal* in 1880–81. Of his many operas only *Hänsel und Gretel* (1893) is still popular: it blends German folklore with Wagnerian operatic techniques.

Humphrey, Hubert Horatio (1911–78) US political leader. As mayor of Minneapolis, Minn. (1945–49), Humphrey gained national prominence as a supporter of civil rights and social legislation. He was elected to the US Senate in 1948 and became active in the leadership of the *Democratic party. In 1964, Humphrey was chosen by Pres. Lyndon Johnson to become his vice presidential running mate and after Johnson's decision not to run for reelection, Humphrey received the Democratic presidential nomination in 1968. Although he was defeated in that election by Richard Nixon, Humphrey remained active in public life, being elected to two more terms in the US Senate, in 1970 and 1976.

humus The black organic matter in soil resulting from the *decomposition of dead plants and animals (humification). It is rich in such elements as carbon, nitrogen, phosphorus, and sulfur, which are useful in maintaining soil fertility and hence in promoting plant growth. Humus also improves water absorption and workability of the soil.

Hunan A province in S central China, mountainous and forested in the S and W. The population includes an aboriginal minority. The chief products are rice, cereals, tea, cotton, timber, and such minerals as lead, zinc, tungsten, and gold. *History*: it was devastated during the Taiping Rebellion (1851–64). Mao Ze-tung was born here. Area: 82,095 sq mi (210,500 sq km). Population (1990): 60,659,754. Capital: Changsha.

hundred A subdivision of the shire in England, first mentioned in the 10th century. Of varying size, it may originally have consisted of a hundred *hides. It corresponded to the *wapentake in the areas under Danish law. An administrative and judicial unit, it had its own court sitting every four weeks until the 13th century, when its importance began to decline.

Hundred Days (Mar 20–June 28, 1815) The period from *Napoleon Bonaparte's return to France, after his escape from Elba, until his final defeat by the allies at *Waterloo.

Hundred Days (Mar 9–June 16, 1933) The first hundred days of Pres. Franklin D. Roosevelt's New Deal administration. During this time Congress passed many of the bills designed to help recovery from the *Depression. Farmers and homeowners were federally subsidized, banks were nationally regulated, and work was created for the unemployed.

Hundred Days of Reform (1898) A program of reforms announced by the Chinese emperor *Guang Xu, with the help of the reformer *Kang You Wei, to modernize the educational system, administration, and the armed forces and to develop trade, commerce, and industrialization on a Western model. Most of the reforms were repealed by Guang Xu's mother *Zi Xi, who with the support of the army imprisoned her son and became regent, thus frustrating a reform movement that might have prevented the overthrow of the *Qing dynasty.

Hundred Flowers A Chinese government campaign to allow greater freedom of speech, particularly among intellectuals. It began in 1956 under the slogan "Let a hundred flowers bloom together, let a hundred schools of thought contend." It led to much open criticism of the government and was harshly suppressed a year later.

Hundred Years' War (1337–1453) A war between England and France. It was precipitated by Edward III's claim to the French throne, although there had long been hostility occasioned by disputes over English territory in France and French support for the Scots. The Treaty of *Brétigny (1360) recognized initial English successes at *Sluys (1340), *Crécy (1346), and Poitiers (1356) but thereafter the war was waged intermittently with frequent truces. Conditions were exacerbated by growing French and Burgundian rivalry, the Burgundians supporting Henry V of England, who achieved recognition as heir to the French throne after his victory at *Agincourt (1415). His early death, the accession of the weak *Henry VI, and more vigorous French prosecution of the war (inspired by *Joan of Arc) reversed his triumph and by 1453 England had been expelled from all French territory except Calais.

Hungarian A language of the *Finno-Ugric branch of the *Uralic family. It is spoken by 14 million people mainly in Hungary, where it is the official language, and in the Czech Republic, Slovakia, Romania, Slovenia, and Croatia. It uses a modified Latin alphabet and has borrowed many words from surrounding languages. Vowel harmony is characteristic of its sound system and its grammar is based on the use of suffixes. *See also* Magyars.

Hungarian National Council (1918–19) A political coalition formed in October 1918, by *Károlyi and dedicated to establishing constitutional government in Hungary. In November, after Károlyi had become prime minister, it proclaimed Hungary a republic but the decline of the economy and the opposition of Hungary's minority nationalities forced its resignation (March 1919) in favor of the communists under *Kun.

Hungarian Revolution (1956) An uprising against Soviet dominance of Hungary. Following the Soviet acceptance of *Gomulka as leader in Poland, a demonstration of students and workers in Budapest demanded the end of the Soviet presence in Hungary and of one-party government. The protestors were joined by army units. Imre *Nagy formed a coalition government, withdrew

Hungary from the *Warsaw Pact, and sought UN help. An opposition government was formed by János *Kádár, and Soviet troops attacked Budapest and crushed the rebellion; Nagy and his associates were captured and executed. About 190,000 people left Hungary as a result of the Revolution.

Hungary, Republic of (Hungarian name: Magyar Népköztársasag) A country in central Europe. It lies mainly in the basin of the middle Danube, which forms the NW boundary with Czechoslovakia before running N–S across the center of the country. To the E of the Danube lies the Great Hungarian Plain, crossed by the Tisza River; to the W an undulating plain rises to some low hills in the SW and in the NW to the hilly Bakony Forest, S of which lies Lake *Balaton. The people are mainly Magyars, with minorities of Germans, Slovaks, and others. *Economy:* agriculture is now organized collectively, though individuals can still own small plots. The main crops are wheat and maize as well as fruit and vegetables. The wine industry is being encouraged, including the redevelopment of the Takaj region in the NE. The only mineral resource of significance is bauxite. Oil and natural gas have been found but most supplies are imported by pipeline. All industry was nationalized and there was considerable expansion after World War II, particularly in engineering and chemicals. From 1968 there was a new system of economic planning, aiming at a certain amount of decentralization and encouragement of individual initiative, while still maintaining overall state control, which rapidly diminished after the communist regime collapsed. The considerable volume of exports includes transport equipment, machinery, fruit and vegetables, and meat. *History:* the Magyars reached the Danube area in the 9th century AD and settled there under the Arpád dynasty. In the 11th century St *Stephen I converted the country to Christianity and became the first Hungarian king. After a long period of dynastic struggles and threats from foreign powers, Hungary was conquered by the Turks in 1526 and in the 17th century it became part of the Hapsburg Empire. The 19th century saw the rise of Hungarian nationalism. A revolt under *Kossuth in 1848 was suppressed by the Austrians but in 1867 Hungary gained internal self-government as part of the Dual Monarchy of *Austria-Hungary. Following the collapse of the Dual Monarchy in 1918 Hungary became a republic but, after a short period of communist rule, a constitutional monarchy was formed with *Horthy de Nagybanya as regent. Although allied to the Germans in World War II, it was occupied by them in 1944 and liberated by Soviet troops in 1945. After the war it became a republic and in 1949 the communists gained control. In 1956 an anti-Stalinist uprising was crushed by Soviet forces. In 1967 a treaty of friendship with the Soviet Union was renewed and during the 1980s some reforms and a certain amount of liberalization took place. Effective power was in the hands of János *Kádár, first secretary of the Central Committee. Hungary, regarded as the showcase of Eastern European communism, pursued an economic course of "market socialism." Kádár was replaced by Károly Grósz in 1988, who, as prime minister, had instituted more liberal economic programs. In 1989 the name of the country was changed to Republic of Hungary, and in 1990 the first free National Assembly elections were held. Democracy and ensuing privatization of industry created a shaky economy during the early 1990s. Official language: Hungarian (Magyar). Official currency: forint of 100 fillér. Area: 35,911 sq mi (93,035 sq km). Population (1990 est): 10,546,000. Capital: Budapest.

Huns Nomadic people, originating in Mongolia, who overran much of SE Europe in the late-4th and 5th centuries, overthrowing the *Ostrogoths and then invading the Roman Empire. Renowned and feared for their military prowess, especially their use of cavalry, the failure of the Empire to continue payment of tribute to them inspired *Attila, under whom the Huns were now united and controlled, to invade Greece, Gaul, and finally Italy (452). The death of Attila

(453) fragmented their empire and after defeat by a coalition of tribes at Nedao (455) they ceased to be of importance.

Hunt, (James Henry) Leigh (1784–1859) British poet and journalist. In essays and criticism for many periodicals he supported Keats and other Romantic poets and promoted various political reforms. In 1813 he was imprisoned for his attacks on the Prince Regent. His books include *Imagination and Fancy* (1844) and *Autobiography* (1850).

Hunt, William Holman (1827–1910) British painter, born in London. After studying in the Royal Academy, he helped found the *Pre-Raphaelite Brotherhood, to the principles of which he alone remained faithful. His symbolic but technically realistic paintings, often biblical in subject, include *The Light of the World* (Keble College, Oxford) and *The Scapegoat* (Port Sunlight), inspired by a visit to Syria and Palestine (1854).

Hunter River A river in SE Australia, in New South Wales. It rises in the Eastern Highlands and flows generally S though Glenbawn Reservoir to enter the Pacific Ocean at Newcastle. Length: 290 mi (467 km).

Huntsville 34 44N 86 35W A city in NE Alabama. Founded in 1805, it is a center for rocket and guided-missile research. Industries include textiles and agricultural implements. Population (1990): 159,789.

Hunyadi, János (c. 1387–1456) Hungarian military leader and statesman. Following his successful Long Campaign against the Turks (1443–44), he was elected (1446) governor and regent for King Ladislas (1440–57). In 1456, shortly before dying of the plague, he routed the Turkish forces before Belgrade, thus securing a 70-year peace.

Hupa An Athabascan-speaking North American Indian people of the lower Trinity River region of N California. They lived along the river banks in villages consisting of women's houses and men's lodges. They hunted elk and deer, fished for salmon, and gathered acorns. Wealth consisted of dentalium shells and woodpecker scalps of which village headmen possessed the largest amounts. Their religion was characterized by *shamanism and the performance of seasonal ceremonies.

Hupei. *See* Hubei.

hurdling A track event in athletics in which sprinters jump 10 hurdles in the course of each race. The standard distances are 110 m and 400 m for men and 100 m for women. For the 110 m the height of the hurdles is 3.5 ft (106.7 cm), for the 400 m it is 3 ft (91.4 cm), and for the 100 m, 2.75 ft (84 cm). Racers are not normally disqualified for knocking over hurdles.

hurdy-gurdy A stringed instrument sounded by a rosined wheel, turned by the right hand, and stopped by a set of keys played by the left hand; there are also two drone strings. It was very popular in medieval times and survives as a folk instrument in parts of Europe.

hurling (*or* hurley) An Irish 15-a-side stick-and-ball field game similar to field hockey, dating back at least 3000 years. The ball is hit or carried through the air with a broad-bladed curved stick, the hurley (Gaelic word: *caman*), and may be caught in the hand. A standard field measures 150 × 90 yd (137 × 82 m). A goal, hit under the crossbar, scores three points, a hit between the posts but above the bar scores one point.

Huron An Iroquoian-speaking North American Indian people who originally inhabited the St Lawrence River region. Supporting themselves primarily by agriculture, they cultivated maize, beans, squash, and tobacco and occupied villages of bark-covered dwellings. In 1650 they were defeated by the *Iroquois and driven from their lands. Some of the Huron survivors were resettled in Ohio where they were known as the Wyandot Indians. The present Huron population living in small communities in Ohio, Kansas, and Ontario, Canada, is approximately 1250.

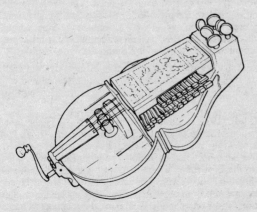

HURDY-GURDY

Huron, Lake The second largest of the Great Lakes in North America, situated between the US and Canada. It is an important shipping route carrying iron ore, coal, grain, and oil. Area: 23,000 sq mi (59,570 sq km).

Hurrians A people living in E Anatolia and N Mesopotamia during the 2nd millennium BC. The Hurrians probably originated in the Armenian mountains before their expansion. Their language, which is extinct, was neither Indo-European nor Semitic, but may be related to *Georgian and the Caucasian languages. It is largely known from cuneiform tablets from Hattusas, the capital of their neighbors, the *Hittites, whose civilization the Hurrians greatly influenced. There was never a Hurrian empire, but the powerful kingdom of Mitanni (1550–1400 BC) was largely Hurrian in population. *See also* Nuzi.

hurricane 1. A tropical *cyclone with surface-wind speeds in excess of 64 knots (107.3 ft or 32.7 m per second) that occurs around the Caribbean Sea and Gulf of Mexico. Tropical cyclones also occur in the W Pacific Ocean, and Bay of Bengal, but are identified by their own local names (*see* typhoon). The center (eye) of a hurricane is an area of light winds around which strong winds, cloud, and rain bands spiral. **2.** Any wind reaching force 12 on the *Beaufort scale (in excess of 64 knots per second) whether or not it is related to a tropical cyclone.

Hurstmonceux. *See* Herstmonceux.

Hus, Jan (c. 1369–1415) Bohemian religious reformer and martyr. Ordained as a priest in 1401, he became a university teacher in Prague and a popular preacher. Under the influence of the writings of *Wycliff, he criticized the ecclesiastical establishment, chiefly on moral grounds, emphasizing the role of the Scriptures.

Husaynids The ruling dynasty of Tunisia from 1705 to 1957. Their founder, al-Husayn ibn Ali, was recognized as governor of Tunisia by the Ottomans, but he and his successors, who had the title of *bey*, were practically independent. In 1883 their land became a French protectorate. The *beys* lost popularity because it was thought they were too servile to the French and in 1957, when Tunisia became a republic, the dynasty came to an end.

husky One of several breeds of compact sturdy deep-chested dogs used for pulling sledges in Arctic regions. The Siberian husky has small erect ears, a long muzzle, and a brushlike tail curved over the back. The dense double-layered coat may be of various colors and provides insulation against the severe climate. The Eskimo dog, bred in Greenland, closely resembles the Siberian husky, from which it is probably descended. The Alaskan malamute is a similar breed of sled dog. Height: 20–25 in (51–63 cm). *See also* Samoyed.

hussars Light-cavalry regiments originating in Hungary in the 15th century. Most European armies have used hussars for reconnaissance and raids. Their uniform included the characteristic dolman, a cloak worn hanging from the left shoulder.

Hussein (ibn Talal) (1935–) King of Jordan (1952–). He became king following the deposition because of mental illness of his father Talal. Hussein led Jordan into the 1967 Arab-Israeli War, in which its possessions on the West Bank of the Jordan River were occupied by Israel. The large Palestinian population of the area moved to the East Bank, where al-*Fatah guerrillas established themselves, posing a threat to Hussein's government. In 1970 he crushed the guerrillas, but in 1974, under pressure from other Arab countries, accepted the claims of the Palestine Liberation Organization to the West Bank. His support of Iraq's Saddam Hussein in the 1990–91 Middle East crisis cost Jordan Western and Arab aid.

Hussein, Saddam (1937–) President of Iraq (1979–). Under his presidency Iraq waged war with Iran (1980–88) and then invaded and annexed Kuwait (1990), an action that led to his defeat in *Operation Desert Storm in 1991. A member of the Ba'th party from his youth, Hussein took part in several coup attempts and was exiled twice before the Ba'th party successfully took control of the government in 1968. As president, he directed a harsh dictatorship, one threatened by domestic unrest after defeat in Kuwait.

Husserl, Edmund (1859–1938) German philosopher, influential in the phenomenological tradition (*see* phenomenology). He taught at Halle, Göttingen, and Freiburg Universities. Husserl's philosophy rejected presuppositions about what actually exists (and why it does) and studied purely "subjective" data.

Hussites The followers of the Bohemian heretic Jan *Hus (1372–1415). They demanded a reformed national Church with a vernacular liturgy. In spite of papal and imperial crusades led by the Holy Roman Emperor *Sigismund, the Hussites remained undefeated until a compromise was reached at the Council of *Basle in 1433. The moderate Utraquists gained many of their demands and, in spite of schisms, survived until the 17th century. *See also* Moravian Brethren.

Huston, John (1906–87) US film director. He began his career as a scriptwriter. His first film as director was *The Maltese Falcon* (1941), and subsequent films included *The Treasure of the Sierra Madre* (1948), for which he wrote the script and in which he also acted, *The African Queen* (1951), *The Misfits* (1960), *Fat City* (1972), *The Man Who Would Be King* (1975), and *Annie* (1982).

Hutchinson, Anne (Marbury) (1591–1643) US colonist and religious leader; born in England. She came to Boston in 1634 with her husband and children and began preaching against institutional organized religion. She felt that religion came from within a person, a theory many took to be against Puritanism. Banished from Massachusetts (1637), she and her followers established Portsmouth, R.I. In 1643, while living on Long Island, she and her family were killed by Indians.

hutia A large *rodent of the family *Capromyidae* (which also includes the *coypus), found in Cuba and the West Indies. Hutias are 8–24 in (20–60 cm) long excluding the naked tail (1.2–12 in; 3–30 cm). They are mainly vegetarian and are either diurnal and arboreal (genus *Capromys*; 4 species) or nocturnal and terrestrial (genus *Geocapromys*; 3 species).

HUSSEIN *The king has encountered considerable opposition within Jordan and makes frequent tours of his country, piloting his own helicopter.*

Hutten, Ulrich von (1488–1523) German humanist, who became poet laureate of the Holy Roman Empire in 1517. His reputation was established as a wit and satirist before he devoted himself to the cause of the Reformation and German nationalism. Joining the war against the German princes, he was driven into exile shortly before his death.

Hutton, James (1726–97) Scottish physician, often considered the founder of geology. His investigations led him to believe that the earth was very much older than generally believed at that time. These views were expressed in his book *Theory of the Earth* (1785), which met with strong objections from those who accepted the views of creation contained in Genesis.

Huxley, Thomas Henry (1825–95) British biologist, whose impact spanned both biology and philosophy. A qualified surgeon, he was a staunch supporter and friend of Charles *Darwin and led the debate against opponents of Darwinism at Oxford in 1860. Huxley was instrumental in bringing enlightened change to educational methods. From 1880 onward he challenged orthodox theology and coined the term agnosticism to describe his own position. Three of his grandsons achieved fame in the fields of science and literature. **Sir Julian Huxley** (1887–1975) was a zoologist and scientific administrator, who also made valuable contributions to the philosophy of science. He was appointed first director general of UNESCO (1946–48). His views on evolution appeared in *Evolution: The Modern Synthesis* (1942). His brother **Aldous Huxley** (1894–1964) was a novelist and writer. During the 1920s he lived mostly in Italy and later settled in California. The witty satirical novels *Antic Hay* (1923) and *Point Counter Point* (1928) were followed by *Brave New World* (1932), *Eyeless in Gaza* (1936), and *After Many A Summer Dies the Swan* (1939). His later works, including *The Doors of Perception* (1954) and *Heaven and Hell* (1956), explore such subjects as mysticism and the use of drugs. **Sir Andrew Fielding Huxley** (1917–), half-brother to Sir Julian and Aldous, is a biologist noted for his researches into the mechanisms of nerve-impulse conduction and muscle contraction. For their work on nerve impulses Huxley and his collaborator A. L. *Hodgkin shared a Nobel Prize (1963) with Sir John *Eccles.

Huygens, Christiaan (1629–95) Dutch astronomer and physicist, who discovered Saturn's rings in 1656. He also built the first pendulum clock and designed an arrangement of lenses called a Huygens eyepiece, which is still in use on some telescopes and microscopes. He devised a wave theory of light to explain his observation of double refraction. He claimed to have invented the hairspring (a claim also made by *Hooke).

Huysmans, Joris Karl (1848–1907) French novelist. In his best-known novel, *A rebours* (1884), he epitomized the contemporary taste for decadent aestheticism in the character of Des Esseintes, who devoted his life to the sensual indulgence of his esoteric tastes. He also wrote art criticism and a series of partly autobiographical novels, including *Là-bas* (1891), that charted his spiritual progress and ultimate acceptance of Roman Catholicism.

hyacinth A perennial herbaceous plant of the genus *Hyacinthus* (about 30 species), native to the Mediterranean region and tropical Africa and widely planted as ornamental garden and pot plants. Growing from bulbs, the flower stems, up to 14 in (35 cm) high, bear a dense head of bell-shaped flowers, varying from white and yellow to deep purple. The plants have slender leaves, up to 12 in (30 cm) long. The common garden hyacinths are derived from *H. orientalis*. Family: *Liliaceae*.

Hyades A young open *star cluster in the constellation Taurus, the brightest stars forming a V-shaped group that can be seen with the naked eye. The star *Aldebaran lies in the direction of the cluster but is actually much nearer the sun.

hyaena. *See* hyena.

hybrid The offspring resulting from the mating of two unrelated individuals. The hybrid offspring often shows greater general fitness than either of the two parents, a phenomenon called hybrid vigor (or heterosis). This is commonly used by plant breeders to produce a generation of crop plants giving higher yields and showing improved resistance to disease. Hybrid vigor cannot be maintained in subsequent generations and new hybrids have to be produced for each season.

Hyde, Douglas (1860–1949) Irish scholar, whose translations of Irish literature influenced such writers as Yeats and Synge. He was also the first president of Eire (1938–45). He founded, and was first president (1893–1915) of, the Gaelic League. His books include *The Love Songs of Connacht* (1893), *A Literary History of Ireland* (1899), and *Legends of Saints and Sinners* (1915).

Hyderabad 17 22N 78 26E One of the largest cities in India, the capital of Andhra Pradesh situated on the Musi River. Formerly the capital of the princely state of Hyderabad, it was founded in 1590 by the Muslim Qutb Shahi sultans. The old city was planned around the Charminar (1594), a rectangular building surmounted by four minarets; other notable buildings include the Mecca Masjid, a mosque modeled on the one at Mecca. An educational center, Hyderabad is the site of Osmania University (1918), an agricultural university, and several research institutes. There has been considerable industrial growth in recent years, giving Hyderabad a higher standard of living than many other Indian cities. The chief manufactures include bus and railroad equipment, textiles, and pharmaceutical goods. Population (1991): 2,991,884.

Hyderabad 25 23N 68 24E A city in SW Pakistan, on the Indus River. A focal point of rail and road routes, it has light industries and several institutions of higher education, including the University of Sind (1947). Population (1981): 751,529.

Hyder Ali (1728–82) Muslim Indian ruler of Mysore. A volunteer in the Mysore raja's army from 1749, he became a commander (1759) and in about 1761 deposed the raja. When the British refused to support him against his Indian enemies, he invaded British territory and was narrowly defeated near Madras, coming closer than any other Indian ruler to ousting the British from S India.

Hydra In Greek legend, a monster with many heads who grew two more whenever one was cut off. It was killed by *Heracles, whose own death was later caused by the monster's poisonous blood or gall.

Hydra A widely distributed genus of solitary freshwater invertebrate animals belonging to an order (*Hydroida*) of *coelenterates. They are flexible *polyps, 0.40–1 in (10–30 mm) long, with the mouth at the top surrounded by 6–10 tentacles. Hydras are usually attached to stones, sticks, or aquatic vegetation and feed on small animals. Reproduction is asexual in summer and sexual in winter. Class: *Hydrozoa*.

Hydrangea A genus of shrubs (about 80 species) native to Asia and North and South America, including several popular ornamentals. The showy heads of white, pink, or blue flowers may be sterile and sometimes change color according to the acidity or alkalinity of the soil. *H. macrophylla* is a popular pot plant. Family: *Hydrangeaceae*.

hydraulics The study of the applications of *hydrostatics and *hydrodynamics to design problems. In civil engineering it is used to study the flow of water in pipes, rivers, canals, etc., especially with reference to the construction of dams, reservoirs, and hydroelectric power stations. In mechanical engineering, applications include the design of machinery involving fluids, such as hydraulic presses, *turbines, propellers, etc. Hydraulics is concerned with the bulk properties of fluids, such as density, viscosity, elasticity, and surface tension, rather than their molecular properties.

hydraulis (Greek: water pipe) An early type of *organ in which the air pressure was maintained by water. A clay model found in the ruins of Carthage has three ranks of pipes and suggests an actual height of about 10 ft (3 m). The loud sound it produced made it useful for signaling in battle; it was also played in Roman amphitheaters, the Emperor Nero being an enthusiastic performer.

hydrocarbons Compounds containing carbon and hydrogen. The saturated hydrocarbons are classified as *alkanes. Unsaturated hydrocarbons include the *alkenes and *alkynes. *Aromatic hydrocarbons include *benzene and its many derivatives.

hydrocephalus An excess of fluid in the brain. The brain is normally bathed in cerebrospinal fluid, which is constantly being produced and reabsorbed. A block in the flow or reabsorption of the fluid will result in hydrocephalus. In a baby, the bones of whose skull are not yet joined, the head becomes enlarged.

Congenital defects, meningitis, tumors, and injury can all be causes. Hydrocephalus may resolve spontaneously or may require surgical treatment.

hydrochloric acid A solution in water of the colorless pungent gas hydrogen chloride (HCl). It is made by the action of sulfuric acid on salt or by the direct recombination of hydrogen and chlorine from the electrolysis of sea water. It is very soluble in water and forms a strong acid. Concentrated hydrochloric acid contains about 40% HCl by weight and is a clear fuming corrosive liquid. The acid in the human stomach is dilute hydrochloric acid (0.4%).

hydrocyanic acid (*or* prussic acid; HCN) A highly toxic colorless liquid. It is made from ammonia and methane reacted with air in the presence of a catalyst. HCN forms weakly acidic solutions in water and is used in making synthetic fibers and as a fumigant.

hydrodynamics (*or* fluid dynamics) The branch of mechanics concerned with the study of ideal fluids in motion. An ideal fluid is assumed to be incompressible and to be free from frictional forces. Although never achieved, this simplification is often necessary to analyze a complex situation. The velocity, acceleration, and pressure at each point in the flow of an ideal liquid gives an indication of what will happen in a real liquid. *See also* aerodynamics; hydraulics.

hydroelectric power Electricity generation using the energy of falling water. The water turns a *turbine connected to an alternator, generating electricity with an efficiency of over 90% at full load and generally over 60% at quarter-load. Water is led through pipes from high-level natural or artificial reservoirs to the power station. Lower-level reservoirs and dammed rivers are also used in some situations. The higher the reservoir, the less water is needed for the same power output. Hydroelectric power is, therefore, a cheap power source in mountainous areas with high rainfall. Unfortunately these are not usually near the industrial communities that consume the most power. Also, because it depends on rainfall, hydroelectricity has to be backed by other power sources (*see* power station). In pumped storage stations, electricity is stored by using it to drive pumps that raise the water to a high-level reservoir. In times of high demand this water is run back through the turbines. Hydroelectric power stations can have an output of 10,000 megawatts.

hydrofoil A type of ship the hull of which is raised out of the water by foils as its speed increases. The foils provide lift in much the same way as an airfoil; once the hull is clear of the water the drag is greatly reduced and the speed can be increased far above that of a normal ship of the same size and weight. The first hydrofoil was built in 1906 by Enrico Fortanini (1848–1930); this had a stack of foils arranged like a ladder. Modern craft use a large V-shaped foil, to provide stability in turns or in rough seas, or small totally submerged foils, which support the hull on streamlined struts. Propulsion is by propeller or by pumped-water jet. Hydrofoils of 150 tons are in use in many parts of the world; some are capable of reaching speeds of up to 70 mph (112 kph).

hydrogen (H) The lightest of all gases, recognized as an element by Cavendish in 1766 and named by Lavoisier after water (Greek *hudro*, water). Hydrogen makes up about three-quarters of the mass of the universe. It is the simplest element, its nuclei consisting of one proton. Heavier elements are formed by nuclear fusion (*see* nuclear energy) from hydrogen in stars. The heavier isotope of hydrogen, *deuterium (D *or* ^{2}H), occurs as about one part in 6000 of ordinary hydrogen. *Tritium (^{3}H) also occurs but is unstable. As well as the gaseous element (H_2) and water (H_2O), hydrogen occurs in organic compounds and in all inorganic *acids and *alkalis. The gas itself is used as a fuel for rockets, in welding, for filling balloons, and in chemical manufacture. It combines (explosively if in the right proportions) with oxygen to form water and can be obtained from water by electrolysis. Liquid hydrogen is used for experiments in low-temperature physics. At no 1; at wt 1.00797; mp −434.45°F (−259.14°C); bp −423.17°F (−252.87°C).

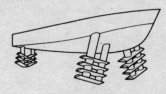

ladder foils

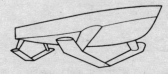

V-shaped foils

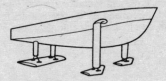

short submerged foils

HYDROFOIL

hydrogen bomb. *See* nuclear weapons.

hydrogen bond A weak attraction (much weaker than a covalent or ionic *chemical bond but much stronger than *Van der Waals forces) between an oxygen, nitrogen, or fluorine atom in one molecule and a hydrogen atom in a neighboring molecule. The hydrogen atom must itself be linked to a similar electronegative atom by a covalent bond. The attraction arises because the atom bonded to the hydrogen atoms exerts a strong pull on the shared electrons and thus confers a partial positive charge on the hydrogen. Consequently electrostatic attraction occurs between this hydrogen atom and the oxygen, fluorine, or nitrogen in the other molecule. Hydrogen bonding is responsible for the anomalous physical properties of many compounds, including water. It is particularly important in biological systems, being responsible for maintaining the structure of proteins and nucleic acids.

hydrography The description, measurement, and charting of the waters of the earth's surface (oceans, seas, lakes, rivers, and streams), particularly for navigational purposes. Tides, currents, and waves are also involved. The term is sometimes used for the shape of the sea floor and the deposits covering it.

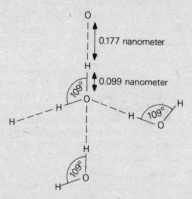

HYDROGEN BOND *The hydrogen bonding between water molecules (H_2O) in ice crystals.*

hydrology The science that studies the occurrence and movement of water on and over the surface of the earth. The **hydrological cycle** is the cyclic movement of water from the sea to the atmosphere and back, via precipitation, streams, and rivers. The main processes with which hydrology is concerned are precipitation, evaporation and transpiration, stream flow, and groundwater flow. It has many important applications, such as flood control and the supply of water for domestic and industrial purposes, irrigation, and hydroelectric power. □water table.

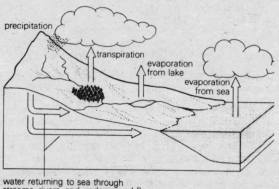

HYDROLOGY *The hydrological cycle.*

hydrolysis The reaction of a chemical compound with water; usually water is the solvent in which the reaction occurs. A common example is the hydrolysis of *esters to form alcohols and carboxylic acids.

hydrometer An instrument for measuring the relative *density of a liquid. It consists of a weighted and sealed glass bulb with a long neck on which a scale is calibrated. The relative density is measured by placing the hydrometer in the liquid and noting the level to which it sinks.

hydrophobia. *See* rabies.

hydrophone A type of *microphone that converts underwater sound waves into electrical signals. It consists essentially of a diaphragm, a *transducer, and an *amplifier. It is used in *sonar equipment, depth sounding, and underwater communications.

hydroponics The cultivation of plants in a liquid nutrient solution instead of soil. A carefully prepared aqueous solution of all the nutrients required for healthy growth is used, usually in conjunction with an inert medium, such as sand or gravel, which provides support for the plant-root system. On a small scale, the solution is simply poured over the substrate and the excess allowed to drain into containers for reuse. On a commercial scale, this is done by an automatic pumping system in which the solution is monitored to maintain nutrient levels and acidity.

Hydroponics enables crops to be produced in arid regions or where the soil is infertile or toxic, but its high cost restricts its use to high-value crops, such as flowers and vegetables.

hydrostatics The branch of mechanics concerned with fluids at rest (*compare* hydrodynamics). It is generally considered to have been instigated by Archimedes. Applications include the design of storage tanks, gates, and valves for hydraulic structures, dams, etc.

Hydrozoa A class of aquatic invertebrate animals (3700 species)—*coelenterates—whose life cycle usually alternates between generations of mainly marine sessile colonial *polyps and free-swimming solitary *medusae. *See also* Hydra; Obelia; Portuguese man-of-war.

hyena (*or* hyaena) A carnivorous ☐mammal of the family *Hyaenidae*. There are three species: the African spotted hyena (*Crocuta crocuta*); the Asian striped hyena (*Hyaena hyaena*); and the brown hyena (*H. brunnea*) of South Africa, also called strandwolf. Hyenas are doglike in appearance, up to 5 ft (1.5 m) long including the tail, and stand about 35 in (90 cm) high at the shoulder. They hunt in packs, feeding on carrion and killing young or sick animals.

Hyères 43 07N 6 08E A resort and spa in S France, in the Var department on the French Riviera. It has a notable beach and offshore are the Îles d'Hyères, a small group of islands (Porquerolles, Port-Cros, I'Île du Levant, and two islets). Population (1975): 39,593.

Hygiea The Greek goddess of health, worshiped together with *Asclepius, god of medicine, and sometimes identified as his daughter or wife. She was usually portrayed in the act of feeding a serpent from a dish.

hygrometer An instrument that measures the relative *humidity of the atmosphere. In mechanical hygrometers, a material (usually human hair) is used, the length of which varies with the humidity, the variations being transformed into the movement of a pointer along a scale. In the wet-and-dry bulb hygrometer, two thermometers are placed side by side, one having its bulb covered by a moist cloth. The cooling caused by the evaporation from this wet bulb depends on the atmospheric moisture and thus the difference between the two thermometer readings can be related by standard tables to the relative humidity.

Hyksos A nomadic Asiatic tribe, known to the ancient Egyptians as Shepherd Kings or Princes of Foreign Lands. Moving southward about 1750 BC through

Palestine and Syria, the Hyksos invaded Egypt and, until driven northward again by the Egyptians about 1570 BC, ruled the Delta area, introducing metallurgy, bronze weapons, the wheel and, traditionally, the use of horse and chariot.

Hymen The greek god of marriage. He was the son of Apollo or of Dionysus and Aphrodite.

Hymenoptera A large worldwide order of insects (over 100,000 species) including the ants, sawflies, ichneumons, wasps, and bees. Many species show a high degree of social organization. Typically they have two pairs of membranous wings and the first segment of the abdomen is constricted to form a "waist." A tubular egg-laying structure (ovipositor) is generally present and in higher groups is modified for sawing, piercing, or stinging. The larvae (except the sawflies) are legless and have well-developed heads. The males develop from unfertilized eggs. Many species are of benefit to man because they pollinate flowering plants and prey on or parasitize insect pests.

Hymettus, Mount (Modern Greek name: Imittós Óros) 37 57N 23 49E A mountain ridge in SE Greece, running N–S for about 9 mi (15 km) immediately E of Athens. The Kara marble used in ancient times was quarried here. Height: 3366 ft (1026 m).

hymn A song of praise in honor of a deity or saint, often in a metrical verse form. Hymns have been an important part of Christian congregational worship since the end of the 4th century. During the Middle Ages polyphonic settings became common but after the Reformation Lutheran chorale became the basis of the German and English hymn traditions. Famous hymn writers include Martin Luther, Charles Wesley, and Isaac Watts (1674–1748); many of the hymns sung in the Anglican church today were written in the 19th century.

Hypatia (d. 415 AD) Neoplatonist philosopher and mathematician. She lectured on philosophy at *Alexandria, where her wisdom and learning endeared her to both pagans and Christians. The patriarch Cyril resented her influence, and she was brutally murdered by a Christian mob.

hyberbola The curve, or pair of curves, formed by a *conic section and defined in Cartesian coordinates (*see* coordinate systems) by the equation $x^2/a^2 - y^2/b^2 = 1$, where a and b are constants. Its two parts have a common axis and are separated by a minimum distance $2a$ along this axis. As it goes out to *infinity, the curve becomes increasingly close to two straight lines, called *asymptotes.

hyperbolic functions A set of mathematical functions written sinh x, cosh x, tanh x, and their inverses csch x, sech x, and coth x respectively. Sinh x is defined as $\frac{1}{2}(e^x - e^{-x})$, where e is the base of natural logarithms; cosh x is $\frac{1}{2}(e^x + e^{-x})$, and tanh x is sinh x/cosh x. Hyperbolic functions are defined by analogy with the trigonometric functions sin x, etc., and are so named because they are related to the *hyberbola in much the same way as the trigonometric functions are related to the circle.

Hyperboreans In Greek mythology, a people who lived in the far north, beyond the north wind (Boreas), in a land of sunshine and luxury. According to *Herodotus, they were devotees of Apollo and sent offerings to him at Delos but did not come themselves.

hyperglycemia A high concentration of sugar in the blood. This occurs in *diabetes mellitus and may, if severe and uncontrolled, lead to coma.

Hyperion In Greek mythology, one of the *Titans, the son of Uranus and Gaea and father of *Eos, *Helios, and *Selene. He was himself a sun god and was often identified with his son Helios.

hypertension High *blood pressure. This is a common condition, which can be caused by kidney disease, hormonal disorders, and some congenital diseases; for most cases, however, no cause can be found (this is known as essential hypertension). Usually there are no symptoms, with the consequent danger that untreated hypertension may lead to heart failure, kidney failure, cerebral hemorrhage, and blindness. In some cases surgery can be curative, but usually only drug treatment is necesary and must continue indefinitely.

hyperthyroidism Overactivity of the thyroid gland, which occurs most commonly in women. It may lead to the syndrome of thyrotoxicosis; restlessness, irritability, heat intolerance, weight loss, and palpitations, sometimes with protruding eyes and swelling of the neck (*see* goiter)—this is called exophthalmic goiter (*or* Graves's disease). It can be treated by surgery, radioactive iodine to destroy part of the gland, or drugs that suppress the production of thyroid hormones.

hypnosis The production of a trance state by means of firm suggestion, with the cooperation of the subject. People who have been deeply hypnotized can carry out instructions that would not be possible in a normal waking state; for instance, they can become insensible to pain or regress to childish behavior. First used for therapeutic purposes by *Mesmer in the 18th century, it was developed (and given the name hypnosis) by James Braid (1795–1860) in the 19th century. In France it was used by *Charcot (under whom *Freud studied), and by the turn of the century it was established as a means of treating certain psychiatric disorders (especially those of psychosomatic origin). It has, however, always been regarded as somewhat disreputable, first because of its misuse on the stage as a form of entertainment and second because the mechanism is still not understood. Although it is alleged that a hypnotist cannot force a patient under hypnotism to do anything he would not be willing to do when awake (e.g. commit a crime), the dangers inherent in one person controlling another's actions are obvious.

hypnotherapy A form of alternative medicine, in which the patient is put into a hypnotic state, during which the therapist suggests that particular symptoms will no longer be felt. Hypnotherapy does not cure medical conditions but has proved useful with some patients in relieving symptoms.

hypnotics Drugs that cause sleep. Although most drugs that depress the brain's activity have this effect, the ideal hypnotic produces natural sleep without "hangover" effects on awakening. Some drugs of the *benzodiazepine group come closest to this ideal and have now almost entirely replaced *barbiturates as hypnotics.

hypoglycemia A low concentration of sugar in the blood. This may occur in otherwise healthy people who have eaten little and exercised considerably, but is more often seen in diabetics who have taken too much insulin. The patient feels weak, sweaty, and shaky. *See* diabetes.

hypothalamus A part of the *brain, surrounding the lower part of the third ventricle, that is an important coordinating center for the functions of the autonomic *nervous system. It is particularly involved with the control of body temperature, with regulating how much is eaten and drunk, and with the emotions. It also releases *neurohormones affecting other organs, especially the *pituitary gland.

hypothermia Lowering of the body temperature. This is most commonly seen in old people and young babies—whose body temperature is less well controlled—if they are living in poorly heated rooms. If the body temperature falls very low severe internal changes may occur, but otherwise gentle warming will help the patient to recover. Hypothermia may be deliberately induced for heart surgery.

hyrax An African *mammal belonging to the order *Hyracoidea* (6 species), also called coney; 12–24 in (30–60 cm) long, hyraxes are related to ungulates (hooved mammals), having hooflike toes and a two-chambered stomach for digesting their vegetable diet. They are nimble and live in small colonies in trees or among rocks, being most active at twilight.

HYRAX *The rock hyrax, or dassie* (Procavia capensis), *lives in colonies of up to about 40 individuals in caves or other shelters in rocky regions of Africa.*

hyssop A perennial herbaceous plant, *Hyssopus officinalis*, native to S Europe, Asia, and Morocco. It is grown elsewhere as a garden ornamental and was formerly cultivated as a medicinal herb. Growing to a height of 24 in (60 cm), it has whorls of violet-blue flowers along the stem. Family: *Labiatae*.

hysterectomy The surgical removal of the womb. A subtotal hysterectomy involves removing the body of the womb but leaving the neck (cervix); in total hysterectomy (or panhysterectomy) the entire womb is removed. It is most commonly performed when the womb contains large fibroids—benign tumors that cause heavy menstrual periods. Other conditions that may require hysterectomy include cancer of the womb or the presence of precancerous cells in the cervix. The operation is usually performed through an incision made in the abdominal wall: it invariably precludes subsequent pregnancy but does not affect sexual activity.

hysteresis Any of several physical phenomena in which an induced effect lags behind the inducing cause. The term is most often applied to magnetic hysteresis in which the magnetic induction produced in a ferromagnetic material lags behind the magnetic field. Thus a graph of magnetic induction plotted against a magnetizing field is a closed S-shaped loop (hysteresis loop). The area within the loop is equal to the energy dissipation per unit volume during one cycle of magnetization. Other forms of hysteresis include thermal, dielectric, and elastic hysteresis.

hysteria A neurotic condition of emotional instability and immaturity in which patients are vulnerable to suggestion and develop physical symptoms. Hysterical symptoms are unconsciously adopted by the individual because they bring some gain. The symptoms may be of "conversion hysteria," characterized by physical symptoms, such as paralysis; or of "dissociative hysteria," with changes in thinking, such as multiple personality. Treatment is usually by *psychotherapy.

Hywel the Good (Howel Dda; d. 950 AD) Welsh prince (c. 909–50 AD). A friend of the English king Athelstan, Hywel eventually united S and N Wales in his remarkably peaceful reign. His famous codification of Welsh law remained effective for more than 300 years.

I

iamb In verse, a metrical foot consisting of an unstressed syllable (or in verse based on quantity, a short syllable) followed by a stressed (or long) syllable. It was developed in quantitative verse by the ancient Greeks, who used it in dramatic dialogue because of its affinity to the natural rhythm of speech, and is the most common type of metrical foot in English poetry.

Iapetus In Greek mythology, one of the *Titans, the son of Uranus and Gaea and father of Atlas and Prometheus. When the rebellion of the Titans was defeated by Zeus, he was imprisoned in Tartarus.

Iaçsi (German name: Jassy) 47 09N 27 38E A city in NE Romania, near the Russian border. The capital of Moldavia, it possesses many historic buildings and academic institutions, including a university (1860). It has metal, chemical, and pharmaceutical industries. Population (1992): 342,994.

Ibadan 7 23N 3 56E The second largest city in Nigeria. The arrival of the railroad (1901) aided its commercial development and it is now an important industrial, commercial, and administrative center although there are few modern industries. Cocoa, palm products, and cotton are traded. It contains the University of Ibadan (1962). Population (1990 est): 1,230,000.

Ibagué 4 35N 75 30W A city in central Colombia, on the E slopes of the Central Cordillera. The surrounding area produces cocoa, tobacco, rice, and sugarcane. Tolima University was founded here in 1945. Population (1985): 293,000.

Ibarruri, Dolores (1895–1989) Spanish politician. The foremost Spanish communist in the 1930s, her oratory earned her the name La Pasionaria. She went into exile in 1939 and lived in the Soviet Union until the legalization of the Communist party allowed her to return to Spain (1977). She subsequently became a member of the Cortes.

Iberian Peninsula A peninsula in SW Europe, occupied by Portugal and Spain. It is separated from the rest of Europe by the Pyrenees and its flora and fauna are similar to those of N Africa. Area: 229,054 sq mi (593,250 sq km).

Iberians A Bronze Age people of S and E Spain in the 1st millennium BC. Their non-Indo-European language, which was displaced by Latin, is known from a variety of inscriptions on stone and other materials. The culture of the tribes of the coastal region of Valencia and in the NE showed considerable Greek influence while that of the SE tribes owed much to the Carthaginians. This is shown, for example, in differences in the alphabets used in each area. The economic basis was agriculture, mining, and metalworking. They lost their identity by cultural assimilation to the *Celts in Roman times.

Ibert, Jacques (1890–1962) French composer. A pupil of Fauré, he won the Prix de Rome in 1919. He directed the Academy of Rome from 1937 to 1955. His compositions include operas, chamber and orchestral music, and songs. His best-known work is the humorous orchestral *Divertissement* (1930).

Iberville, Pierre le Moyne, Sieur d' (1661–1706) French-Canadian explorer. After serving in the French navy he returned to Canada and led raids on the English fur-trading posts on Hudson Bay (1686–97). In 1699 he founded a colony at present-day Biloxi, Miss. and in 1700, the first French colony in Louisiana (near present-day New Orleans).

ibex A rare wild *goat, *Capra ibex*, of Eurasian and N African mountains. About 33 in (85 cm) high at the shoulder, ibexes have backward-curving horns up to 26 in (65 cm) long and their coat is brownish-gray with variable markings.

Other species known as ibex include the tur (*C. caucasica*) of Russia and the Spanish ibex (*C. pyrenaica*).

ibis A long-necked wading bird belonging to the subfamily *Threskiornithinae* (20 species), distributed worldwide in warm regions, 22–30 in (55–75 cm) long, ibises have a characteristic slender downcurved bill, and unfeathered face or head and neck, which may be black or brightly colored. They feed on small fish and aquatic invertebrates. Family: *Threskiornithidae* (ibises and spoonbills); order: *Ciconiiformes* (herons, storks, etc.).

IBIS *The sacred ibis* (Threskiornis aethiopica) *was revered by the ancient Egyptians as a symbol of the god Thoth: mummified birds have been found in the tombs of the pharaohs. Today the species is restricted to Africa S of the Sahara.*

Ibiza (Iviza *or* Ivica) A Spanish island in the Mediterranean Sea, in the Balearic Islands. Its climate and fine beaches have made it a popular tourist center. Exports include almonds, dried figs, apricots, and salt. Area: 209 sq mi (541 sq km). Chief town: Ibiza.

Iblis The Muslim name for the devil, perhaps derived from Greek *diabolos*. He is also called *al-Shaytan* (Satan). Because of his disobedience and pride, the devil was expelled from Paradise by God, but given power to lead astray those who do not serve God. Muslim tradition gives him a number of names before his fall, such as Azazil. It is disputed whether he was an angel, as in the Koran, or a jinni.

Ibn al-'Arabi, Muhyi-l-din (1165–1240) Muslim mystic and poet born in Murcia (Spain). The leading mystic of his age, he was one of the great geniuses of *sufism. In philosophy, he was a Neoplatonist. Some scholars believe that Islamic sufism, as represented by Ibn al-'Arabi, was an imitation of Christian monastic mysticism.

Ibn Battutah (1304–1368?) Arab traveler. From 1325 to 1354 he traveled-extensively in Asia Minor, the Near and Far East, Europe, and Africa. He then settled at Fez and wrote an invaluable and amusing account of his work, the *Rihlah*.

Ibn Ezra, Abraham Ben Meir (1093–1167) Hebrew poet and scholar, born in Toledo, who traveled to England, Italy, France, North Africa, and perhaps to Palestine. His works include a set of famous commentaries on the Hebrew Bible, poems, riddles, and epigrams.

Ibn Gabirol, Solomon (c. 1021–c. 1058) Jewish philosopher and poet, born in Málaga (Spain). He was one of the earliest philosophers of Moorish Spain and a leading Neoplatonist. His outstanding philosophical work, *The Fountain of Life*, influenced generations of Western medieval thinkers. *The Kingly Crown* is the summit of his poetic achievement.

Ibn Khaldun (1332–1406) Arab historian and philosopher, who held court posts in Spain and was chief judge in Cairo, where he died. In the *Kitab al-'ibar* (*Book of Examples*) he outlined the history of Islam and a historical theory of cyclical progress and regression in which nation states develop out of, and are subsequently destroyed by, nomadic communities.

Ibn Saud (c. 1880–1953) The first king of Saudi Arabia (1932–53). With the military help of al-*Ikhwan, he extended his territory from the Sultanate of Najd, which he reconquered in 1902, to encompass much of Arabia by 1924, when he took Hejaz. The name Saudi Arabia was adopted in 1932. In 1933 Ibn Saud came to an agreement with a US oil company, which discovered oil in his country in 1936, using the resultant revenues to introduce modernization programs.

Ibo (*or* Igbo) A people of SE Nigeria who speak Igbo, a language of the Kwa subgroup of the *Niger-Congo family. Subsistence cultivators of yams, cassava, and taro, they traditionally lived in scattered small holdings or village clusters of patrilineal kin headed by the eldest male descendant of the founder. Small federations of villages were the largest political units before colonial times. Many have now adopted Christianity. A growing sense of ethnic identity led to the proclamation of the short-lived Ibo secessionist republic of *Biafra (1967–70).

Ibrahim Pasha (1789–1848) Ottoman general; the son (or adopted son) and right-hand man of the viceroy of Egypt, *Mehemet Ali. In Egypt from 1805, he was given various offices by his father, culminating in the command of the Egyptian army after Mehemet Ali had quarreled with the Ottomans (1831). Ibrahim occupied Syria, becoming governor general (1833), until forced to withdraw by the European powers (1840). His modernizing policies were severely imposed and provoked much opposition. In 1848 he succeeded his infirm father as viceroy of Egypt but died after only 40 days in office.

Ibsen, Henrik (1828–1906) Norwegian playwright and poet, the founder of modern prose drama. The son of a rich merchant who became bankrupt when his son was eight, Ibsen was preparing to study medicine when he wrote his first, unsuccessful, play. After working in theaters in Bergen and Kristiania and continuing to write plays, none of which was outstanding, he wrote *Kongsemnerne* (*The Pretenders*; 1864), for which he was granted a scholarship. He traveled to Rome and from 1864 to 1891 lived in Italy and Germany, with occasional visits to Norway. His fame as a dramatist grew with *Brand* (1865) and *Peer Gynt* (1867). In his next several plays he turned to the presentation of social issues; women's emancipation in *A Doll's House* (1879), inherited disease and guilt in *Ghosts* (1881), and public corruption in *An Enemy of the People* (1882), plays which earned him a wide and controversial reputation. Subsequent works, such as *The Wild Duck* (1884) and *Hedda Gabler* (1890), dealt with the problems of individuals. In his last plays, *The Master Builder* (1892), *John Gabriel Borkman* (1896), and *When We Dead Awaken* (1899), he turned to the treatment of autobiographical themes in a symbolic manner.

Icarus (astronomy) A very small (about 0.6 mi [1 km] diameter) *minor planet with the smallest known *perihelion (0.19 astronomical units). It passed only 372,600 mi (600,000 km) from earth in 1968.

Icarus (mythology). *See* Daedalus.

Ice Age A period in the earth's history when ice spread toward the equator with a general lowering of temperatures. The most recent of these was the *Pleistocene epoch ending about 10,000 years ago, during which four major ice advances occurred. Other ice ages occurred in Permo-Carboniferous times about 250 million years ago and in Pre-Cambrian times about 500 million years ago. Between 1550 and 1850 the **Little Ice Age** occurred, with a significant lowering of temperatures in the N hemisphere.

iceberg A large mass of ice in the sea that has originated on land. Many result from the breaking off, or calving, of ice from glaciers. In the N hemisphere icebergs originate chiefly from Greenland; in the S hemisphere most break off from the Antarctic ice. A large part of an iceberg is submerged, causing a hazard to shipping (e.g. the loss of the *Titanic* in 1912).

icefish A name given to several unrelated fish including the family *Chaenichthyidae* (175 species) of the order *Perciformes*, also called white-blooded fish, which occur in Antarctic waters. Others include the semitransparent icicle or glass fish of E Asia (family *Salangidae*) and certain species of *smelt. Order: *Salmoniformes*.

ice hockey A six-a-side team game played with stick and puck on a rink. It derives from field hockey and was first played on the frozen harbor of Kingston, Ontario (c. 1860). Canada is the true home of the game, but it is widely played in the US, Sweden, Germany, Finland and Eastern Europe, including Russia and other former Soviet republics. Each team consists of a goalkeeper, right and left defense, center, and right and left wing and each team is allowed eight reserves. The premier professional league is the National Hockey League (NHL) (instituted 1917). The championship trophy, the Stanley Cup, has been won by the Montreal Canadiens more than any other team. The Canada Cup is a well-known international tournament, and hockey is also played in the Winter Olympics.

Iceland, Republic of (Icelandic name: Ísland) An island country in the N Atlantic Ocean, just S of the Arctic Circle, off the SE coast of Greenland. It consists mainly of a largely uninhabited plateau of volcanoes, lava fields, and glaciers; most of the population live around the deeply indented coast. *Economy*: some crops and livestock are produced, sufficient for local needs, but the basis of the economy is fishing. Hydroelectricity has been used to power an aluminum plant, and geothermal power (from the numerous geysers and thermal springs) is an important source of energy. There is also a thriving tourist industry. The main exports are fish products and aluminum. *History*: the Vikings reached Iceland about 874 AD and by the 10th century it had become an independent state with its own parliament, the Althing, which is considered to be the oldest in the world. In 1264 it came under Norwegian rule and, together with Norway, it passed to the Danish crown in 1381. In the late 19th century it gained a certain degree of self-government and in 1918 became an independent state under the Danish crown, attaining full independence as a republic in 1944. In recent years, following various extensions of its fishing limits, it has been involved in several

*Cod Wars with the UK. President: Vigdis Finnbogadottir. Official language: Icelandic. Official religion: Evangelical Lutheranism. Official currency: króna of 100 aurar. Area: 39,758 sq mi (103,000 sq km). Population: (1990 est): 251,000. Capital and main port: Reykjavik.

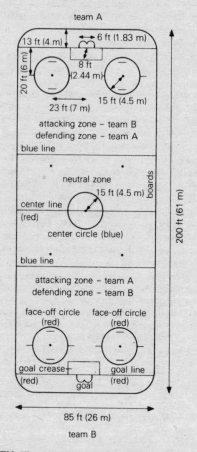

team A

13 ft (4 m)   6 ft (1.83 m)

20 ft (6 m)

8 ft (2.44 m)

15 ft (4.5 m)

23 ft (7 m)

attacking zone – team B
defending zone – team A

blue line

neutral zone

15 ft (4.5 m)

boards

center line (red)

center circle (blue)

blue line

attacking zone – team A
defending zone – team B

face-off circle (red)   face-off circle (red)

goal crease (red)   goal line (red)

goal

200 ft (61 m)

85 ft (26 m)

team B

ICE HOCKEY *The dimensions of the rink.*

Icelandic A North Germanic language of the Western Scandinavian subgroup. It is the official language of Iceland. Developed from the *Old Norse spoken by the original settlers of Iceland during the 9th and 10th centuries, Icelandic remains the most conservative of the Scandinavian languages in vocabulary, grammar, and orthography, but there has been much change in pronunciation.

Icelandic literature The greatest period of Icelandic literature was between 1100 and 1350, when the language was a dialect of *Old Norse and the Roman alphabet had only recently replaced the indigenous *runic script. Much of the material then written down drew upon considerably older oral sources. *Skaldic poetry, originating in Iceland's pre-Christian (pre-1000) era, remained an important form throughout the Middle Ages (*see also* Eddas). In prose, stories previously recited were written down for reading aloud (*see* sagas) and the influence of this classical prose has remained a strong conservative force in subsequent Icelandic writing. Despite the small number of Icelandic speakers there was a considerable revival in prose and poetry during the 19th century. In 1955 the Icelandic novelist Halldor *Laxness won the Nobel Prize in literature.

Iceland moss An edible *lichen, *Cetraria islandica*, that grows on moors and alpine areas of the N hemisphere and on lava slopes and plains of Iceland. Up to about 4 in (10 cm) high, it has a dark-brown to gray-white upright body with numerous flattened branches. It contains about 70% digestible starch and a brown dye.

Iceland spar A variety of *calcite consisting of pure colorless transparent crystals having the property of double refraction. It is therefore used for optical purposes and formerly for prisms in polarizing microscopes. It occurs in large steam cavities in basalt lava in Iceland.

Iceni A British tribe that inhabited the area that is now Norfolk and Suffolk. Their revolt against Roman rule in Britain under the leadership of *Boadicea (60 AD) was brutally suppressed.

ice plant A succulent annual or biennial plant, *Cryophytum crystallinum*, that is covered in glistening papillae and has long prostrate stems reaching 30 in (75 cm). Native to South Africa, it is naturalized in California and the Mediterranean region and widely grown as a garden or pot plant. It is easily propagated from seed. Family: *Aizoaceae*.

ice skating The recreation and sport of sliding over ice on steel-bladed skates. It originated over 2000 years ago and was widely practiced in the Middle Ages in Scandinavia and on Dutch canals. The main forms of the sport, which is governed by the International Skating Union and is predominantly amateur, are speed skating (long-distance outdoor racing) and two events judged on style— figure skating (compulsory exercises followed by a freestyle performance to music, either singly or in pairs) and ice dancing (a combination of dancing and pairs figure skating). *See also* ice hockey.

I-ch'ang. *See* Yichang.

I Ching A Chinese classic work on divination, also called the Book of Changes, attributed to Wen Wang (12 century BC). It is based on eight named trigrams (*bagua* or *pa kua*) made up of broken and unbroken lines (representing *yin and yang respectively) and arranged in different sequences. Study of the I Ching and its cosmology has exercised many Chinese philosophers.

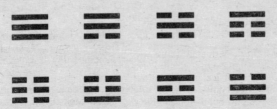

I CHING *The* pa kua *are the basis of the 64 hexagrams of the* I Ching, *each of which has a particular significance.*

ichneumon An insect, also called ichneumon fly and ichneumon wasp, belonging to a family (*Ichneumonidae*; about 40,000 species) occurring in Europe,

North America, and elsewhere. About 0.47 in (12 mm) long, ichneumons resemble wasps but have longer antennae. They are parasitic upon other insects thereby controlling many insect pests. The female uses a long tubular ovipositor to lay eggs on or in the host. The larvae feed on the host's body fluids and eventually cause its death. Order: *Hymenoptera*.

Ichthyornis A genus of extinct seabirds whose fossils date from the Cretaceous period (125–60 million years ago). It was 8 in (20 cm) long and was probably an active flier, having a large-keeled breastbone and strong wing bones.

ichthyosaur An extinct dolphinlike marine reptile that lived through much of the Mesozoic era but was most abundant in the Jurassic period (200–135 million years ago); 40 in–40 ft (1–12 m) long, it had broad flexible paddles, a large tail fin, and a triangular dorsal fin. Most ichthyosaurs had a long snout and jaws armed with sharp teeth and hunted fish near the surface of the sea but some had few or no teeth and fed on mollusks. □fossil.

icon A painted or mosaic image of Christ or a saint, peculiar to the Byzantine and Orthodox churches. Reverence of icons was castigated as idolatry by the Byzantine iconoclasts (*see* iconoclasm) and they were temporarily banned (730–843 AD). The decree reinstating them proclaimed that an icon must be a recognizable portrait of its subject with his accepted attributes, a formula resulting in a high degree of standardization. Unlike other paintings, therefore, icons have undergone little stylistic development and are characterized by a symbolic rather than realistic approach to color, perspective, etc. *See also* Rublyov.

Iconium. *See* Konya.

iconoclasm The rejection of the veneration of *icons in the Byzantine Church. The movement gained much support, especially in Asia Minor, during the 8th and 9th centuries. Imperial prohibition of icons lasted from 730 to 787 and from 815 to 843, during which times icon worshipers were severely persecuted. Iconoclasm was an expression both of longstanding Christological disputes and of the antagonism toward the portrayal of divinity that was also common to Islam and Judaism in the Near East.

iconography The branch of art history dealing with the interpretation of images and symbols associated with a particular subject in art. Although the term was first used in the 18th century in the study of engravings, it was largely promoted by Aby Warburg (1866–1929) and Erwin Panofsky (1892–1968). *See also* iconology.

iconology The interpretation of the content of a picture in relation to its historical context. The term was adopted by Erwin Panofsky (1892–1968) from the title, *Iconologia*, of a 16th-century book on symbols. Iconology attempts to place *iconography in a broader context and to study visual imagery as a bridge to wider aspects of history and civilization.

Ictinus (5th century BC) Greek architect. With *Callicrates, Ictinus designed the *Parthenon, the most perfect of classical Greek buildings. He also helped rebuild the Telesterion for the temple at Eleusis and possibly designed the temple of Apollo Epicurius at Bassae.

id In *psychoanalysis, the part of the unconscious mind that is governed by irrational instinctive forces, such as *libido and *aggression. These forces seek immediate (actual or symbolic) relief and the id is therefore said to be ruled by the pleasure principle and not by reality or logic. *See also* ego; superego; unconscious.

Ida, Mount (Turkish name: Kaz Dağı) A mountain range in NW Asian Turkey, rising to 5797 ft (1767 m). It was important in classical times as it overlooks the plain on which Troy was built.

Idaho A state in the NW, dominated by the N Rocky Mountains. It is bordered by Montana and Wyoming on the E, Utah and Nevada on the S, Oregon and Washington on the W, and British Columbia, Canada, on the N. The valley of the Snake River, famous for its canyons and cataracts, lies in the S of the state. The most spectacular of the river's gorges, Hell's Canyon (7000 ft; 2135 m), is the deepest on the North American continent. Most of the population (70%) lives in the vicinity of the Snake, and the state is sparsely populated. Much of the land is under the control of the federal government in the form of national parks, including Yellowstone National Park. The state is primarily agricultural. On the better soils potatoes (Idaho potatoes are particularly important) are grown while the poorer land supports herds of beef cattle and sheep. Rich in minerals, Idaho is a leading US producer of silver and antimony. Natural gas and oil are increasingly exploited. Idaho is heavily forested, and lumbering is an important activity in the upland regions. *History*: probably first visited by members of the Lewis and Clark expedition in 1805. Fur trappers soon entered the region, establishing trading posts. What is now Idaho belonged to the Oregon Territory, acquired by the US in 1846. The discovery of gold and silver in the 1860s brought a wave of settlers, and labor disputes in the mines dominated the late 19th century. Many of the new settlers also took up ranching and lumbering at the same time. The arrival of the railroads spurred the growth of cities. Idaho became a state in 1890 and has enjoyed prosperity in the 20th century. The state's vast water resources (it has 10 major rivers) have been converted into hydroelectric power with the building of huge dams. From the 1980s environmental issues relating to water pollution and waste disposal and management and conservation of Idaho's natural resources became important. Area: 83,557 sq mi (216,412 sq km). Population (1990): 1,006,749. Capital: Boise.

ide. *See* orfe.

ideal gas A hypothetical gas that exactly obeys the ideal gas equation (*see* gas laws). Such a gas has no intermolecular forces and the volume of its molecules is negligible. Also known as a perfect gas, it is closely approximated by real gases at low pressure.

idealism Any doctrine that equates reality with mind, spirit, person, soul, thought, or, as in *Plato, archetypal ideas. *Berkeley was an idealist in holding that all we perceive is sensible ideas. He escaped from *solipsism on the ground that other people were, like himself, spirits—ideas in the mind of God, perceivers of the collections of ideas that were "material objects." In the early 18th century the term came to be used for the belief that the world of common sense was only a projection of our minds. Later it was publicized by *Kant, who called his theory of knowledge "transcendental idealism," the view that the synthetic knowable is confined to the world of phenomena as contrasted with the real world of ideas, or things-in-themselves. *Hegel's absolute idealism conceived the real as being perfect, whole, and complete. *Bradley postulated that there are degrees of truth. It is Hegelian idealism that has led to the organic theory of the state (*see also* Hegelianism).

ideographic writing systems (*or* ideography) Writing systems in which each concept is represented by a symbol. All ideographic systems were probably derived from *pictographic writing systems, stylized representations of abstract concepts being added to the list of symbols. Languages such as Chinese still use ideographic writing systems. However, the huge number of symbols required to represent even a practical selection of the words in a language places a great strain on a person's memory, and hinders the acquisition of literacy skills. Moreover, ideographic systems are inflexible and cannot easily represent new coinages, words borrowed from foreign languages, etc. They have, therefore, been largely replaced by the more efficient phonetic writing systems (*see* alphabets).

Idomeneus In Greek legend, a king of Crete, grandson of *Minos. He was a suitor of *Helen and fought in the *Trojan War. On returning to Crete he killed his son, having sworn to Poseidon to sacrifice the first being he met. Thereafter he lived in exile in Italy.

If A French islet in the Gulf of Lyons. Its 16-century fortress, Château d'If, was used as a state prison and made famous by Alexandre Dumas in *The Count of Monte Cristo*.

Ife 7 33N 4 34E A city in SW Nigeria. It is the holy city of Yoruba tribe and is famed for its terra-cotta and bronze pieces. Today it is primarily an agricultural trade center, the chief products being cocoa and cotton. It contains the University of Ife (1961). Population (1992 est): 269,000.

Ifni An area in Morocco, on the Atlantic coast. First settled by the Spanish (1476), it formed part of the Spanish West Africa (1946) and was returned to Morocco in 1969. Chief town: Sidi Ifni.

igloo A temporary dome-shaped dwelling made from blocks of snow by Eskimos. The blocks are cut with a long knife and the joints filled with snow. The igloo is entered by a low and narrow semicylindrical passageway about 10 ft (3 m) long.

Ignatiev, Nikolai Pavlovich, Count (1832–1908) Russian diplomat, who was instrumental in expanding Russian interests into the Far East and the Balkans. After successful diplomatic missions to Bukhara and China (1858–60), Ignatiev served as ambassador to Turkey (1864–77). In 1878 he negotiated the Treaty of *San Stefano, which ended the Russo-Turkish War. He was subsequently minister of the interior (1881–82).

Ignatius of Antioch, St (1st century AD) Christian martyr; Bishop of Antioch. Little is known of his life apart from a series of famous letters to Churches in Rome and Asia Minor, written while he was a prisoner on his way to Rome to be executed. They are a valuable source of information on the beliefs and organization of the early Church. Feast day: Feb 1.

Ignatius Loyola, St (1491–1556) Spanish founder of the *Jesuits. Of noble birth, his deep interest in religion dated from 1521, after reading the life of Christ while convalescing from a war wound. After visiting the Holy Land (1523), he studied in Spain and in Paris. There, in 1534 he made vows of poverty, chastity, and obedience, with St *Francis Xavier and other followers. He was ordained in 1537 and then moved to Rome, where he founded the Society of Jesus with the approval of Pope Paul III in 1540. As its first superior general, he sent out missionaries to Japan, India, and Brazil and founded Jesuit schools. His *Spiritual Exercises* (1548) has had lasting influence on the Roman Catholic Church. Feast day: July 31.

igneous rock One of the three major categories of rock (*compare* metamorphic rock, sedimentary rock) consisting mostly of crystalline rocks cooled directly from magma. That cooled at the surface forms extrusive rocks—volcanic lavas with small crystals because they have cooled rapidly (*see also* pyroclastic rock). Some extrusive rocks, such as obsidian, are like glass. Igneous rocks cooled at depth are called intrusive or plutonic. They have larger crystals, granite being a common example. A third category contains the hypabyssal rocks, cooled in dikes or sills at intermediate depth and usually having intermediate crystal sizes, for example dolerite. Silica is the dominant chemical constituent of igenous rocks and the silica content, resulting from the chemical composition of the magma from which the rock cooled, determines whether the rock is acidic (over 66% silica), intermediate (55–66%), basic (45–55%), or ultrabasic (under 45%).

ST IGNATIUS LOYOLA *An engraving after a painting by Rubens. The Latin motto is* Ad Maiorem Dei Gloriam *(To the greater glory of God).*

ignis fatuus (*or* will-o'-the-wisp) A phenomenon sometimes observed on marshy ground or graveyards, appearing as a small bluish light. It is believed to be the flame of burning marsh gas (mostly methane), ignited by traces of hydrogen phosphide sometimes found near decaying organic matter.

Iguacú Falls (*or* Iguassú Falls) 25 35S 54 22W A waterfall in South America, on the border between Brazil and Argentina on the Rio Iguaçú. The spectacular falls are divided by forested rocky islands and are a major tourist attraction. Height: 269 ft (82 m). Width: about 2.5 mi (4 km).

iguana A lizard belonging to the predominantly New World family *Iguanidae* (700 species), comprising desert-dwelling, arboreal, and amphibious species. The green common iguana (*Iguana iguana*) reaches a length of 6 ft (1.8 m) including the long tail (about 4 ft [1.3 m]) and has a short spiny crest along the back; males have a dewlap beneath the throat. They feed on vegetation and are excellent swimmers. The marine iguana (*Amblyrhynchus cristatus*) of the Galapagos is the only lizard that feeds in the sea. *See also* anole; basilisk; chuckwalla.

Iguanodon A large dinosaur that lived in the Jurassic and Cretaceous periods (200–65 million years ago). It stood on powerful hind legs about 16 ft (5 m) tall and measured 36 ft (11 m) from its head to the tip of its heavy balancing tail. Iguanodons were herbivorous, tearing off leaves with their tongues and cutting them with bladelike teeth. Order: **Ornithischia*.

Iguvine tablets Nine inscribed bronze plaques, discovered (1444) at Gubbio (ancient Iguvium) in central Italy. Seven survive, containing ritual records of a priestly brotherhood between 400 and 90 BC. They are important evidence for ancient Italian religion and the extinct Umbrian language.

IJmuiden 52 28N 4 38E A port in the central Netherlands, in North Holland province on the North Sea. It is connected to Amsterdam by canal and has major iron and steel and fishing industries. Population: 66,474.

IJsselmeer (*or* Ysselmeer) A freshwater lake in the NW Netherlands, formed from the S part of the *Zuider Zee by the dam completed in 1932. Out of the original area of 1328 sq mi (3440 sq km) much of the planned 888 sq mi (2300 sq km) has already been drained and cultivated.

Ik A small tribe of N Uganda, also known as the Teuso. They are one of the remnants of the original East African hunter-gatherers of Paleolithic times. Their language is unrelated to any other. Recently resettled and forbidden to hunt game they adopted farming but unsuitable conditions and lack of agricultural knowledge have resulted in rapid social and moral disintegration.

ikebana The art of Japanese flower arrangement, first practiced in Japan in the 6th century for Buddhist rituals. Thereafter it evolved into a formal art, being practiced only by men until the 19th century. Famous styles of ikebana include the *shoka*, developed in the 18th century and using three asymmetrically arranged branches.

Ikhnaton. *See* Akhenaton.

Ikhwan, al- (Arabic: the Brethren) Arabian tribesmen united to extend the power of *Ibn Saud in Arabia between 1912 and 1930. Ibn Saud organized the Ikhwan in encampments and with their military help conquered most of Arabia. They then attempted revolt but were defeated by Ibn Saud at the battle of Sabala (1929). He later incorporated the Ikhwan into the National Guard of Saudi Arabia.

Île-de-France A former province in N France, surrounding Paris and enclosed by the Seine, Marne, Beuvronne, Thève, and Oise rivers. It was made a dukedom during the 9th century AD. Following the French Revolution it was divided into departments.

Ilesha 7 38N 4 45E A city in SW Nigeria. Cocoa is exported from there and it is the center of a gold-mining area. Population (1975 est): 224,000.

Ilhéus 14 50S 39 06W A port in E Brazil, in Bahía state on the Atlantic Ocean. Formerly an important export center for cocoa, chief exports now include timber and piassava. Population (1975 est): 119,488.

Ilipa, Battle of (206 BC) A battle in S Spain between *Scipio Africanus and the Carthaginians. Scipio's victory established Roman control of Spain, opening the way for his invasion of Africa.

Illinois A group of Algonkian-speaking North American Indian tribes of Wisconsin, Illinois, Missouri, and Iowa. Their villages were of rush-mat-covered dwellings, each housing several families. Separate chiefs were responsible for matters of war and for civil affairs. Men hunted forest game and prairie bison. Women cultivated maize and corn. The Illinois were much reduced in population through wars with other tribes and eventually dispersed from their territory.

Illinois A state in the Midwest. It is bounded by Wisconsin to the N; the S tip of Lake Michigan forms a 60-mi (95-km) border in the NE; Indiana lies directly to the E and Kentucky to the SE and S, where the Ohio River forms the boundary; Missouri and Iowa lie to the W with the Mississippi River forming the boundary. Illinois consists largely of flat prairies drained by over 275 rivers, most notably the Illinois and the Kaskoskia. Approximately half its population is concentrated in the Chicago metropolitan area, the principal grain market of the US interior. Primarily an agricultural state, its farmers are major producers of soybeans, as well as maize, corn, pork, beef, and dairy products. Manufacturing includes machine tools, electrical machinery, printing and publishing, chemicals, iron and steel, motor vehicles, and food processing. It is also an important coal-mining state. A deep division exists between upstate Illinois, which contains the Chicago metropolitan area, and the predominantly rural area downstate. *History*: the area was inhabited by Illinois, Fox, and Sac Indians in the 17th century when the French first visited what is now Illinois. Marquette and Jolliet and La Salle subsequently conducted explorations of the region. It formed part of the French province of Louisiana but was ceded to Britain (1763) after the French and Indian Wars. It came under US control (1783) after the American Revolution, becoming a territory in 1809 and a state in 1818. The Black Hawk War (1832) marked the final subjugation of the Indians in Illinois. The Illinois and Michigan Canal (1848) ensured the importance of Illinois as a national transportation center by linking Lake Michigan with the Mississippi River. Abraham Lincoln began his political career in Illinois and in the 1858 senatorial race the now famous debates between Lincoln and Stephen A. Douglas on the slavery issue won national attention. Lincoln went on to become president in 1861 and although Illinois entered the Civil War on the Union side, the populace was divided on the states' rights and slavery questions. Bitter labor disputes characterized the 19th century, but as a consequence Illinois became one of the bellwether states in workers' rights legislation. In 1958 the completion of the St Lawrence Seaway linked Illinois to the Atlantic, making Chicago an important overseas shipping center. Area: 56,400 sq mi (146,075 sq km). Population (1990): 11,430,602. Capital: Springfield.

Illinois River A river in NE Illinois southwest of Joliet. Formed by the function of the Des Plaines and Kankakee rivers, it flows SW to the Mississippi River at Grafton, Ill. It is part of the Illinois Waterway, a barge system that begins in Chicago. Length: 273 mi (440 km).

illiteracy The inability to read or write. The ever-increasing demands of a technological society and the concomitant need for a numerate and literate population has led to a growing awareness of the scale of the problem. Anti-illiteracy campaigns are generally run by voluntary helpers.

ILLUMINATED MANUSCRIPTS *An elaborate capital C from an English writing master's copy sheet (c. 1600).*

illuminated manuscripts Manuscripts of gospels, books of hours, prayers, etc., decorated with designs in opaque or transparent watercolor and frequently gold leaf. The art was first practiced by monastic scribes in the early Middle Ages, as in the 8th-century Book of Kells. Although it began as the elaboration of capital letters and decoration of margins, by the time printing was invented (mid-15th century) it had become a form of miniature painting, perfected by professional illuminators. The Duke of Berry's book of hours by the de *Limburg brothers is an outstanding example of late medieval illumination. Such illumination laid the basis for medieval panel painting.

Illyria The Adriatic coastal region W of the Balkans. Inhabited from the 10th century BC by warlike but independent tribes, Illyria constantly harassed Macedonia and Epirus, expanding when their power declined. Piratical raids in the Adriatic provoked Roman intervention from 228 BC and Illyria became the Roman province of Illyricum in 167 BC.

ilmenite A black metallic mineral of composition $FeTiO_3$, found in basic igneous rocks, in veins, and as a detrital mineral in sand. It is an ore of titanium.

Iloilo 10 41N 122 33E A port in the central Philippines, in SE Panay. The island's commercial center, famed for its fabrics, it exports sugar and rice. Population (1980): 244,211.

Ilorin 8 32N 4 34E A city in W Nigeria. It is an important trading center for local agricultural and manufactured products, with modern industries producing sugar, matches, and cigarettes. Its university was founded in 1976. Population (1975 est): 282,000.

Ilyushin, Sergei Vladimirovich (1894–1977) Soviet aircraft designer. He first became known for the Il-2 Stormovik, a dive bomber widely used by the Soviet Union during World War II. He later worked on commercial aircraft, designing the jet airliner Il-62.

imaginary number. *See* numbers; complex numbers.

imagism A literary movement begun in Britain in 1909 that was dedicated to composing poetry characterized by the concise expression of pure visual images. It profoundly influenced British and American poetry for a decade. Its theories derived from criticism of T. E. *Hulme, who rejected the prevailing sentimental romanticism in favor of clarity and hardness. *Des Imagistes* (1914), an anthology edited by Ezra Pound, included poems by Richard Aldington, Hilda Doolittle (H. D.), John Gould Fletcher, and Amy Lowell, who succeeded Pound as leader of the movement.

imago (zoology) The sexually mature adult form of any insect.

imam (Arabic: leader) A Muslim title. **1.** Among Shiite Muslims, the title of the successors of Mohammed, who must be descendants of the fourth caliph *Ali. The imams were regarded as infallible and exercised complete authority. Various Shiite sects recognize different lines of imams and believe that the last of the line (usually considered either the 7th or the 12th after Ali) will return at the end of time. **2.** A title often used by the caliphs and also honorifically given to certain religious leaders, such as *Abu Hanifah. **3.** The title of the leader of prayers in a mosque.

Imbros. *See* Imroz.

Imhotep (c. 2600 BC) Egyptian physician, architect, and adviser to pharaoh *Djoser of the 3rd dynasty. Revered in later times as a healer and magician, Imhotep was eventually deified. He was identified with Asclepius by the Greeks.

Immaculate Conception A dogma of the Roman Catholic Church stating that the Virgin Mary was conceived free from *original sin. It had long been a belief, connected with the feast of the Conception of the Blessed Virgin Mary (Dec 8), which had been celebrated since 1471; but it was the subject of controversy and was opposed by prominent theologians, such as St Bonaventure and St Thomas Aquinas. It was promulgated as dogma in 1854 by Pope Pius IX.

immigration. *See* migration, human.

Immigration and Naturalization Service US Department of Justice division that oversees aliens. It was established in 1891 to enforce the laws that provided for naturalization or deportation of immigrants to the US.

immortelle. *See* everlasting flowers.

immunity In medicine, resistance to infection. Nonspecific immunity is achieved by such agents as polymorphic white blood cells (which engulf invading bacteria) and *interferon, but the term immunity usually refers to that specifically acquired due to the presence of *antibodies. This may be passive, when antibodies derived from another individual are introduced into the body. For example, newborn babies have a temporary passive immunity from antibodies transferred from the mother's blood through the placenta. Active immunity is produced when an individual forms his (or her) own antibodies after exposure to an antigen, such as occurs following an infection. There are two different kinds of immune response produced by antibodies derived from two populations of lymphocytes (white blood cells). Cell-mediated immunity is due to activity of the T-lymphocytes (produced by or dependent on the *thymus). In the presence of antigens these lymphocytes produce cells with antibody bound to their surface. They can attack whole cells and are responsible for such reactions as graft rejection, allergic responses, and delayed hypersensitivity reactions. Humoral immunity is produced by the B-lymphocytes, so called because they are formed in an organ in chickens called the bursa of Fabricius. In man they are probably formed by lymphatic tissue in the gut. B-lymphocytes produce cells that release free antibody into the blood, neutralizing bacterial toxins and coating bacteria to facilitate their ingestion by the polymorphic blood cells.

immunization The production of immunity by artificial means. This may be achieved by injecting antibodies against specific diseases (e.g. tetanus and diphtheria), providing temporary passive immunity, or by *vaccination to produce active immunity.

immunology The study of the biological processes by which the body reacts to foreign substances. This includes the action of *antibodies both in protecting the body against infection (*see* immunity) and in rejecting foreign tissues (*see* transplantation). Immunologists are also concerned with disorders of the immune system, including *allergy and *autoimmunity.

immunosuppression The condition in which the *immunity of the body is reduced. This can occur in various diseases (e.g. leukemia and severe infections) or it may be deliberately induced by certain drugs (e.g. azathioprine and cyclophosphamide). Immunosuppressive drugs are administered after transplant surgery to enable the body to accept the foreign tissue or organ; they are also used to treat rheumatoid arthritis and other conditions associated with *autoimmunity.

impala A common antelope, *Aepyceros melampus*, of central and S African savanna. About 40 in (100 cm) high at the shoulder, impalas have a red-brown coat and white underparts; males have lyre-shaped ridged horns. In the rutting season the herds, numbering several hundred, break up into smaller groups, each led by a mature male. Impala are known for their agile springing leaps, which are most marked when the animals are alarmed.

Impatiens A genus of annual and perennial herbaceous plants (about 700 species), widely distributed in temperate and tropical regions. They have irregular often spurred flowers and (usually) fleshy stems. The genus include *touch-me-not and various cultivated species, such as the garden *balsam and busy Lizzies—red-, pink-, purple-, and orange-flowered hybrids that are popular pot plants. Family: *Balsaminaceae.*

IMPALA *These antelopes usually remain within the cover of dense trees and bushes, like this male. When disturbed they can leap to a height of 10 ft (3m), covering a distance of over 30 ft (9 m).*

impeachment A criminal proceeding against a public official. Under the Constitution (Article I), the House of Representatives has the sole power to impeach a federal officeholder, such as the president or vice president, and the Senate has the sole power to try the accused. Pres. Andrew *Johnson was impeached (1868) by the House and acquitted by the Senate.

impedance A measure of the ability of a circuit to resist the flow of an alternating current. It is given by $Z = R + iX$, where Z is the impedance, R is the *resistance, and X is the reactance. The reactance of an inductance L is ωL and that of a capacitance C is $1/\omega C$, where ω is the angular frequency. Impedance and reactance are measured in *ohms.

imperial cities The German cities of the Holy Roman Empire subject directly to the Emperor (by whose officials they were governed). They grew in number during the Middle Ages, when cities took advantage of political disturbance to assert their freedom. Those that survived flourished, forming themselves into leagues (of which the *Hanseatic League was the most important) and from

1489 were represented in the imperial diet (assembly). In subsequent centuries most cities lost their free status and were incorporated into the provinces; only Hamburg and Bremen maintain their free status today.

Imperial Conferences Meetings between the British government and representatives of the self-governing dominions held between 1907 and 1937 to discuss questions of common interest. Imperial Conferences discussed such matters as migration, naturalization, defense, trade, intraimperial relations, and dominion status. The last Conference discussed the foreign policy of the newly established *Commonwealth of Nations. The Conferences gave way during World War II to the meetings of Commonwealth prime ministers. *See also* Ottawa Agreements.

imperialism The territorial expansion of a nation and its domination over other countries. Powerful nations generally formed their empires by conquest until the 19th century, when imperialism became an economic policy. European powers, especially Britain (*see* Empire, British), ambitious for prestige and anxious for new industrial trading outlets, established their rule over countries in other continents (□Africa). Until World War I ended such imperialism, these countries depended on their rulers for government, commerce, and protection. Since World War II imperialism has been used to describe the efforts of world powers to impose, by persuasion or force, their political ideologies on less prosperous nations.

Imperial Valley A former desert area in S California, now an irrigated valley, part of the Colorado Desert, extending from the Salton Sea to just S of the Mexican border. Watered by the All-American Canal, a man-made outlet of the Colorado River, the valley produces alfalfa, milo, cotton, melon, and garden vegetables.

impetigo A highly infectious skin disease, usually caused by staphylococci. Children are most commonly affected and epidemics may occur in crowded schools. Usually occurring on the face, hands, and knees, it starts with a red mark that develops into a blister, which later forms yellow crusts. Antibiotics, applied locally or internally, will cure the condition.

Imphal 24 47N 93 55E A city in India, the capital of Manipur. During World War II, Imphal was the scene of an Anglo-Indian victory over the Japanese. Population (1991): 196,268.

impotence Sexual inadequacy in men, with failure to achieve or maintain an erection or to ejaculate at orgasm. It may be temporary, resulting from tiredness, illness, drunkenness, depression, or taking certain drugs. Long-term impotence is likely to have a deeper cause reflecting the sufferer's fear of women or of castration. It can usually be treated by specialist counseling or by psychotherapy.

impressionism A French art movement that flourished from the late 1860s to the late 1880s. Its name was derived from Monet's painting *Impression: Sunrise* (1872; Musée Marmottan, Paris), shown at the first of the eight impressionist exhibitions (1874, 1876, 1877, 1879, 1880, 1881, 1882, 1886). The leading impressionists were *Monet, *Pissarro, *Sisley, and *Renoir. Among their many forerunners were *Constable, *Turner, *Boudin, *Daubigny, and *Corot. *Manet shared some of their aims and *Degas, although stylistically independent of them, participated in their exhibitions. Painting mainly in the open air, the impressionists aimed to capture fleeting effects of light and weather in paint with dabs of bright color and a minimum of drawing.

imprinting In *ethology, a rapid and irreversible form of learning that takes place in some animals in the first hours of life. Animals attach themselves in this way to whatever creatures they are exposed to at that time—usually, but not necessarily, their mothers. This type of behavior was first described by Konrad *Lorenz working with newly hatched ducks and geese.

inbreeding Mating between closely related individuals. (The term is also used for self-fertilization in plants). Inbreeding often occurs in small isolated populations of organisms. The effect is to increase the tendency for harmful *recessive genes to express themselves among the population, thus affecting the fitness and survival of individuals. For example, inbreeding in rats reduces fertility and increases mortality. In human societies close inbreeding is prevented by custom and law (*see* incest).

incandescent lamp An electric lamp in which light is produced by passing an electric current through a filament, usually inside a glass bulb containing an inert gas. The filament, of tungsten in the common lightbulb, is heated to over 4717°F (2600°C) so that it glows with a white light.

Incarnation A central tenet of Christian belief, that the second person of the Trinity took human form and became man. Although in other religions gods temporarily appear in human form (i.e. a theophany), in Christianity the Incarnation is a unique event occurring at a particular time; the union of the divine and human in Christ is permanent and the integrity of both the divine and human natures is maintained. The doctrine is stated in the opening of the Gospel of St John and in St Paul's Epistle to the Colossians and was further defined by the Councils of *Nicaea (325) and *Chalcedon (451).

Incas A Quechua-speaking South American Indian people of the Peruvian Andes. From their capital of *Cuzco, they established, during the 15th century, an empire extending from Ecuador to central Chile. It was destroyed in the 16th century by the Spaniards. The Incas assimilated much of the culture of such people as the *Chimu, whom they conquered. Their hierarchical society, ruled by the king of Inca and a class of aristocratic officials, was highly centralized. Although the wheel and writing were unknown, imperial messengers and an extensive road system enabled the ruler to maintain contact with all parts of his empire. The complex religion was concerned with the propitiation of the sun god Inti, object of the state cult, the creator god Viracocha (*see also* Kon-Tiki), the rain god Apu Ilapu, and others. *See also* Machu Picchu.

incense A mixture of gums and spices (especially gum benzoin) that is burned for its aroma (*see also* frankincense). It was employed in pagan rituals in ancient Egypt, Greece, and Rome as well as in Judaic ritual and was a valued trade commodity. In the Book of Revelation it is a symbol of the prayers of saints and has been used in Christian worship since the 6th century AD. It is used predominantly by the Orthodox and Roman Catholic Churches. The vessel for burning incense is called a censer or thurible.

incense cedar A conifer, *Calocedrus* (or *Libocedrus*) *decurrens*, native to W North America and planted for ornament in Europe, where it is usually narrow and columnar and may reach a height of 148 ft (45 m). It has small scalelike leaves covering the twigs and branches and bright-yellow pointed cones, 0.8 in (2 cm) long, which split open to release the seeds. Family: *Cupressaceae* (cypress family).

incest Proscribed sexual relations between close kin. Such proscriptions are universal, but vary considerably in terms of the categories of kin to which they apply. The most common and universal prohibitions apply to members of the same nuclear family, such as relations between parents and children and between brothers and sisters. These taboos, founded in folklore, have a sound basis in genetics (unfavorable recessive genes can become dominant when consanguineous relatives breed). However, folklore is not always a reliable guide to what constitutes consanguinity, as in the case of taboos forbidding marriage between a man and his mother-in-law.

Inchcape Rock. *See* Bell Rock.

Inchŏn 37 30N 126 38E A city in NW South Korea, Seoul's main seaport on the Yellow Sea. It has a private university (1954). A UN attack there (1950) during the Korean War halted the North Korean invasion. Population (1990): 1,818,293.

income tax A direct tax on income and a major source of government revenue in many countries. In most countries, including the US, it is a progressive tax (the rate charged increasing with the taxable income) in which a certain amount can be earned without attracting tax. Thus, those with higher incomes pay more tax in proportion to their incomes than the lower paid; therefore the tax, to a certain extent, balances unequal distribution of incomes in the community. However, it acts as a disincentive to increasing income and makes it difficult for the low paid to escape from poverty. Income tax makes no distinction between income that is spent and income that is invested (furthering the productive potential of the economy); higher indirect taxation and lower direct taxation is advocated as a remedy for this disadvantage.

incunabula Books printed during the infancy of modern printing (before 1500) after the invention of movable type by *Gutenberg. N European incunabula have a heavy type design known as black letter; Italian books have a more elegant roman typeface; both were based on current manuscript writing. Paper leaves and a binding of calf leather over wooden boards were usual. Editions were small (200–500), the preferred subjects being religious or scientific.

Independence 39 04N 94 27W A city in Missouri. Situated in an agricultural area, its industries include oil refining and cement. It was the home of Pres. Harry S. Truman. Population (1990): 112,301.

Independence Day The national holiday of the US. It marks the anniversary of the adoption of the *Declaration of Independence by the Continental Congress on July 4, 1776.

indeterminacy principle. *See* Heisenberg uncertainty principle.

indexation. *See* price index.

Index Librorum Prohibitorum (Latin: *Index of Prohibited Books*) In the Roman Catholic Church, a list of publications considered dangerous to spiritual well-being and not to be read without a bishop's permission. The first formal list of this sort was produced under Pope Paul IV (1555–59); a more comprehensive guide was issued in 1564. The Second *Vatican Council (1962–65) resolved that no new revisions should be undertaken, and the specific limitation on suitable reading is no longer in effect.

India, Republic of (Hindi name: Bharat) A country in S Asia, the seventh largest in the world and the second most populous. Bordering on Pakistan, China, Nepal, Bhutan, Bangladesh, and Myanmar (formerly Burma), it comprises 22 states and 9 Union Territories, reorganized since 1946 according to linguistic groupings. The Himalayas, in which the Ganges River rises, form a natural barrier to the N. Central India consists of a plateau (the Deccan), flanked by the mountains of the Western and Eastern Ghats. N of this lies the Indo-Gangetic plain, with the Thar Desert in the W. The population comprises many ethnic and cultural groups and about 1600 languages and dialects are spoken. The chief religions are Hinduism (83% of the population) and Islam (11%). The *caste system still survives, although untouchability has been abolished. *Economy*: helped by foreign aid, 70% of the workforce is engaged in agriculture,

with rice, pulses, and cereals as the main food crops; tea, jute, cotton, and tobacco are also important. Despite land irrigation and reclamation, production is
hampered by floods, droughts, insufficient mechanization, and the small size of
agricultural units; food supplies are therefore inadequate for the country's needs.
Fishing and forestry are also important. India's large mineral resources include
iron ore, manganese, bauxite, mica, and ilmenite. Coal is mined, oil is produced
from the Arabian Sea, and India also has nuclear power. Industry, much of it
state owned, employs only 10% of the workforce, but India is the world's 10th
greatest industrial power. Industries include steel, chemicals, electronics, cotton
and silk textiles, and handicrafts. The new economic policy of 1977 channeled
resources into agriculture and aimed to stimulate rural employment by allowing
new capital-intensive industries to be established only for goods that could not
be produced by cottage or small-scale industries. Chief exports are cotton
goods, tea, leather, iron ore, and jute, while chief imports are petroleum, wheat,
and machinery. _History_: the *Indus Valley was the site of a civilization for a millenium before the invading Aryans established theirs (c. 1500) between the
Indus and the Ganges. From this civilization Hinduism evolved and it has remained India's dominant religion. The Mauryan Empire followed (c. 320–c. 185
BC), which unified most of India. The 4th–6th centuries AD saw a flowering of
Hindu culture in the N under the *Gupta dynasty. Muslim raids on the N from
the 10th century culminated in the establishment of a Muslim sultanate based on
Delhi (1129), under which much of India was again unified. A later Muslim invasion resulted in the magnificent *Mogul Empire (established 1526). At this
time Europeans were also arriving. The British *East India Company, grown
powerful in the 17th century, fought with French traders in the 18th century for a
monopoly as the Mogul Empire declined. With Robert Clive's victory at
*Plassey (1757), the British established their supremacy and from 1784 a series
of *Government of India Acts shifted power from the East India Company to the
British government. Some of the territory was directly administered by Britain
and came to be called British India. The rest of India was administered by Indian
princes, with Britain only exercising general supervision; such areas were called
princely states. The Indian economy suffered under British trading arrangements, which allowed British goods into India duty free but barred Indian goods
from Great Britain by high tariffs, thus provoking social and political unrest.
After the *Indian Mutiny (1857–59) reforms were introduced, including the
transfer of the East India Company's administrative powers to the India Office,
represented by a viceroy and provincial governors. Subsequent reforms allowed
greater Indian involvement in government, and in 1919 a parliament was created, the majority of members of which were elected. However, the nationalist
movement (_see_ Indian National Congress) became increasingly forceful in its
demand for home rule and, under the leadership of Mahatma *Gandhi, pursued a
policy of civil disobedience. During World War II Gandhi and other Nationalist
leaders were imprisoned for refusing to support Britain unless independence
was immediately granted. This was finally achieved in 1947 on condition that a
Muslim state should be established to satisfy the Muslim faction, active since
the late 19th century (_see_ Muslim League). The creation of *Pakistan (1947)
was followed by violent upheavals in which five hundred thousand people were
killed and by war between the two countries over Kashmir. Trouble between
Hindus and Muslims continued, with riots in 1978, while hostility between India
and Pakistan erupted again in 1965 and 1971 (_see also_ Bangladesh). India,
which became a sovereign state in 1950, has been consolidated by the incorpo-
ration of former French and Portuguese territories (1956 and 1961) and the in-
clusion of Sikkim (1975), although the Kashmir question has not yet been settled. Nevertheless, economic problems and the difficulty of dealing with the

large population, coupled with inefficient or corrupt administrations, aggravated separatist and terrorist reactions, especially during the 1970s. Indira *Gandhi, who served as prime minister from 1966–77 and was returned to power in 1980, sometimes dealt forcefully with the problems confronting her. In 1984 she suppressed a movement of militant Sikhs advocating autonomy for Punjab. Later that year Mrs Gandhi was assassinated by Sikh members of her bodyguard. She was succeeded by her son, Rajiv Gandhi. In the December 1984 elections, voters rallied behind candidates allied with Rajiv Gandhi, who remained prime minister. In 1989, however, he lost the election and was succeeded by Vishwanath Pratap Singh, whose government collapsed in 1990; subsequently, Chandra Shekhar was elected prime minister. In 1991, Rajiv Gandhi was assassinated by a bomb while campaigning for a return to leadership. P. V. Narasimha Rao of the Congress (I) party became the new prime minister and faced economic problems and ethnic strife during his first two years in office. Official languages: Hindi and English. Official currency: Indian rupee of 100 paise. Area: 1,269,072 sq mi (3,287,590 sq km), including Jammu and Kashmir. Population (1991): 844,000,000. Capital: New Delhi.

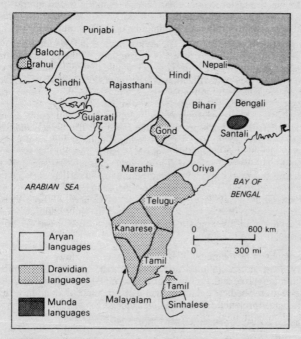

INDIA *The distribution of major language groups in the Indian subcontinent.*

Indiana A state in the Midwest, forming part of the Mississippi Basin. It is largely undulating prairie with glacial lakes in the N. Agriculture is important in the fertile central plain, the major crops being soybeans, corn, wheat, and vegetables (especially tomatoes); pigs are the primary livestock. Its manufacturing industry, concentrated in the NW, near Lake Michigan, produces steel, diamond tools, agricultural machinery, motor vehicles, and domestic appliances. Coal and building stone are also exploited. It is an important transport center with the Ohio River linking Indiana with the Mississippi River and Lake Michigan giving access to the Great Lakes and thereby to the St Lawrence Seaway. *History*: explored by the French in the 17th century, the area was ceded to Britain in 1763. During the American Revolution, US troops occupied the region. Increased settlement followed a defeat of the Indians (1794), and Indiana became a territory in 1800. The Indians were subdued by 1811, and Indiana became a state in 1816. The state remained primarily agricultural and rural until the 20th century, when industrialization grew rapidly. Area: 36,291 sq mi (93,993 sq km). Population (1990): 5,544,159. Capital: Indianapolis.

Indian Affairs, Bureau of (BIA) US Department of the Interior division that oversees Indian reservations. It was established in 1832 as part of the War Department to supervise the removal of Indians to reservations and a new lifestyle. Transferred to the Department of the Interior in 1849, it manages the reservations and educates Indians.

Indianapolis 39 45N 86 10W A city in the US, the capital of Indiana. A rail, road, and air center, its varied manufactures include car and aircraft parts and chemicals. It is the scene of annual speedway races, including the **Indianapolis 500**, a 500-mile race for 33 cars first held in 1911. Population (1990): 731,327.

Indian art and architecture The styles evolved in the Indian subcontinent. Evidence for many older art forms is incomplete, as the hostile climate militates against the survival of objects in perishable materials, such as wood. The art of the *Indus Valley civilization is best represented by carved steatite sealstones and miniature sculptures and its architecture by the massive brick ruins at *Harappa and *Mohenjo-Daro. Between about 324 and 185 BC the characteristic Buddhist architectural form of the *stupa appeared, decorated with stone or stucco reliefs depicting scenes from the Buddha's life. Greek and Roman influence is apparent in the art of the N Indian Buddhist kingdom of Gandhara (1st–7th centuries AD). The 10th-century Muslim invasions drove indigenous art to the S. The central spire of Hindu temples became increasingly massive, symbolizing the mythological cosmic mountain; luxuriant carvings, often of erotic scenes, covered every available surface, as in the 13th-century Sun Temple at Konarak (Orissa). The Tamil kingdom of Cola (c. 850–1279) is famous for its exquisite small bronzes. With the spread of Mogul dominance, *Mogul art and architecture became the main tradition until that too declined under British rule.

Indian corn. *See* maize.

Indian hemp A North American perennial herb, *Apocynum cannabinum*, that grows to a height of 5 ft (1.5 m) and bears small greenish-white flowers. The stem fibers were used by Indians to make matting and ropes and the dried roots have medicinal properties. Family: *Apocynaceae*.

True *hemp is also sometimes called Indian hemp.

Indian languages A classification based on the geographically defined area of the Indian subcontinent. Within this area are found languages of widely differing origins. The two major language families to be found are the *Indo-European and the *Dravidian. On the NW borders of India, Baluchi and *Pashto, members of the *Iranian subgroup of the Indo-European family, are spoken. Most of the other Indo-European languages of India are of the *Indo-Aryan subgroup. This includes the lingua franca Hindustani; *Hindi, the official national language; Rajasthani, *Punjabi, *Gujarati, and *Sindhi in the west; *Bengali and *Bihari in the east; and Kashmiri. Most of S India is covered by the Dravidian language family. In addition to these two large families, there are scattered languages of the *Munda group in the NE, and languages of *Sino-Tibetan origins are spoken in the Himalayas.

Indian licorice An Indian plant, *Abrus precatorius*, the roots of which have been used as a substitute for licorice although they contain poisonous resins. The poisonous red and black seeds are used to make necklaces and as weights. Family: *Leguminosae*.

Indian literature Sanskrit literature, the most important division of ancient Indian literature, is divided into three periods: the Vedic period (c. 1500–c. 200 BC), during which the vast and complex sacred literature of Hinduism was accumulated (*see* Vedas; Upanishads); the Epic period (c. 400 BC–c. 400 AD), in which the great Indian epic, the *Mahabharata*, which includes the *Bhagavad Gita*, and the shorter epic, the *Ramayana*, were composed; and the Classical period (from c. 200 AD), characterized by various literary forms including romances, drama, and lyric poetry. *Kalidasa is considered the greatest writer of this period. During the 19th century various regional vernacular literatures of India developed, adopting new Western forms and reviving traditional ones. Leading writers of this period include the Bengali poet Rabindranath *Tagore and the Urdu poet Muhammad *Iqbal.

Indian Mutiny (1857–59) A revolt of about 35,000 sepoys (Indian soldiers in the service of the British East India Company), which developed into a bloody Anglo-Indian War. It began with a massacre of Europeans at Meerut in May 1857, following which the mutineers captured Delhi. The sepoys then rose in many other N Indian towns and were joined by local princes. Extensive British reinforcements were able under Colin *Campbell to regain Delhi in September and relieve besieged Lucknow in November by July 1858, the revolt had largely been contained. The consequent Government of India Act (1858) transferred the administrative powers of the East India Company to the British crown.

Indian National Congress The political party, founded in 1885, that governed India after the declaration of independence in 1947. Though earlier a moderate party, a section of it took up the cause of home rule in 1917. For the next 20 years, chiefly under the guidance of Mahatma *Gandhi, it advocated noncooperation with the British and in World War II refused to support Britain without being promised Indian independence. The party was led by Jawarhalal *Nehru from 1951 to 1964, by Lal Bahadur Shastri (1904–66) until 1966, and then by Mrs Indira *Gandhi until her assassination in 1984, when the leadership passed to her son Rajiv Gandhi (assassinated 1991).

Indian Ocean The world's third largest ocean, extending between Asia, Africa, Australia, and Antarctica. Lying mainly in the S hemisphere, most is within the tropical and temperate zones. It contains coral and volcanic islands while others, such as the Seychelles, are the peaks of underwater ridges or, like Madagascar, are continental. The ocean floor is extremely rich in minerals.

Indian pipe A fleshy waxy-white to pinkish herb, *Monotropa uniflora*, of North America and Asia, also called corpse plant. Up to 12 in (30 cm) high, it has tiny scalelike leaves, lacks chlorophyll, and obtains nutrients from woodland humus. The stem and single cup-shaped flower resemble a small pipe. Family: *Monotropaceae*.

Indian Removal, Policy of (1830) US program that provided for the removal of Indians in the E to lands W of the Mississippi River. In an effort to prevent hostilities along the expanding US frontier, tribes were moved to Arkansas, Missouri, Iowa, Wisconsin, Minnesota, Kansas, Nebraska, and Oklahoma.

Indian Reorganization Act (Wheeler-Howard Act, 1934) US law designed to encourage Indian self-determination and increase self-sufficiency. It allowed for greater self-government regarding internal affairs and provided funds for credit and education.

Indian Territory The land W of the Mississippi, corresponding to present-day Oklahoma, set aside (1834) for settlement of Indians ejected, sometimes forcibly, from the E. These included the Cherokee, whose journey was known as the Trail of Tears because of the hardships and deaths endured on the way.

indicator A substance used to indicate through changes in color, fluorescence, etc., the presence of another substance or the completion of a chemical reaction. Indicators are usually weak organic acids or bases that yield ions of a different color to the unionized molecule. For example, litmus is red in the presence of acids but blue in the presence of alkalis.

indigestion (*or* dyspepsia) Abdominal discomfort due to disordered digestion. Most people experience indigestion at some time and there is usually no serious cause, but peptic ulcers, a hiatus hernia, and gall bladder disease may all give symptoms that are described as indigestion.

indigo A blue *dye formerly obtained from plants, particularly of the genus *Indigofera*, and present in the woad plant (*Isatis tinctoria*). It is now synthesized from *aniline.

indium (In) A soft silvery metal, named for the bright indigo line in its spectrum. It is used in making transistors, rectifiers, thermistors, and alloys of low melting point. At no 40; at wt 114.82; mp 314°F (156.6°C), bp 2645°F (1450°C).

Indo-Aryan languages A subgroup of the *Indo-Iranian language group, spoken in India, Sri Lanka, and Pakistan. Sometimes called the Indic group, it descends from *Sanskrit, and the earliest Indo-Aryan language dates from about 1100 AD. The most important languages of the group are *Hindi and *Urdu, which are the national languages of India and Pakistan respectively; these are both literary languages with many borrowings of Persian and Arabic words dating from the Mogul period. More colloquial *Hindustani is also a member of this group, as are the widely spiken *Sindhi, *Bengali, *Gujarati, *Punjabi, and Sinhalese. The Dardic (*see* Dards) languages of Pakistan, Afghanistan, and Kashmir, of which the best known is Kashmiri, are often included in the Indo-Aryan group.

Indochina The area of SE Asia comprising present-day *Vietnam, *Kampuchea (formerly Cambodia), and *Laos. It was so called by Europeans because it has been influenced by both Indian and Chinese culture. During the 19th century the French established control over the region, forming (1887) the Union of Indochina from *Cochin China, Cambodia, *Tonkin, and *Annam; Laos was added in 1893. Its capital was Saigon (now Ho Chi Minh City). Except in Cochin China the royal families were retained, although most power lay with the federal government under a French governor general. During World War II the Japanese occupied Tonkin (1940) and then all Indochina (1941). Following Japan's defeat France established the Federation of Indochina, to which Laos and Cambodia submitted while nationalists in Annam, Tonkin, and Cochin China demanded complete independence for a new state of Vietnam (*see* Ho Chi Minh). In 1946 fighting broke out between nationalists (*see* Viet Minh) and the French, the bitter conflict continuing until 1954, when the *Geneva Conference ended French control of Indochina (*see also* Dien Bien Phu).

Indo-European languages The largest language family of the world, sometimes called Indo-Germanic. They are spoken throughout Europe as well as in India, Iran, and in parts of central and E Asia and the family is generally thought to include the following subgroups: *Germanic; *Italic; *Indo-Iranian; *Celtic; *Baltic; Slavid (*see* Slavonic); *Albanian; *Greek; *Armenian; *Tocharian; and *Anatolian. Of these, the oldest recorded is Anatolian and the most recent Albanian. Armenian and Greek are single languages rather than subdivided groups like Indo-Iranian or Germanic. Anatolian and Tocharian are now extinct. The only living languages of Europe that do not come from Indo-European origins are *Turkish, *Finnish, *Hungarian, and *Basque. The Indo-European group relates languages as apparently separate as English, a subgroup of Germanic, and *Sanskrit, an ancestor of modern Indian languages. Most of the research needed to support this wide grouping was done by German philologists in the 19th century, *See also* Indo-Hittite languages.

INDIGO *This ornamental shrub (Indigofera gerardiana) is closely related to the species formerly used as a source of indigo. It has red flowers and silvery branches.*

Indo-Hittite languages A language family proposed by some scholars to include the *Indo-European and *Anatolian languages as subgroups. There has been some confusion about the relation of *Hittite, an Anatolian language, to the Indo-European group. Indo-Hittite has been suggested as an ancestor of both Indo-European and Anatolian. It is more generally accepted that Indo-European is the parent language and Anatolian a subgroup on the same level as the *Celtic or the *Germanic languages.

Indo-Iranian languages A subgroup of the *Indo-European language group, spoken in India, Pakistan, Bangladesh, Nepal, and Sri Lanka. It is subdivided into two branches: *Indo-Aryan and *Iranian. These are among the oldest of the Indo-European group, spoken originally in Turkistan, and there is still much debate about the relation of these languages to the Hittite languages of Anatolia. *Sanskrit was a language of Indo-Iranian origin and the *Romany language spoken by *Gypsies is a member of this group.

Indonesia, Republic of (name from 1798–1945: Dutch East Indies) A country in SE Asia, consisting of a series of islands extending E–W for some 3200 m (5150 km) in the Pacific and Indian Oceans. The main islands are Sumatra, Java and Madura, Bali, Sulawesi, Lombok, the Moluccas, and Timor together with part of Borneo (Kalimantan), and Irian Jaya (the W half of New Guinea). Most of the islands are mountainous and volcanic. Its ethnically diverse population, which belongs mainly to the Malaysian race, may be broadly divided into three main groups: the rice growers of Java and Bali (who make up over half the population), the Islamic coastal peoples, and a group of tribal peoples. The Chinese are the largest nonindigenous group. *Economy*: although rich in natural resources, with large deposits of oil, natural gas, and other minerals as well as some of the richest timber stands in the world, it is a mainly agrarian economy of which the staple crop is rice; cash crops include rubber, palm oil, copra, sugar cane, and coffee. Agricultural output, however, is generally low. The manufacturing sector, which includes shipbuilding, textiles, chemicals, and glass, has been slow to develop. The main exports include oil, timber, and rubber. *History*: in the Middle Ages, kingdoms and empires flourished, including the Hindu Srivijaya empire (7th–13th centuries), based on Palembang, and the Majapahit, which, centered on Java, ruled most of the area in the 15th century. In the 16th century it was occupied successively by the Portuguese, the British, and the Dutch, and from 1602 to 1798 it was ruled by the Dutch East India Company. It became a colony of the Netherlands and, after Japanese occupation during World War II, declared itself a republic in 1945. Dutch colonial interests continued in conflict with the Indonesian nationalists until the country was formally granted independence (1949–50) as a single state. In 1956 ties with the Netherlands were broken off. During the period 1957–65 Dr Sukarno became the central figure pursuing an essentially nationalist policy; Irian Jaya was incorporated in 1963 and there was confrontation with Malaysia (1963–66). A military coup in 1965 under the leadership of General Suharto overthrew Sukarno's moderately right-wing authoritarian government replacing it with a harsh military dictatorship; left-wing elements were virtually eliminated. Despite subsequent moves to increase the number of civilian cabinet ministers, the regime remains predominantly military. Changes in foreign policy have led to an influx of capital from the West and Japan and an improvement in relations with Malaysia, but despite the substantial increases in revenue from oil there has been little change in the standard of living for the majority of the population. By the end of 1977, criticism of the Suharto regime increased and there was a series of student riots. Separatist movements have continued in Irian Jaya and East Timor, which was formally incorporated as a province in 1976. Suharto was elected to his sixth five-year term in 1993. He served as chairman of the nonaligned nations movement in 1991. President: General Suharto. Official language: Bahasa Indonesia. Official currency: rupiah of 100 sen. Area: 735,000 sq mi (1,903,650 sq km). Population (1989 est): 187,726,000. Capital and main port: Jakarta.

Indore 22 42N 75 54E A city in India, in Madhya Pradesh. Formerly the capital of the princely state of Indore, it is an important trading center with cotton mills and engineering works. Its university was established in 1964. Population (1991): 1,086,673.

Indra The principal Hindu deity of the Vedic period, god of war and storm, who slew the dragon Vritra, releasing the fertile water and light necessary to create the universe. He is portrayed as wielding a thunderbolt. In later Hinduism, he is supplanted by *Vishnu, *Shiva, and *Krishna and appears as the relatively powerless ruler of the firmament and the East.

indri The largest Madagascan woolly lemur, *Indri indri*. Up to 26 in (70 cm) long, it is gray and black, with long hind legs, a short tail, and a doglike head. It lives in treetops, eating leaves, and has a loud howling cry. Indris are threatened by the destruction of their forest habitats. Family: *Indriidae*.

induction (electromagnetism). *See* electromagnetic induction.

induction (embryology) The process by which an embryonic tissue influences adjacent cells to develop in a certain way, i.e. to differentiate into a particular adult tissue. Absence of the inducer tissue may result in abnormal development or nondevelopment of the induced cells.

induction (logic) The process of making an empirical generalization by observing particular instances of its operation. The conclusion goes beyond the facts, since not all possible instances can be examined. From induction predictions can be made but they are always liable to falsification. *Compare* deduction.

indulgences In the Roman Catholic Church, remissions of the temporal penalties incurred for sins already forgiven by God in the sacrament of penance. Indulgences are based on the belief that a sin, although forgiven, must still have a penalty on earth or in purgatory. The Church may remit these penalties by virtue of the merits of Christ and the saints. The practice of indulgences arose in the early Church when confessors and those about to be martyred were permitted to intercede for penitents and so mitigate the discipline imposed on them. During the later Middle Ages, indulgences came to command a financial value, which led to widespread abuse and was one of the chief causes of Luther's attack on the Church at the Reformation. Their sale was prohibited in 1567. Today the grant of indulgences, to encourage piety and good works, is largely the prerogative of the pope.

Indus River A river in S central Asia, one of the longest in the world. Rising in SW Tibet in the Himalayas, it flows NW through Kashmir, then SSW across Pakistan to its large delta near Karachi on the Arabian Sea. Its main tributary is the Panjnad, which is formed from the Jhelum, Chenab, Ravi, Beas, and Sutlej rivers. The Indus carries large amounts of sediment and it is also subject to severe flooding but it is an important source of irrigation and hydroelectric power. Waterlogging and salinization have threatened cultivation on the Indus plain and projects have been undertaken to provide an effective drainage system. The Indus contained one of the earliest organized cultures, which lasted from about 2500 until 1700 BC (*see* Indus Valley civilization). Length: 1800 mi (2900 km).

industrial democracy The participation of workers in decisions regarding their work, factory, or company. Various forms of industrial democracy are used in different countries. In the US, the method widely advocated is an extension of *collective bargaining. In Germany, workers' representatives sit on supervisory boards, which monitor the decisions of the board of directors. In some countries there is full worker representation, with three-quarters of a management board consisting of production workers. Other methods of encouraging workers' participation include *profit-sharing plans and *works' councils.

industrial relations Relations between the two sides of industry, employers and employees, usually represented respectively by management and labor unions. In industries with good industrial relations, strikes and lockouts are rare or nonexistent and both sides cooperate to achieve, and to share in, their objectives, whether they be profits, the provision of an efficient service, or simply job satisfaction. Poor industrial relations are easily recognized by frequent and damaging strikes. The key to good industrial relations is probaby some measure of *industrial democracy, *profit sharing, and *collective bargaining.

industrial revolution The name given to the process of change that transformed Britain and then other countries from agricultural to industrial economies. The industrial revolution began in Britain about 1750 when the *agricultural revolution was well under way. Inventions were made in the textile industry by such men as James *Hargreaves, Richard *Arkwright, and Samuel *Crompton, which made the production of cloth much faster and the yard produced of better quality. These new machines could not be used in the home and necessitated the building of factories to house them, at first near rivers for water power and then, when the steam engine was invented, near coal fields. In the factories working conditions were usually intolerable: long hours were worked for low wages and the employment of children was common. Industrial towns sprang up, where living conditions were pitiable, but the current belief in *laissez-faire meant little was done to interfere with the progress of industrial growth. Advances were also made in the production of iron and in communications. The *canals were extended and from about 1830 *railroads were built. By the mid-19th century British industrial methods had spread to continental Europe and the US, laying the foundations for further progress in the 20th century.

Industrial Workers of the World (IWW) US labor organization, established (1905) to organize unskilled workers. Radical in nature, it was founded by socialist leaders whose ultimate goal was to do away with capitalism. Led by William D. *Haywood, nicknamed the "Wobblies," and drawing its membership particularly from the West, it advocated violence, sabotage, and strikes. It went underground after 1919 and was virtually nonexistent by the mid-1920s.

Indus Valley civilization A homogeneous culture flourishing between about 2500 and 1700 BC in the area of modern Pakistan. Excavations from the 1920s onward in the great centers of *Mohenjo-Daro and *Harappa have revealed grid-planned streets, municipal drainage, workmen's barracks, granaries and other large public buildings of baked brick, and a standardized system of weights and measures, all testifying to effective centralized administration. Sealstones bearing undeciphered hieroglyphics have also been found. The economy was primarily agricultural but there was some trade with *Sumer and *Akkad. The final downfall of the civilization (c. 1500 BC) was probably because of the *Aryans' incursion.

Ine (died c. 726) King of Wessex (688–726), whose code of law provides valuable information on economic and social life in his time. A patron of the Church, he abdicated (726) to retire to Rome.

inequality A mathematical statement that one quantity is greater or less than another.

$a < (>) b$ means a is less (greater) than b.

$a \leq (\geq) b$ means a is less (greater) than or equal to b.

inert gases. *See* noble gases.

inertia A property of a body that causes it to resist changes in its velocity or, if stationary, to resist motion. When the body resists changes in its linear motion its mass is a measurement of its inertia (*see* mass and weight). When it resists changes in rotation about an axis its inertia is given by its *moment of inertia.

inertial guidance A means of guiding a missile or submarine without communicating with its destination or point of departure. It consists of a set of three gyroscopes, with their axes mounted mutually perpendicular to each other, connected to a computer. The gyroscopes provide a frame of reference, which enables the computer to adjust the controls of the vehicle to steer a preset course.

INDUS VALLEY CIVILIZATION *A seal, probably used for trading purposes, showing a humped bull and pictographic letters. It was found at Mohenjo-Daro (Pakistan).*

infallibility A dogma of the Roman Catholic Church promulgated at the first *Vatican Council (1870). It stated that the pope cannot err in defining the Church's teaching in matters of faith and morals when speaking *ex cathedra* (Latin: from the throne), i.e. when intending to make such a pronouncement. The pope is not held thereby to be inspired by God but only to be preserved from error when making such a pronouncement.

infanticide The killing of newborn children. In advanced societies it is generally considered a crime but in many communities, especially in India and China, it has been used to limit population numbers in circumstances of poverty, over-population, or famine. Frequently female children and the weak or deformed were at greater risk because they were considered unproductive. In some societies, for instance among the ancient Phoenicians, a firstborn child would be offered as a sacrifice to the gods.

infant mortality The number of deaths that occur in infants under one year of age. This includes neonatal mortality, occurring in the first four weeks of life, from such causes as asphyxia and other birth injuries, prematurity, and developmental abnormalities. Neonatal deaths account for about two-thirds of infant mortalities in prosperous countries. The quality of a country's obstetric and antenatal care is reflected in its perinatal mortality rate: the number of stillbirths and deaths occurring in the first week of life per 1000 births.

infantry A force of soldiers who fight on foot, even though they may be transported to the battle by air, sea, or mechanized transport. Infantry was predominant in ancient warfare, declined when the emphasis shifted to cavalry (c. 400 AD), and became important again with the development of firearms in the late Middle Ages. World War I, with its trench warfare, was still essentially an infantry war. The development of fast-moving armor, air power, and the landing craft made World War II a war of combined operations in which infantry played a decisive but not exclusive role. In modern warfare the extensive use of armor and guided missiles has turned the emphasis away from confrontation between massed infantry toward infiltration and *guerrilla warfare.

infection Illness caused by microorganisms, including bacteria, viruses, fungi, and protozoa. Examples of bacterial infections are diphtheria, plague, pneumonia, scarlet fever, tuberculosis, venereal disease, and whooping cough. Viruses cause chickenpox, the common cold, influenza, measles, polio, rabies, and smallpox (among others); malaria and sleeping sickness result from protozoan infection, and fungi cause ringworm. Infectious diseases (also called contagious or communicable diseases) are the commonest cause of sickness and—except in modern industrial societies—have always been the main cause of death. Infections flourish in dirty crowded impoverished conditions, where the inhabitants are malnourished. Methods of transmission include direct contact with an infected person, contact with a human or animal carrier or contaminated objects, and contact with infected droplets produced by coughing and sneezing. The spread of infectious diseases can be prevented by such measures as improving public health, isolation of infected persons, and *vaccination. *Antibiotics are active against a wide range of disease-causing organisms, but as yet there are few effective drugs for viral diseases.

inferiority complex An unconscious belief, first described by Alfred *Adler, that one is severely inadequate in some particular way. This leads to defensive behavior and often to an overcompensation, such as open aggressiveness. *See also* complex.

infinity In mathematics, a quantity larger than any that can be specified. The symbols $+\infty$ and $-\infty$ are read as "plus infinity" and "minus infinity," respectively. They indicate infinitely large positive and negative values. $x \rightarrow +\infty$ means that the value of a variable quantity, x, continues to increase and has no maximum.

inflammation The reaction of the body's tissues in response to injury, infection, chemicals, and poisons, which is characterized by redness, heat, swelling, and pain. Blood flow to the inflamed area increases and white blood cells infiltrate the tissues and begin to engulf the invading bacteria (or other foreign particles). This may result in the accumulation of dead cells and bacteria, which form pus. Inflammation is an essential part of the healing process.

inflation A general sustained increase in prices resulting from excessive demand for goods (demand-pull inflation), increased pricing by sellers in the absence of increased demand (cost-push inflation), or an expansion of the money supply (monetary inflation). **Deflation** is the opposite process and causes a reduction in both output and employment. In the 19th century periods of deflation and inflation alternated regularly. However, the abnormal length and severity of deflation in the 1930s has been followed in the postwar years by a protracted period of inflation, rising in the 1970s to over 10% per annum in many countries. Remedies vary according to the importance ascribed to each contributory factor: control of wages and prices (*see* prices and incomes policy), increased taxation, reduced government spending, and a controlled money supply are among current policies. However, none of them is likely to succeed when the basic cause is an increase in the cost of imported raw materials, such as oil. *Compare* depression.

inflorescence The arrangement of a group of flowers borne on the same main stalk, of which there are two basic types. In a racemose (or indefinite) inflorescence the tip of the main stem continues to grow and flowers arise below it. Examples are the raceme (e.g. foxglove) and the spike, which is similar but the flowers lack stalks (e.g. wheat). Flat-topped racemose inflorescences include the umbel (*see* Umbelliferae), the capitulum (e.g. daisy), and the corymb (e.g. candytuft). A cymose (or definite) inflorescence, or cyme, is one in which a flower is produced at the tip of the main stem, which then ceases to grow. Growth—and further flower production—is continued either by one lateral bud below the tip, to produce a monochasium (e.g. buttercup), or by a pair of buds, giving a dichasium (e.g. stitchwort).

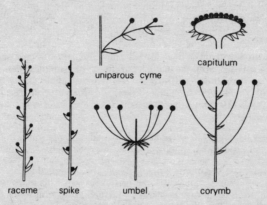

INFLORESCENCE *All plants except those with solitary flowers show characteristic arrangements of their flowers on the main flowering stalk. All the types shown here, with the exception of the uniparous cyme, are racemose inflorescences.*

influenza An acute viral infection characterized by chills, fever, headache, and a slight cough. Muscle weakness, aching joints, and loss of appetite may follow. Cases vary from mild to very severe and possibly fatal (particularly if a secondary bacterial infection occurs). Bed rest, aspirin, and fluids provide the only treatment. Usually small outbreaks of influenza occur regularly in winter, but occasionally epidemics sweep across the world. The worst epidemic in the 20th century occurred in 1918–19, when as many as 20 million people died. These epidemics occur because of the development of new strains of influenza viruses, which are not recognized by the body's immune system. Because of this, it is difficult to produce a vaccine, although new ones are constantly produced and are partially effective.

information theory The mathematical theory of communication, involving analysis of the information content of messages and the processes used in their transmission, reception, storage, and retrieval. Statistical concepts, such as probability, are used to assess the extra information (redundancy) necessary to compensate for spurious signals (noise) occurring during communication. The *bit is the basic unit of information and the channel capacity is a measure of the ability of the transmission medium, e.g. a telegraph line, to carry information. Information theory was developed in the 1940s by Claude E. Shannon. It has been applied widely in such fields as computer science and *cybernetics and has greatly aided the understanding of many processes, ranging from the laws of thermodynamics to the use of language.

infrared radiation Electromagnetic radiation with wavelengths between about 750 nanometers and 1 millimeter. In the electromagnetic spectrum it lies between the red end of visible light and microwaves. It was discovered in 1800 by William *Herschel, who noticed that the solar spectrum contained invisible rays with a heating effect. Infrared radiation is emitted by all bodies at temperatures above absolute zero and is the predominant radiation emitted up to temperatures of about 3000°C.

infrasonics The study of the properties and production of sound waves with a frequency below the threshold of human hearing, i.e. below about 20 hertz. They are produced naturally by earthquakes and tidal waves; in cars traveling at high speeds they have been suspected of having adverse effects on the drivers.

Inge, William (Motter) (1913–73) US dramatist. His plays are set in his native Midwest and deal with the fears, frustrations, and complex feelings of average people, especially in small towns. His works include *Come Back, Little Sheba* (1950), *Picnic* (1953; Pulitzer Prize), *Bus Stop* (1955), *The Dark at the Top of the Stairs* (1957), and the screenplay for *Splendor in the Grass* (1961; Academy Award).

Ingenhousz, Jan (1730–99) Dutch physician and plant physiologist, who discovered the process of *photosynthesis in green plants. Ingenhousz found that plants took in carbon dioxide and gave off oxygen, but only when exposed to light. This oxygen replenished that used by animals and plants in respiration.

Ingolstadt 48 46N 11 27E A city in S Germany, in Bavaria on the Danube River. The Bavarian university was situated here from 1472 to 1800. The cathedral (1425–1500) and castle (1417) survived World War II. An industrial center, it has oil-refining and motor-vehicle industries. Population (1991 est): 105,500.

Ingres, Jean-Auguste-Dominique (1780–1867) French painter, born in Montauban, the son of an artist. He became a pupil of *David in Paris in 1797. His three paintings of the Rivière family (Louvre) established him as a skilled portraitist. From 1806 to 1820 he lived in Rome, where he produced numerous pencil portraits as well as paintings. Many of his historical and mythological paintings aroused criticism but, on returning to Paris in 1824, his *Vow of Louis XIII* (Cathedral, Montauban) received acclaim and established Ingres as an opponent of the romantic movement (*see* romanticism). After holding several posts in the École des Beaux-Arts, he returned to Rome as the director of the French Academy there (1834–41). He is noted for his nudes, e.g. *Valpinçon Bather* (Louvre), and his draftsmanship, which influenced *Degas and *Picasso.

inhibitor A substance that retards a chemical reaction; often called a negative *catalyst. Examples include antioxidants, enzyme inhibitors, and antipolymerization agents.

initiation rites Rituals performed on the transition from childhood to adult status or on joining certain professions, societies, or associations. During the period of transition, adolescents among primitive peoples often undergo intensive education in the duties of adulthood. *Circumcision may be practiced at this time. Initiation rites are frequently performed on admission to religious orders, secret societies, and craft guilds. *See also* passage rites.

initiative. *See* referendum and initiative.

JEAN-AUGUSTE-DOMINIQUE INGRES Self-portrait
(1804; Musée Condé, Chantilly).

injection The introduction of medicinal fluids into the body using a syringe and hollow (hypodermic) needle. The three basic injection routes are under the skin (subcutaneous), for example for insulin; into a muscle (intramuscular), for drugs to be slowly absorbed; and into a vein (intravenous), for drugs to be rapidly absorbed. Drugs are injected when high concentrations are needed or when they are poorly absorbed by the intestines.

injection molding A process, similar to die-casting, for molding thermoplastic materials (plastics that soften on heating and harden on cooling). Injection-molding machines are often fully automatic; the plastic is heated in a cylinder until it has melted and is then forced under pressure into a cooled molding chamber.

ink A colored fluid for writing or printing. Ordinary permanent blue-black writing ink contains ferrous sulfate, mineral organic acid, and other dyes. Colored inks contain only synthetic dyes, while washable ink uses water-soluble synthetic dyes. Marking ink is a mixture of inorganic and organic salts that precipitates aniline black on the surface being marked. India ink, used mainly for drawing, is a black waterproof ink containing carbon black and *shellac. Printing ink consists of pigments suspended in linseed oil, resins, and solvents, the composition depending on the printing process. Ballpoint pen ink is more like printing ink than writing ink since it consists of synthetic dye dissolved in organic liquids with a resinous binder.

ink cap A *mushroom belonging to the genus *Coprinus*, the gills of which are digested after release of the spores to form an inky fluid that drips from the cap. The common ink cap (*C. atramentarius*) grows in tight clusters, usually at the base of trees and shrubs, and has a pale brownish-gray cap, 1.2–2.8 in (3–7 cm) high, and a whitish stalk.

Inkerman, Battle of (Nov 5, 1854) A decisive battle of the Crimean War, in which the French and British defeated the Russians at Inkerman, near Sevastopol. In spite of poor direction the Anglo-French force withstood the Russian attack: the Russians lost about 12,000 men, the British, about 2,500, and the French, about 1,000.

Inland Sea A shallow section of the NW Pacific Ocean between the Japanese islands of Honshu, Shikoku, and Kyushu.

Inner Mongolia Autonomous Region (Chinese name: Nei Menggu AR) An administrative division in NE China, bordering on Mongolia and the Gobi Desert in the W. Its steppes are now partly irrigated and cultivated, producing mainly wheat, and the nomadic Mongol herdsmen, now comprising only 7% of the population, are beginning to settle. Some coal is mined. Area: 459,225 sq mi (1,177,500 sq km). Population (1990): 21,456,798. Capital: Hohhot.

Inner Temple. *See* Inns of Court.

Innocent III (Lotario de' Conti de Segni; 1160–1216) Pope (1198–1216). He was an outstanding canon lawyer, and as pope his policy was directed to the extension of papal power in all areas of temporal and spiritual government. He successfully intervened in the disputed imperial succession in Germany. In France he condemned the marital behavior of *Philip II Augustus and in England forced the submission of King *John, who recognized the pope as feudal overlord. He also proclaimed the fourth *Crusade (1204). The fourth *Lateran Council (1215) represents the climax of his spiritual rule. In its proclamation of the supremacy of spiritual over temporal power, his pontificate marks the apogee of the medieval papacy.

Innocent IV (d. 1254) Pope (1243–54). Before election to the papacy he was a renowned teacher of canon law at Bologna. Much of his pontificate was taken up with attempts to resolve the conflict between the papacy and Emperor *Frederick II. Innocent was forced to flee Rome (1244) and at the Council of Lyon (1245) condemned and deposed the emperor. Only after Frederick's death, however, did Innocent return to Rome (1253).

Innsbruck 47 17N 11 25E A city in W Austria, the capital of the Tirol on the Inn River. Chartered in 1239, it developed as the junction of several important trade routes, including the *Brenner Pass. It has many fine medieval buildings, and a university (1677). It is a popular tourist and winter sports center and the 1964 Olympic Winter Games were held here. Industries include glass and textiles. Population (1991): 114,996.

Inns of Court Associations in the UK with the exclusive right to confer the rank or degree of barrister-at-law, known as "calling to the Bar." The Inns are Lincoln's Inn (established 1310), Middle Temple (1340), Inner Temple (1340), and Gray's Inn (1357). They are administered by a body of senior barristers and judges known as "benchers," who have absolute discretion as to admission of students to the Bar.

inoculation. *See* vaccination.

Inönü, Ismet (1884–1973) Turkish statesman; prime minister (1923–37, 1960–65) and president (1938–50). After a successful military career he joined *Atatürk and commanded the fighting against the Greeks in Anatolia (1921). He was prime minister under Atatürk, after whose death (1938) Inönü became president. Following defeat in the elections of 1950 he led the Republican People's party opposition to the Democratic party government and after the 1960 coup formed three successive coalition governments (1961–65). He remained in Turkish politics until 1972.

inorganic chemistry. *See* chemistry.

inquilinism An animal relationship in which one species lives in the nest of another species or makes use of its food. For example, some termites live only in the mounds of certain other termite species, although in completely separate compartments.

Inquisition (*or* Holy Office) An institution of the medieval and early modern Church designed to combat heresy and moral offenses. Formally instituted (1231) by Pope *Gregory IX in response to the growing threat of heresy, especially of the *Cathari and *Waldenses, it attempted to place all control of heresy in papal hands. Inquisitors, appointed by the pope, especially from the Dominican and Franciscan orders, and possessing considerable powers, often merited their reputation for cruelty. The use of torture was authorized in 1252 and trials were held in secrecy; fines and various penances were imposed on those who confessed, while those who refused were imprisoned or executed by burning. Almost entirely confined to S Europe, the Inquisition lapsed during the 14th and 15th centuries but was revived in Spain in 1478 against apostate Jews and Muslims. Operating with great severity, especially under the first grand inquisitor, de *Torquemada, the Spanish Inquisition later operated against Protestants in Spain and (with little success) the Netherlands, and achieved some notoriety for its arrest of St *Ignatius Loyola. The growth of Protestantism led to the establishment (1542) of a Roman Inquisition by Pope Paul III. It was given complete independence in matters of doctrine and control of heresy and among its victims was *Galileo. In 1965 the Holy Office became a branch of papal bureaucracy and was renamed the Sacred Congregation for the Doctrine of the Faith; it is now concerned with maintaining Roman Catholic discipline.

In re Gault (1967) US Supreme Court decision that upheld juvenile rights under the 14th Amendment. Gerald Gault, a juvenile, claimed violation of rights, having been denied legal counsel, notification of charges, and appeal of sentence.

In re Neagle (1890) US Supreme Court decision on executive branch powers. The decision upheld the right of the executive branch to carry out its constitutional duties despite previous congressional action, or lack of it.

INRI Abbreviation for *Iesus Nazarenus Rex Iudeorum* (Jesus of Nazareth King of the Jews). According to John 19.19–20, this inscription, written in Hebrew, Greek, and Latin, was placed by order of Pilate on the cross upon which Jesus was crucified. The initials often appear on the representation of the cross in Christian painting and sculpture.

insanity In law (although not a legal term), defect of reason caused by disease of the mind, making a person not responsible for his acts. A person is presumed sane until the contrary is proved. If a jury finds an accused person committed an act as charged but was insane, it must return a verdict of not guilty by reason of insanity. According to **M'Naghten's Rules** (established following the acquittal in 1843 on the ground of insanity of Daniel M'Naghten, charged with murder) an accused person is insane if he was unaware of the nature or quality of the act or did not know it was wrong. Insanity may affect a person's capacity to make binding contracts or a will or his fitness to plead, i.e. answer to a criminal charge and therefore to stand trial. An insane person contracting with someone aware of his insanity is only bound by contracts for necessaries, such as food, but is liable to pay only a reasonable price irrespective of the contract price. In cases of a person with partial insanity, i.e. with intermittent periods of lucidity, a defense must show that at the relevant time the person was insane.

insect An invertebrate animal, 0.008–14 in (0.2–350 mm) long, belonging to the largest class in the animal kingdom (*Insecta*; about a million known species). Insects occur throughout the world and account for 83% of all animal life. An insect's body, covered by a waterproof cuticle, is divided into three sections: the head, which bears a pair of antennae; the thorax, with three pairs of legs and typically two pairs of wings; and the abdomen. With biting or sucking mouth-parts they feed on almost all plant or animal materials. The majority of insects lay eggs, which go through a series of changes (*see* metamorphosis) to reach the adult stage. In the more primitive orders, for example *Orthoptera and *Hemiptera, the young (called nymphs) resemble the adults, but in the higher orders, for example *Hymenoptera, Diptera* (flies), and *Coleoptera* (beetles), the young (called larvae) are unlike the adults, often have a different diet, and go through a resting pupal stage.

Insects play an important role in nature as predators, parasites, scavengers, and as prey. Many are plant or animal pests and disease carriers. Others are useful in pollinating crops or killing insect pests and some produce useful substances, such as honey, beeswax, and silk. Phylum: *Arthropoda*.

insecticides Substances used to kill insects by chemical action. Previously, strong inorganic poisons, such as arsenic compounds and cyanides, were used but these were also toxic to humans and livestock. Synthetic organic substances, beginning with DDT in 1945 and including aldrin, endosulfan, and parathion, are now widely used, mainly because of their selectivity, but also because of their cheapness and ease of application. Insecticides are classified according to mode of action or application; for example, **contact insecticides** are applied directly to the insects, while **residual insecticides** are sprayed on surfaces that the insects touch. Problems of insect immunity and environmental pollution have encouraged research into alternative methods involving *biological control.

Insectivora The order of *mammals, comprising about 375 species, that includes *shrews, *tenrecs, *hedgehogs, *moles and *desmans, *golden moles, and *solenodons. Feeding mainly on invertebrates, insectivores are fairly primitive mammals with narrow snouts and sharp simple teeth; their eyes and brains are generally small. Inconspicuous and frequently nocturnal, insectivores are found in nearly all regions; they are absent from the Poles and Australasia and only a few species live in South America.

insectivorous plant. *See* carnivorous plant.

insolvency The inability of a person or company to pay their debts. A creditor may petition a court to declare an insolvent debtor bankrupt (*see* bankruptcy), in which case all his property is sold and the proceeds distributed to his creditors. An insolvent company or partnership is put into liquidation, the court appointing a liquidator, who realizes its assets for distribution to creditors. Although there are state insolvency laws they have generally been superseded by the Federal Bankruptcy Act.

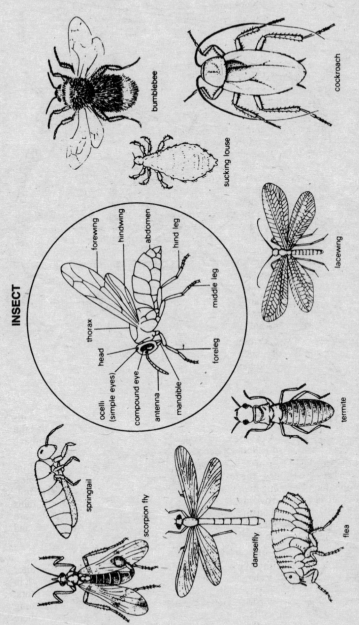

INSECT *The structure of a typical insect (center), with representatives from all the principal insect orders.*

INSECT

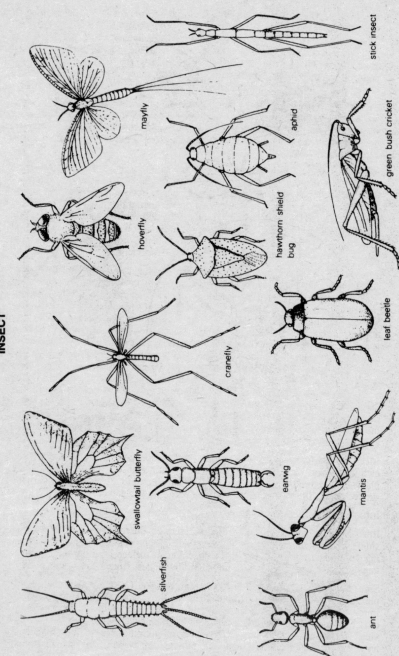

stick insect

mayfly

aphid

green bush cricket

hoverfly

hawthorn shield bug

leaf beetle

cranefly

swallowtail butterfly

earwig

mantis

silverfish

ant

instinct 1. A complex pattern of behavior, the form of which is determined by heredity and is therefore characteristic of all individuals of the same species. Although the behavior may be released and modified by environmental stimuli, its basic pattern does not depend on the experience of the individual. Birdsong and the complex behavior of social insects (such as bees) are striking examples. It is doubtful whether any human activities are, in this sense, instinctive. 2. An innate drive, such as hunger or sex, that urges the individual toward a particular goal.

insulator A material that is a poor conductor of electric current and therefore has a high resistivity. Solids, such as glass, rubber, ceramics, and PVC, are used in electric circuits to separate conducting wires and prevent current loss. In overhead power transmission, air acts as the insulator between high-voltage lines. *See also* energy band.

insulin A protein hormone that is secreted by the islets of Langerhans in the *pancreas in response to a high concentration of glucose in the blood, which occurs, for example, after a meal. It stimulates the uptake of glucose and amino acids from the blood by the tissues and the formation of *glycogen. Its effects are counteracted by the hormone *glucagon. Insulin was first isolated in 1921 by *Banting and *Best and its amino acid composition and three-dimensional structure were revealed by Frederick *Sanger and Dorothy *Hodgkin. A deficiency of insulin causes the symptoms of *diabetes mellitus.

insurance A method of providing monetary compensation for a misfortune or loss that may not occur. Events that must occur at some time, such as death, are provided for by life insurance. In many countries insurance against unemployment, sickness, and retirement is provided by the government. Other types of insurance are undertaken by the private sector. Almost any risk can be insured against, the most common being marine and aviation insurance; automobile insurance; fire, burglary, and household insurance; private medical insurance; and weather insurance. The public does not deal directly with the underwriters (insurers) but arranges to cover a risk through an insurance broker, who works for a commission paid by the insurer and advises the client as to the best coverage available, taking into account the cost and reliability of the insurer. Claims are also settled through brokers. The cost to the insured of covering the risk (premium) is calculated by the insurer's *actuary on the basis of the probability of the risk occurring. If the event occurs, the insured's claim is paid by the insurer, as calculated by an insurance assessor or as stipulated in the insurance policy.

intaglio The production of a sunken image, especially in metal or stone, by etching or engraving. It is used in sculpture, gems, and seals, and for making the plates for gravure printing, in which ink is transferred to the paper from only the sunken areas of the plate, the rest having been wiped clean.

integers. *See* numbers.

integrated circuit (IC) A solid-state *semiconductor circuit contained in a single wafer of semiconductor. ICs are made by a process of etching and diffusing a pattern of impurities into the semiconductor surface, forming tiny positive-negative junctions, which make up individual diodes, *transistors, etc.

Since the 1970s computers have been used to make ICs smaller and more complex, in spite of the fact that further reducing the size makes the doping pattern imprecise. A silicon chip is covered with circuits, and computer-controlled microscopic probes search out the best points for connections for each specific device. The application of this technique has revolutionized many areas of industry and commerce, making cheap *microprocessors available for the automation of production processes.

intelligence The ability to reason and to profit by experience. An individual's level of intelligence is determined by a complex interaction between his heredity and environment; the Swiss psychologist Jean *Piaget has greatly contributed to present-day understanding of intellectual development. The first **intelligence tests** were devised by Alfred *Binet in 1905 and there are now many tests for assessing intellectual ability. An individual's performance in a test is represented by his **intelligence quotient** (IQ), the product of 100 and the ratio of mental age (obtained from the test results) to actual age. Tests are constructed so that the average IQ is 100 and over 95% of the population come between 70 and 130. However, since it is now widely thought that true intelligence can be expressed only through speech and writing (and is therefore inaccessible to testing) and since each test reflects the constructor's view of the nature of intelligence, the predictive value of the tests as a basis for selection for secondary education is questionable. Tests that measure a wide range of abilities, such as the Weschler Intelligence Scale for Children (WISC), are now regarded as the most useful and relevant for diagnosing educational difficulties.

intelligence service The government department responsible for obtaining information about the military and economic capabilities and political intentions of another country (intelligence) or for thwarting the attempts of a foreign country to obtain such information for itself (counterintelligence). Sources of intelligence information may be open, such as diplomatic reports, newspapers, and radio broadcasts, or secret, such as aerial reconnaissance, "bugging," and the fieldwork of spies. Intelligence services existed in antiquity and the first known treatise on the subject is Sun Tzu's *The Art of War* (c. 400 BC). Elizabeth I of England had a notable intelligence service, as did Cardinal de Richelieu in 17th-century France and Frederick the Great in 18th-century Prussia. The first specifically military service was established in France under *Fouché (1802) during the Napoleonic Wars, which the British countered (1808) with the Peninsular Corps of Guides in Spain. Intelligence services subsequently grew in complexity and sophistication. The best-known US intelligence services are the *Central Intelligence Agency, the *Federal Bureau of Investigation (counterintelligence), and the National Security Agency (dealing with cryptology).

The development of intelligence services since World War II is linked with technological advances. Modern methods of obtaining secret information about a foreign state, including photoreconnaissance by such aircraft as the U-2 and by satellites, as well as the work of spies, depend on the use of microfilm, recording machines, and computers. The activities of spies have become less significant but remain an enduringly popular theme for books and films and those real-life agents who have been uncovered, such as *Mata Hari, the *Rosenbergs, Burgess and *Maclean, and *Philby, have attracted enormous interest.

Inter-American Development Bank An international bank founded in 1959 to provide assistance for developing countries in Latin America and the Caribbean by making loans at very low *interest rates.

interest The amount of money charged by a lender to a borrower for the use of a loan. The principal (P) is the amount on which interest is calculated; the term (t), the length of time in years for which the money is lent; and the interest rate (r), the annual rate of return per 100 units of principal. In simple interest, the principal each year is the sum originally lent. The lender is paid $Prt/100$ in interest and repaid P after t years. In compound interest, the interest each year is not paid to the lender but is added to the principal, so that the principal for the next year becomes $P + r/100$. After t years the lender is paid $P(1 + r/100)^t$.

interference A wave phenomenon in which two waves combine either to reinforce each other or to cancel each other out, depending on their relative phases.

The pattern of light and dark strips so produced is called an **interference pattern** (*or* interference fringe). The effect occurs when the two beams have the same frequency and have approximately the same amplitude. Interference was discovered in 1801 by Thomas *Young and provided strong evidence for the wave theory of light.

An **interferometer** is used to produce interference patterns, mainly for the accurate measurement of wavelengths. Several different types are in use, the older instruments being devices for splitting a beam into two parts and then recombining them to form interference patterns after each part has traveled a different distance. In the Michelson interferometer (□Michelson-Morley experiment) the beam is split by a half-silvered mirror in which part of the beam is reflected and the rest transmitted. In the Fabry-Perot interferometer two parallel half-silvered mirrors are placed close to each other. In more modern instruments two lasers are used as separate coherent sources.

interferon A protein that appears in the plasma during viral infections: it is released from infected cells and inhibits the growth of the viruses. Interferon plays an important role in *immunity because it can enter uninfected cells and render them immune to all viral infections. It was discovered in 1957 by a British virologist, Alick Isaacs (1921–67).

Interior, Department of the US cabinet-level executive branch department that oversees nationally owned public lands and natural resources. It decides on the use of land and water resources; protects fish and wildlife; preserves national parks, forests, and historical places; provides outdoor recreation; assesses and develops mineral resources; and administers Indian reservations and US territories. Directed by the secretary of the interior, it was established in 1849.

interior design The part of architectural design that deals with the placing and layout of rooms within a building. It chiefly involves the decoration of walls and ceilings and design of normally immovable types of furniture, such as mirrors and fireplaces. It has increasingly concerned movable furniture as well, a field previously left to the skill of the individual craftsman. In the 20th century greater attention has been given to creating a harmonious and functional style for buildings, down to the smallest object of furniture. A notable practitioner of this was Arne Jacobsen, who sometimes specified exact positions for his furniture.

Interlaken 46 42N 7 52E A resort in central Switzerland in the Bernese Oberland between Lakes Brienz and Thun. One of Switzerland's oldest tourist resorts, it is surrounded by spectacular mountain scenery with a fine view of the Jungfrau mountain. Population: 4735.

intermediate vector boson (*W*) A hypothetical elementary particle thought to be exchanged by particles undergoing a *weak interaction. It would be an unstable *boson, either charged or neutral, and have a mass greater than about 800 MeV. *See also* particle physics.

internal-combustion engine A *heat engine in which fuel is burned inside the engine, rather than in a separate furnace (*see* steam engine). This category includes all piston engines, *jet engines, and *rockets. The first practical internal-combustion engine was patented by N. *Otto in 1876. This was a four-stroke engine using gas as a fuel. It was the invention of the □carburetor and the development of the *oil industry that made the liquid-fueled Otto engine a practical source of power for the horseless carriages emerging in the late 19th century (*see* car). Since then the gasoline engine has powered most road vehicles.

The modern gasoline engine has a compression ratio of 8 or 9 to 1, which requires special fuels (*see* tetraethyl lead) to avoid *knocking. A simpler but less efficient variety of the gasoline engine is the two-stroke. This does not have the complicated inlet and exhaust valves of the Otto engine, the explosive mixture entering and leaving the cylinder through ports in its walls that are covered and uncovered by the movements of the piston. Two-stroke engines are used where low power is required and in some cars and motorcycles.

The main alternative to the gasoline engine is the oil engine, based on a cycle invented by the German engineer Rudolf Diesel (1858–1913). In the diesel engine, air is compressed alone inside the engine, causing its temperature to rise to over 1023°F (550°C); oil is then pumped into the combustion chamber as a fine spray and ignites on contact with the hot air. In this case the compression ratio has to be 15 or 16 to 1, making the engine considerably heavier and more expensive than the gasoline engine. The efficiency of both Otto and diesel engines is limited by their compression ratios and thus their working temperatures (□heat engines). Also, combustion is intermittent and therefore incomplete, causing pollution problems. Moreover, both being reciprocating engines, they have inherent vibrations. This last problem is overcome to some extent in the *Wankel engine. The *gas turbine, however, uses continuous combustion and with a compression ratio of up to 30:1 can reach a working temperature of 2194°F (1200°C). It is therefore more efficient and creates less pollution than piston engines. Jet engines based on the gas turbine are used widely in aircraft and as an easily started and shut down prime mover in some power stations.

Internal Revenue Service (IRS) US Treasury Department arm that enforces tax laws and collects taxes. Established in 1862, the IRS has 8 administrative districts, each with its own director, and has facilities for audit, review, and collection.

Internal Security Act (McCarran Act, 1950) US law passed to curb communist activity. Sponsored by Sen. Patrick A. McCarran, it authorized a commission to require subversive organizations to register as communist, to detain people suspected of sabotage or espionage in times of national emergency, and to bar such individuals from national defense work. The act was amended (1968) to exclude registration requirements.

International An association of national socialist or labor parties formed to promote socialism or communism. The **First International** was an organization of labor and socialist groups founded in London in 1864 as the International Working Men's Association. Karl Marx soon assumed its leadership and its first congress was held in Geneva in 1866. Although the First International was successful in disseminating socialist ideas among workers, it failed to make any political changes, largely because of the conflicting socialist views of its members, especially those of Marx and *Bakunin. Its last meeting was held in 1876 in Philadelphia.

The **Second International** was founded in Paris in 1889; its headquarters were in Brussels. The organization was composed primarily of European, North American, and Japanese social democratic parties, which believed in parliamentary democracy, and of labor unions. Its leaders included Ramsay *Macdonald. At the outbreak of World War I, the organization collapsed because of division between pro- and anti-war groups. A postwar attempt to revive it failed.

The **Labor and Socialist International** was founded in Vienna in 1921; its goal was to create a socialist commonwealth. It has been called the "second and a half International" because it was composed of those out of sympathy with the Second and Third Internationals. It opposed fascism and also communist dictatorships while supporting the Soviet Union. The organization came to an end following Hitler's invasions in W Europe in 1939.

The **Third International** (*or* Comintern), an organization of world communist parties, was founded by Lenin in March 1919, to encourage worldwide prole-

ideal Otto cycle

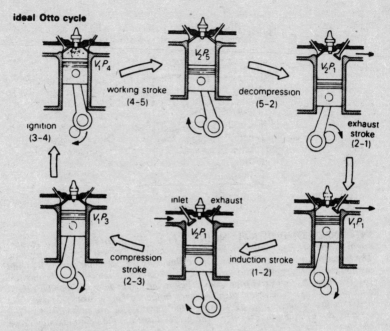

ideal Diesel cycle

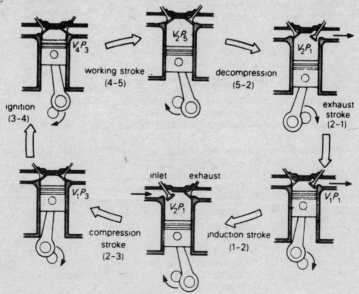

INTERNAL-COMBUSTION ENGINE

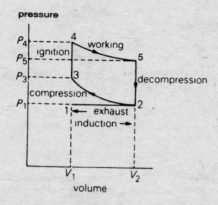

INTERNAL-COMBUSTION ENGINE

In the ideal Otto-cycle (four-stroke) engine, there are four piston strokes (movements up and down) for each explosion. The petrol-air mixture is drawn into the cylinder by the induction stroke (1-2) and compressed by the compression stroke (2-3). A spark the ignite (3-4) the mixture causing the pressure to rise from P_3 to P_4 before the piston descends (combustion at constant volume). The piston then descends in the working stroke (4-5) and rises again in the exhaust stroke (2-1), when the burnt gases are pushed out of the cylinder through the exhaust valve. The graph illustrates the pressure and volume changes during the cycle. In the Diesel cycle, ignition is caused by the high compression achieved by the compression stroke (2-3) and the piston descends, increasing the volume of the burning gas from V_3 to V_4, before the pressure has time to rise (combustion at constant pressure).

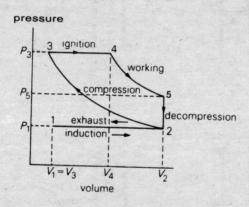

INTERNAL-COMBUSTION ENGINE

tariat revolution. Throughout its existence it adjusted its program to political exigencies and to the power struggles within the Soviet party leadership. As a gesture of reconciliation with his Western allies, Stalin dissolved the International in 1943 (*see also* Cominform).

The **Fourth International** was founded by *Trotsky in Mexico City in 1937 in opposition to Stalin and the Third International. It held its first conference in France in 1938 and was composed primarily of those who supported Trotsky's transitional program, which aimed to undermine capitalism in preparation for its revolutionary overthrow.

The **Socialist International** was founded in 1951 as an association of socialist parties that believe in parliamentary democracy and oppose communism. Its headquarters are in London.

International Bank for Reconstruction and Development (IBRD) A specialized agency of the *United Nations, known as the World Bank, with headquarters in Washington, DC. Its function is to finance development in member countries by making loans to governments or under government guarantee. It was set up by the 1944 *Bretton Woods agreements to facilitate reconstruction after World War II. All members must belong to the *International Monetary Fund.

International Brigades A volunteer army recruited during the Spanish Civil War (1936–39) by the Comintern to aid the Republicans against Franco. Comprising at its largest some 20,000 volunteers, of which about 60% were communists, it was organized by nationality into seven brigades. Ill-armed and badly led, it was disbanded in 1938. Many Americans sympathetic to the Republican cause joined the brigades.

International Civil Aviation Organization (ICAO) A specialized agency of the *United Nations established in 1947 to promote high operating standards and fair competition among international airlines. With headquarters in Montreal, it formulates agreed standards in telecommunications, personnel training, and air-traffic protocols. Its council of representatives of 27 of the member countries implements the decisions of the assembly, its legislative body, and when necessary settles disputes between members.

international commodity agreements Agreements between producers of primary products to regulate their production and sale in order to stabilize prices and conserve supplies; examples include the Tin Agreement (1956), Coffee Agreement (1962), and Rubber Agreement (1976). Natural factors, such as crop failures, and the discovery of new mineral deposits cause fluctuations in the supply and hence the price of commodities. Producers, which are mostly developing countries, have agreed to limit production, fix minimum prices, and establish marketing organizations to build up buffer stocks by buying surpluses, which are sold when prices exceed a specific ceiling.

International Confederation of Free Trade Unions (ICFTU) An international body of national trades-union federations formed in 1949 by federations that had withdrawn from the *World Federation of Trade Unions (WFTU) following disagreements with the communist members of the WFTU.

International Court of Justice The judicial body set up by the UN to pass judgment on disputes between states. The court, which normally sits at The Hague, comprises 15 judges, each from a different state, elected by the UN General Assembly. The court may only hear disputes between states that have agreed to be brought before it by any other state, either generally or in a specific case. Judgments of the court are enforced by application to the UN Security

Council. The court also advises the UN and other specified bodies on questions of *international law.

International Criminal Police Organization. *See* Interpol.

International Date Line A line following the 180° meridian, deviating to avoid some land areas. The date immediately E of the line is one day earlier than to the W since 180°E is 12 hours ahead of *Greenwich Mean Time and 180°W is 12 hours behind.

Internationale The national anthem of the Soviet Union until 1944, composed by P. Degeyter (1848–1932).

international gothic A style of painting and sculpture dominant in W Europe between about 1375 and 1425. Originating in France and Burgundy, it later spread to Italy, Bohemia, and other German states. International gothic retained the figure stylizations of *gothic but introduced naturalism in the depiction of landscape, animals, and costume. Leading exponents were the de *Limburg brothers and Claus *Sluter in Burgundy and *Gentile da Fabriano and *Pisanello in Italy.

International Labor Organization (ILO) A specialized agency of the *United Nations dedicated to the improvement of working conditions and living standards. It was first convened in 1919, when it was affiliated to the *League of Nations, and its headquarters are in Geneva. The organization advocates a world labor code to protect the interests of workers, supports labor research projects, monitors labor legislation, and provides technical assistance to developing nations. In 1977 the US withdrew from the ILO on the grounds that it had come to be dominated by political interests but rejoined in 1980.

international law The rules that determine the legal relationship between independent states (public), or between citizens of such states (private). Public international law, also called the law of nations and administered by the *International Court of Justice, is based on: (1) natural law, being laws recognized by civilized nations; (2) agreements between states, i.e. conventions; (3) customs followed in practice; and, to a lesser extent (4) the writings and opinions of respected jurists. Private international law, also called conflict of laws, determines the laws of which country should apply in given circumstances and which courts should have jurisdiction.

International Monetary Fund (IMF) A specialized agency of the *United Nations, with headquarters in Washington, DC, set up by the 1944 *Bretton Woods agreements to stabilize exchange rates and facilitate international trade. Each member country contributes to the fund in both gold and its own currency. A member with balance-of-payments difficulties can obtain the currency it requires from the fund in exchange for its own, which it must repurchase within five years. The higher a member's contribution the greater its voting rights. *See also* Special Drawing Rights.

International Organization for Standardization (ISO) An organization, situated in Geneva, for establishing and controlling international scientific, industrial, and commercial standards of measurement and design. It was founded in 1946.

International Phonetic Alphabet (IPA) An augmented version of the Roman alphabet, developed by the International Phonetic Association in the late 19th century and kept under continous revision since. It attempts to symbolize, on phonetic principles, every sound that can be made in human language. It is used internationally in dictionaries to represent the pronunciation of words.

international style The predominant architectural style of the 20th century, so called because it was the first style effectively to breach all national and cultural barriers. Originating in W Europe and the US with such architects as *Gropius, *Wright, *Behrens, and *Le Corbusier, the international style evolved from the new tastes, materials, and advanced technology produced by industrialization. It is chiefly characterized by the use of concrete, often roughcast, a tendency toward monolithic uniformity in the use of undecorated cubic forms, and a functional asymmetry.

International Telecommunication Union (ITU) A specialized agency of the *United Nations founded in 1934 to promote international agreement on standards of use and development of telecommunications systems. It makes recommendations on the regulation and use of radio frequencies, general operating procedures, and the establishment of telecommunications systems in developing countries, including radio, telegraph, telephone, cable, and television. Its headquarters are in Geneva.

International Working Men's Association. *See* International.

Interpol (*Inter*national Criminal *Pol*ice Organization) An association of about 120 national *police forces formed in 1923 to provide a means of international cooperation in the prevention of crime. Its constitution strictly precludes activities of a political, military, religious, or racial nature. Its major concerns are the exchange of police information and the arrest of those who are the subject of an extradition order. Interpol has been most effective in the control of smuggling, particularly of gold and narcotics, and of currency offenses and counterfeiting.

Interregnum. *See* Commonwealth.

interstellar medium The matter, mainly gas and some dust, contained in the region between the stars of the *Galaxy. The gas is mainly hydrogen with some helium. It can exist, for example, as hot ionized clouds, cooler and more tenuous neutral areas, or dense clouds of molecular hydrogen and other molecules. Small dust particles are found throughout the interstellar region. The gas and dust is probably material cast off from old stars, with young stars forming out of the denser clouds.

interstitial An atom that exists in the spaces (interstices) between the atoms or molecules in a crystal lattice. Some interstitial compounds are important *alloys and some are *semiconductors.

intestine The part of the digestive tract, in the abdomen, that extends from the stomach to the anus. It is divided into two parts. The small intestine, which includes the duodenum, jejunum, and ileum, is the principal site of digestion and absorption of food. It secretes digestive enzymes and mucus and its inner surface is thrown into fingerlike processes, which increase the absorptive area. The duodenum is a common site for a *peptic ulcer, since it receives the acid contents from the stomach. The large intestine consists of the colon, cecum, rectum, and anus. It is largely concerned with the absorption of water from digested food and the formation of *feces, which are expelled from the anus. The intestines contain specialized muscle whose rhythmic contractions (called peristalsis) propel food toward the anus.

intimism A branch of postimpressionist painting, specializing in domestic interiors having an atmosphere of intimacy. The chief practitioners were the *Nabis painters Pierre *Bonnard and Édouard *Vuillard.

Intolerable Acts (*or* Coercive Acts; 1774) British parliamentary Acts intended to enforce stricter control over the American colonies following the *Boston Tea Party. The Boston Port Bill (1774) closed the port until reparation for the lost tea had been made. The Massachusetts Government Act repealed the colony's charter and imposed a military government on Massachusetts; the Administration of Justice Act allowed British officials to return home for trial in a criminal case; and the Quebec Act gave the lucrative fur trade between the Ohio and Mississippi rivers to Quebec. The Acts contributed to the outbreak of the *American Revolution.

intoxication Any form of acute poisoning; in popular language it usually refers to alcoholic poisoning. This is characterized by excited, often abusive, behavior, unsteady gait, confused memory, flushed skin, and poor coordination.

intrauterine device (IUD). *See* contraception.

introversion (*or* intraversion) A quality of personality characterized by interest in oneself rather than in the outside world: it is the opposite of *extroversion. Introverts are reflective and introspective, with a tendency to have a small circle of friends. They are good at persisting for a long time at one task; their interests tend to be philosophical; and they are highly susceptible to permanent *conditioning.

intrusive rock. *See* igneous rock.

intuitionism Any doctrine in which what appears to be self-evident is regarded as the basis of knowledge ("I just *know* that such-and-such is the case"). From the model of mathematics, the Pythagoreans believed that intuition is superior to observation and in modern times the mathematical school of *Brouwer was called intuitionist regarding its views about the nature of mathematics. In contemporary philosophy, intuitionism has been most emphasized in *ethics.

Inuit The *Eskimos of Alaska, Greenland, and Canada. The assertiveness of the Inuit tribes, especially in Canada, brought civil, economic, and social reforms in the late 1970s and early 1980s.

Invar An *alloy of iron with 36% nickel, which expands by only 0.9 mm per km for each centrigrade degree temperature rise. This is about $1/10$ the expansion of platinum and titanium and less than $1/20$ of that of most other metals. It was discovered in 1896 and since then has been used for accurate measuring tapes and chronometer parts.

Invercargill 46 26S 168 21E A city in New Zealand, in S South Island on the Waihopai River. It is the center of a sheep- and dairy-farming region. Population (1980 est): 53,700.

Inverness 57 27N 4 15W A city in N Scotland, at the head of the Moray Firth. Inverness is a tourist center and has boatbuilding, distilling, iron-founding, and woolen industries. It has a 19th-century cathedral and castle, which occupies the site of an earlier castle destroyed in 1746. Population: 44,000.

invertebrate Any animal without a backbone. All animals except vertebrates belong to this category, including the *protochordates—animals that possess a rodlike skeletal notochord. Although widely used, the term is seldom employed in taxonomic systems.

invert sugar A mixture of the sugars glucose and fructose resulting from the action of heat or the enzyme invertase on cane or beet sugar (sucrose). It is sweeter than sucrose and widely used in foods and confectionary.

investiture controversy A dispute between the papacy and the Holy Roman Empire during the late 11th and early 12th centuries concerning the right of secular rulers to appoint bishops and invest them with their office in return for pledges of loyalty. The conflict arose between Pope *Gregory VII and the Holy Roman Emperor *Henry IV and later also involved the Norman kings of England. Compromise was reached with England in 1106 and with the emperor in 1122. This issue provided a focus for the struggle for supremacy between lay and ecclesiastical powers.

investment 1. The purchase of capital goods (plant and machinery) used in the production of consumer goods and services. Investment and consumption together comprise the national income. A high level of investment is a necessary part of a nation's economic well-being and helps to promote *economic growth. In most countries incentives, in the form of tax relief, are available on investment expenditure. What actually motivates investment is a matter of debate: some economists believe the rate of interest is the most important factor, while others assign more importance to the level of demand in the economy. Certainly investment varies a great deal over the *trade cycle. **2.** The use of money to obtain an income or a capital gain in the future. This can be achieved by depositing it with a bank or other financial institution to provide income without capital growth. Investment also includes the purchase of any asset that can be expected to increase in value and can also be linked with insurance policies.

investment bank A financial institution that acts as an intermediary between a company seeking to raise capital on a stock exchange and those wishing to invest. It advises a client on when and how to make a new issue of *securities, advertises it to the public, and often underwrites the issue (i.e., guarantees to buy all the securities that have not been applied for).

investment company. *See* closed-end investment company.

Io In Greek legend, a priestess of Hera, loved by Zeus, who transformed her into a heifer to protect her from discovery. Hera ordered Argus, a herdsman with eyes covering his entire body, to guard her, but she escaped with the help of Hermes and was finally restored to Zeus in Egypt.

Ioánnina (*or* Yannina) 39 40N 20 51E A city in NW Greece, in Epirus on Lake Ioánnina. Conquered by the Turks in 1430, it became the seat (1788–1822) of Ali Pasha. It was captured by the Greeks in 1913. The university was founded in 1970. Population: 40,130.

iodine (I) A purple-black lustrous solid *halogen that evaporates slowly at room temperature to give a purple gas. It was discovered in 1811 by B. Courtois (1777–1838). It is insoluble in water but dissolves readily in organic solvents, such as chloroform ($CHCl_3$) or carbon tetrachloride (CCl_4), to give pink-purple solutions. Iodine is present in sea water and concentrated by seaweeds; it also occurs in saltpeter deposits, such as those in Chile. Potassium iodide (KI) is widely used in photography. The radioactive isotope ^{131}I, with a half-life of 8.1 days, is produced in nuclear reactors; its accidental release into the atmosphere would cause serious problems. It is also used in the diagnosis and treatment of thyroid disorders as it is concentrated in the thyroid gland. Tincture of iodine is used as an antiseptic. At no 53; at wt 126.904; mp 236°F (113.5°C); bp 363.8°F (184.35°C).

io moth A large common American *saturniid moth, *Automeris io*. Males are yellow and the larger females reddish brown, with a wingspan of 3 in (70 mm). The greenish spiny larvae feed on trees and are poisonous to touch.

ion An atom or group of atoms that has lost or gained one or more electrons and consequently has an electric charge. Positively and negatively charged ions are called **cations** and **anions** respectively. The sign and magnitude of the charge is indicated by a superscript, as in the potassium ion, K^+, or the doubly charged sulfate ion, SO_4^{2-}. Many compounds (electrovalent compounds) are combinations of positive and negative ions; sodium chloride, for example, is formed from sodium ions (Na^+) and chloride ions (Cl^-). *See also* chemical bond; ionization.

Iona 56 19N 6 25W A small sparsely populated island in NW Scotland, in the Inner Hebrides. It has many religious associations; St Columba landed there in 563 AD, establishing a monastery that became the center of the Celtic Church. It later became a burial ground for Scottish, Irish, and Norwegian kings. Area: 3.3 sq mi (8.5 sq km).

Ionesco, Eugène (1912–94) French dramatist. He was born in Romania of French and Romanian parents and settled permanently in France in 1938. He inaugurated the *Theater of the Absurd with his first play, *The Bald Prima Donna* (1950), which exposed the poverty of language as a means of communication. His later plays, which include *The Lesson* (1951), *The Chairs* (1951), *Rhinoceros* (1960), *Exit the King* (1962), and *Man With Bags* (1977), use a variety of surrealistic techniques to express a nihilistic vision of society.

Ionia In antiquity, the central W coast of Asia Minor and the adjacent islands, settled by Greeks about 1000 BC. Between the 8th and 6th centuries BC *Miletus, *Samos, *Ephesus, and other Ionian cities led Greece in trade, colonization, and culture. The first Greek philosophers, including *Thales, *Pythagoras, and *Anaximander, were Ionian. After 550 BC Ionia passed under the domination of *Lydia and later Persia. The Ionian revolt against Persian rule (499–494 BC) resulted in defeat, economic ruin, subjugation by outsiders, and comparative eclipse.

Ionian Islands A group of Greek islands in the Ionian Sea, extending from Corfu in the N to Zacynthus in the S and including Páxos, Lévkas, Ithaca, and Cephalonia. They belonged to Britain from the Treaty of Paris (1815) until 1864, when they were ceded to Greece. Several were devastated by earthquakes in 1514, 1893, and 1953. Total area: 891 sq mi (2307 sq km).

Ionian Sea The section of the central Mediterranean Sea, bounded by Italy, Sicily, and Greece, that contains the Ionian Islands.

Ionic order. *See* orders of architecture.

ionization The process of producing *ions from neutral atoms or molecules. Solvation (surrounding of an ion by polar solvent molecules), heating (thermal ionization), or bombardment with particles or radiation provide the necessary energy for the process. The minimum energy required to ionize an atom A (i.e. $A \rightarrow A^+ + e^-$) is called its **ionization potential**, which is usually measured in electronvolts.

ionization chamber An instrument used for measuring the intensity of *ionizing radiation. It consists of a gas-filled chamber containing two electrodes with a large potential difference between them. When radiation enters the chamber it ionizes some of the gas atoms or molecules. The ions flow toward the electrodes creating a current, the magnitude of which is a measure of the intensity of the radiation. The *Geiger counter is an example of an ionization chamber.

ionizing radiation Any radiation that ionizes the atoms or molecules of the matter through which it passes. It may consist of particles (such as *electrons) or it may be electromagnetic radiation (*see* ultraviolet radiation; X-rays; gamma radiation). Ionizing radiation occurs naturally in *cosmic rays and is emitted by radioactive substances. It is also produced artificially in X-ray machines, particle accelerators, nuclear reactors, etc. Ionizing radiations are used in medical diagnosis and therapy and in sterilization of food. In biological tissue these radiations create reactive free radicals, especially by ionizing water molecules, which attack proteins, nucleic acids, etc., and can cause damage by changing their structure and function.

ionosphere A region of the upper □atmosphere that reflects short radio waves, enabling transmissions to be made around the curved surface of the earth by sky waves. The gases in the ionosphere are ionized by absorption of radiation from the sun. Its existence was suggested in 1902 by A. E. Kennelly and independently by O. Heaviside. Sir Edward Appleton (1892–1925) provided proof by bouncing radio waves off the different layers of the ionosphere, which vary in behavior with the position of the sun and with the sunspot cycle. The ionization of the D region, at between 30 and 55 miles (50 and 90 km) altitude, disappears during the day. The E region is between 55 and 100 miles (90 and 160 km) high and the F region (sometimes called the Appleton layer) is from 100 miles up to about 250 miles (160 to 400 km). The lower part of the ionosphere (E region) is sometimes called the Kennelly-Heaviside layer. The gas particles in the F region do not lose their charge as quickly as those below because the gas is less dense and therefore ions and electrons are subject to fewer collisions. This enables radio transmissions to continue at night.

Iowa A state in the Midwest. The Mississippi River forms it boundary with Wisconsin and Illinois in the E; Missouri lies to the S; the Missouri River forms its boundary with Nebraska and South Dakota in the W; and Montana lies to the N. The land rises slowly from the Mississippi Valley to form a gentle rolling landscape, with the higher land in the NW. Iowa is predominantly an agricultural state, and its agricultural sector is one of the most important in the country although industry produces more revenue. In the 1930s Iowa moved to diversify its economy, encouraging agriculturally associated industries including the manufacture of agricultural machinery and food processing. It is famed for its livestock, particularly pigs. Major crops are corn, oats, soybeans, and other fodder crops. There is also some mining for portland cement and gypsum. The scattered population and lack of urban areas limit the cultural institutions the state can support. *History*: the Mound Builders were the earliest known inhabitants. When French explorers arrived in the 17th century, they found Sac, Fox, Iowa, and Sioux tribes. *Marquette and Jolliet explored the region in 1673 and La Salle in 1681–82. It formed part of the Louisiana Purchase (1803). The Black Hawk Wars virtually ended the tenure of the Indians in the state, and settlers from the East and from Europe migrated W. With the growth of rural communities, agrarian protest groups, such as the Granger Movement, sprang up. They served as political forums seeking to improve farmers' economic status. Iowa remains essentially agricultural and rural with one of the lowest rates of population growth in the US. Area: 56,290 sq mi (145,790 sq km). Population (1990): 2,776,755. Capital: Des Moines.

Ipatieff, Vladimir Nikolaievich (1867–1952) US physicist, born in Russia. While working in Germany he discovered the structure of *isoprene (1897); returning to Russia in 1899 he investigated the catalytic breakdown of *hydrocarbon molecules at high temperatures. In 1930 he emigrated to the US, where he worked on the development of high-octane fuels for internal-combustion engines.

ipecacuanha A South American herbaceous plant, *Uragoga ipecacuanha*, cultivated in the tropics for its root, which yields medicinal alkaloids used as an expectorant and emetic. Large doses cause vomiting and diarrhea. Family: *Rubiaceae*.

Iphigenia In Greek legend, the eldest daughter of *Agamemnon and *Clytemnestra. When the Greek fleet was delayed at Aulis at the beginning of the *Trojan War, Agamemnon was told that Artemis demanded the sacrifice of his daughter before the fleet could sail to Troy. He was about to comply when

Artemis took pity on Iphigenia and transported her to Tauris, where she became a priestess of Artemis. The story is the subject of two plays by *Euripides.

I-pin. *See* Yibin.

Ipoh 4 36N 101 02E A city in NW Peninsular Malaysia, the capital of Perak state. The tin-mining center of Malaysia, it has noted Chinese rock temples. Population (1980): 300,727.

Ipswich 52 04N 1 10E A city in SE England, at the head of the Orwell estuary. It is a port with engineering, printing, brewing, flour-milling, plastics, fertilizers, tobacco, and textile industries. Cardinal Wolsey was born here. Population (1981): 120,447.

Ipswich 27 38S 152 40E A city in Australia, in SE Queensland. It is the state's second largest coal producer. Population (1991): 71,861.

Iqbal, Mohammed (?1875–1938) Indian Muslim poet and philosopher, born in Sialkot (Punjab). He came to England in 1905 (already a noted romantic poet and promoter of Indian nationalism) to study at Cambridge University. From 1908 Iqbal lived in Lahore where he became a leading member of the *Muslim League. He is generally credited with the formulation of the political theory of Pakistan as a separate Muslim state in the Indian subcontinent.

Iquique 20 15S 70 08W A port in N Chile, on the Pacific Ocean. Industries include fish-meal plants and canneries; the chief exports are nitrates, iodine, and fish meal. Population (1987 est): 133,000.

Iquitos 3 51S 73 13W A port in NE Peru, on the Amazon River 2300 mi (3700 km) from its mouth. The furthest point upstream accessible to oceangoing vessels, it exports rubber, timber, and nuts. Its university was founded in 1962. Population (1988 est): 248,000.

IRA. *See* Irish Republican Army.

Iráklion (*or* Herakleion; Italian name: Candia) 32 20N 25 08E The chief port of the Greek island of Crete, on the N coast. It is picturesque, possessing many Venetian fortifications, and has become a tourist center. Exports include raisins, grapes, and olive oil. Population (1971): 78,209.

Iran, Republic of (name until 1935: Persia) A country in the Middle East lying between the Caspian Sea and the Persian Gulf. Its central plateau, containing deserts and marshes, is surrounded by mountains, the *Zagros Mountains in the W, the *Elburz Mountains and the Kopet Mountains in the N, and a barren region of peaks and sand in the E. It suffers great extremes of temperature and severe earthquakes. The most populous areas are the NW and the Caspian coast, which have the greatest rainfall. The population is mainly Persian with groups of Turks, Kurds, Armenians, Arabs, and such tribes as the Bakhtyari. *Economy*: agriculture supports 75% of the population, although lack of rain hampers productivity and much food has to be imported. The development of irrigation has been a high priority. Wheat, rice, tobacco, fruit, sugar beet, and tea are grown; sheep and goats are kept. Iran's chief source of revenue is its oil; it possesses 10% of the world's reserves. The main oil fields are in the Zagros Mountains, where oil was first discovered (1908). Other minerals include coal, copper, iron ore, lead, natural gas, and precious stones. The textile industry uses local cotton and silk, and carpet manufacture is an important handicraft. Among Iran's other industries, its steel industry is the largest in the Middle East. Oil revenues have been used to diversify the economy; to this end many capital goods, such as machinery, are imported. *History*: the Caspian coast and the plateau are among the earliest centers of civilization. Early Persian dynasties include the *Achaemenians and the *Sasanians (*see* *also* Greek-Persian wars). Arab domination, which established Islam in the area, was followed by that of the Turks and Mongols before the Persian Safavid dynasty (1502–1736) came into power. Following a period of great prosperity (1587–1629) Persia again declined, encroached on by Uzbeks, Arabs, Afghans, Turks, and Russians. The next great dynasty, the Kajar dynasty (1794–1925), was marked largely by rivalry for domination between Britain and Russia. Western influence was felt increasingly during the latter half of the 19th century. Repressive rule provoked opposition that became open in about 1900 and was intensified by resentment against the concessions granted to Britain and Russia, made necessary by the Shah's financial difficulties. The Shah was forced to grant a constitution and National Assembly (the Majlis; 1906); his successor disbanded this and was then deposed and replaced (1909). Further disorders resulted in the army coup that established Reza Khan in power (1921), from 1925 as *Reza Shah Pahlavi. Under his virtual dictatorship order returned and the country was industrialized and extensively Westernized; he was forced to abdicate in favor of his son *Mohammed Reza Pahlavi (1941). Iran's oil was a major source of political unrest. In 1945 the Soviet Union supported a revolt to gain oil concessions (later withdrawn). Oil was also a major issue for the militant National Front movement, which nationalized the oil industry (1951); the British responded with a blockade resulting in serious economic difficulties and the Shah was forced to flee the country temporarily. Martial law was ended after 16 years in 1957 but economic and political instability continued; the Shah's reform program, which included in 1963 the enfranchisement of women, the redistribution of land, and compulsory education, was opposed by major religious and political groups. Unrest was further provoked by harsh repression, with many dissidents executed or imprisoned. By 1978 different opposition groups had united under the exiled Muslim leader Ayatollah Ruholla *Khomeini. There were demonstrations and riots in 1977–78, and in early 1979 the Shah left the country, later dying in exile (1980). Ayatollah Khomeini took over the government in the so-called Islamic Revolution and gradually eliminated opposition through a strict Muslim administration. In 1979 students occupied the US embassy in Tehran and took 52 hostages who were held until January 1981. In September 1980, Iraq attacked Iran, but the invasion was repelled. A stalemate ensued until 1988 when a ceasefire was agreed upon. Ayatollah Khomeini died in 1989, and Ali Akbar Hashemi Rafsanjani was elected to the presidency. In 1990–91, Iran appeared to be exploiting Iraq's weakness after its defeat in Kuwait during *Operation Desert Storm by encouraging dissent among Shiite Muslims in Iraq. Rafsanjani, regarded as less anti-Western than his rivals, strengthened his hold on the government in 1992 parliamentary elections and won reelection as president in 1993. Official language: Persian (Farsi). Official currency: Iranian rial of 100 dinars. Area: 636,160 sq mi (1,648,000 sq km). Population (1989 est): 51,005,000. Capital: Tehran.

Iran-Contra Affair (1987) An illegal operation in which the US sold arms to Iran in return for help in releasing hostages in the Middle East and for money, used to support the Contra rebels in Nicaragua. US Marine Lt. Col. Oliver L. North, on the staff of the National Security Council, testified at Senate hearings that individuals in the executive branch condoned the diversion of funds. He and others were later indicted for their role in the affair, but most were convicted only of minor offenses.

Iranian languages A subgroup of the *Indo-Iranian language family. Iranian languages are spoken in Iran, Afghanistan, Turkey, and parts of the Caucasus. The Iranian languages are closely related to *Sanskrit. Modern Iranian languages include Persian, Kurdish, *Pashto, and *Ossetic.

Iraq, Republic of A country in the Middle East, bordering on the Persian Gulf. The SE consists of an alluvial plain around the delta of the Tigris and Euphrates Rivers; this floods in spring. The W is a vast desert while the N is mountainous. The population is about 90% Muslim divided evenly between Shiite and Sunnite sects. The Kurds, who live in the mountainous NE, form about 15–20% of the population. *Economy*: mainly agricultural, the chief crops being wheat, barley, rice, maize, sorghum, sesame, dates, and cotton. Since 1958 cooperative and collective farms have been set up and mechanization and irrigation schemes have increased production. The main industry is oil (first discovered at Kirkuk in 1927) and Iraq is a member of OPEC. Natural gas is also produced, as are textiles, processed foods, cement, and electrical and leather goods. Cereals, meat, machinery, vehicles, chemicals, and consumer goods are imported, chiefly from Japan, Germany, the US, and France. *History*: as *Mesopotamia, Iraq was the site of the world's first civilization; it is extremely rich in archeological remains. It was conquered by Arabia and became Muslim in the 7th century AD and was part of the Ottoman Empire from 1534 until World War I, when UK troops expelled the Turks. As a British mandate (1920–32), Iraq became a kingdom (1921). From this period on it has been politically unstable, with ethnic and religious unrest and frequent coups; the monarchy was overthrown in 1958. During the 1960s and 1970s the Kurds rebelled and, from 1968, Muslims and communists opposed the socialist government. Even though Iraq was a member of the *Arab League, it quarreled with Iran and Syria before a military union with Syria was signed in 1978. Taking advantage of disorder in Iran, Iraq attacked (1980) its neighbor. Iran repelled the invasion, and the war dragged on at enormous cost to both countries until a ceasefire was agreed upon in 1988. In August 1990, Pres. Saddam *Hussein ordered the invasion of *Kuwait, against which Iraq had territorial and economic claims. Kuwait was overrun with great brutality and looted before Iraq announced its "annexation." The US, other Western countries, and most Arab nations opposed Iraq's aggressiveness, obtaining UN condemnation of the invasion and in January 1991 launching *Operation Desert Storm. Forced by sustained bombing and then a coalition attack to withdraw from Kuwait, Iraq's leaders then had to face internal unrest and renewed pressure from Iran. Faced with a strained economy hampered by international sanctions and with Kurdish and Shia Muslim unrest, President Hussein remained defiant of the world community and determined to retain his power. President: Saddam Hussein. Official language: Arabic. Official currency: Iraqi dinar of 1000 fils. Area: 169,248 sq mi (438,466 sq km). Population (1992 est): 18,000,000. Capital: Baghdad.

Ireland The second largest island in the British Isles, separated from Great Britain by the North Channel, the Irish Sea, and St George's Channel. It consists of a central lowland area of fertile plains, bogs, and moorland, rising to hills and mountains in the N and S. The River Shannon is the chief river, draining N–S, and Ireland contains many lakes, particularly in the N and W, including Lough Neagh. Since 1920 Ireland has been politically divided, the NE part forming Northern Ireland in the UK and the remainder comprising the Republic of Ireland. *History*: rich in archeological remains, Ireland was invaded in the 4th century BC by the Celts. The country came to be divided into the five tribal kingdoms (the Five Fifths) of Ulster, Meath, Leinster, Munster, and Connaught, which nominally acknowledged the overlordship of the High Kings of Ireland (the rulers of Tara). In the 5th century the country was converted to Christianity—a process in which St Patrick was the outstanding figure—and in the following centuries the Irish Church fostered scholarship, art, and missionary work. The 9th and 10th centuries saw Viking invasions, which were brought to an end by Brian Boru's great victory at Clontarf (1014). In the mid-12th century

Ireland was invaded by the Norman conquerors of England and Henry II gained the allegiance of the Irish kings. English law and administration were introduced in the 13th century, and an Irish parliament (composed of the Anglo-Irish and subordinate to the English Crown) began to meet. However, English rule was restricted to the area around Dublin (called the Pale) until the 16th century, when the subjection of the Irish became the aim of the Tudor monarchs of England. Revolts, inspired in part by Roman Catholic opposition to the Reformation, were suppressed and the *Plantation of Ireland by English and later by Scottish settlers was begun. Irish resistance continued, culminating in the rebellion of 1641, which was not suppressed until 1649–50. The subsequent confiscation of the rebels' land and its redistribution among English colonists established the economic and political ascendancy of the Protestant minority in Ireland. It was strengthened by the Restoration settlement and by events after William of Orange's defeat (1690) of the Irish supporters of the deposed Catholic king, James II: the usual land confiscations were accompanied on this occasion by new anti-Catholic penal laws. In the 18th century Ireland's subservience to England came to be opposed by many Irish Protestants and in 1782, under the leadership of Henry Grattan, the Irish parliament obtained legislative independence. However, the abortive Irish rebellion of 1798 led to the complete union of Britain and Ireland (1800; *see* Union, Acts of). Eventually, Catholics received civil rights in 1829 (*see also* O'Connell, Daniel). The appalling social conditions suffered by the majority of Irish renewed Catholic militancy in the 19th century. Nationalist agitation was taken up after the Irish (potato) famine first, abortively, by the *Fenians and then by the *Home Rule movement. While the *Land League pursued agrarian reform with some success, Home Rule was delayed. It was nominally obtained in 1914 but was opposed both by the Republicans, who wanted a greater degree of independence, and the Protestant Ulster Unionists, who feared for their future in a self-governing country with a Catholic majority. Following the proclamation of an Irish republic by Sinn Fein (1919) and virtual civil war Britain proposed partition (1920), with the establishment of separate parliaments in the predominantly Protestant NE and Catholic S and W. The formula was unacceptable to the Republicans and in 1921 the Irish Free State, with dominion status, came into being. The NE (Northern Ireland) immediately withdrew, accepting self-government within the UK.

Northern Ireland The province comprises the counties of Antrim, Armagh, Down, Fermanagh, Londonderry, and Tyrone. *Economy*: there has been a significant change since the 1950s, the traditional industries of shipbuilding and linen manufacture as well as agriculture having declined in importance. Diversification of industry has taken place (chemicals, rubber products, man-made fibers, and engineering) and there has been a large rise in the number of people employed in the service sector. The economy has suffered, however, from the political upheavals of the last decade. *History*: the Government of Ireland Act (1920) established a parliament, which met at Stormont Castle in Belfast and had legislative responsibility for most matters other than foreign affairs. Executive power lay with a prime minister and cabinet. Some 12 representatives were also (and continue to be) returned to the UK Parliament. The Protestant majority in Northern Ireland predominantly supports the union with Great Britain, while many of the Roman Catholic minority, dissatisfied with Protestant dominance, seek union with the Republic of Ireland. Violent conflict broke out between the two groups in 1969; the British army has since maintained a peacekeeping force in Northern Ireland. Terrorist activities both in Ireland and Great Britain led to the imposition (1972) of direct rule of Northern Ireland by the UK Parliament. An Anglo-Irish treaty signed in 1985 gave the Republic of Ireland a consulting role in the governing of Northern Ireland. During 1981 violent reprisals followed the deaths of a number of hunger strikers, who had been demanding political status while serving sentences for terrorism. Sporadic bombings and terrorist attacks continued into the 1990s. Area: 5452 sq mi (14,121 sq km). Population (1986): 1,567,000. Capital: Belfast.

Republic of Ireland (Irish name: Éire) The country is administratively divided into 26 counties. *Economy*: predominantly agricultural, cattle rearing being of major importance, especially in the E lowlands, where cattle are fattened for beef production. Dairy farming is also extensively practiced, particularly in the S. Arable crops produced include barley, wheat, oats, potatoes, and sugar beet. Tourism is the second major source of revenue. Industries have expanded considerably since the 1950s, largely under foreign companies, and are oriented to the export market. They include food processing, brewing, distilling, textiles, and clothing. Peat is extensively cut as a fuel for power stations and as a household fuel. In 1977 Europe's largest lead-zinc mines were opened at Navan. Although the Republic has an extensive coastline its fishing industry is relatively small. *History*: Republican opposition to partition continued immediately after the establishment of the Irish Free State but was quelled by 1923. In 1932 De Valera, leader of Fianna Fáil, became prime minister and, in 1937, introduced a new constitution by which the Irish Free State was renamed Éire. In 1949 a coalition led by Fine Gael took the country, as the Republic of Ireland, out of the British Commonwealth. Since 1969 Irish politics have been dominated by the violent conflict in Northern Ireland and successive Irish governments have declared their desire to see the establishment there of a form of government acceptable to both Roman Catholics and Protestants. In 1973 Ireland became a member of the EEC. Charles J. Haughey who, as Jack Lynch's successor, led a Fianna Fáil government (1979–81; 1982), was ousted in November 1982, and Dr Garret FitzGerald became prime minister for a second term, heading a Fine Gael–Labour coalition. In 1983 a "Forum for a New Ireland" that included representatives of the Republic, Northern Ireland, and Britain began to study issues affecting Northern Ireland and the Republic of Ireland. The 1985 Anglo-Irish treaty made the Republic's role in Northern Ireland's affairs more formal. When FitzGerald's government collapsed in 1987, Haughey was returned for a third time. In 1990, Mary Robinson became the first female president of Ireland. Haughey resigned amid corruption charges in 1992 and was followed by Albert Reynolds. In December 1993, Ireland and the UK agreed on a framework for resolving issues in Northern Ireland. President: Mary Robinson. Official languages: Irish and English. Chief religion: Roman Catholic. Official currency: Irish pound of 100 pence. Area: 26,599 sq mi (68,893 sq km). Population (1989 est): 3,734,000. Capital and main port: Dublin.

Ireland, John Nicholson (1879–1962) British composer, a pupil of Stanford and teacher of Britten and E. J. Moeran (1894–1950). His works include orchestral and chamber music, songs, and piano pieces. Many of these, including *The Forgotten Rite* (for orchestra; 1913) and *Sarnia* (for piano; 1941), were inspired by the history of the Channel Islands.

Irene (c. 752–803 AD) Byzantine empress and saint of the Greek Orthodox Church. After the death of her husband Leo IV (reigned 775–80), Irene ruled jointly with their son Constantine VI (771–797?) until 790, when she was banished from court. In 797 she returned, blinded and imprisoned Constantine, and ruled alone. She fought against the iconoclasts (*see* iconoclasm) for the restoration of icons in Christian worship. In 802 she was overthrown and exiled to Lesbos.

Ireton, Henry (1611–51) English soldier, who fought for the parliamentarians in the English *Civil War. In 1646 he became Cromwell's son-in-law. Initially favoring negotiations with Charles I, he proposed a constitutional solution to the conflict of power but in 1649 he was a signatory to the king's death warrant. During the Commonwealth, Ireton served in Ireland, where he died of fever at the siege of Limerick.

Irian Jaya. *See* West Irian.

iridium (Ir) A hard brittle metal, discovered in 1803 by C. Tennant (1768–1838), in the residue left after dissolving platinum in aqua regia. Its salts are highly colored, whence its name (Latin *iris*, rainbow). Its principal use is as a hardening agent for platinum and in electrical contacts. At no 77; at wt 192.22; mp 4374°F (2410°C); bp 7473°F (4130°C).

iris (anatomy) The muscular tissue in the □eye that surrounds the pupil and is situated immediately in front of the lens; it is responsible for eye color. Reflex contraction of the muscles in the iris cause it to become smaller in dim light (which enlarges the pupil and allows more light to enter the eye) and larger in bright light (thus decreasing the size of the pupil).

Iris (botany) A genus of perennial herbaceous plants (about 300 species), native to N temperate regions and widely planted in gardens. Irises grow from bulbs or rhizomes (underground stems) and their flowers, which have three erect inner petals and three drooping outer sepals, can be three or more colors, often with a contrasting "beard" on the lower petals. Many garden varieties are derived from *I. germanica*: up to 40 in (1 m) high, they have purple, white, or yellow flowers and grow from rhizomes. Family: *Iridaceae. See also* flag.

Iris (mythology) The Greek goddess of the rainbow and messenger of the gods, especially of *Hera. She is portrayed as carrying a herald's staff and often bearing water that could put perjurers to sleep.

Irish elk A large extinct European *deer belonging to the genus *Megaloceros*, which was abundant during the Pleistocene epoch (2.5 million–10,000 years ago). It stood 71 in (1.8 m) at the shoulder and its massive palmate antlers spanned up to 13 ft (4 m). Several species are known and remains of the largest have been found in Irish bog deposits.

Irish famine (1846–51) The starvation and death of almost a million Irish following a blight that ruined the potato crop (the staple diet of most Irish) in 1846. Another million emigrated.

Irish Literary Renaissance A period of literary activity in Ireland in the late 19th and early 20th centuries inspired by the contemporary resurgence of political nationalism and of interest in traditional Gaelic culture. The strongest individual influence was that of W. B. *Yeats, especially through his *The Wanderings of Oisin* (1889) and *The Celtic Twilight* (1893). Other writers included the poet George Russell (pseudonym AE; 1867–1935), the novelist George Moore (1852–1933), and the dramatist J. M. *Synge.

Irish literature The Gaelic literature of Ireland. The earliest literature, as in other parts of the Celtic world, was the responsibility of an official learned class, the *filid* (or *Druids), who transmitted orally the ancient traditions of the people. The earliest written literature, however, dates from the 7th to 10th centuries. Of most interest in this period are the heroic sagas, written in prose and preserved mainly in three 12th-century manuscript collections, the Book of the Dun Cow, the Book of Leinster, and the Yellow Book of Lecan. These epics, which are shorter than Icelandic sagas, deal with both heroic (warfare, voyages, etc.) and romantic elements. They were grouped in the Middle Ages into two cycles, the early pagan Ulster cycle and the much later *Fenian cycle. *Deirdre and *Cuchulain are the prominent figures in the Ulster cycle and appear in the two most famous stories, the *Longes Mac Nusnig* (*Exile of the Sons of Usnech*) and the *Táin Bó Cúalnge* (*Cattle-Raid of Cooley*). From the 13th century bardic poets preserved Gaelic culture from the impact of Norman English; their main productions were panegyrics written for aristocratic patrons, but they also responded to influences introduced by the Normans and English, such as, for example, the theme of courtly love. Despite a revival of Gaelic poetry in the 16th century, it declined with the submergence of the Irish aristocracy, particularly after the coming of Cromwell (1649). The work of the poet and historian Geoffrey Keating (c. 1580–c. 1645) is the most important prior to this date; the two outstanding poets of the period were David O'Bruadair (1625–98) and Egan O'Rahilly (1670–1728). Gaelic literature was at its lowest ebb during the 18th century, but was revived in the 19th century, having splintered in the meantime into several dialects. Such 20th-century writers as Liam *O'Flaherty and Brendan *Behan have produced distinguished work in Gaelic, but generally there has been nothing to equal the work of the major modern Irish poets and writers, who have almost without exception written in English. *See also* Irish Literary Renaissance.

Irish moss. *See* carrageen.

Irish Republican Army (IRA) A militant organization established in 1919. It fought a successful war against British forces (1912–21) but the subsequent partition treaty was rejected by many IRA members. The antitreaty faction (keeping the name IRA) was defeated by 1923 and declared illegal but continued to press for an all-Ireland republic. A bombing campaign against England in 1939 and an "offensive" against Northern Ireland (1956–62) both failed. The movement was then quiescent until the present troubles began in 1968. In 1969 both the IRA and *Sinn Féin, to which many IRA members belong, split into the Officials, desiring a socialist 32-county republic, and the Provisionals, concerned only with expelling the British from the North. The Irish National Liberation Army is a breakaway terrorist group.

Irish Republican Brotherhood. *See* Fenians.

Irish Sea A section of the Atlantic Ocean, separating England, Scotland, and Wales from Ireland. Area: about 40,000 sq mi (100,000 sq km). Maximum width: 150 mi (240 km).

Irish terrier A breed of dog originating in Ireland and used for hunting. It has a sturdy streamlined body, a long head, and an alert appearance. The hard wiry coat is red to yellowish-red. Height: 16–18 in (41–46 cm).

Irish wolfhound An ancient breed of large hunting dog originating in Ireland. It has a powerful body and a long narrow head with small ears. The rough wiry coat is long on the brow and under the jaw and can be gray, brindle, red, black, white, or fawn. Height: 31 in (78 cm) minimum (dogs); 28 in (71 cm) minimum (bitches).

Irkutsk 52 18N 104 15E A city in N Russia. It is a major railroad junction and is the industrial, cultural, and educational center of E Siberia. Its industries include ship, aircraft, and vehicle production and repair; machinery, chemicals, textiles, and food are also produced. Population (1990 est): 640,000.

iron (Fe) A metallic transition element that has been known and used since prehistoric times. It is the fourth most abundant element in the earth's crust, occurring in the ores hematite (Fe_2O_3), magnetite (Fe_3O_4), and siderite ($FeCO_3$). It is widely used in toolmaking, construction, shipbuilding, car manufacture, and a host of other applications, almost always alloyed with other elements, such as carbon, manganese, chromium, titanium, and vanadium (*see* steel). It is obtained from its ores by smelting in a *blast furnace to give pig iron, which is then converted into cast iron, wrought iron, or steel. Iron has two important valence states forming iron II (ferrous) and iron III (ferric) compounds. Common compounds include the sulfates ($FeSO_4$, $Fe_2(SO_4)_3$), chlorides ($FeCl_2$, $FeCl_3$), and oxides (FeO, Fe_3O_4, Fe_2O_3). Iron is vital to animal life owing to its presence in *hemoglobin. Studies of meteorites and of the magnetic and seismic properties of the earth suggest that the earth has an iron-nickel core, molten on the outside but solid in the interior. At no 26; at wt 55.847; mp 2798°F (1535°C); bp 4987°F (2750°C). *See also* ferromagnetism.

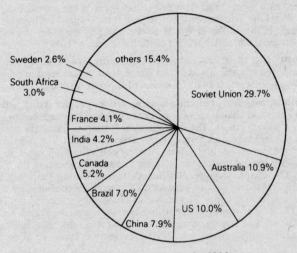

IRON *World production of iron ore in the 1980s.*

Iron Age The cultural phase during which iron replaced bronze metal technology (*see* Bronze Age). Despite spasmodic earlier use of meteoric iron, it was not until about 1500 BC that iron-working techniques were perfected by the *Hittites. Initially a prestige metal, the superior hardness of which was prized for weapons, iron gradually spread throughout the Middle East after about 1100 BC. It was used in *Hallstatt Europe in the 7th century BC. The Chinese were both forging and casting iron about 500 BC, preceding Europe by about 1700 years in casting. Australia and pre-Columbian America never developed iron metallurgy but African societies moved directly from stone to iron technologies.

ironclad A wooden warship protected by iron armor, the forerunner of the modern battleship. Both the French and the British used ironclad barges against the Russians in the Crimean War (1854–56) but the first ironclad warship, the *Gloire*, was built by France in 1859. The first battle between ironclads occurred off the Virginia coast in 1862 in the Civil War.

Iron Cross The highest German decoration for bravery in battle, instituted by Frederick William III of Prussia in 1813. An iron Maltese cross edged in silver, it was reinstituted by Hitler in 1939.

Iron Curtain The ideological division between the Soviet Union and its satellite countries in E Europe on the one hand, and the democratic countries of W Europe on the other. The term was first used by Winston Churchill in 1946 and came to symbolize the strained relations that persisted well into the 1950s.

Iron Gate (Romanian name: Porțile de Fier; Serbo-Croat name: Gvozdena Vrata) 44 40N 22 30E The deepest gorge in Europe, on the Romanian-Yugoslav border, through which the Danube River flows. A canal, which is used by larger shipping, bypasses the gorge on the Romanian side. A Romanian-Yugoslav hydroelectric plant was opened there (1972). Length: about 2 mi (3 km).

iron lung. *See* respirator.

Ironside, William Edmund, 1st Baron (1880–1959) British field marshal. Disguised as a railroadman he was a secret agent in the second Boer War. In World War I he commanded the Allied forces against Soviet Russia at Archangel (1918). In World War II he was chief of the imperial general staff (1939–40) and commander in chief of the home forces (1940).

ironwood One of several unrelated trees with very hard wood, including *Mesurea ferrea* of India and Malaysia (family *Guttiferae*), used in cabinetwork, and a *hop-hornbeam, *Ostrya virginiana*, of E North America.

Iroquois A coalition of North American Indian peoples living between the Hudson River and Lake Erie, who spoke the Iroquois language belonging to the Iroquois Caddoan family. The Iroquois were farmers and hunters who lived in villages of longhouses, each occupied by several families. The individual clans were grouped into tribes and nations ruled by councils of delegates. In the 16th century, they formed the famous **Iroquois League**, composed of the *Mohawk, Oneida, Onondaga, Cayuga, and Seneca tribes. During the **Iroquois War** (1642–53), these five nations expanded their territory considerably at the expense of neighboring tribes. The Iroquois Confederacy, joined by the Tuscarora tribe in 1722, allied itself with the British in wars against the French and, except for the Oneida and Tuscarora, against the colonists in the *Revolutionary War. The League finally collapsed following the second Treaty of *Fort Stanwix (1784).

irrational numbers. *See* numbers.

Irrawaddy River The chief river in Myanmar (formerly Burma), flowing SSW across the entire country. Joined by the Chindwin River at Mandalay, it enters the Andaman Sea through a swampy delta (one of the great rice-growing areas of Asia). Length: 1250 mi (2010 km).

Irredentists Italians who sought to bring all Italian-speaking areas into newly unified Italy in the late 19th century, in particular the Austrian-controlled Trentino in the NE. The Irredentists, so called from *Italia irredenta* ("unrecovered Italy"), urged Italy to join the UK and France in World War I. The postwar distribution of territories, giving Italy the Trentino and the Istrian peninsula on the N Adriatic, realized their chief ambitions.

irrigation The artificial watering of land for crop production. Irrigation was practiced in ancient Egypt; traditional systems linked to seasonal changes in river level, using earth banks and channels with water-lifting devices, are still used in many areas. Modern methods involve artificial reservoirs, canals, and pumping systems; the entire field may be flooded, as in rice growing, or the water may run in channels between the rows of the crop. High-pressure sprinklers are also used, especially where the land is undulating. Irrigation may be essential for crop production in arid regions but is also used to supplement rainfall in other regions.

Irtysh River (*or* R. Irtish) A river in central Asia. Rising in the Altai Mountains of China, it flows W and NW to join the Ob River in Russia. Length: 2760 mi (4444 km).

Irving, Sir Henry (John Henry Brodribb; 1838–1905) British actor and manager. He established his reputation in London during the early 1870s and remained the leading actor of the London stage for the next 30 years. From 1878 to 1902 he was manager of the Lyceum Theatre, where, with Ellen *Terry as his leading lady, he acted in a notable series of Shakespearean productions. He made several tours in the US, and in 1895 became the first actor to receive a knighthood.

SIR HENRY IRVING *As Shylock in* The Merchant of Venice, *one of his most famous roles.*

Irving, Washington (1783–1859) US author and historian. Educated as a lawyer, Irving began to publish satirical essays, the most famous of which, *History of New York* (1809), was written under the pen name Diedrich Knickerbocker. From 1815 to 1832 he lived in Europe where he wrote *The Sketch Book* (1819–20), which contains some of his best short stories, including "Rip Van Winkle" and "The Legend of Sleepy Hollow." While in Europe, Irving also served in a diplomatic capacity at the US embassies in Madrid and London. After returning to the US, he was acclaimed as the country's leading man of letters, publishing more short stories, novels, and biographies, among them his five-volume *Life of George Washington* (1855–59).

Isabella (*born* Elizabeth Farnese; 1692–1766) The second wife of Philip V of Spain, whom she dominated throughout their marriage (1714–46). Her ambitions centered on the acquisition of Italian possessions for her sons, the eldest of whom ruled Naples and Sicily before becoming *Charles III of Spain.

Isabella (I) the Catholic (1451–1504) Queen of Castile (1474–1504). Her marriage (1469) to Ferdinand of Aragon brought about the union of the two major Spanish kingdoms, to which Granada was added following its reconquest from the Moors in 1492. The introduction of the Inquisition (1480) and the expulsion of the Jews (1492) were largely due to Isabella's influence. She also supported Columbus's voyages of discovery. *See also* Ferdinand V and II.

Isabella II (1830–1904) Queen of Spain (1833–68). Isabella's reign saw almost continual political turmoil. Her succession was contested by her uncle Don Carlos and only secured in 1839, after the first Carlist War (*see* Carlism). Her governments became increasingly unpopular and she was deposed.

Isabella of France (1292–1358) The wife (1308–27) of Edward II of England; the daughter of *Philip (IV) the Fair. Increasingly isolated by Edward's favorites, she left England in 1325. She became the mistress of Roger *Mortimer and together they returned to overthrow and murder Edward (1327). In 1330 her son Edward III executed Mortimer and confined Isabella to a nunnery.

Isabey, Jean Baptiste (1767–1855) French portrait painter and miniaturist, born in Nancy. He trained under *David and was patronized successively by Marie Antoinette, Napoleon, and the restored Bourbon kings. His son **Eugène Isabey** (1804–86) was also a painter.

Isaiah (8th century BC) Old Testament prophet. He was influential at the court of the rulers of Judah until the Assyrian invasion (701 BC) and, according to tradition, was later martyred.

The Book of Isaiah contains his prophecies, although some scholars attribute chapters 40–66 to others. The prophecies condemn the corruption of both Judah and the surrounding nations, counsel against entering foreign political alliances, and predict the captivity of the nation in Babylon and its return. Several sections announce the coming of a Messiah. These passages formed the basis of the messianic expectations of the Jews and were interpreted by the Christian writers of the New Testament as referring to Jesus.

ISBN (International Standard Book Number). *See* library.

Ischia, Island of 40 44N 13 57E A volcanic island in Italy, at the entrance to the Bay of Naples. A popular resort, it is noted for its picturesque scenery and mineral springs. Area: 18 sq mi (47 sq km). Chief town: Ischia.

Ise 34 29N 136 41E A city in Japan, in S Honshu on the Pacific Ocean. It is the site of Japan's most sacred Shinto shrines, some of which possibly date back to the 1st century BC. Population (1990): 104,164.

Isfahan (*or* Esfahan) 32 41N 51 41E A city in central Iran. It has some fine examples of Persian architecture, including the 17th-century royal mosque. An industrial quarter was established in the 1930s, and a university was founded in 1950. The city was prominent in the unrest that preceded the Shah's departure from Iran in February 1979. Population (1986): 986,753.

Isherwood, Christopher (1904–86) British novelist. His experiences while teaching in Berlin in the 1930s are described in the novel *Mr Norris Changes Trains* (1935) and in the stories *Goodbye to Berlin* (1939), portrayed in the film *Cabaret* (1968). He collaborated with his friend W. H. *Auden on several plays. In 1939 he moved to California, where he cultivated an interest in Hindu philosophy. His other works include *The World in the Evening* (1954), *Down There on* *a Visit* (1962), and *A Single Man* (1964). In these and several autobiographical works, including *Christopher and His Kind* (1977), homosexuality is a recurrent theme.

Ishtar The supreme Babylonian and Assyrian goddess, the daughter of the sky god Anu or of the moon god Sin. She combined aspects of a beneficent mother goddess and fierce goddess of war and fertility. She descended to the underworld in search of her lover *Tammuz.

Isidore of Seville, St (c. 560–636 AD) Spanish churchman; Doctor of the Church and the last of the western Fathers of the Church. Archbishop of Seville from about 600, he is famous for his encyclopedia of knowledge, the *Etymologiae*, which was much used by medieval scholars. In dealing with such subjects as grammar, mathematics, history, and theology Isidore included etymological explanations of words (hence the title), but these were allegorical rather than scientific. Feast day: Apr 4.

isinglass A form of gelatin, about 90% pure, made from the swim bladders of fish. It is used in glues and to clarify jellies and alcoholic drinks.

Isis An Egyptian goddess, the sister and wife of *Osiris, whose dismembered body she magically restored to life, and mother of *Horus. She was usually portrayed as holding the child Horus and wearing on her head the solar disk and a cow's horns, the same attributes as *Hathor. She was essentially a goddess of protection, being the perfect mother and having magical powers of healing. Her cult eventually spread throughout the Roman Empire.

Iskenderun (former name: Alexandretta) 36 37N 36 08E A port in central S Turkey. Its main activities are fishing and trading in tobacco, silk, bananas, and cereals. Until 1939 it was in Syria. Population (1980): 124,824.

Islam (Arabic: submission to God) A major world religion, which originated in Arabia in the 7th century AD. The essential creed of Islam, whose adherents are called Muslims, is that there is one God, Allah, and that *Mohammed is his prophet. The revelations received by Mohammed are recorded in the *Koran, which is the basis of Islamic belief and practice and the source of a complex legal and social system (*see also* Islamic law). Islam shares a number of beliefs with Judaism and Christianity and accepts the Books of Moses and the Gospels of Jesus as parts of the same divine scripture that is definitively expressed in the Koran. There is no formally organized church or priesthood. Instead, five fundamental duties are incumbent upon the individual Muslim: expression of belief in the one God, Allah, and in the prophethood of Mohammed; observance at set times of five daily prayers, which are recited facing toward Mecca; fasting during the month of *Ramadan; payment of a special tax for charitable purposes; and performance of the pilgrimage to Mecca (*see* hajj) at least once, if means permit. Given the impetus of the *jihad* or holy war against unbelievers originally prescribed as a duty, the Muslim armies of Arabia extended Islam through the Middle East and N Africa in the 7th and 8th centuries AD. It later spread to sub-Saharan Africa, India, China, SE Asia, parts of Russia, the Balkans, and Spain. It early divided into sects, which originally differed as to who should be the leader of Islam and what should be his powers. The main sects are the *Sunnites (*or* Sunni) and the *Shiites (*or* Shia; *see also* Ahmadiya; Wahhabiya). There are an estimated 1 billion Muslims.

Islamabad 33 40N 73 08E The capital of Pakistan, situated in the N of the country on the Potwar Plateau. The site was chosen in 1959 and construction began in 1961. The government's first cabinet meeting was held in 1967. The Quaid-i-Azam University was founded in 1965 and the People's Open University in 1974. Population (1981): 204,364.

Islamic art and architecture A distinctive style of art and architecture created and developed by the Muslims in the countries they conquered. Islamic art is generally classified by scholars into five regional groupings: Syrian-Egyptian; Persian; Ottoman-Turkish; Moorish (i.e. North African and Spanish); and Indian. Its most distinctive feature is its elaborate patterning in architecture, painting, ceramics, metalwork, woodwork, glassware, textiles, and carpets. Of all these arts architecture is the most individual, its main characteristics being the dome and the horseshoe ☐arch. Religious objections to the depiction of human and animal forms inhibited the development of sculpture. Islamic painting is usually associated with Persian, Mogul, and Turkish miniatures, although there were many schools of painting during the Middle Ages and later. Calligraphy, particularly in decoration, is regarded as an art form in a class of its own. *See also* Mogul art; Persian art.

Islamic law The sacred law of Islam, *shari'ah*, prescribes not only religious duties (*see* Islam) but covers every aspect of the life of a Muslim. Its basic principles were elaborated in the 9th century AD, when the *Koran and the practice of Mohammed (the *sunna*) came to be generally accepted as the main sources of the law. The law covers marriage, divorce, and inheritance; it forbids usury, the depiction of living beings, the drinking of alcohol, the eating of pork, etc., and prescribes penalties and punishments for crimes. When a problem could not be solved by reference to the Koran or *sunna*, other sources were allowed and different legal interpretations developed. Thus among the *Sunnite majority, four equally orthodox schools have arisen, which agree on fundamentals but differ in their interpretation of specific points. In modern times most Muslim states have adopted secular legal systems at least in part and especially with regard to criminal, financial, and property law.

island A piece of land surrounded by water (excluding the continents). The world's largest island is Greenland (840,000 sq mi; 2.2 million sq km). Continental islands, such as Britain, lie on the continental shelves, separated usually by a narrow shallow stretch of water from the mainland. Oceanic orogenic islands, such as the Japanese islands, frequently occur in island arcs at the junction of two lithospheric plates (*see* plate tectonics); they are volcanic in origin. Oceanic volcanic islands, such as the Hawaiian islands, occur in the central parts of the deep oceans, particularly the Pacific. They are believed to be formed over "hot spots" in the earth's crust, where molten magma rises to the surface. Many coral islands have a volcanic base. *See also* reef.

Ismaili A *Shiite Muslim sect. In the 8th century AD a group of Shiites recognized Ismail the son of Jafar al-Sadiq as *imam, while the rest of the Shiites supported his brother Musa. In 909 the Fatimid caliphate was established, the rulers of which were Ismaili imams. The Ismaili Fatimids ruled in Egypt and N Africa until 1171, contesting control of the Muslim world with the *Abbasid dynasty of Baghdad. They developed several doctrines that diverge considerably from non-Ismaili Islam and eventually split into many subsects. Today the best-known Ismaili sect is that headed by the *Aga Khan.

Ismailia (Arabic name: al Isma'iliyah) 31 36N 32 15E A city in NE Egypt, midway along the Suez Canal on Lake Timsah. Dependent on the canal trade, much of the population moved elsewhere during the canal's closure (1967–75). It is the center of an irrigated area producing market-garden crops. Population (1986): 212,567.

Isma'il Pasha (1830–95) Viceroy of Egypt for the Ottoman Empire (1863–79). He introduced important reforms but the huge foreign debts that his policies incurred eventually supplied the pretext for British intervention (1882) and led the Ottomans to depose him. Under Isma'il the *Suez Canal was opened in 1869.

ISO. *See* International Organization for Standardization.

Isocrates (436–338 BC) Athenian teacher of rhetoric and political pamphleteer. After developing his highly polished style as a professional speechwriter, Isocrates opened a school, where his method of teaching rhetoric as a preparation for life began the literary tradition of education. His appeals to successive military leaders to unite the feuding Greek states against Persia culminated in the *Philippus* (346 BC), addressed to *Philip of Macedon.

isolationism The policy that opposes participation in world affairs, except in self-defense. The term is most usually used to describe US policies pursued after World War I, when isolationism reached its peak in the Neutrality Acts (1935–37). The Japanese attack on Pearl Harbor in World War II ended isolationism.

structural isomers *Ethanol and dimethyl ether have the same atoms in the molecule but different functional groups.*

cis-trans isomers *A form of stereoisomerism occurring as a result of a double bond.*

optical isomers *Another form of stereoisomerism in which two forms of tartaric acid have different optical properties.*

ISOMERS

isomers Chemical compounds that have the same molecular formulae but different arrangements of atoms in their molecules. In **structural isomerism** the molecules have different molecular formulae. Thus, ethanol (C_2H_5OH) and dimethyl ether (CH_3OCH_3) both have the formula C_2H_6O, although they are quite different compounds. A form of structural isomerism is that in which functional groups occur at different positions in the molecule. For example, there are two alcohols derived from propane: propan-1-ol ($CH_3CH_2CH_2OH$) and propan-2-ol ($CH_3CH_2OHCH_3$), which differ in the position of the OH group on the chain. In **stereoisomerism** the molecules have the same structure and groups but the isomers differ in their spatial arrangements. **Cis-trans isomerism** occurs as a result of the positioning of groups in a planar molecule. A common type occurs in organic molecules with double bonds. Since rotation cannot occur about the bond it is possible to have two isomers: one with groups on both sides of the bond (the cis isomer) and the other with groups on opposite sides of the bond (trans isomer). Similar types of isomer are found in square inorganic complexes depending on opposite (trans) or adjacent (cis) positioning of ligands. Another form of stereoisomerism is **optical isomerism**, in which the two isomeric forms of the molecule are asymmetric and differ in that one molecule is a mirror image of the other. Asymmetric molecules of this type exhibit optical activity, i.e. they rotate *polarized light passed through their solutions. One isomer rotates the light in one sense, the other rotates the light the same amount in the opposite sense. Many naturally occurring organic compounds are optically active. Isomers of all types have different physical properties and, to a greater or lesser extent, different chemical properties. In some cases isomers can exist in equilibrium, a phenomenon known as **tautomerism**.

isomorphism The existence of different chemical compounds with the same crystal structure. Usually it is a reflection of analogous chemical bonding patterns. The *alums, for instance, are all isomorphic compounds.

Isopoda A widely distributed order of *crustaceans (4000 species). The group includes the most successful terrestrial crustacean—the *woodlouse—as well as aquatic forms, such as the *gribble; some marine species are parasites. Isopods have oval flattened bodies, covered by armorlike plates, and—usually—seven pairs of walking legs. The young develop within a brood pouch on the female.

isoprene (CH_2:$C(CH_3)CH$:CH_2) A colorless volatile liquid. It is made from chemicals extracted from oil, coal, or tar and is used to make synthetic rubber. Natural rubber consists mainly of a polymer of isoprene. *See also* polymerization.

isostasy The principle that segments of the earth's outer crust of equal area have the same mass; the higher the feature rises, the deeper the sial of which it is composed extends into the denser sima below. If a change in this equilibrium condition occurs, movements of the crust occur to restore the equilibrium (this is called isostatic compensation). For example, areas of deposition sink, while areas of erosion rise.

isotherm A line on a map joining points of equal temperature. Corrections are usually made to compensate for the effect of altitude on temperature.

isothermal process Any process that occurs without a change in the temperature of a system (*compare* adiabatic process).

isotopes Atoms of the same element that contain equal numbers of *protons but different numbers of *neutrons in their nuclei. They have identical chemical properties but different physical properties. An isotope is indicated by combining its nucleon number and its name or symbol in various ways, for example uranium-235, U-235, ^{235}U. All naturally occurring elements are mixtures of isotopes; hydrogen, for example, consists mainly of ^1H (98.44%) with small amounts of ^2H (deuterium). A third isotope, ^3H (tritium), also exists in nature in minute quantities (1 part in 10^{17}) but can be made artificially. Radioactive isotopes (radioisotopes) are important in nuclear reactors and nuclear weapons. For these purposes sophisticated methods of separation have had to be devised, based on differences in their physical properties. Methods used depend on different rates of gaseous and thermal diffusion, centrifuging, electrolysis, and electric or magnetic effects.

isotopic spin (*or* isospin) A *quantum number used to distinguish between elementary particles (*see* particle physics) having the same properties, except that of electric charge. The concept is not based directly on the idea of rotation but it is analogous in mathematical terms to angular momentum, different charge states of the same particle (e.g. the nucleon) being regarded as having different orientations in a fictitious "isotopic space."

isotropy Any property of a body or medium that is independent of the direction in which it is measured. A body or medium that is not isotropic is said to be anisotropic.

Israel, State of A country in the Middle East, bordering on the Mediterranean Sea. There are mountains in the N, a narrow coastal plain in the W, and the Negev Desert in the S. The Jordan River flowing through the *Great Rift Valley forms part of the E border. The population varies greatly in language and culture, as it consists largely of Jews who have immigrated since 1948. Many Palestinian Arabs left the area when Israel was created but some have since returned. The remaining Arab population lives mainly in the N, with some nomadic Bedouins in the Negev Desert. In 1948 the population consisted of 650,000 Jews and 155,000 Arabs; the population since then has more than quadrupled, with Jews now forming 85% and Arabs 11%; immigration is now decreasing. Some 8% of the population live in *kibbutzim* and *moshavim* (*see* kibbutz); rural settlements established since 1948 are usually on these lines. *Economy*: both industrial and agricultural output has increased rapidly since 1948, boosted by investments and gifts of capital from abroad. There are resources of copper ore and phosphates; potash and bromine from the Dead Sea are also exploited. One of the chief centers of diamond cutting and polishing, Israel also has food-processing, textile, chemical, and electronics industries and exports finished diamonds and light manufactures. Fishing and tourism are also important. Six percent of the work force is employed in agriculture, which depends heavily on artificial irrigation. Between 1949 and 1970 the area of irrigated land increased by six times, with a corresponding increase in production. There has also been extensive reforestation, with a land reclamation scheme in the Negev Desert. Thus, although in 1948 Israel produced only 30% of its food requirements, it now imports only grain in large quantities and exports citrus and other fruit, vegetables, and flowers. Hampered since 1950 by an Arab trade boycott, Israel has had difficulty in building up an export market and still has a large trade deficit. *History*: Israel's history prior to 1948 is that of *Palestine, in which Jewish Zionists had demanded the creation of a Jewish state since the late 19th century. According to a UN recommendation and against Arab opposition, Palestine was to be divided into a Jewish state, an Arab state, and a small internationally administered zone around Jerusalem. As soon as the state of Israel was proclaimed following British withdrawal (1948), however, Arab forces (those of Egypt, Transjordan, Iraq, Syria, and Lebanon) invaded; by early 1949 Israeli forces had not only repulsed them but had gained control of 75% of Palestine, while the rest had been annexed by Jordan (the *West Bank of the Jordan River) and Egypt (the *Gaza Strip). Jerusalem was divided between Jews and Arabs. In 1956, following Nasser's nationalization of the Suez Canal, Israeli forces occupied the Gaza Strip and the *Sinai Peninsula and gained access to the Red Sea, which boosted its international trade. In the Six-Day War (1967) Israel defeated Egyptian, Syrian, and Jordanian forces and again occupied the Gaza

Strip and the Sinai Peninsula as well as the *Golan Heights, the West Bank, and the Arab sector of Jerusalem. Jerusalem was administered by Israel thereafter as a single unit. Following the Yom Kippur War (1973; so called because the Israelis were taken unawares by Egyptian forces on the Day of Atonement—Yom Kippur) peace talks opened in Geneva. Adjourned in 1974, they were reopened between Israel and Egypt following the visit to Jerusalem of President *Sadat (1977). The Camp David talks, initiated by Pres. Jimmy Carter, resulted in a peace agreement in 1979 following which Israel withdrew from Sinai (1980–82). In 1982, Israel invaded Lebanon, destroyed the Palestine Liberation Organization (PLO) base there, and occupied the southern part until completely withdrawing troops by 1988. The unpopularity within Israel of the Lebanon campaign, coupled with raging inflation, led to indecisive results in the 1984 elections. The ruling right-wing Likud party, led by Yitzhak Shamir, was forced into an uneasy coalition with Shimon Peres's Labor party, in which Peres led the government until 1986, when Shamir took over, until 1988, when he formed his own government. In 1990–91, despite numerous missile attacks by Iraq, Israel kept its forces out of the Middle East conflict that ended with Iraq's defeat after it invaded Kuwait. From November 1991, Israel engaged in its first direct talks with Arab nations, in an attempt to resolve Middle East disagreements. The Labor party, with Yitzhak Rabin as prime minister, regained power in 1992. In September 1993, Israel and the PLO reached a historic agreement, recognizing each other and establishing a basis for Palestinian self-government within Israel. Israel also signed an agreement with Jordan, setting an agenda for peace. Head of State: Chaim Herzog. Official languages: Hebrew and Arabic. Official currency: Israeli shekel of 100 new agorot. Area: 8018 sq mi (20,770 sq km). Population (1992 est): 5,000,000. Capital: Jerusalem. Main port: Haifa.

Issachar, tribe of One of the 12 *tribes of Israel. It claimed descent from Issachar, son of Jacob and Leah. It occupied territory to the S and SE of the Sea of Galilee.

Issus, Battle of (333 BC) The battle in which Alexander the Great of Macedon defeated an enormous Persian army under Darius III, which was caught in a narrow pass and outmaneuvered. Victory here opened Alexander's way from Asia Minor into Persia proper.

Istanbul (*or* Stamboul) 41 02N 28 57E A city in W Turkey, on both sides of the Bosporus. There are many ancient buildings in the city, including the mainly 6th-century Hagia Sophia (originally a church and now a museum), the Blue Mosque, and the Topkapi Palace (the former sultans' harem). It is a major port and industrial center and has three universities (15th century, 1773, and 1971); tourism is a major source of revenue. *History*: ancient Byzantium was renamed Constantinople in 330, when the emperor Constantine I declared it the capital of the Eastern Roman Empire. It was the capital of the Byzantine Empire until its capture by the Ottoman Turks in 1453, although it had been held by Crusaders from 1204 to 1261. The Ottomans renamed it Istanbul and made it the capital of their empire in 1457. After having been taken by the Allies in World War I, Istanbul became the largest city of the Turkish Republic (established in 1923). Population (1985): 5,495,000.

Isthmian Games In ancient Greece, the biennial festival held near Corinth in Poseidon's honor. Established in 581 BC these games, more lighthearted than the other major Greek festivals, included music and poetry competitions as well as the more usual athletic events and horse racing. The victor's prize was a crown of wild celery.

Istria A peninsula in Croatia between the Gulf of Trieste and the Bay of Kvarner. Passing to Italy at the end of World War I, it was ceded to Yugoslavia

(1947) except for the Territory of Trieste, which was divided between Italy and Yugoslavia in 1954.

Itaipu Dam. *See* Paraná, Rio.

Italian A language of the *Romance family spoken in Italy. The standard literary and official form is based upon the Tuscan dialect of Florence, the dialect used by *Dante.

Italian art The style of art found in Italy after the collapse of the Roman Empire. Antique motifs continued but were gradually replaced by Christian imagery and the influence, especially in Ravenna and Venice, of *Byzantine art and architecture. The *romanesque style of the 11th and 12th centuries gave way to the *gothic in the 13th century. A truly Italian art developed in the late-13th and 14th centuries, when the foundations of *Renaissance art were laid by *Giotto, *Duccio, and the sculptor Nicola *Pisano. Independent styles arose in the regional centers of Italy, especially in Florence (which dominated the 15th century), Venice (where the Venetian school was founded by the *Bellini family), and Rome. The giants of the Renaissance, *Leonardo, *Michelangelo, *Raphael, and the Venetians *Giorgione and *Titian dominated the late 15th and early 16th centuries. Their work merged into □mannerism, exemplified by the architect *Giulio Romano, the painter *Parmigianino, and in Venice the painters *Tintoretto and *Veronese. Mannerism gave way around 1600 to the *baroque, the outstanding Italian exponents of which worked in Rome: the architects *Bernini (also a sculptor) and *Borromini and the painter *Caravaggio. After the 17th century Italian art lost its impetus, except in Venice, where it briefly flowered in the 18th century with the work of *Canaletto, *Guardi, and *Tiepolo. A revival occurred in the early 20th century under the influence of *futurism and the outstanding Italian painters of the modern period are *Modigliani and de *Chirico.

Italian East Africa. *See* Somaliland.

Italian literature Latin remained the literary language of Italy until the 13th century, when poets at the Sicilian court of Frederick I (later Emperor Frederick II) began to imitate the poetry of Provence in native Italian. The delicate love poetry of the *dolce stil nuovo school of Florentine poets was followed in the 14th century by the allegorical works of *Dante, the love sonnets of *Petrarch, and the prose tales of *Boccaccio. The gradual development of the Italian language culminated in the Renaissance works of *Ariosto, *Machiavelli, and *Tasso. There followed a long period of decadence until, in the late 18th century, a literary revival was brought about by the dramatists *Alfieri and *Goldoni and the poet *Foscolo. In the 19th century the influence of romanticism, epitomized in the poetry of *Leopardi, was followed by a reaction represented by the classicism of the poet *Carducci and the realism of the novelist and dramatist Giovanni Verga (1840–1922). Major writers of the early 20th century include the poet *D'Annunzio, the dramatist *Pirandello, and the critic Benedetto *Croce. Literary exploration of social and moral themes was curbed during the fascist regime from 1922 to 1943, but recommenced after World War II, with such writers as Alberto *Moravia, Cesare *Pavese, and Italo Calvino.

Italic languages A subgroup of the *Indo-European language family spoken in central and NE Italy in the thousand years before the rise of Rome. A parent of modern *Romance languages, this group comprised four related dialects: *Latin, Faliscan, Osco-Umbrian, and Venetic. At the beginning of the 1st millenium BC Osco-Umbrian was the most widely spoken, but with the growth of Roman civilization, Latin quickly came to dominate other dialects, which are now known only through Latin sources.

italic script A style of handwriting adopted in 15th-century Italy by papal scribes and later (c. 1500) adapted for printing. Italic cursive letters eliminate unnecessary lifts of the pen, permitting rapid legible handwriting. *In print its characteristic sloped letters, such as those used in this sentence, are used mainly for display, emphasis, or to indicate that a word is in a foreign language.*

Italy, Republic of A country in S Europe, occupying a peninsula bordered by the Tyrrhenian Sea (W), the Ionian Sea (S), and the Adriatic Sea (E). The principal offshore islands are Sicily and Sardinia. Except for small coastal areas and the Po Valley in the N, the country is generally rugged and mountainous. The main rivers are the Po, Tiber, Arno, and Adige. *Economy*: agriculture is still important, the main crops being wheat, maize, grapes, and olives. Industry, however, has expanded considerably since World War II and is now the most important sector. The principal manufactures are textiles (including silk) and clothing, and machinery, motor vehicles, and chemicals, which together with fruit and vegetables are the principal exports. The wine industry is growing in importance and exports have increased in recent years. Mineral resources are not large and Italy is heavily dependent on imported fossil fuels, although oil is now being extracted, especially in Sicily, and hydroelectricity has been considerably developed. There are also plans to develop nuclear energy. Tourism is an important source of revenue. During the 1970s, however, Italy was faced with severe problems of inflation and economic stagnation and the longstanding problem of integrating the poorer predominantly agricultural S with the industrial N remained unresolved. *History*: pre-Roman Italy was inhabited from the 7th century BC by the *Etruscans in the N, Italics (including the Samnites) and Latins in central Italy, and Greek colonists in the southern mainland and Sicily. By 275 BC most of the peninsula had come under the rule of Rome (*see* Roman Republic). As the Western *Roman Empire declined from the 4th century AD, Italy was invaded by a succession of barbarian tribes, including the Visigoths and the Vandals. The last Roman emperor was deposed in 476 by the German king, Odoacer, who in 493 was in turn overthrown by the Ostrogoths. They were expelled in the early 6th century by the Eastern (Byzantine) Roman Empire, the position of which was threatened from the mid-6th century by successive invasions: the Lombards were followed by the Franks in the 8th and 9th centuries, a period that also saw the origins of the pope's temporal power (*see* papal states); the Muslims invaded the S in the 9th and 10th centuries, Magyars, the N in the 10th century, and Normans, the S in the 11th century. The claim of the German kings to rule Italy was established in 962, when Otto the Great was crowned Holy Roman Emperor in Rome. The conflict from the 11th century between successive popes and emperors over the *investiture controversy embroiled the Italian city-states (notably Milan, Pisa, Genoa, Venice, and Florence), which in the 12th century were further divided by the struggle between *Guelfs and Ghibellines. The economic and political development of the city-states in the first half of the 14th century was facilitated by the removal of the papacy to Avignon and the preoccupation with German affairs of the Holy Roman Emperors. Many of the Italian cities came to be dominated by single families, such as the *Visconti and then the Sforza in Milan and the *Medici in Florence, who during the Renaissance were often outstanding patrons of culture and learning. Following the French invasion of Italy in 1494, Italy became the scene of conflict between France and Spain and from the 16th to early 18th centuries was largely dominated by the latter. Spain ruled Milan, Naples, Sicily, and Sardinia directly and influenced Savoy, Genoa, and Tuscany; of the major Italian states only the papal states and Venice remained independent. During the 18th century Spanish hegemony was destroyed, passing to Austria until 1796, when Italy was conquered by the French Revolutionary armies under Napoleon. The French occupation gave Italy the experience of unity. After Napoleon's fall and the restoration of Austrian rule this developed into the movement for independence and unification (the *Risorgimento). By 1861, under the leadership of Victor Emmanuel II of Sardinia-Piedmont and his chief minister Cavour, aided by Garibaldi in the S, the Austrians had been expelled and the kingdom of Italy proclaimed with Victor Emmanuel as its first king; unification was virtually complete by 1870. In the late 19th century Italy acquired a colonial empire, notably Somaliland and Eritrea in East Africa, but its attempt to seize Ethiopia was defeated at Adowa in 1896. In 1915 Italy entered World War I on the side of the Allies, obtaining the Trentino and the Istrian peninsula (*see* Irredentists). The postwar rise of fascism brought Mussolini to power in 1922. In 1936 he conquered Ethiopia and in 1939, Albania. In 1940, loyal to his alliances (1936, 1939) with Hitler, Mussolini took Italy into World War II on Germany's side (1940). The Allied conquest of Sicily (1943) brought Mussolini's fall and in 1946 Umberto II abdicated following a referendum rejecting the monarchy. Since the establishment of the Republic there have been over 40 governments, led by the Christian Democrats. However, their repeated failure to deal effectively with a stagnating economy, widespread corruption, and growing lawlessness exacerbated by such groups as the *Red Brigades and fascists led to an increase in the strength of the Communist party, which in 1977 achieved a measure of participation in government. In 1983, after an election in which the Christian Democrats received a third of the vote and the Communists slightly less, a Socialist, Bettino Craxi, became premier of a government of center-left parties. The government pursued a policy of fiscal conservatism while successfully suppressing terrorists and intensifying a campaign against the Mafia. A caretaker government in 1987 was followed by a coalition government that collapsed in 1988. In 1991 Giuseppe Andreotti formed his seventh coalition government, but he was forced to step down in 1992 to make way for new leadership. Government and business corruption charges mounted in 1993. Official language: Italian. Official religion: Roman Catholic. Official currency: lira of 100 centesimi. Area: 116,350 sq mi (301,425 sq km). Population (1990 est): 57,657,000. Capital: Rome. Main port: Genoa.

itch mite A parasitic *mite, *Sarcoptes scabei*, that produces *scabies in man and mange in domestic animals. The female burrows into the skin, where it lays eggs and causes intense itching and irritation. Family: *Sarcoptidae*.

Ithaca (Modern Greek name: Itháki) A Greek island in the Ionian Sea, one of the Ionian Islands. It is widely believed to have been the home of Homer's Odysseus. Area: 33 sq mi (85 sq km).

Ithaca 42 27N 76 30W A city in central New York, on the S tip of Cayuga Lake. Cornell University (1865) is there. Settled in 1789, it is a center for the agricultural products of the area and also produces office machinery and clothing. Population (1990): 29,541.

Ito Hirobumi (1841–1909) Japanese statesman, who played a leading part in the abolition of feudalism and the adoption of modern methods and institutions. During the 1880s he assumed responsibility for drafting the Meiji constitution (1889) and between 1885 and 1901 he was prime minister four times. During his second ministry Japan defeated China in the *Sino-Japanese War (1894–95). Ito was assassinated by a Korean nationalist.

Itúrbide, Agustin (1783–1824) Mexican soldier prominent in the independence movement; emperor (1822–23). He used the general unrest in Mexico to further his own advancement in the army. Appointed commander of the combined rebel forces when Mexico declared itself independent of Spain (1820), he subsequently proclaimed himself emperor. Within months *Santa Anna forced his abdication; Itúrbide returned from exile in 1824 but was executed.

Ivanovo 57 00N 41 00E A city in Russia, on the Uvod River. It played an important part in both the 1905 and 1917 Russian Revolutions. It is one of the country's major textile centers. Population (1987): 479,000.

Ivan (III) the Great (1440–1505) Grand prince of Muscovy (1462–1505). Ivan greatly expanded Muscovite territory and ended Russian subordination to the Tatars. In 1497 he introduced a new legal code. Ivan married (1472) Zoë Palaeologus (d. 1503), the niece of the last Byzantine emperor, and adopted the Byzantine two-headed eagle as his arms.

Ivan (IV) the Terrible (1530–84) Grand prince of Muscovy (1533–84), who was crowned tsar in 1547. Ivan reformed the legal code and local administration (1555), conquered Kazan and Astrakhan, and established commercial relations with England. After 1560 his reign was marred by his brutality: thousands were executed and in a fit of rage Ivan murdered his son (1581). The effects of his tyranny were aggravated by the financial strains resulting from the abortive *Livonian War (1558–82).

Ives, Charles (Edward) (1874–1954) US composer. An early experimenter with polyrhythms, polytonality, quarter tones, and the superimposition of disparate musical styles, he composed four symphonies, five violin sonatas, songs, and other works. His second piano sonata, subtitled *Concord, Mass* (1909–15), was inspired by writers associated with the town of Concord. Its movements were subtitled "Emerson," "Hawthorne," "The Alcotts," and "Thoreau." One of his best-known works is *Central Park in the Dark* (1898–1907). Of the more than 500 works he composed, most remained unpublished. For his *Symphony No. 3* (1904) he was awarded a Pulitzer Prize. He was also senior partner of the insurance firm of Ives and Myrick.

ivory The close-grained white tissue forming the tusks of elephants, walruses, and narwhals and the teeth of hippos. So-called fossil ivory is obtained from mammoths. Plastics have now generally replaced ivory for such mundane domestic artifacts as knife handles, but, being easy to carve and polish, ivory is still such a valuable commodity that its main source, the African elephant, is threatened with extinction. Ivory carving is a very ancient art; objects from France date to Paleolithic times and fine examples survive from Egyptian, Minoan, Mycenaean, Assyrian, Greek, and Roman civilizations. In Europe ivory plaques with relief carving became important during the early Middle Ages for small religious icons, book covers, caskets, etc. India, SE Asia, China, and Japan (*see* netsuke) have ancient traditions of skilled ivory carving. American Eskimo carvings in walrus ivory are greatly prized by connoisseurs.

ivory-billed woodpecker A rare black-and-white *woodpecker, *Campephilus principalis*, occurring in North American forests; 18 in (45 cm) long, it has a white bill and the male has a red crest. It feeds on woodboring insects and requires a large feeding territory, hence its decline due to the expansion of the timber industry.

Ivory Coast, Republic of (French name: Côte d'Ivoire) A country in West Africa, on the Gulf of Guinea. Swamps and tropical forests give way to savanna on higher land to the N. The diverse African population includes Baule, Bete, Senufo, and Malinke. *Economy*: chiefly agricultural, livestock being important as well as crops, including maize, yams, and other tropical plants. The main cash crop is coffee, of which, together with timber (particularly mahogany), Ivory Coast is Africa's leading exporter. Other exports include cocoa, pineapples, and rubber. Mineral resources are on the whole sparse, although some manganese is mined, diamond fields are being exploited, and some oil was found in 1977. Industry is being developed, including tourism. *History*: explored by the Portuguese in the late 15th century, the area was disputed by several European trading nations over the centuries, becoming a French colony in 1893. It became part of French West Africa in 1904 and an overseas territory in 1946. It possessed internal self-government as a member of the French Community from 1958 and became fully independent in 1960. The Ivory Coast's slumping economy prompted austerity measures that were met with violent protests across the country in 1990. The economy was further strained by an influx of refugees from Liberia. The first free elections since independence, held in late 1990, were tinged by accusations of cheating. The death in December 1993 of Felix Houphouet-Boigny, president since independence, set off a struggle for political power. Official language: French. Official currency: CFA (Communauté financière africaine) franc of 100 centimes. Area: 124,470 sq mi (322,463 sq km). Population (1990 est): 12,070,000. Capital: Yamoussoukro. Main port: Abidjan.

ivy An evergreen woody climbing plant, *Hedera helix*, that has glossy three- to five-lobed leaves, aerial roots (with which it clings to supports), clusters of small greenish-yellow flowers, and small round fruits ripening from green to black. Native to Europe and W Asia, it is widely cultivated (ornamental ivies often have variegated foliage). Family: *Araliaceae*.

Ivy League A group of seven universities and one college in the NE of high academic and social prestige. They include *Harvard, *Yale, *Princeton, Brown, Dartmouth, Cornell, Columbia, and Pennsylvania and are all members of an athletic conference for intercollegiate sports known as the Ivy League, which dates back to the 1870s.

Iwo 7 38N 4 11E A city in SW Nigeria. Its main activity is the export of agricultural products, especially cocoa. Population (1990 est): 312,000.

Iwo Jima 24 47N 141 19E A Japanese island in the W Pacific Ocean, the largest of the Volcano Islands. Captured by US forces after a severe struggle (1945), it was returned in 1968. Sulfur and sugar are produced. Area: 8 sq mi (20 sq km).

Iwo Jima, Battle of (1944) World War II battle. US troops invaded the Japanese island stronghold of Iwo Jima and, after more than three weeks of fighting, secured it for a strategic US airplane landing strip. Casualties were heavy, well over 20,000 for each side. The photograph of US Marines raising the flag atop Mt Suribachi has been immortalized in statuary and paintings as a symbol of courage.

Izanagi and Izanami In Japanese mythology, the male and female creator deities of Japan. They stirred the sea with a spear and drops from its tip formed the Japanese islands, for which they then created other *kami* (spirits) as inhabitants and guardians (*see* Amaterasu).

Izhevsk 56 49N 53 11E A city in Russia, the capital of the Udmurt Republic. It is a major metallurgical center. Population (1991 est): 647,000.

Izmir (former name: Smyrna) 38 25N 27 10E A port in W Turkey, on the Aegean Sea. Much was destroyed by fire in 1922, the rebuilt town being a modern commercial center with a university (1953). There is trade in silk, cotton, carpets, figs, raisins, and sponges. Population (1985): 1,490,000.

Izmit 40 47N 29 55E A city in NW Turkey, on the Sea of Marmara. As ancient Nicomedia it was the seat of the kings of Bithynia, and it is now a naval port. Population (1985): 236,200.

J

Jabalpur (*or* Jubbulpore) 23 10N 79 59E A city in India, in Madhya Pradesh. An important railroad junction and industrial center, its manufactures include cement, textiles, and military equipment. Its university was established in 1957. Population (1991): 739,961.

Jabir. *See* Geber.

jabiru A large *stork, *Jabiru mycteria*, ranging from Mexico to Argentina; 55 in (140 cm) long, it is white with a dark-blue head and neck with a red patch at the base and has a long slightly upturned heavy bill.

jaborandi A tropical American plant of the genus *Pilocarpus* (22 species), the dried leaves of which yield an alkaloid, pilocarpine, used medicinally in eye-drops to constrict the pupil and to treat glaucoma. Family: *Rutaceae*.

jacamar A bird belonging to a family (*Galbulidae*; 15 species) occurring in tropical American forests; 5–11 in (12–27 cm) long, jacamars have a large head tapering to a long narrow tail and iridescent blue, green, or bronze plumage. They feed on insects caught in flight. Order: *Piciformes* (woodpeckers, etc.).

jacana A waterbird belonging to a family (*Jacanidae*; 7 species) occurring in tropical regions worldwide, also called lily trotter. Jacanas are characterized by long legs with elongated toes and claws, which enable them to run over floating vegetation; 10–13 in (25–32 cm) long, they are commonly reddish to dark-brown in color and can swim and dive well, feeding on aquatic plants and animals. Order: *Charadriiformes* (gulls, plovers, etc.).

Jacaranda A genus of ☐trees and shrubs (50 species) of South and Central America and the West Indies, often grown as ornamentals. *J. mimosifolia*, up to 49 ft (15 m) tall, has finely divided compound leaves and clusters of blue or violet tubular flowers. In cooler climates it can be cultivated in warm greenhouses. Some species yield commercially valuable timber. Family: *Bignoniaceae*.

jackal A carnivorous mammal of the genus *Canis*, found in Asia and Africa. Jackals are closely related to dogs and have pricked ears and bushy tails. The African black-backed jackal (*C. mesomeles*) is up to 43 in (110 cm) long including the tail (10–13 in; 25–33 cm) and often hunts in packs for carrion, usually at night. The African side-striped jackal (*C. adustus*) is smaller and shyer.

jackdaw An intelligent Eurasian crow, *Corvus monedula*, about 13 in (32 cm) long, having a black plumage with a gray nape, an erectile crest, and pale-blue eyes. Often found in colonies, jackdaws may be seen flying around cliffs, ruins, and large buildings. They feed on insects, grain, and carrion and may rob nests of eggs and chicks.

Jack Russell terrier A breed of dog developed in England from the fox terrier by the Rev. John Russell (1795–1883) for flushing foxes from earth. It has a stocky body and a strong muscular head with small drooping ears. The short coat is white, black, and tan. Height: up to 15 in (38 cm).

Jackson 32 20N 90 11W The capital city of Mississippi, on the Pearl River. Founded in 1821, it was virtually destroyed by General Sherman in 1863. More recently (1960s) it has been the scene of considerable racial tension. Its industries include the production of oil and gas, textiles, and glass. Population (1990): 196,637.

Jackson, Andrew (1767–1845) US military leader and statesman; 7th president of the United States (1829–37). A Tennessee frontiersman, Jackson fought in the *Revolutionary War, served in the US House of Representatives (1796–97) and in the US Senate (1798), and later became a national hero when his defense of New Orleans boosted American morale at the end of the *War of 1812. After the war, he commanded US forces in an invasion of Florida (1818), where he defeated the *Seminoles. Jackson was again elected to the US Senate (1823–25) and ran unsuccessfully for the presidency in 1824. As the leader of an emerging faction of the Jeffersonian Republicans, Jackson is generally credited with the foundation of the modern *Democratic party. As the victorious presidential nominee of that party in 1828, reelected in 1832, he relied on support from the middle class and opposed the power of aristocrats and professional politicians. His economic policy strengthened *states' rights and one of the most controversial acts of his presidency was his withdrawal of federal deposits from the *Bank of the United States. After leaving office, he spent his later years at his home, The Hermitage, near Nashville, Tenn.

ANDREW JACKSON *President (1829–37) who, as a general in the War of 1812, had been the hero of the Battle of New Orleans.*

Jackson, Glenda (1936–   ) British actress. She has acted in many Royal Shakespeare Company stage productions, but first achieved popular success with her portrayal of Elizabeth I in a television series (1971). Her movies include *Women in Love* (1969), *A Touch of Class* (1972), *Hedda* (1976), *The Incredible Sarah* (1976), and *Stevie* (1978). She later served in Parliament as a Labour representative.

Jackson, Jesse (1941–) US minister and civil rights leader. He worked closely with Martin Luther *King, Jr. during the 1960s and established and led Operation Breadbasket, an antidiscriminatory project of the Southern Christian Leadership Conference, and PUSH (People United to Serve Humanity). He campaigned unsuccessfully for the Democratic presidential nomination (1984, 1988) and worked successfully for US disinvestment in South Africa.

Jackson, Michael (1958–) US singer, dancer, and composer, known for his high tenor voice. A member of the Jackson Five, a group with four of his brothers, he sang and danced from the age of five. Signed by Motown Records in 1969, the group rose to stardom and by 1975 had changed record companies and been renamed The Jacksons. Michael, usually the lead singer in the group, went on to unprecedented success as a solo act with sold-out tours and such hit recordings/videos as *Thriller* (1983), *Bad* (1987), and *Dangerous* (1991).

Jackson, Robert Houghwout (1892–1954) US lawyer and jurist; US Supreme Court justice (1941–54). He worked as a lawyer for the Bureau of Internal Revenue (1934) and the Securities and Exchange Commission (1935) and as assistant attorney general (1936–37), solicitor general (1938), and attorney general (1940) before being appointed to the Supreme Court. He was chief prosecutor at the Nazi war crime trials in Nuremberg, Germany (1946–47). As an associate justice he was known as a moderate in favor of separation of church and state and against the seizure of the steel mills by Pres. Harry S. Truman in 1952.

Jackson, Stonewall (Thomas Jonathan J.; 1824–63) US Confederate general. A graduate of West Point (1846), he served in the Mexican War and then left the army (1852). He joined the Confederate cause when the Civil War began. In the first battle of *Bull Run (1861), he and his brigade were described as standing "like a stone wall" in the face of the Federal advance. Jackson was a master of rapid tactical movement, shown particularly in the Shenandoah Valley campaign (1862) and he was considered Lee's best lieutenant. His untimely death at Chancellorsville left a gap in the Confederate command that was never filled.

Jackson Hole A valley and wildlife preserve near the Teton Range in NW Wyoming. Part of the valley has been included in Grand Teton National Park since 1950. American elk herds feed here during the winter. Area: 376 sq mi (974 sq km).

Jacksonville 30 20N 81 40W A city and port in NE Florida, on the St Johns River near its mouth on the Atlantic Ocean. Named for President Jackson (formerly the first territorial governor of Florida), it is the state's largest city and main commercial center. A major naval base, its industries include ship repairing, paper, and chemicals. Population (1990): 635,230.

Jack the Ripper An unidentified murderer who killed and mutilated at least seven prostitutes in the East End of London, England, in late 1888. One recent theory suggests that he was Vassily Konovalov, a Russian who committed similar murders in Paris and St Petersburg and who died in a Russian asylum.

Jacobins An extremist group in the *French Revolution. The Jacobin Club was founded in 1789 and (meeting in a Dominican [*or* Jacobin] monastery) became increasingly radical. Helped by *Danton's rabble-rousing speeches, they proclaimed the republic, had the king executed, and overthrew the *Girondins (1792–93). Through the Committee of *Public Safety, the Jacobins, under the influence of *Robespierre, instituted the *Reign of Terror. They collapsed after Robespierre's execution.

Jacobites Supporters of the exiled *Stuart king, James II, and his descendants. Between 1688, when the Glorious Revolution overthrew James II, and 1745, the Jacobites (mainly Roman Catholics and/or Tories), were the rallying point for opposition to the Hanoverian monarchs. Two Jacobite rebellions, in 1715 and 1745, were suppressed and thereafter the movement lost its political force.

Jacob's ladder A perennial herb, *Polemonium caeruleum*, native of Eurasia and widely cultivated as a garden flower. Growing to a height of 35 in (90 cm), it has bright-blue flowers and leaves consisting of paired ladderlike leaflets. Family: *Polemoniaceae*.

Jacopo della Quercia (c. 1374–1438) Italian Renaissance sculptor, who was the Sienese counterpart to *Donatello. His Sienese works include the Fonte Gaia (1416–19), the now dismantled fountain for the Piazza del Campo, and the Baptistry font, on which he collaborated with *Ghiberti. However, Jacopo's most powerful works are the marble reliefs (1425–35) of scenes from Genesis, which surround the portal of S Petronio, Bologna.

Jacopone da Todi (c. 1236–1306) Italian religious poet. On the death of his wife, he joined the Franciscans as a member of the "Spirituals," the strictest group of the order. In 1298 he was imprisoned by Pope Boniface VIII, whom he had attacked in verse, but was released on the pope's death in 1303. The famous Latin poem *Stabat mater dolorosa* is attributed to him, but most of his poetry was written in the Umbrian dialect of Italian. His *laudi spirituali* (spiritual praises) are vivid devotional poems covering a wide range of mood, from mystical love of God to bitter denunciation of the world.

Jacquard, Joseph-Marie (1752–1834) French inventor of the Jacquard loom, completed in 1801. Its design allowed for the weaving of figured patterns by means of punched cards, which were later employed in the calculator developed by Charles *Babbage and in subsequent computers.

Jacquerie (1358) A peasant revolt in NE France during the Hundred Years' War with England. Its name refers to the aristrocrats' contemptuous nickname for a peasant—Jacques Bonhomme. Caused by famine, plague, and war, the rebellion was rapidly suppressed.

jade An extremely hard semiprecious stone, usually green or greenish white, consisting of a tough compact variety of either jadeite (a pyroxene, $NaAlSi_2O_6$) or nephrite (an amphibole). Many highly prized stones come from Upper Burma, where they are found in river terraces or beds.

Jadotville. *See* Likasi.

Jaén 37 46N 3 48W A city in S Spain, in Andalusia. It has a fine Renaissance cathedral. Once famous for silk, it now produces chemicals and has rich lead mines nearby. Population (1970): 78,156.

Jaffa. *See* Tel Aviv-Yafo.

Jagger, Mick (1944–) British rock singer; lead singer of the *Rolling Stones. He became notorious for his aggressive performances on stage and was arrested in 1967 for possessing drugs. He acted in the films *Ned Kelly* (1969) and *Performance* (1970).

Jagiellons The ruling dynasty of Poland and Lithuania (1386–1572), Hungary (1440–1441, 1490–1526), and Bohemia (1471–1526). The dynasty was founded by Jagiełło (1350–1434), grand duke of Lithuania, who became king of

Poland as Władysław II in 1386, when he married Queen Jadwiga of Poland (1370–99; reigned 1384–99). He was succeeded by his son Władysław III (1424–44), who also became king of Hungary (1440). Władysław III's nephew Władysław (1456–1516) became Vladislav II of Bohemia in 1471 and of Hungary in 1490. The Jagiellons lost Hungary and Bohemia to the Turks at the battle of *Mohács (1526). The last Jagiellon ruler was Sigismund II Augustus (1520–72; ruled Poland 1548–72), under whom a Polish-Lithuanian commonwealth was created by the Union of *Lublin.

jaguar The largest New World *cat, *Panthera onca*, found in the southern US and Central and South America. Up to 8 ft (2.5 m) long including the tail (28–35 in; 70–90 cm), it has dark rosette-shaped spots on its yellow coat. Jaguars inhabit forest and scrub and can swim well and may catch fish. They also hunt peccaries, turtles, and capybaras and may attack domestic livestock.

jaguarundi A weasel-like *cat, *Felis yagouaroundi*, of Central and South America. Up to 43 in (110 cm) long, it stands only 11 in (28 cm) high at the shoulder. It has a red or gray coat, long tail, and small ears. In addition to birds, jaguarundis eat such fruits as grapes, figs, and bananas.

Jahangir (1569–1627) Emperor of India (1605–27); the son of *Akbar the Great, from whom he inherited a powerful empire. After expanding it further he ruled wisely and justly, fostering sports and the arts. He enjoyed good relations with the British *East India Company.

Jainism The religion of between two and three million Indians, followers of *Mahavira. Founded in the 6th century BC in opposition to Vedic religion, Jainism stresses *ahimsa, asceticism, and meditation. Right belief, knowledge, and conduct are the means of release from the perpetual round of rebirth caused by *karma. This release is possible only for monks; the laity aim only for a better rebirth. Jainism is atheistic, although lesser spirits and demons proliferate. The universe, containing heavens and hells revolving eternally in ascending and descending cycles, is seen as the mechanistic interaction of six principles: souls, space, time, matter, right, and wrong. These constitute the opposing categories of life and nonlife.

Jaipur 26 53N 75 50E A city in India, the capital of Rajasthan. Formerly the capital of the princely state of Rajasthan, it has many fine buildings built of pink sandstone, an 18th-century observatory, and a university (1947). Jaipur is famous for its enamel work and jewelry, textile printing, and stone, marble, and ivory carving. Population (1991): 1,454,678.

Jakarta (*or* Djakarta; name until 1949: Batavia) 6 09S 106 49E The capital of Indonesia, in NW Java linked by canal to its port, Tanjung Priok. The Dutch set up a fort here in the early 17th century and it became a major commercial center as the headquarters of the Dutch East India Company. The University of Indonesia was founded in 1950. Population (1980): 6,503,500.

jalap A climbing plant *Ipomoea purga*, of Mexico and South America, that has crimson flowers. The dried tubers yield a resin that is used medicinally as a laxative. Family: *Convolvulaceae*.

Jamaica, State of An island country in the Caribbean Sea, off the S coast of Cuba. A high plateau is crossed by the Blue Mountains, which reach 7400 ft (2255 m). The population is mainly of African and mixed African and European descent. *Economy*: sugar, bauxite, and tourism form the basis, although the tourist trade was badly affected for several years by domestic unrest. Jamaica is the world's second largest producer of bauxite and alumina and has increased its control of the industry, which was previously handled by US companies. Alumina-processing smelters and a bauxite and alumina complex have been built in partnership with other countries. *History*: discovered by Columbus in 1494, it was occupied by the Spanish, who exterminated the original Arawak inhabitants. Captured by the British in 1655, it became a colony and a center of the slave trade until the abolition of slavery in 1833. Self-government was introduced in 1944 and extended in 1959, and in 1962 Jamaica became an independent state within the British Commonwealth. There has been considerable political unrest in recent years between the Labour party (JLP) and the People's National party (PNP) led by Michael *Manley, an advocate of democratic socialism and republican status for Jamaica. A state of emergency existed in 1976–77 following riots. In 1980 Manley lost the election to Edward Seaga. In 1989, Manley came back and served until 1992, when he resigned due to illness. He was succeeded by Percival J. Patterson. Enjoying a particularly favorable relationship with the US, Jamaica was the chief beneficiary of the US-sponsored Caribbean Basin Initiative. Jamaica is a member of the OAS and CARICOM. Prime minister: Percival J. Patterson. Official language: English. Official currency: Jamaican dollar of 100 cents. Area: 4244 sq mi (10,991 sq km). Population (1990 est): 2,513,000. Capital and main port: Kingston.

James (I) the Conqueror (1208–76) King of Aragon (1213–76). James, who became effective ruler in 1227, was the greatest medieval Aragonese monarch. He reconquered the Balearic Islands and Valencia from the Moors and thus laid the basis for Aragonese expansion in the Mediterranean in the next century. James also contributed to the cultural achievements of his reign, prompting the compilation of the *Chronicle* of his exploits.

James I (1394–1437) King of the Scots (1406–37), whose actual rule began on his release (1424) from English imprisonment. He strengthened royal authority at the expense of the nobles, whom he treated with some harshness, and extended royal control over the administration of justice and commerce. He was assassinated by a group of disaffected nobles. He is believed to be the author of the poem "The Kingis Quair" ("The King's Book").

James I (1566–1625) The first Stuart king of England and Ireland (1603–25) and, as James VI, king of the Scots (1567–1625). He succeeded his mother Mary, Queen of Scots, and was brought up by a series of regents. As king he reasserted royal authority against the encroachments of the nobility and the Presbyterians. In England, James encountered opposition from his parliaments, which resented his assertion of the *divine right of kings. James was also unpopular for his choice of favorites and for his attempts to obtain a Spanish marriage for his son. One of the great achievements of his reign was the publication (1611) of the *King James or Authorized version of the Bible. He was the first king to rule both Scotland and England.

James II (1430–60) King of the Scots (1437–60). He established his authority over rival factions and continued the extension of royal control and justice begun by his father James I. He was killed while besieging the English at Roxburgh Castle.

James II (1633–1701) King of England, Scotland, and Ireland (1685–88). The second son of Charles I, James (as duke of York) escaped to Holland (1648) after his father's defeat in the Civil War. In 1659 he married the daughter of the Earl of Clarendon, Anne Hyde (1637–71), by whom he had two daughters (later Queens Mary II and Anne). A few years after the Restoration (1660) of his brother Charles II, James became a Roman Catholic. Successive attempts to exclude him from the succession failed and in 1685 he became king. The Protestant rebellion of the Duke of *Monmouth was suppressed, Roman Catholics were admitted to public office, and religious freedom for all denominations was announced (1687). The threat of a Roman Catholic succession was increased with the birth of a son (*see* James Edward Stuart, the Old Pretender) to his second wife, Mary of Modena (1658–1718), and precipitated his overthrow in the *Glorious Revolution. James was forced to flee and his subsequent attempt to regain the crown from Ireland failed with his defeat by William III's forces at the *Boyne (1690) and Aughrim (1691). He died an exile in France.

James III (1452–88) King of the Scots (1460–88). Until 1469 Scotland was ruled by a regency and his personal rule was marked by baronial revolts. He was killed after defeat by rebel barons near Stirling.

James IV (1473–1513) King of the Scots (1488–1513). In 1503 he married *Margaret Tudor. He defeated the rebels who had killed his father James III, procuring internal stability and respect for the monarchy. Recurrent hostility with England culminated in the invasion of Northumberland (1513) and his defeat and death, with most of his nobles, at *Flodden.

James V (1512–42) King of the Scots (1513–42). During his minority (1513–28) Scotland was controlled by rival pro-French and pro-English factions. James favored the French, to whom he was allied by his marriage to Mary of Guise (1515–60). He died shortly after the failure of an invasion of England and was succeeded by his daughter Mary, Queen of Scots.

James VI (King of the Scots). *See* James I (king of England).

James, Henry (1843–1916) US novelist and critic. Much of his childhood was spent in Europe, and in 1875 he moved to Paris, where he met Turgenev, Flaubert, and others who influenced his concern with the technique of fiction. From 1876 he lived mainly in England, becoming a British citizen in 1915. His novel *Roderick Hudson* (1875) introduced the international theme of Americans confronting European culture that he was to develop in many other novels, such as *The Portrait of a Lady* (1881), although he occasionally returned to strictly American settings, as in *Washington Square* (1881) and *The Bostonians* (1886). He wrote more than a hundred shorter works of fiction, of which *The Turn of the Screw* (1898) is perhaps the best known. In his later novels, *The Wings of the Dove* (1902), *The Ambassadors* (1903), and *The Golden Bowl* (1904), action is subordinated to a searching psychological analysis rendered in a highly elaborate style. He was an influential critic; the prefaces to his novels are important theoretical statements on the novel. He also wrote plays, but they were not successful, although many of his works have been adapted for dramatic performance. His brother **William James** (1842–1910) was a psychologist and philosopher, who developed the theory of *pragmatism in ethics. He held that the truth or falsity of classical philosophical systems made little difference to everyday life and that the function of a theory should be to solve practical difficulties: thus a theory was only true in so far as it successfully helped to solve problems. Religious and moral beliefs were treated in the same nondogmatic way, especially in his influential *Varieties of Religious Experience* (1902) and *The Meaning of Truth* (1909).

James, Jesse (Woodson) (1847–92) US outlaw. He and his brother Frank fought with southern guerrilla groups during the Civil War before they became outlaws. By 1867 he had formed the James gang and was robbing banks, stagecoaches, and trains in his native Missouri and surrounding states. A $10,000 reward offered by the state of Missouri in 1881 was claimed by a James gang member, Robert Ford, who shot Jesse, living as Thomas Howard in St Joseph. The legends surrounding Jesse James range from those depicting him as a Robin Hood to those portraying a cold-blooded killer.

James, St In the New Testament, the name of three followers of Christ. **1.** A leader, with St Peter, of the early Christians of Jerusalem. He is described as "the Lord's brother" (Mark 6.3), but the exact relationship is uncertain. He was a devout follower of Jewish practice, being converted to Christianity at the time of the resurrection. He was condemned to death by the Sanhedrin in 62 AD. The **Epistle of James** in the New Testament was traditionally attributed to him and was possibly written early in the 1st century AD. **2.** The Apostle, known as St James the Great, son of Zebedee and brother of *John. He was present with his brother at many events in the life of Christ recounted in the Gospels. He was beheaded by Herod Agrippa I in 44 AD. In the Middle Ages it was believed that he had preached in Spain and was buried at Santiago de Compostela, the center of international pilgrimages. Feast day: July 25. **3.** The Apostle, known as St James the Less, son of Alphaeus. Nothing further is certainly known about his life. Feast day: May 1.

James Edward Stuart, the Old Pretender (1688–1766) The son of James II, the deposed Roman Catholic king of England. In exile, he was urged by his supporters, known as *Jacobites, to claim the English throne. After their invasion of Scotland failed in 1715, James abandoned his claim and lived in permanent exile in Rome.

Jameson, Sir Leander Starr (1853–1917) South African statesman, born in Scotland, who worked closely with Cecil *Rhodes; prime minister of Cape Colony (1904–08). In 1895 he led the **Jameson Raid** into the Transvaal to support British immigrants against the Afrikaners. Imprisoned for three months in England he returned to Cape Colony to become a member of Parliament and, on Rhodes's death, leader of the Progressive party.

James River A river in the central US, flowing generally ESE through Virginia to *Chesapeake Bay. Jamestown, the first permanent English settlement in America, was established along its lower course in 1607. Length: 340 mi (547 km).

Jamestown The first permanent English colony in America, established May 14, 1607 on a peninsula in the James River (Virginia) by the London Company. Although many settlers died from disease, lack of food, and Indian attacks in the early years, by 1610, under the leadership of Capt. John Smith, the settlement was secure. The marriage of John Rolfe to the daughter of Chief Powhaton, Pocahontas, temporarily improved relations with the Indians. The colonists cultivated tobacco, which became an important crop. The House of Burgesses, the first representative government in the colonies, was established there in 1619. Jamestown was the capital of Virginia until 1699. It is preserved as a colonial historical park.

Jammu and Kashmir A state in N India, forming part of the disputed area of *Kashmir. Area: 38,820 sq mi (100,569 sq km). Population (1991): 7,718,700. Capital: Jammu (winter); Srinagar (summer).

Jamnagar 22 28N 70 06E A city in India, in Gujarat on the Gulf of Kutch. Formerly the capital of the princely state of Nawanagar, it has a fine palace. Industries include textiles and cement. Population (1991): 325,475.

Jamshedpur 22 47N 86 12E A city in India, in Bihar. Founded in 1907 by the industrialist Dorabji Jamsetji Tata, it is the site of India's principal iron and steel works. Population (1991): 461,212.

Janáček, Leoš (1854–1928) Czech composer. He studied at the Leipzig and Vienna conservatories and became professor of composition at Brno conservatory in 1919. He was over 60 before he gained wide recognition as a composer. In his vocal works he attempted to reproduce natural speech rhythms; he was also influenced by folk music. His works include the operas *Jenufa* (1894–1903), *The Excursions of Mr Broucek* (1908–17), and *The Makropulos Case* (1923–25), two string quartets, piano music, songs, vocal works, and the *Glagolithic Mass* (1926).

Janissaries The elite troops of the Ottoman sultans. First raised by Sultan Orkhan (1279–1359; reigned 1326–59) about 1330, and organized by his successor Murad I (1319–89; reigned 1359–89) as a professional army, the Janissaries were carefully selected from the Ottoman subject peoples, especially from Christian families. Highly trained, powerful, and close to palace politics, during the 17th and 18th centuries they engineered palace coups, murdering two sultans, and forcing others to abdicate. After their insurrection in 1826 *Mahmud II killed the entire corps.

Jan Mayen 70 10N 9 00W A volcanic island in the Arctic Ocean. It was annexed to Norway in 1929 and has a meteorological station and a NATO radio and navigation station. Area: 144 sq mi (373 sq km).

Jansen, Cornelius Otto (1585–1638) Dutch Roman Catholic theologian and founder of *Jansenism. The director of episcopal colleges in Bayonne (1612–14) and Louvain (1617–30), he became dean of the University of Louvain in 1635 and Bishop of Ypres in 1636. His major work, *The Augustinus* (1640), is the basis of Jansenist doctrine and was condemned as heretical by Pope Innocent X in 1653.

Jansenism A movement in the Roman Catholic Church in the 17th and 18th centuries based on the teaching of Cornelius *Jansen. Stressing the more rigorously predestinarian aspects of St *Augustine's teaching, it brought the Jansenists into conflict with the Jesuits and was condemned by the Church as constituting a threat to traditional sacramentalism. Among other points, Jansenists argued that the efficacy of the sacraments depended on the moral character of the recipient. Jansenism was condemned in 1653 by Pope Innocent X. One of the most famous Jansenists was *Pascal. *See also* Port Royal.

Jansky, Karl Guthe (1905–50) US radio engineer, who discovered a source of radio waves outside the solar system (1932), while investigating static interference. Jansky's discovery led to the new science of *radio astronomy.

Januarius, St (Italian name: San Gennaro; d. 305?) Italian churchman; Bishop and patron saint of Naples. He was probably martyred during the persecution of *Diocletian. The phial of solidified blood in the cathedral in Naples, which is believed to liquefy miraculously several times each year, is revered as one of his relics. Feast day: Sept 19.

January First month of the year. It is named for the Roman god Janus, whose name means "door", and indicates beginning. It has 31 days. New Year's Day (Jan 1) is a major holiday. The zodiac signs for January are Capricorn and Aquarius, the flowers are the carnation and the snowdrop, and the birthstone is the garnet.

January Insurrection. *See* Congress Kingdom of Poland.

Janus The Roman god of doors, thresholds, and beginnings, after whom the month January is named. He is usually portrayed as having two heads facing forward and backward. His blessing was invoked for the sowing of crops and the beginning of any other major activity.

Japan (Japanese name: Nippon *or* Nihon) A country in E Asia, consisting of a series of islands lying between the Pacific Ocean and the Sea of Japan. The four main islands are *Honshu, *Kyushu, *Hokkaido, and *Shikoku. They have long indented coastlines and much of the land is mountainous, with the highest mountain, *Fujiyama, rising to 12,399 ft (3778 m). The country has long been subject to earthquakes. The population is of mixed Malay, Manchu, and Korean descent; the original inhabitants, the *Ainu, survive in small numbers on Hokkaido. *Economy*: during the past two decades Japan has developed into a highly industrialized country, manufacturing electrical goods, motor vehicles, and petrochemicals; it now produces about half the world's ships. The electronics, paper, and textile industries are also important. Mineral resources, which include limestone, copper, chromite, and coal, are on the whole sparse and Japan relies heavily on imports. There is some oil and natural gas; hydroelectricity is an important source of power. Agriculture is intensive and, although rice is still the main crop, there have been efforts to diversify with such crops as wheat, barley, and soybeans. Vast forests cover over half the land and there is considerable timber production. Although fishing is proportionately less important than before World War II, Japan is still one of the world's leading fishing nations and in 1977 fishing limits were extended to 200 miles. The large volume of exports includes machinery, motor vehicles, metals, textiles, and chemicals. *History*: about 200 BC the country was united under the *Yamato dynasty, already rulers of one of its component kingdoms for about 500 years. Their religion formed the basis of *Shinto, the native religion of Japan, and until 1946 Japanese emperors were regarded as divine descendants of the sun goddess. From 1186 AD real power was in the hands of the military *shoguns until Emperor *Mutsuhito regained power for the House of Yamato in 1867. In 1871, Hoken Seido (the feudal system) ended and from the mid-19th century the country was once again opened up to Western communications and ideas, from which it had been virtually isolated for 200 years. It expanded colonially, especially in successful wars against China and Russia, and it occupied several Asian countries. It fought against the Allies in World War II and surrendered after atomic bombs were dropped on Hiroshima and Nagasaki in 1945. Until the peace treaty of 1951 it was under US occupation. In 1956 Japan joined the UN and in 1972 regained the Ryukyu Islands. By a new constitution of 1947 the emperor renounced his former claim to divinity and became a constitutional monarch. Relations with the US, Japan's principal trading partner, are clouded by a huge trade surplus in Japan's favor. US exporters claim that the Japanese create obstacles to the entry of American goods into Japan while Japanese goods, often enjoying price advantages made possible by government policy, have unobstructed access to the US market. The US continues to provide the chief military defense of the Japanese islands. Emperor Hirohito's death (1989) ended a 62-year reign. Domestically, Japan was rocked during the late 1980s and early 1990s by a series of political and financial scandals. In 1993 elections, a coalition of minority parties defeated the entrenched Liberal Democratic party (LDP), in power since 1955. Head of state: Emperor Akihito. Prime minister: Morohiro Hosokawa. Official language: Japanese. Official currency: yen of 100 sen and 1000 rin. Area: 143,777 sq mi (372,483 sq km). Population (1990): 123,778,000. Capital: Tokyo. Main port: Yokohama.

Japan, Sea of A section of the NW Pacific Ocean between Japan and the Asian mainland.

Japanese The language of the Mongoloid people of Japan. Its relationship to other languages is uncertain but it is probably related to *Korean. It is polysyllabic and tonal. There are many very different regional dialects; the standard and official form is based on the speech of Tokyo. Japanese writing systems are extraordinarily complex. The basic kana system has about 1850 characters derived (c. 2nd century AD) from *Chinese script but used to indicate both a syllabic value (the *on*) and a conceptual value (the *kun*). This has two forms, each with 50 characters, developed in the 9th to 10th centuries: the formal hiragana style used for literary works and the katakana or cursive style used for practical purposes and for loanwords.

Japanese art Neolithic Japanese art consisted of crudely executed terra-cotta figurines and some ceramic ware. The introduction of Buddhism via Korea in the 6th century and the influence of Chinese culture initiated a great period of temple building, sculpture (chiefly of the Buddha), and the development of the art of flower arrangement (*see* ikebana). In the Kamakura period (12th–14th centuries) the refined *Fujiwara style was replaced in sculpture by a vigorous naturalism. In painting, a uniquely Japanese style developed in continuous narrative paintings on horizontal scrolls and realistic landscapes. Another entirely Japanese art form was the colored woodblock print of the Tokugawa period (1630–1867). These prints, portraying the transient world of theater, teahouse, etc., and produced by such artists as *Hokusai and *Kitagawa Utamaro, enjoyed a popularity in Europe in the late 19th century, being particularly influential among impressionist painters (*see* ukiyo-e). Examples of Japanese applied arts are the small wood and ivory carvings (called netsuke) and the gold inlaid sword guards (tsuba). Japanese ceramic art is best illustrated by the *cha-no-yu wares.

JAPANESE ART *Mount Fuji (background) from* The Village of Sekiya on the Banks of the Sumida *(1835) by Hokusai, color print from wood blocks.*

Japanese cedar A conifer, *Cryptomeria japonica,* native to China and Japan, where it is an important timber tree reaching a height of 180 ft (55 m); elsewhere it is grown for ornament and rarely exceeds 115 ft (35 m). Japanese cedar has narrow curved leaves that point toward the tips of the branches and globular spiny cones, 0.8 in (2 cm) across, ripening from green to brown. Family: *Taxodiaceae.*

Japanese literature Before the mid-8th century AD Chinese was the more prestigious language in Japan and in the 8th century Chinese characters were adapted to render spoken Japanese (*see* Japanese). Vernacular Japanese folk songs, however, gave rise to a type of lyric poem, the *waka,* which remained a standard poetic form for over a millennium. This native form appears in the earliest Japanese anthology, the *Manyoshu* (compiled after 759), which contains about 4500 poems. The emperors of the Heian period (794–1185) encouraged literature, and further anthologies were published, as well as prose tales (*monogatari*) and fictionalized diaries (*nikki*). Fiction writing was particularly the province of women; its most famous practitioner was *Murasaki Shikibu, the author of the *Genji Monogatari (Tale of Genji*; c. 1015). Unsettled conditions in the following 500 years led to a decline in this essentially aristocratic literary output. The last official anthology appeared in 1439. The *no drama, mainly Buddhist in inspiration, however, flowered during the late 14th and early 15th centuries, and the *haiku* (an epigram comprising 17 syllables) was a product of the early 16th century.

In the Tokugawa period (1603–1867) literature of all kinds enjoyed a renaissance under the patronage of the leisured warrior class and the new mercantile middle class. The *haiku* reached its peak in the hands of *Matsuo Basho. Fiction encompassed many forms and moods, and nationalistic pride led to official encouragement for writers of philosophy, history, and other learned works. The *joruri* (puppet theater) at first prospered with playwrights of the caliber of Monzemon writing for it but during the late 18th century it declined in competition with the popular *kabuki* theater.

After 1868 European influence manifested itself in every branch of literature, mainly with adverse effects as writers strove to imitate Western models. In the years after World War II, however, several novelists and poets established international reputations, including *Kawabata Yasunari and Yukio *Mishima.

Japanese maple A *maple tree, *Acer palmatum,* up to 43 ft (13 m) tall, the 5–11 lobed leaves of which turn scarlet in autumn. Native to Japan, it is a popular ornamental in many cultivated varieties, including purple-leaved and dwarf types. They require shelter in cooler climates.

japonica A shrub or tree of the genus *Chaenomeles* (or *Cydonia*), native to Japan but widely cultivated as an ornamental. Flowering quince (*C. japonica*) and Japanese quince (*C. speciosa*) are the most popular species. These have toothed oval glossy leaves and clusters of flame-pink or scarlet five-petaled flowers, 2 in (5 cm) across. The hard greenish-yellow applelike fruit has a spicy scent and is used in marmalade and jelly. Family: *Rosaceae.*

Japurá River A river in NW South America, rising as the Río Caquetá in SW Colombia and flowing generally SE to join the Amazon River near Tefé in Brazil. Length: 1750 mi (2800 km).

Jaques-Dalcroze, Émile (1865–1950) Swiss composer and educator. While professor of harmony at the Geneva conservatory he developed a system of coordinating musical rhythms and bodily movement, which he called *eurhythmics. He founded a number of schools throughout Europe to teach his methods.

jarrah A shrub or tree, *Eucalyptus marginata,* of W Australia, that has extremely durable weather-resistant timber, known as West Australian mahogany. It can grow to a height of 52 ft (16 m) and is found in dry areas. Family: *Myrtaceae.*

Jarry, Alfred (1873–1907) French dramatist. His play, *Ubu Roi* (1896), is an outrageous satire on bourgeois conventions of respectability. He wrote several sequels and also novels and poems and is regarded as a precursor of *surrealism and the *Theater of the Absurd.

jasmine A shrub of the genus *Jasminum* (about 300 species), native to tropical and subtropical regions and widely cultivated. Many species are fragrant and yield an essential oil used in perfumery. Two species suitable for temperate gardens are the common jasmine (*J. officinalis*) from S Asia, which has fragrant white flowers and grows to a height of 20 ft (6 m), and the Chinese winter jasmine (*J. nudiflorum*), 10–20 ft (3–6 m) tall, the yellow flowers of which open in winter before the leaves. (Winter jasmine can be distinguished from *Forsythia by its green stems.) Family: *Oleaceae.*

Jason A legendary Greek hero, heir to the throne of Iolcos in Thessaly. Sent by his uncle, the usurper Pelias, to fetch the *Golden Fleece, he and the *Argonauts underwent many adventures before finally recovering the Fleece from Colchis with the help of *Medea. After many years of wandering he died at Corinth.

jasper An impure variety of *chalcedony, usually red or reddish brown. It is slightly translucent and is regarded as a semiprecious stone. It is an abundant mineral, occurring mainly in veins and in cavities in volcanic rocks.

Jasper National Park A national park in Canada, in W Alberta, N of Banff National Park and part of the Rocky Mountains. Established in 1907, it is well known as a recreation center. The park's attractions are numerous: glaciers, mountains, hot springs, lakes, rivers, valleys, canyons, and wildlife. The highest point is Mt Columbia (12,294 ft; 3,748 m). Area: 4,200 sq mi (10,878 sq km).

Jaspers, Karl (Theodor) (1883–1969) German philosopher, a forerunner of *existentialism. Interested in the relation between science and philosophy, he studied medicine and psychology and believed philosophers were better for an acquaintance with the scientific method. His philosophy, expounded in *Philosophie* (1932), is about the possibilities and quality of human choice. He thought *Kierkegaard and *Nietzsche were exceptional in exhibiting the variety of possibilities open to man.

Jassy. *See* Iaşi.

Jatakas In the Pali Buddhist canon, a collection of 550 moral tales describing previous existences of the Buddha before his enlightenment. Each story is related to an event in the Buddha's present life. The collection is also a valuable source of folklore.

jaundice Yellowing of the skin and whites of the eyes due to the presence of *bile pigments. Bile pigments are normally produced by the liver from the breakdown of red blood cells and then excreted in bile into the gut. Jaundice may result if there is excessive breakdown of red blood cells, as in hemolytic anemia, or in disease of the liver, such as *hepatitis, or blockage of the bile duct by *gallstones.

Jaurès, Jean (1859–1914) French socialist leader and journalist; a proponent of the international unity of the working class. He was a vehement supporter of Dreyfus and advocated the separation of church and state. In 1905 he was instrumental in founding the French socialist party (the Section française de l'internationale Ouvrière). He helped found *L'Humanité* in 1904 and was its editor until 1914, when he was assassinated.

Java An Indonesian island, the smallest of the Greater *Sunda Islands. Its chain of volcanic mountains has formed exceptionally fertile soil, and its many rivers feed its intensive wet-rice agriculture. Other food crops, sugar cane, and kapok are grown and forest products include teak. Indonesia's administrative and industrial center, Java has its three largest cities and is heavily overpopulated. The textile industry is of particular importance, especially synthetic textiles, although the village batik industry has declined. Java is subsidized by other islands, which has provoked much unrest. *History*: Indian colonies in the early centuries AD developed into Hindu and Buddhist kingdoms, with Hindu-Javanese culture reaching its height in the 14th century. Later Islamic control barely influenced the culture. The Dutch East India Company was centered here from 1619. During the anticommunist purges (1965–67) between 500,000 and 1,000,000 people were killed. Area: 51,032 sq mi (132,174 sq km). Capital: Jakarta.

javelin throw A field event in track and field in which a spearlike javelin is thrown as far as possible. The men's javelin is 8.5–8.9 ft (2.6–2.7 m) long and weighs 1.8 lb (800 g). The women's measures 7.2–7.5 ft (2.2–2.3 m) and weighs a minimum of 1.3 lb (600 g). It is thrown with one hand, over the shoulder, after an approach of approximately 120 ft (36 m), and the metal head must hit the ground first. Each competitor has six attempts.

jaw One of the two bones of the face that form a framework for the mouth and provide attachment for the teeth. The lower jaw (or mandible) is a horseshoe-shaped bone with a vertical process at each end that forms a joint with the temporal bone of the skull, just in front of each ear. The upper jaw consists of bones (maxillae) that are closely connected to each other and to the other facial bones. Each contains an air *sinus.

Jawara, Sir Dawda (1924–) Gambian statesman; president (1970–). A Muslim, he became minister of education in 1960 and prime minister in 1962, in which post he led his country to independence in 1965. When The Gambia became a republic in 1970 Jawara became president.

Jawlensky, Alexey von (1864–1941) Russian expressionist painter, who spent most of his life in Germany (see expressionism). His chief influences were *Kandinsky, with whom he was associated in several artistic groups, notably *Neue Kunstlervereinigung, and *Matisse. Typical of his vibrantly colored and heavily outlined style is his series of heads resembling icons.

jay A crow, *Garrulus glandarius,* of Eurasia and N Africa. It is about 13 in (34 cm) long and brownish pink, with a black tail, white rump, black-barred blue wing patches, and a black-and-white erectile crest. Jays are found mainly in woodland, feeding on insects and larvae in summer and storing acorns and other seeds for winter food. The N American **blue jay** (*Cyanocitta cristata*) lives E of the Rocky Mountains. About 12 in (30 cm) long, it is bright blue above with a white breast, black face markings, and an erectile crest. It also stores acorns and other seeds.

Jay, John (1745–1829) US political leader, diplomat, and jurist. Entering public life as secretary to the N.Y.–N.J. Boundary Commission (1773), Jay emerged as an early advocate of American independence and served in the First and Second *Continental Congresses (1775–76). In 1779, after having helped to draft the N.Y. state constitution, he was sent to Spain as US minister plenipotentiary and later joined Benjamin *Franklin and John *Adams in Paris in the peace negotiations with Great Britain (1782) to end the Revolutionary War. Jay returned to the US and was named secretary of foreign affairs by the Congress (1784), but the restrictions on his policy-making power imposed by the *Articles of Confederation led him to support the formulation of a stronger federal government. Collaborating with Alexander *Hamilton and James *Madison, he published the *Federalist Papers (1787–88), which helped to sway public opinion in favor of the ratification of the US *Constitution. In 1789, Pres. George *Washington appointed Jay to become the first chief justice of the US Supreme Court. While still serving as chief justice, Jay was sent to London to resolve lingering disagreements between the US and Great Britain. The result of his efforts, the **Jay Treaty** (1794), averted war between the two countries, but was seen by many in the US as a surrender to British demands. Jay resigned from the Supreme Court in 1795 to become governor of New York, an office that he held until 1801.

Jaya, Mount (or Mount Sukarno) 4 05S 137 09E The highest mountain in Indonesia, in West Irian in the Sudirman range. Height: 16,503 ft (5029 m).

Jayawardene, J(unius) R(ichard) (1906–) Sri Lankan statesman; prime minister (1977–78) and then president (1978–88). He became a significant politician in the years before Ceylon (Sri Lanka from 1972) obtained independence in 1948 and as a member of the United National party, which he led from 1970, held various posts before becoming prime minister.

jazz A form of popular music that originated in New Orleans around 1900, characterized by improvisation and syncopated rhythms. The musical influences responsible for its creation included French and Spanish popular music, ragtime, blues, brass-band music, and African slave songs. It first became popular in the Storyville district of New Orleans and as an accompaniment to funerals, weddings, and country outings. Early jazz bands featured improvised solos on such instruments as the cornet, clarinet, and trombone. Louis Armstrong and Jelly Roll Morton are associated with New Orleans jazz (*see* New Orleans style). In the 1920s jazz spread to larger cities, such as New York and Chicago; the original band was enlarged with saxophones and additional cornets and trumpets. Large dance bands emerged in the era of *swing (the 1930s), in which the bandleaders Paul Whiteman, Benny Goodman, Glenn Miller, and Count Basie were especially important. In the 1940s Dizzy Gillespie and Charlie "Bird" Parker revolted against swing with *bop, using a smaller band and introducing harmonic and rhythmic innovations. *Cool jazz of the late 1940s and 1950s adopted a relaxed behind-the-beat approach as in the playing of Miles Davis and Stan Getz. In the 1960s and 1970s such musicians as Gunther Schuller and John Lewis integrated jazz idioms with classical forms and techniques to form *third stream. Ornette Coleman and John Coltrane expanded the boundaries of jazz to include atonality in a style called *free-form jazz.

Jean de Meun (c. 1240–c. 1305) French poet. His conclusion (18,000 lines) of the verse allegory *Roman de la rose,* contrasting in both style and content with the earlier part written by *Guillaume de Lorris, is valued chiefly for its lengthy and informative digressions on topics of contemporary interest.

Jean Paul (Johann Paul Friedrich Richter; 1763–1825) German romantic novelist. His novels, such as *Hesperus* (1795) and *Das Leben des Quintus Fixlein* (1796), combine fantasy with humor and psychological realism and later influenced *Keller and *Mörike.

Jeans, Sir James Hopwood (1877–1946) British mathematician and astronomer. His early work was on the kinetic theory of gases and on the quantum theory. Later he concentrated on cosmogony, putting forward a now discredited theory of planetary formation. After 1928 he devoted himself to writing books popularizing science: *The Universe around Us* (1930), *Science and Music* (1937), and *The Growth of Physical Science* (1947) are examples.

Jedda. *See* Jiddah.

Jeffers, Robinson (1887–1962) US poet. From 1916 he lived in isolation near Carmel on the coast of California. *Tamar and Other Poems* (1924) and other volumes of long narrative poems and short lyrics express a bleak view of mankind. He also wrote plays, notably an adaptation of Euripides' *Medea* (1946).

Jefferson, Thomas (1743–1826) US statesman; 3rd president of the United States (1801–09). Educated as a lawyer, Jefferson began his political career in the Virginia House of Burgesses (1769–75). As one of the most eloquent supporters of the cause of American independence, he wrote an influential pamphlet, *A Summary of the Rights of British America* (1774), which earned him a national reputation and gained him election to the Second *Continental Congress in 1775. In the following year, Jefferson was the principal author of the

*Declaration of Independence. During the *Revolutionary War, Jefferson served in the Virginia legislature and as governor (1779–81). He returned to the US Congress in 1783 and was appointed US minister to France in 1784. With the ratification of the US *Constitution and the election of George *Washington, Jefferson became the first US secretary of state (1789–93).

Jefferson, however, opposed the aristocratic policies of the *Federalists and as the leader of the Jeffersonian-Republicans (later to become the *Democratic party) he resigned from the Washington cabinet in 1793. He later served as vice president under John *Adams (1796–1801) and was elected to the presidency himself in 1800. During Jefferson's two terms in office, he oversaw the war with the *Barbary pirates (1801–05), approved the *Louisiana Purchase (1803), dispatched the *Lewis and Clark Expedition to explore that territory (1804), and encouraged US neutrality in the Napoleonic Wars through the *Embargo Act of 1807. After leaving public office, Jefferson retired to his Virginia estate, Monticello, and was one of the founders of the University of Virginia in 1819.

THOMAS JEFFERSON

Jefferson City 38 33N 92 10W The capital city of Missouri, on the Missouri River. Primarily an administrative center, it is the site of Lincoln University (1866). Population (1990): 35,481.

Jeffries, John. *See* Blanchard, Jean Pierre François.

Jehol. *See* Chengde.

Jehovah. *See* Yahweh.

Jehovah's Witnesses A religious movement founded in 1872 by Charles Taze Russell (1852–1916) in Philadelphia. They were first known as the International Bible Students and from 1884 as the Watch Tower Bible and Tract Society. Although based on Scriptural teaching, the movement's beliefs reject Christ's divinity, regarding him as God's prophet. They expect the end of the world in the near future, although the mooted date of 1975 proved incorrect. They originally believed that only the 144,000 elect would be saved but, since the movement increased in numbers, this limitation has been modified. They accept Jehovah as their sole authority and they refuse military service as they will not kill their fellow humans.

Jellicoe, John Rushworth, 1st Earl (1859–1935) British admiral; commander of the grand fleet (1914–16) in World War I. He was criticized for his command at the battle of *Jutland, in which the German fleet escaped relatively unscathed.

jellyfish A free-swimming aquatic invertebrate animal belonging to a class (*Scyphozoa*; about 200 species) of *coelenterates. The translucent gelatinous body, 0.05–79 in (1.5–2000 mm) in diameter, is bell- or umbrella-shaped, with a central tubular projection that hangs down and bears the mouth. Jellyfish occur in all oceans, especially in tropical regions, and usually propel themselves through the water by contracting muscles around the edge of the bell. Stinging tentacles are used to capture and paralyze prey, ranging from plankton to small fish, and can seriously affect man.

The term jellyfish is also used for the free-swimming sexual form of any other coelenterate (*see* Medusa).

Jena 51 00N 11 30E A city in S Germany, on the Saale River. Its university (1558) became famous in the 18th century when Fichte, Hegel, Schelling, Schiller, and August Schlegel taught there. As well as the Zeiss optical works (*see* Jena glass), founded in 1846, Jena has chemical and engineering industries. Population (1990): 110,000.

Jena and Auerstädt, Battles of (Oct 14, 1806) Simultaneous battles in which Napoleon defeated the Prussians. Following Prussia's challenge to Napoleon after his defeat of Austria at *Austerlitz, Auerstädt and Jena broke Prussia as a military power and left Russia to face Napoleon alone. Prussia remained in the orbit of the French Empire until 1813, when it rejoined the alliance against Napoleon.

Jenkins' Ear, War of (1739–48) A war that arose out of Britain's illicit trade in Spanish America and merged into the War of the *Spanish Succession (1740–48). It followed the accusation of Captain Robert Jenkins that his ear had been cut off by Spanish coast guards in the West Indies.

Jenner, Edward (1749–1823) British physician, who developed the first effective vaccine—against smallpox. Jenner noticed that people who caught the mild disease cowpox never contracted smallpox. In 1796 he inoculated a small boy with cowpox and, two months later, with smallpox. The boy did not get smallpox. Jenner published his findings in 1798 and the process of vaccination—a word that Jenner coined—became a widespread protective measure against smallpox.

Jensen, Johannes (Vilhelm) (1873–1950) Danish novelist and poet, many of whose works were inspired by his travels in the US and the Far East. His most important work was the novel sequence *Den lange Rejse* (*The Long Journey*; 1908–22), a Darwinian account of the origin and early history of mankind.

Jenson, Nicolas (c. 1420–80) French printer, who produced the first distinctive roman typeface, which replaced Gothic (*or* black letter) type. After studying printing under Johann Gutenberg, Jenson opened a printing shop in Venice in 1470.

jerboa A small hopping *rodent belonging to the family *Dipodidae* (25 species) of Asian and N African deserts, also called desert rat. Jerboas are 1.6–6 in (4–15 cm) long and have kangaroo-like hind feet, a long balancing tail, large eyes and ears, and soft sandy-colored fur. They spend the day in tightly closed burrows and emerge at night to feed on seeds and tubers.

Jeremiah (7th century BC) An Old Testament prophet. He is believed to have been born about 650 BC in a village near Jerusalem. The **Book of Jeremiah** contains his prophecies relating to the fall of Judah, its conquest by the Babylonian king Nebuchadnezzar, and the *Babylonian exile of the Jews. A Messiah is prophesied, who will be a descendent of David and who will rule over Jews and Gentiles.

Jerez de la Frontera 36 41N 6 08W A city in SW Spain, in Andalusia. It is renowned for its wine industry and gave its name to sherry. It is also famous for its horses. Population (1991): 182,939.

Jericho 31 52N 35 27E A village in the Jordan Valley (Israel), N of the Dead Sea, now in the Israeli-occupied West Bank area. The nearby site of the old city was excavated by Kathleen *Kenyon, revealing one of the earliest known towns (before 8000 BC), with massive stone fortifications surrounding circular brick-built houses. Later Neolithic burials yielded skulls with features modeled in plaster and shells inset for eyes. Of the biblical Bronze Age city attacked by *Joshua (Joshua 6) nothing remains. The extensive ruins of the magnificent palace, Khirbat al-Mafjar, built (739–44 AD) by the Umayyad caliph Hisham (d. 743) can still be seen.

Jerome, St (c. 342–420 AD) Italian biblical scholar; Doctor of the Church and author of the *Vulgate Bible, the first Latin translation of the Bible from the Hebrew. After a period as a hermit, he was ordained by St *Paulinus of Nola in Antioch. A secretary to Pope Damasus I (reigned 366–94) from 382 until 385, he later settled in Bethlehem, where he established a monastery. He also wrote biblical commentaries and theological works, which are famous for their prose style. Feast day: Sept 30.

Jersey 49 13N 2 07W The largest of the Channel Islands, in the English Channel. Colonized from Normandy in the 11th century, French influence remains strong and French is the official language. It consists chiefly of a plateau incised by deep valleys. Agriculture, particularly dairy farming, is important and the famous Jersey cattle are bred for export. Tourism is also a major source of income. In 1959 the Jersey Zoological Park was founded by Gerald Durrell to protect rare species of wildlife. Area: 45 sq mi (116 sq km). Population (1981): 77,000. Capital: St Helier.

Jersey cattle A breed of dairy cattle originating from the English island of Jersey. Relatively small and fine-boned, Jerseys are golden-brown to black in color, adaptable, and mature rapidly. They produce high-quality creamy milk.

Jersey City 40 44N 74 04W A city in N New Jersey. Founded in 1629, it is connected to nearby New York City by the Hudson River tunnels. Its 12 mi (20 km) of waterfront forms part of the port of New York. A major industrial

and commercial center with oil refineries, its products include paper and cigarettes. Population (1990): 228,537.

Jerusalem (Arabic name: El Quds) 31 47N 35 13E The capital of Israel, in
the Judea Heights between the Mediterranean and the Dead Seas. Jerusalem is a
religious center for three major world religions: Christianity, Judaism, and
Islam. Most employment is found in government and the city's main industry,
tourism. The Hebrew University of Jerusalem was founded in 1918. The modern
city spreads out extensively on the W side of the Old City, which is walled
(1537–40) and contains most of the religious shrines, including the Western
(Wailing) Wall (Jewish), the Dome of the Rock (begun 661 AD; Islamic), and the
Church of the Holy Sepulcher, which was founded in about 335 on the traditional site of Christ's burial and resurrection, although most of the present structure is 19th-century. *History*: Jerusalem was occupied by Alexander the Great
(4th century BC) and the Romans (63 BC), under whose fifth procurator, Pontius
Pilate, Jesus Christ was put to death in the city. Occupation by the Turks was
succeeded by the establishment of the Kingdom of Jerusalem, a feudal state created in 1099 following the conquest of the city by the Crusaders under *Godfrey
of Bouillon. It was enlarged in the early 12th century by *Baldwin I and his successors, but their authority was gradually undermined by the religious orders of
the knighthood, such as the *Hospitallers and the *Templars, and the Kingdom
ended when Jerusalem fell to Saladin in 1187. The Turks took the city again in
1517 and held it until 1917, when it was taken by the British, who held it under
mandatory rule until 1948. Jerusalem was then divided between the new Zionist
state of Israel, of which it became the capital (1950), and Jordan. Israel occupied
the whole city in June 1967, and the status of Jerusalem, of supreme religious
and symbolic importance to both Jew and Arab, is the greatest obstacle to settling the *West Bank question. Population (1990 est): 504,000.

Jerusalem artichoke A North American perennial herb, *Helianthus tubero-
sus*, that grows to a height of 7 ft (2 m), and has edible sweet-tasting knobbly tubers up to 4 in (10 cm) long. They bloom only in hot summers, producing yellow flowers like those of the *sunflower. Family: *Compositae*.

Jerusalem cherry A small shrub, *Solanum pseudocapsicum*, probably of Old
World origin, growing to a height of 5 ft (1.3 m) and bearing cherry-sized red or
yellow highly poisonous fruits. The false Jerusalem cherry (*S. capsicastrum*) of
Brazil is similar. Both are grown as ornamentals. Family: *Solanaceae*.

Jespersen, Otto (1860–1943) Danish linguist. His principal works are
Growth and Structure of the English Language (1905), *A Modern English
Grammar on Historical Principles* (1909–31), *The Philosophy of Grammar*
(1924), and *Analytic Syntax* (1937). His approach to language is traditional and
historical; his writing is noted for its lucidity.

Jesselton. *See* Kota Kinabalu.

Jesuits Members of the Society of Jesus, an order founded by St *Ignatius
Loyola in 1533 to propagate the Roman Catholic faith. The order was organized
along military lines; in addition to the traditional vows of chastity, poverty, and
obedience, Jesuits were sworn to go wherever the pope might send them. They
quickly established themselves as educators and missionaries, becoming one of
the dominant forces of the *Counter-Reformation; their argumentative subtlety
was proverbial. They also played a prominent role in missions to the New World
and the East. Their power and rigorous organization eventually brought them
into conflict with civil authorities throughout Europe, and they were expelled
from several states. In 1773 Pope Clement XIV suppressed the order, and it was
not reinstated until 1814. Today Jesuits are active in most countries and are

noted for their schools and universities, including the Gregorian University in Rome; they continue to play a leading role in intellectual life and missions.

JERUSALEM *At the ancient Wailing Wall, men and women each have their own areas of worship.*

Jesus (c. 6 BC–c. 30 AD) The founder of *Christianity; called by his followers the Messiah or Christ (Greek *khristos*, anointed one). Most of the information concerning Jesus comes from the New Testament *Gospels of Matthew, Mark, and Luke. This material was arranged in order to proclaim and interpret his life and teachings to early Christians and therefore does not provide neutral biographical detail, although it is based on historical facts. According to these sources, Jesus was born at Bethlehem in the last years of the reign of *Herod the Great; he was the son of the Virgin *Mary, of Nazareth in Galilee, who belonged to the tribe of Judah and the family of David. Mary's husband, Joseph, was a carpenter, and Jesus was apparently trained as a carpenter in Nazareth. About 27 AD, *John the Baptist, who was related to Jesus, began to preach that the Kingdom of God (a divine last judgment) was approaching and to urge repentance and baptism as a preparation for it. Jesus was baptized by John and shortly (after John had been imprisoned by Herod Antipas) began his public ministry, traveling in Galilee and in the area NW of Lake Gennesaret. He taught in synagogues and in the open, not using sacred texts but adopting a popular style by preaching in parables and proverbial expressions. His teaching, which is summarized in the Sermon on the Mount (Matthew 5–7), emphasized the approaching kingdom of God, the need for repentance, and the importance of such virtues as charity, faith, and humility instead of the ceremonial observance of the Law. Miracles were attributed to him, including healing, driving out demons, and miraculously feeding a multitude of 5000. The beginnings of a movement are evident in Galilee when Jesus summoned the disciples, traditionally 12 in number, instructing them to leave their families and their work in order to preach the imminence of the Kingdom of God. The Gospels devote most attention to the last week of Jesus' life. He went with the disciples to Jerusalem for Passover, apparently aware of the serious opposition that awaited him. There he was acknowledged as the Messiah by many people, but, after betrayal by Judas, was arrested and condemned to death by the chief Jewish tribunal, the Sanhedrin, for the blasphemous claim to Messiahship. The Gospels tend to exonerate Pontius *Pilate in the proceedings against Jesus, but he was executed according to Roman law as a criminal (*see* crucifixion). In the New Testament his death is presented as the fulfillment of a divine purpose that was made clear to the disciples only at the resurrection (on the next day but one after the crucifixion) and by a number of appearances to individuals and groups of disciples. His ascension into heaven is mentioned in the Gospels and in Acts (1.3), where it is said to have occurred 40 days after the resurrection.

jet engine A form of *gas turbine (*see also* internal-combustion engine) in which part of the energy released by burning the fuel is used to drive a turbine, which in turn drives a compressor to increase the pressure of the air required for combustion, and part is used as a high-velocity jet to provide thrust to drive an aircraft. It was first developed in the 1930s. Except for light aircraft, all military and commercial aircraft are now powered by jet engines. Thrust in these engines is equal to the mass of the gas produced multiplied by its acceleration and is due to the forward reaction of the gas jet on the engine itself rather than on the air through which it is flying. It is therefore more efficient at higher altitudes, where the atmosphere is thinner and drag is less.

Early postwar commercial aircraft used a turboprop engine, in which a propeller is driven by the turbine shaft—strictly, therefore, these are not jet engines. For greater speed and economy the turboprop has now been replaced by the turbojet (with reheat) or the turbofan. At over twice the speed of sound (Mach 2), the forward pressure of the air is sufficient for the compressor, and therefore the turbine, to be dispensed with. The resulting engine is called a ramjet. The main drawback of the ramjet is that it needs a rocket-assisted take-off to attain a speed of Mach 2 before it starts to operate. Turboshaft engines, similar to the turboprop, are also in use for driving helicopters, hovercraft, ships, trains, turbogenerators in power stations, and (experimentally) automobiles. In these the turbine shaft is used to provide all the working power. *See also* rockets.

Jewish autonomous region (*or* Birobidzhan) An autonomous region (*oblast*) in E Russia. Formed in 1934 for Soviet Jews, the harsh climate discouraged settlers, and Russians and Ukrainians outnumber Jews, although there is a Yiddish theater, newspaper, and broadcasting service. Industries include metallurgy, timber, and engineering. Area: 13,895 sq mi (36,000 sq km). Population (1990 est): 220,000. Capital: Birobidzhan.

Jews A predominantly Semitic people, claiming descent from the ancient Israelites. The Jews spread or were dispersed in antiquity from the land of Israel, and there are now communities in most countries (*see* Ashkenazim; diaspora; Sephardim). Although they do not share distinctive racial characteristics, they have a strong sense of cultural identity (*see* Bene Israel; Falashas). Their religion is *Judaism (but in recent times some Jews have professed an attachment to the people while rejecting the religion). Under Persian, Greek, and Roman rule the Jews gradually evolved a system of internal self-government and communal administration that enabled them to survive as minority communities through many centuries of Christian and Muslim domination, despite adverse discrimination and frequent persecution (*see* anti-Semitism). Since the late 18th century they have gradually achieved equal rights as citizens in most countries, although the Nazi slaughter of six million Jews in Europe (*see* holocaust) is one of the ugliest episodes in human history. It did, however, provide the Zionist claim for a national home for the Jews with unanswerable force (*see* Israel; Zionism).

Jew's harp A musical instrument consisting of a metal tongue set in a small frame, held between the teeth. The tongue vibrates when stroked by the finger; the mouth cavity acts as a resonator, different notes being produced by varying its size.

Jezreel, Valley of. *See* Esdraelon, Plain of.

Jhansi 25 27N 78 34E A city in India, in Uttar Pradesh. The heroism of the Rani (female ruler) of Jhansi during the Indian Mutiny has become legendary in modern Indian history. Primarily an agricultural trading center, Jhansi also has a steel-rolling mill. Population (1981): 281,000.

Jiang Qing (*or* Chiang Ch'ing; 1912–91) Chinese communist politician; the third wife (from 1939) of Mao Tse-tung. A former actress, she attempted with three leftist associates (Zhang Chunjao, Wang Hungwen, and Yao Wenyuan) to seize power on Mao's death. Known as the **Gang of Four**, they were arrested within a month. She remained in prison after a public trial at which she refused to recant.

Jiangsu (Chiang-su *or* Kiangsu) A low-lying province in E China on the Yangtze delta. It is the most densely populated area and one of the richest agricultural regions. It was the center of European trade after 1842 and was badly damaged by Japanese occupation (1937–45). It produces wheat, rice, tea, cotton, salt, fish, and silk. Area: 39,860 sq mi (102,200 sq km). Population (1990): 67,056,519. Capital: Nanjing.

Jiangxi (Chiang-hsi *or* Kiangsi) A mountainous province in SE China. It was a center of Confucianism (960–1279), and in the 20th century the Communist-Nationalist conflict originated here (*see* Jiangxi Soviet). One of China's main rice-producing areas, it has mineral resources, including coal and uranium, and is known for its porcelain. Area: 64,300 sq mi (164,800 sq km). Population (1990 est): 37,710,281. Capital: Nanchang.

Jiangxi Soviet (*or* Kiangsi Soviet; 1931–34) A communist republic proclaimed in the Chinese province of Jiangxi. It was a revolutionary base from which Mao Tse-tung and *Zhu De were able to build up their forces in the civil war with the *Guomindang under Chiang Kai-shek. They withstood four encirclement campaigns by the Guomindang but in 1933 Chiang Kai-shek launched a massive fifth campaign in response to which Mao evacuated the base and set off on the *Long March.

Jiddah (*or* Jedda) 21 30N 39 10E A city in Saudi Arabia, on the Red Sea coast. It is a modern industrial city and the chief port for Muslim pilgrims to

Mecca. The King Abdulaziz University was opened there in 1967. Population (1980 est): 1,500,000.

Jilin (Chi-lin *or* Kirin) A province in NE China, in Manchuria. The E is mountainous, while the W lies on the fertile Manchurian plain. Soybeans, cereals, timber, and minerals are produced. Area: 72,930 sq mi (187,000 sq km). Population (1990): 24,658,721. Capital: Changchun.

Jilong (Chi-lung *or* Keelung) 25 10N 121 43E A port and naval base in N Taiwan. It was developed under Japanese occupation (1895–1945). Industries include fishing, chemical, coal and gold mining, and ship building. Population (1991 est): 353,000.

Jim Crow Laws Legislation passed by southern states in the late 19th century to enforce racial segregation; the name derives from that of an African-American character in a popular song. Under a "separate but equal" doctrine, schools and public facilities were established for each race. Legislation in Oklahoma, for example, provided separate telephone booths for African-Americans and whites and in Arkansas separate gambling tables were required. Most of the laws were invalidated by the civil-rights legislation of the 1960s.

Jiménez, Juan Ramón (1881–1958) Spanish poet. His early works, such as *Sonetos espirituales* (1915), were influenced by French symbolism but he later developed a pure abstract style in such works as *La estación total* (1946). He also wrote *Platero y yo* (1914), a portrait of a boy and his donkey.

Jimmu The legendary first ruler of Japan. According to the oldest Japanese writings, Jimmu was descended from the sun-goddess Amaterasu and embarked upon the unification of Japan in 660 BC. This legend was intended to glorify the imperial dynasty and anticipated the dynasty's actual establishment by about seven centuries.

jimsonweed. *See* thorn apple.

Jinan (Chi-nan *or* Tsinan) 36 41N 117 00E A city in E China, the capital of Shandong province. A city since the 8th century BC, it is a cultural center. Industries include textiles, chemicals, and machine building. Population (1990): 1,480,915.

jinja A Shinto shrine dedicated to a deity or nature spirit, situated in a place of exceptional natural beauty. It consists of three parts: the *haiden*, a hall where the laity pray and worship; the *heiden*, where religious ceremonies are performed; and the *honden*, the main inner sanctuary usually accessible only to priests. Before the jinja is a sacred gateway. The architecture is simple and traditional. Large jinja may incorporate other elements, such as a dance platform, an ablution basin, and animal statues.

Jinja 0 27N 33 14E The second largest city in Uganda, on the N shore of Lake Victoria. Founded by the British (1901), it has developed as an industrial center since the opening of the Owen Falls Dam (1954) with steel rolling, copper smelting, and other industries. Population (1991 est): 61,000.

Jinjiang (Chen-chiang *or* Chinkiang) 32 15N 119 20E A port in E China, in Jiangsu province at the junction of the Yangtze River and the *Grand Canal. It is a major trading center, its industries including food processing. Population (1990): 383,316.

Jinmen (Chin-men *or* Quemoy) 24 26N 118 20E A Taiwanese island in Taiwan Strait. It is near the Chinese mainland and was bombed from there in 1958, an event that caused an international incident. Area: 50 sq mi (130 sq km).

Jinnah, Mohammed Ali (1876–1948) Indian statesman, who was largely responsible for the creation of Pakistan. Born in Karachi, he studied law in England and embarked on an extremely successful legal practice in India before becoming involved in politics. As a member of both the *Muslim League and the *Indian National Congress he championed Hindu-Muslim unity after 1920, when he resigned from the Congress in opposition to Gandhi's policies. He was president of the League in 1916 and 1920 and from 1934, and came to advocate the establishment of a separate state for Indian Muslims. This was achieved with the creation in 1947 of Pakistan, of which he was the first governor general.

Jiulong (*or* Kowloon) 22 20N 114 15E A port in SE China, on the Jiulong peninsula, opposite Hong Kong island and part of the British colony (ceded 1860). Population (1991): 2,030,683.

Joachim, Joseph (1831–1907) Hungarian violinist and composer. A child prodigy, he studied with Ferdinand David (1810–73) at the Leipzig conservatory. His interpretations of Bach and Beethoven and his musical perfectionism influenced many composers: Brahms dedicated his violin concerto to him.

Joachim of Fiore (c. 1132–1202 AD) Italian mystic and abbot. He is best known for his philosophy of history, which divided history into three periods: The Age of the Father (Old Testament), The Age of the Son (New Testament and 42 subsequent generations), and The Age of the Spirit, in which all humanity would be converted. Joachim's monastic order, which he founded at San Giovanni in Fiore, was dissolved in 1505.

Joan, Pope A legendary female pope first referred to in the 13th century. She is said to have been elected pope in male disguise about 1100 or earlier, to have ruled for more than two years, and then to have given birth to a child while in a procession, dying immediately thereafter. The legend may be based on a Roman folktale.

Joanna the Mad (1479–1555) Queen of Castile (1504–16). The death of her husband, Philip the Handsome of Castile in 1506, drove her mad. Her father Ferdinand (V and II) of Aragon ruled for her until his death, when he was succeeded by her son, later Emperor *Charles V. He kept Joanna imprisoned in the castle of Todesillas, where she died.

Joan of Arc, St (French name: Jeanne d'Arc; c. 1412–31) French patriot, known as the Maid of Orléans, whose courageous military and moral leadership against the English invaders led to a reversal of French fortunes in the *Hundred Years' War. Of peasant origin, she claimed to have been told by Saints Michael, Catherine, and Margaret that it was her divine mission to expel the English from France and enable Charles VII to be crowned. She persuaded Charles to allow her to lead an army to relieve the besieged city of Orléans. Her success resulted in Charles's coronation at Rheims (July 1429). Other victories followed but she failed to recapture Paris and was subsequently seized by the Burgundians, who sold her to their English allies. They tried her and burned her as a heretic. She was canonized in 1920.

João Pessoa (name until 1930: Paraíba) 7 06S 34 53W A port in E Brazil, the capital of Paraíba state near the mouth of the Rio Paraíba do Norte. The chief exports are cotton, sugar, and coffee. Population (1980): 290,424.

Job An Old Testament figure. **The Book of Job**, probably written between the 5th and 2nd centuries BC, develops the theme of the suffering of the innocent. Job experiences the loss of his family, property, and health, but adamantly denies his friends' suggestions that sin is the cause of his misfortunes, for he knows himself to be innocent. No final explanation of the dilemma is reached, but Job is brought to see that man cannot understand the ways of God. Humbled by this knowledge, he prays for his friends and is ultimately granted greater prosperity than he formerly had.

JOAN OF ARC *This portrait of the great French heroine dates to 1584.*

Jocasta. *See* Oedipus.

Jochho (d. 1057) Leading Japanese sculptor of the Fujiwara period (*see* Fujiwara style). His serene and refined statues of the Buddha for the Fujiwara family temple and his joined-wood technique were influential.

Jodhpur 26 18N 73 08E A city in India, in Rajasthan. Formerly the capital of the princely state of Jodhpur, the city is noted for its handicraft industries, such as ivory carvings and lacquerware. It also gave its name to a style of riding breeches that were introduced into Britain during the 19th century. Jodhpur University was established in 1962. Population (1991): 648,621.

Jodl, Alfred (1890–1946) German general, who was responsible for much of German strategy in World War II. He was executed as a war criminal.

Joel An Old Testament prophet of Judah. **The Book of Judah** records his prediction of a plague of locusts and other disasters as punishment for Judah's sins, followed eventually by a restoration of God's favor and the nation's final triumph over its enemies.

Joffre, Joseph Jacques Césaire (1852–1931) French marshal; commander in chief of the French armies (1915–16) in World War I. As chief of staff he won the victory of the Marne (1914) but the French failure at Verdun (1916) led to his resignation. □Lloyd George, David, 1st Earl.

Jogjakarta (*or* Djokjakarta) 7 48S 110 24E A city in Indonesia, in S Java. It was the capital of the 1945–49 Indonesian Republic. A cultural center, its university was established in 1949. It is rich in Buddhist monuments, notably the temple of Borobudur. Population (1980): 398,727.

Johannesburg 26 10S 28 02E The largest city in South Africa, in the Transvaal of the Witwatersrand. It was founded in 1886 following the discovery of gold in the area and developed rapidly as the center of the gold-mining industry. During the second Boer War it was taken by the British (1900). Today it is a major industrial, commercial, and banking center containing the South African Stock Exchange (1887). Its industries include engineering, chemicals, and textiles. Linked to the city is the complex of towns known as *Soweto, inhabited by black Africans. Johannesburg has a number of cultural and educational institutions, notably the University of Witwatersrand (1922) and the Rand Afrikaans University (1966). The fine Johannesburg Art Gallery (1911) was designed by Sir Edwin Lutyens. Population (1991): 632,369.

Johannsen, Wilhelm Ludvig (1857–1927) Danish geneticist, whose work with plants demonstrated that the physical appearance (phenotype) of individuals was the result of the interaction of their hereditary constitution (genotype) and their environment. He also provided supporting evidence for the mutation theory of *de Vries. Johannsen coined the word *gene* for a unit of heredity as well as the terms phenotype and genotype.

John (1167–1216) King of England (1199–1216), nicknamed John Lackland; the youngest son of Henry II, he succeeded his brother Richard I. His reign saw the renewal of war with *Philip II Augustus of France, to whom he had lost several continental possessions, including Normandy, by 1205. He came into conflict with his barons and was forced to sign the *Magna Carta at Runnymede. His subsequent repudiation of the charter led to the first *Barons' War (1215–17), during which John died.

John I (1357–1433) King of Portugal (1385–1433). The head of the military order of Aviz, John led the nationalist opposition to the succession to the Portuguese throne of John I of Castile (1358–90; reigned 1379–90). After securing the throne, John soundly defeated the Castilians at Aljubarrota. In 1415 he captured Ceuta, the first possession of any European nation in Africa.

John I Tzimisces (925–76 AD) Byzantine emperor (969–76). He increased the power of the Byzantine empire by subjecting the Bulgarians and defeating the Russians (971) and by conquering cities in Syria (974–75).

John (II) the Good (1319–64) King of France (1350–64), who was taken prisoner by the English at the battle of Poitiers (1356) during the *Hundred Years' War. He remained in captivity in London, where he was forced to sign the unfavorable Treaty of *Brétigny, until 1360. Released in 1360, he was unable to raise the ransom demanded by the English and was forced to return to London, where he died.

John (II) the Perfect (1455–95) King of Portugal (1481–95). John encouraged Portugal's overseas expansion, supporting Bartolomeu Dias, and concluded the treaty of Tordesillas with Spain (1494), which demarcated their respective fields of action in the New World. His home policies reduced the power of the aristocracy.

John II Casimir (1609–72) King of Poland (1648–68), whose reign is known as the Deluge. John faced a revolt of the Ukrainian Cossacks, on whose behalf Russia invaded Poland in 1654, and in 1667 John Casimir was forced to cede the eastern Ukraine. Sweden's invasion of Poland in 1655 resulted in the loss of N Livonia (1660). John Casimir abdicated and died in France.

John III (1502–57) King of Portugal (1521–57). John's reign saw the flourishing of culture in the works of Camoens and others. Spending his country's wealth on his lavish court (rather than economic development), he was responsible for the start of Portugal's decline.

John III Sobieski (1624–96) King of Poland (1674–96), famous as an adversary of the Turks. A brilliant military commander, John Sobieski was elected king after defeating the Turks at Khotin (1663). In 1683 he saved Vienna from the Turks in the great victory at Kahlenberg. His subsequent failure to conquer Moldavia and Wallachia led to a loss of personal prestige, which aggravated the domestic unrest that was a feature of his reign.

John (IV) the Fortunate (1604–56) King of Portugal (1640–56). As duke of *Bragança, John led a revolt in 1640 against Spanish rule that brought him to the throne. He revived the Cortes and formed foreign alliances against Spain but lost most of Portugal's Asian possessions to the Dutch.

John VI (?1769–1826) King of Portugal (1816–26), having been prince regent from 1799. John lived in Brazil during Napoleon's occupation of Portugal. Returning to Portugal in 1821, he faced a revolt of the reactionaries against constitutional monarchy, which was only defeated with French and British help. In 1825 John recognized the independence of Brazil, which was ruled by his son *Pedro I.

John XXII (Jacques d'Euse; c. 1249–1334) Pope (1316–34) during the *Avignon papacy, a man of great administrative and financial ability. In 1317 he dissolved the austere group of the *Franciscans known as Spirituals, whose cause was taken up by Emperor Louis IV. Aided by the philosophers Marsilius of Padua and William of Ockham, Louis denounced papal supremacy and in 1328 set up an antipope in Rome. John's last years were dominated by theological disputes.

John XXIII (Baldassare Cossa; d. 1419) Antipope (1410–15), one of three claimants to the papacy during the *Great Schism. In 1414 John summoned the Council of *Constance to end the Schism but fled when it demanded his resignation. He was arrested, imprisoned, and deposed.

John XXIII (Angelo Roncalli; 1881–1963) Pope (1958–1963). A papal diplomat and then patriarch of Venice (1953–58) before his election at the age of 77, John was the most popular and innovative pope of modern times. In 1962 he summoned the second *Vatican Council, which marked the climax of John's pursuit of Church reforms and Christian unity. His best-known encyclical *Pacem in Terris* (*Peace on Earth*; 1963), advocated reconciliation between the Western democracies and Eastern communist countries. His diary was published as *The Journal of a Soul* (1965).

John, Augustus (Edwin) (1878–1961) British painter. He studied at the Slade School, London (1894–98), displaying a precocious drawing talent, and exhibited at the *New English Art Club from 1903. A flamboyantly unconventional character, he traveled widely, often in Gypsy style. His strongly characterized portraits of contemporaries, such as James Joyce and T. E. Lawrence, are indebted to tradition.

John, Elton (Reginald Kenneth Dwight; 1947–) British rock pianist and singer, who became popular in the US with such songs as "Rocket Man" and "Daniel." He is well known for wearing large and colorful glasses on stage.

John, St In the New Testament, one of the 12 Apostles, son of Zebedee and brother of James. He was present at a number of events in the life of Jesus as recounted in the Gospels and is also thought to be the anonymous disciple "whom

Jesus loved" present at the crucifixion. Tradition states that he escaped martyrdom and died at Ephesus. Feast day: Dec 27.

The Gospel according to St John is the fourth book of the New Testament traditionally ascribed to St John and probably written in the late 1st century AD. It is markedly different in a number of details from the other three synoptic Gospels and was specifically written with the intention of inspiring faith in Jesus as the Son of God. It begins with a prologue portraying Jesus as the *Logos* or Word, a theme familiar to current Greek philosophy. Having spoken of his incarnation, it concentrates on his public ministry and especially on claims made in a number of discourses and conversations not recorded in the other Gospels. Over half the book is devoted to the events and teaching occurring during the last week before the crucifixion.

The Epistles of John are three New Testament books traditionally ascribed to St John and written toward the end of the 1st century. The first is addressed to the Churches at large and defines the distinctive marks of a true Christian. The others are brief personal letters: the second warns an unnamed lady against false teachers, while the third commends and encourages a certain Gaius. Tradition also ascribes the Book of *Revelation to John.

John Birch Society A right-wing group founded in 1958 by Robert Welch, Jr. John Birch was a US Army intelligence officer who was killed by the communist Chinese in August 1945, and is represented by the Society as the first hero of the *Cold War.

John Bull The personification of England or the English national character. The character first appeared in *The History of John Bull* (1712) by John Arbuthnot, and was popularized in 18th- and 19th-century political cartoons. He is usually portrayed as a stocky countryman noted for his honesty and stubbornness.

John Dory (*or* dory) A fish of the family *Zeidae*, found worldwide in moderately deep marine waters. It has a round narrow body with deep sides, each having a black spot surrounded by a yellow ring, and spiny-rayed fins extended into filaments. *Zeus faber*, up to 35 in (90 cm) long, is a food fish of the Atlantic and Mediterranean. Order: *Zeiformes*.

John Frederick (I) the Magnanimous (1503–54) Elector of Saxony (1532–47), who led the Protestant Schmalkaldic League against Emperor *Charles V. John Frederick was imprisoned (1547–52) after the League's defeat at the battle of Mühlberg and was deprived of his territory and electoral rank.

John of Austria, Don (1545–78) Spanish soldier. The illegitimate son of Emperor *Charles V, his half-brother *Philip II entrusted him with major military commands. He suppressed the revolt of the Moriscos (Moors converted to Christianity) in S Spain in 1569 and in 1571 he commanded the combined fleets of Spain, Venice, and the papacy against the Turks, winning a great victory at *Lepanto. In 1573 he conquered Tunis and in 1576 became governor general of the Netherlands, where he died.

John of Damascus, St (c. 675–c. 749 AD) Greek Orthodox theologian and Doctor of the Church, born in Damascus. While a tax official at the caliph's court at Damascus he wrote several treatises defending the use of images in church worship against *iconoclasm. In about 716 he retired to a monastery near Jerusalem, where he was ordained. There he wrote his most influential work, *The Fount of Wisdom*, which deals with philosophy, heresies, and the Orthodox faith. Feast day: Mar 27.

John of Gaunt (1340–99) The fourth son of Edward III of England, born at Ghent; duke of Lancaster from 1362. After a distinguished career in the *Hundred Years' War he assumed an increasingly important role in domestic government during the senility of Edward and the minority of Richard II. From 1386 to 1389 he attempted without success to realize his claim, through his second wife, to Castile. In 1396 he married his mistress Catherine Swynford, and in 1397 their descendants were legitimized but excluded from the royal succession. They included Margaret *Beaufort, the mother of Henry VII.

John of Leiden (Jan Beuckelszoon; 1509–36) Dutch *Anabaptist leader. In 1534 he pronounced himself king of Münster, an Anabaptist stronghold in Germany that had expelled its civil and religious authorities. During his brief rule he legalized polygamy and made property communal. The town was recaptured in 1535 and he was executed.

John of Luxembourg (1296–1346) Count of Luxembourg (1310–46) and, by marriage, king of Bohemia (1311–46); son of Emperor Henry VII. His almost constant warfare and consequent levy of high taxes made him unpopular in Bohemia. He died at Crécy fighting for the French.

John of Nepomuk, St (c. 1340–93) The patron saint of Bohemia. As vicar general of Prague, he opposed Wenceslas IV's plans to create a second bishopric in the city. At the king's instigation he was tortured and drowned. Feast day: May 16.

John of Salisbury (c. 1115–80) English churchman, philosopher, and a leading classical scholar of his age. After studying in Paris under *Abelard he became secretary to Thomas Becket and later bishop of Chartres (1176). His principal works are the *Polycraticus*, a treatise criticizing contemporary political and courtly life, and the *Metalogicon*, a defense of the study of grammar, logic, and rhetoric.

John of the Cross, St (Juan de Yepes y Alvarez; 1542–91) Spanish mystic, poet, and since 1926 Doctor of the Church. With St *Teresa he founded the Discalced *Carmelites, a reformed branch of the Carmelite order. His poems, which include *Cántico espiritual* and *Noche oscura del alma*, are regarded as the finest examples of Spanish mystical literature. Feast day: Nov 24.

John O'Groats 58 39N 3 02W A village at the NE tip of Scotland, site of the house of John de Groot, a 16th-century Dutch immigrant. John O'Groats is 603 mi (970 km) in a straight line from Land's End, Cornwall.

John Paul II (Karol Wojtyła; 1920–   ) Pope (1978–   ). A Pole, he is the first non-Italian pope since 1522. He taught at Lublin and Kraków Universities before becoming archbishop of Kraków (1964). He has outspokenly defended the Church in communist countries, especially in Poland, and has condemned the politicization of the Church. In 1979 he visited Poland, becoming the first pope to go to a communist state. In 1981 he survived an assassination attempt. His extensive travels have taken him to the US, Britain, South America, and the Far East. He succeeded **John Paul I** (Albino Luciani; 1912–78; reigned August–September 1978), who took the names of his two predecessors, John XXIII and Paul VI, thus symbolizing his desire to combine the charismatic and intellectual qualities for which they were respectively known.

Johns, Jasper (1930–   ) US artist, who was a major influence on *pop art. He worked as a commercial artist before establishing his reputation at a one-man show in New York (1958) with paintings of targets and flags. The collages and constructions that followed made a similar use of everyday objects, for example the bronze *Beer Cans* (1960).

Johnson, Andrew (1808–75) US statesman; 17th president of the United States (1865–69). A tailor by trade and with no formal education, Johnson became active in the *Democratic party, serving as a member of the US House of Representatives (1843–53) and as governor of Tennessee (1853–57). Later elected to the US Senate (1857–62), he was one of the few southern political leaders who maintained his allegiance to the Union at the outbreak of the Civil War. In 1862, Pres. Abraham *Lincoln appointed Johnson military governor of Tennessee, and Johnson was elected vice president as Lincoln's running mate in 1864. Johnson succeeded to the presidency in the following year, after Lincoln's assassination. During his single term of office, Johnson was a supporter of a conciliatory policy towards the defeated South and came into increasing conflict with the *Radical Republicans who overrode his veto and passed the harsh *Reconstruction Act of 1867. His dismissal of Secretary of War Edwin *Stanton in violation of the Tenure of Office Act led to impeachment proceedings against him by the US Senate, but he was acquitted by a single vote. Johnson did not run for reelection in 1868, but shortly before his death in 1875, he was elected to the US Senate.

JOHN PAUL II *At the Jasna Gora monastery, Czestochowa, during his 1979 visit to Poland. The monastery, a famous place of pilgrimage, contains the image of the Virgin known as* The Black Madonna.

Johnson, Cornelius (Janssen van Ceulen; 1593–1661) English portrait painter, born in London of Dutch parents. Until Van Dyck's arrival (1632), Johnson was the leading portraitist at the courts of James I and Charles I, where he specialized in oval-shaped bust portraits. He settled in Holland in 1643.

Johnson, Jack (John Arthur J.; 1878–1946) US boxer. He began fighting professionally in 1897 and became the first African American to hold the heavyweight championship, which he gained in 1908. He held the title until 1915, when he lost to Jess Willard. His self-confidence and showmanship angered many whites, and in 1912 he was charged with taking a white wife-to-be across state lines in violation of the Mann Act. Arrested and convicted, he fled to Canada and Europe. Upon his return to the US in 1920, he served one year in prison.

Johnson, James Weldon (1871–1938) US writer and statesman. After brief careers as a teacher and lawyer, he began writing songs with his brother John. Together they wrote for Broadway musicals from 1901, as well as "Lift Every Voice and Sing," widely popular among African Americans. He served as consul to Venezuela (1906–09) and Nicaragua (1909–14), and held several executive positions in the National Association for the Advancement of Colored People (NAACP) (1916–30). His poetry collections include *Fifty Years and Other Poems* (1917) and *God's Trombones* (1927). Other works are *The Autobiography of an Ex-Colored Man* (1912), *Black Manhattan* (1930), and *Along the Way* (1933).

Johnson, Lyndon Baines (1908–73) US statesman; 36th president of the United States (1963–69). Beginning his career as a teacher, Johnson was a strong supporter of the New Deal programs of Pres. Franklin *Roosevelt and was named Texas director of the National Youth Administration in 1935. Johnson later served in the US House of Representatives (1937–49) and Senate (1949–61), becoming majority leader in 1957. An unsuccessful candidate for the Democratic presidential nomination in 1960, he was chosen as John F. *Kennedy's vice presidential running mate. He succeeded to the presidency after Kennedy's assassination in 1963. As president, Johnson initiated the Great Society program, the most comprehensive plan of social legislation since the New Deal. Among the most important achievements of this program were the establishment of Medicare for senior citizens and the passage of the Civil Rights Act of 1964. Reelected by a substantial margin in 1964, Johnson became increasingly concerned during his first full term in office with the American involvement in the *Vietnam War. He faced growing domestic criticism for his policies and declined to run for reelection in 1968.

Johnson, Richard Mentor (1780–1850) US lawyer and politician; vice president (1837–41). A hero in the War of 1812, he served in the US House of Representatives (1807–19; 1829–37) and the Senate (1819–29). As running mate to Martin Van Buren in the presidential election of 1836, he did not receive a majority of votes; his election to the vice presidency was decided by the Senate.

Johnson, Samuel (1709–84) British poet, critic, and lexicographer. He left Oxford without taking a degree and went to London in 1737. His early publications include a biography of his friend Richard *Savage (1744) and a long didactic poem, *The Vanity of Human Wishes* (1749). From 1750 to 1752 he produced the weekly *Rambler* almost single-handedly. His *Dictionary* appeared in 1755 and was well received. His major writings include *Rasselas* (1759), a moral fable, an edition of Shakespeare (1765), and *Lives of the Poets* (1779–81). From the early 1760s he enjoyed the friendship of Reynolds, Goldsmith, Burke, and other men of letters, including his biographer *Bowell, who met him first in 1763 and became a close friend in the 1770s.

Johnson, Virginia Eshelman. *See* Masters, William Howell.

Johnson, Walter Perry (1887–1946) US baseball player. A pitcher (1907–27) for the American League Washington Senators, he was nicknamed "The Big Train" because of his fastball. He won 416 games during his career and struck out 3,508 batters. He later managed and was one of the first players inducted into the Baseball Hall of Fame (1936).

Johnston, Joseph (Eggleston) (1807–91) US Confederate general. After resigning from the US Army at the beginning of the Civil War, he was made a general in the Confederate Army, won the first battle of *Bull Run (1861), and fought at Fair Oaks (1862) where he was critically wounded. In 1863 he lost Vicksburg to *Grant, and in 1864 he led the attempt to hold General *Sherman's march through Georgia. Johnson was then relieved of command, primarily due to a long-standing feud with Confederate President Jefferson. He fought again in the Carolinas (1865) and was forced to surrender to Sherman. After the war, Johnston served in the US House of Representatives (1879–81) and was commissioner of railroads (1885–91).

LYNDON B. JOHNSON *President (1963–69) during the Vietnam War who initiated Great Society domestic programs.*

Johnstown 40 20N 78 55W A city of SW Pennsylvania, on the Conemaugh River, E of Pittsburgh. The Johnstown Flood National Memorial here commemorates 2,100 people who lost their lives in the flood of 1889, when a reservoir dam to the SW burst and flooded the city. Although flood control projects have alleviated the problem, another severe flood occurred in 1977. Industries include coal mining, synthetic fuel and steel making, and clothing and furniture manufacturing. Population (1990): 28,134.

John the Baptist, St In the New Testament, the son of a priest, Zacharias, and Elizabeth, a relative of the Virgin *Mary; known as the "Forerunner of Christ." Born in his mother's old age, he was six months older than Jesus. After living in the desert, he began about 27 AD preaching on the banks of the Jordan River, urging repentance and baptism because of the imminent approach of the Kingdom of God (Matthew 3.2). He baptized Christ, recognizing him as the Messiah. He was beheaded by *Herod Antipas, at the request of *Salome, for denouncing his second marriage to Herodias as illicit. Feast days: June 24 (birth); Aug 29 (beheading).

John the Fearless (1371–1419) Duke of Burgundy (1404–19), a great military leader who earned his nickname on a Crusade in 1396. He competed with the Armagnacs for control over the mad Charles the Well-Beloved of France and arranged the assassination (1407) of their leader (and his cousin) Louis, duke of Orleans. His own death, however, was at the hands of an Armagnac assassin.

Johor A swampy forested state in S Peninsular Malaysia. It is economically linked to Singapore, depending on it for trading facilities and supplying it with water. Chief products are rubber, copra, pineapples, palm oil, tin, and bauxite. Area: 7330 sq mi (18,958 sq km). Population (1990): 2,106,500. Capital: Johor Baharu.

Johor Baharu 1 29N 103 44 E A city in S Peninsular Malaysia, the capital of Johor state. A trading center with a notable sultan's residence, it is linked to Singapore by a causeway across the Johor Strait. Population (1980): 249,880.

joint The point at which two or more bones are connected to each other. There are three broad categories. Immovable joints allow no movement of the bones; examples are the sutures between the bones of the skull. Slightly movable joints allow a certain degree of movement, as in the joints connecting the individual bones of the spine. Freely movable joints (diarthrodial, or synovial, joints) permit a variety of movements. They include the hinge joints at the knee and elbow, the ball-and-socket joints at the hip and shoulder, and the gliding joints at the wrist and ankle. The bone ends at movable joints are covered by *cartilage and enveloped in a tough capsule thickened in parts to form *ligaments. The inside of the capsule is lined by synovial membrane, which secretes a lubricating fluid.

Joint Chiefs of Staff (JCS) US military advisers who advise the president, National Security Council, and the secretary of defense. Composed of a chairman appointed by Congress and the heads of the *Army, *Navy, and *Air Force, it was established in 1947. The commandant of the *Marines was included from 1978. The JCS coordinates the activities of the armed services as directed by the secretary of defense.

Joinville, Jean de (c. 1224–1317) French chronicler. His record of the seventh Crusade (1248–54), on which he accompanied Louis IX and shared his captivity, constitutes the main part of his *Histoire de Saint Louis*. His work is noted for its vivid descriptions and its honesty and human sympathy.

Joliot, Frédéric, and Irène Joliot-Curie. *See* Curie, Marie.

Jolliet, Louis. *See* Marquette, Jacques.

Jolson, Al (Asa Yoelson; 1886–1950) US popular singer and songwriter, born in Russia. He sang in circuses, vaudevilles, and minstrel shows, becoming famous for his blacked-up face and the song "Mammy." In 1927 he appeared in the first full-length sound film *The Jazz Singer* and subsequently made the films *The Singing Fool* (1928) and *Swanee River* (1940).

Jonah (8th century BC) An Old Testament figure. **The Book of Jonah** was probably written after the *Babylonian exile of the Jews. It relates how Jonah was commanded by God to preach to the Gentiles in Nineveh, the Assyrian capital. Attempting to escape this task, he fled by ship, but was thrown overboard, swallowed by a great fish (probably a whale), and after three days was safely cast ashore. He repented of his disobedience and fulfilled God's commandment. The purpose of the story was to emphasize that God was the God of the Gentiles as well as the Jews.

Jones, (Alfred) Ernest (1879–1958) British psychoanalyst. A follower and friend of Sigmund *Freud, Jones helped to establish psychoanalysis in Britain and North America. He wrote many papers, especially on the psychology of literary works, including a famous analysis of *Hamlet* in *Hamlet and Oedipus* (1949). In 1920 he founded the *International Journal of Psychoanalysis* and he also wrote *Sigmund Freud: Life and Work* (3 vols, 1953–56).

Jones, Bobby (Robert Tyre J.; 1902–71) US amateur golfer. Between 1923 and 1930 he won four US and three British Open championships, five US amateur championships, and one British amateur championship. In 1930 he won all four championships, after which he retired from competition.

Jones, Henry. *See* Cavendish.

Jones, Inigo (1573–1652) English classical architect. One of the first Englishmen to study architecture in Italy and to understand the rules of classicism, Jones was particularly influenced by *Palladio in his two best-known buildings, the Queen's House, Greenwich (1616–35), and the Banqueting Hall, Whitehall (1619–22). His style was strongly influential in England in the 18th century.

Jones, James (1921–77) US writer. After serving in the Army (1939–44), he wrote the novel *From Here to Eternity* (1951) about military life at Pearl Harbor, which was made into a movie in 1953. He followed with *The Thin Red Line* (1962; film, 1964) and *Whistle* (1978; published posthumously), also about army life. Other works include *Some Came Running* (1957; film, 1958), *Go to the Widow-Maker* (1967), and *A Touch of Danger* (1973).

Jones, John Paul (1747–92) American naval commander, born in Scotland. On the outbreak of the American Revolution he was commissioned into the American navy (1775). Jones captured and sank a number of ships in American and British waters (1776, 1778). In 1779 in the *Bon Homme Richard* Jones defeated the British frigate *Serapis* in a desperate battle lasting almost four hours. He subsequently became a rear admiral in the Russian navy, fighting in the Black Sea against the Turks (1788–89).

Jones, LeRoi (1934–   ) US dramatist and poet. In *Dutchman* (1964) and other plays and volumes of poetry he deals with social relationships between African Americans and whites. As a leading African-American editor and publisher he has encouraged many other African-American writers. He changed his name to Imamu Baraka to emphasize his identity with his African-American heritage and culture.

Jongkind, Johan Barthold (1819–91) Dutch landscape painter and etcher, who settled in Paris in 1846. He was influenced by the Dutch landscape tradition but the atmospheric effects he achieved in his seascapes and watercolors anticipate *impressionism.

Jönköping 57 45N 14 10E A town in S Sweden, at the S end of Lake Vättern. Its manufactures include matches, paper, textiles, footwear, and machinery. Population (1978 est): 107,561.

jonquil. *See* Narcissus.

Jonson, Ben (1572–1637) English dramatist and poet. In *Every Man in His Humour* (1598) he introduced the "comedy of humors," each character being driven by a particular obsession. Other major satirical plays include *Valpone* (1606), *The Alchemist* (1610), and *Bartholomew Fair* (1614). He also published two collections of poems and translations. Ranked above Shakespeare in the 17th century, Jonson based his finest work on classical principles and influenced a number of younger poets.

Joplin, Scott (1868–1917) US pianist and composer of *ragtime music. One of the first to write down such music, Joplin is remembered for his skillful syncopation in such rags as "Maple Leaf Rag" and "The Entertainer." The revival of the latter, in the film *The Sting* (1973), sparked a renewed interest in Joplin's music. His ragtime operas *A Guest of Honor* (1903), now lost, and *Treemonisha* (1907) were failures and Joplin, having known success, died in poverty.

Jordan, Hashemite Kingdom of A country in the Middle East, its only sea outlet being on the tip of the Gulf of Aqaba. It is mainly desert but more fertile in the W and N, where the population is concentrated. The people are Arab, and most are Sunnite Muslims, with Christian and other minorities. *Economy*: Jordan's major industries are the extraction and some processing of phosphates, which are exported from Aqaba and also used locally in fertilizers. Agriculture is concentrated in the irrigated Jordan Valley. Produce includes cereals, vegetables, wool, and such fruit as melons and olives. Potash from the shore of the Dead Sea is also exploited and some copper is mined. *History*: the area that is now Jordan appears to have flourished in the Bronze Age and was part of the Roman Empire by 64 BC. It was controlled by Arabs from the 7th century, Crusaders in the 11th and 12th centuries, and Turks from the 16th century until 1916, when the part E of the Jordan River was named Transjordan and a League of Nations mandate for its control was given to the UK. It became an independent kingdom in 1946 and was named the Hashemite Kingdom of Jordan in 1949. In the Arab-Israeli War of 1948–49, Jordan overran the *West Bank, but it was occupied by Israel in the Six-Day War of 1967. Palestinians, many of whom were refugees from the West Bank, then began raids on Israel from the East Bank; they were, however, subdued by Jordanian forces in the civil war of 1970–71 to avoid Israeli retaliation against Jordan. This brought Jordan into disfavor with other Arab states, which was only temporarily alleviated by Jordanian participation in the Arab-Israeli War of 1973. Under Arab pressure, Jordan recognized the *Palestine Liberation Organization as the body entitled to govern the West Bank and, in 1988, renounced all claims to the area. The present monarch, King Hussein, succeeded to the throne in 1952. U.S. policymakers hoped that Hussein would represent the interests of the PLO in peace negotiations with Israel after Israel in 1982 had driven PLO fighters out of Lebanon, but the king refused. He also refused to be part of the coalition that condemned and fought Iraq in the Persian Gulf War of 1991. Prior to the war, he had sought a peaceful solution to Iraq's invasion of Kuwait, and later in the year he supported the Middle East peace conference in Madrid. By 1993, Jordan's relations with Iraq had deteriorated. Also in 1993, Jordan signed a historic agreement with Israel, setting an agenda for peace between the two nations. Official language: Arabic. Official currency: Jordanian dinar of 1000 fils. Area: about 37,738 sq mi (97,740 sq km), including the West Bank. Population (1990 est): 3,065,000, including the West Bank. Capital: Amman.

Jordan, Michael (1963–   ) US basketball player. A collegiate star at the University of North Carolina at Chapel Hill, he left after his junior year (1984), played in the Olympics, and turned professional. He was an immediate star with the Chicago Bulls of the National Basketball Association (NBA), leading the league in scoring and being named rookie of the year and to the NBA's all-star team. Jordan continued his scoring success thereafter, becoming known for his acrobatic shots. His domination of the game in the early 1990s led to unprecedential recognition and contracts for commercials, especially sneakers and beverages. He led the Bulls to NBA championships in 1991–93 and played on the US Olympic team in 1992. Jordan unexpectedly retired before the 1993–94 season.

Jordan River A river in the Middle East. It rises in Syria and Lebanon and flows due S through the Sea of Galilee, finally entering the Dead Sea. It forms for some of its course part of the border between Israel and Jordan. Length: 199 mi (320 km).

Joseph, Chief (1832–1904) Nez Percé Indian chief. An advocate of passive resistance, he was forced by more aggressive members of his tribe to go to war (1877) against US troops sent to remove the Indians from their lands in Washington. He spent his time during the fighting caring for women, children, and the wounded. The tribe was finally captured during a retreat to Canada. They were relocated to Oklahoma and then, in 1885, to a reservation in Washington.

JORDAN *Camels on the Gulf of Aqaba, the country's only sea outlet.*

Joseph, St In the New Testament, the husband of the Virgin *Mary. He was a devout Jew belonging to the line of David but worked humbly as a carpenter. He eventually settled in Nazareth. *Jesus grew up there and remained in his house for at least 12 years. He was certainly dead by the time of the crucifixion. Feast day: Mar 19.

Joseph II (1741–90) Holy Roman Emperor (1765–90), ruling with his mother *Maria Theresa until 1780. As sole ruler, Joseph, an enlightened despot (*see* Enlightenment), introduced religious freedom and reforms in education, law (issuing a legal code in 1786), and administration, and emancipated the serfs. His sweeping reforms encountered some opposition, especially in Hungary and the Austrian Netherlands, and his attempt to subject church to state involved the dissolution of over 700 monasteries and much hardship for monks.

Joséphine (1763–1814) The wife (1796–1809) of Napoleon Bonaparte and Empress of the French from 1804. Her first husband was Alexandre, Vicomte de *Beauharnais, who was guillotined in the French Revolution. She presided over a brilliant court until divorced by Napoleon because of their childlessness.

Joseph of Arimathea, St In the New Testament, a man described as a councillor. He asked Pontius Pilate for the body of Christ after the crucifixion and arranged for its burial on the same day. According to medieval legend, he came to England after the crucifixion, bringing with him the *Holy Grail, and built the first English church, at Glastonbury. Feast day: Mar 17.

Josephson, Brian David (1940–) British physicist, who shared the 1973 Nobel Prize for his work on tunneling effects in superconductors and semiconductors. He discovered that when two superconductors are separated by a thin dielectric an oscillating current is set up if a steady potential difference is applied between them (**Josephson effect**).

Josephus, Flavius (Joseph ben Mattityahu; c. 38–c. 100 AD) Jewish historian and apologist. During the Jewish revolt of 66 AD against the Romans he helped organize the defense of Galilee, but was captured and subsequently accompanied *Vespasian to Rome. Here he wrote his surviving works: a history of the Jewish war, a history of the Jews from the creation up to the war, a defense of Judaism (*Against Apion*), and an autobiography.

Joshua In the Old Testament, the successor of Moses as leader of the Israelites in the period shortly after the *Exodus. **The Book of Joshua**, which follows Deuteronomy in the Old Testament, relates the history of the Israelites between the death of Moses and the death of Joshua. It describes the invasion and conquest of Canaan (Palestine) and its division among the 12 tribes. Among the well-known episodes in the narrative are the Israelites' miraculous crossing of the Jordan River and the capture of Jericho, the walls of which collapsed at the blast of the Israelites' trumpets.

Joshua tree A treelike plant, *Yucca brevifolia*, native to desert regions of the SW US. Growing to a height of more than 33 ft (10 m), its branching stem can assume unusual shapes: the name is said to derive from its supposed resemblance to the prophet Joshua extending his arms in blessing. It has stiff sword-shaped leaves and bears waxy white flowers in dense clusters at the tips of the branches.

Josquin des Prez (c. 1450–1521) Flemish composer. A pupil of Ockeghem, he served at the courts of Milan, Ferrara, and Rome and sang in the papal choir between 1486 and 1494. He was choirmaster at Cambrai Cathedral from 1495 to 1499. His compositions were either elaborately contrapuntal or expressively homophonic; they include masses, motets, and chansons.

Jotunheimen A mountain range in S central Norway. It rises to 8110 ft (2472 m) at Glittertinden, the highest mountain in the country.

joule (J) The *SI unit of work or energy equal to the work done when the point of application of a force of one newton moves through a distance of one meter. Names for James *Joule.

Joule, James Prescott (1818–89) British physicist, who performed a series of experiments during the 1840s to determine the mechanical equivalent of heat. His result, announced in 1847, attracted little attention at first but, supported by Lord *Kelvin, his work greatly contributed toward *Helmholtz's formulation of the law of conservation of energy. He also investigated the heating effect of an electric current (*see* Joule's law) and, with Lord Kelvin, discovered the fall in temperature that occurs when a gas expands adiabatically (*see* Joule-Kelvin effect). The unit of energy is named for him.

Joule-Kelvin effect (*or* Joule-Thomson effect) The change in temperature of a gas when it is expanded adiabatically. In most gases it produces a cooling as energy is needed to overcome the attractive forces between molecules when the gas is expanded. The effect is utilized in *refrigeration and in the *liquefaction of gases. It was discovered by James *Joule and William Thomson (later Lord *Kelvin).

Joule's law A law formulated by James *Joule describing the rate at which a resistance in an electrical circuit converts energy into heat. The heat energy produced per second (in watts) equals the product of the resistance (in ohms) and the square of the current (in amperes).

journalism The gathering, writing, and publication or broadcasting of news. Journalism developed together with *newspapers and *periodicals and its modern English-language origins lie in the 17th century. Most early English journalists were essentially propagandists for political parties, although a campaign for freedom from government control was hotly fought throughout the 18th century. The role of journalists became that of objective reporters and investigators only after newspapers became independent of direct political control in the mid-19th century, a period that saw the work of some of the most celebrated journalists. The late 19th century saw the introduction of sensational journalism (the "yellow" press) in the US, particularly by William Randolph Hearst and Joseph Pulitzer, which greatly increased circulation. The first academic courses providing training in journalism were established around the beginning of the 20th century. Awareness of the social responsibilities of journalists and the new specialized demands of radio and television broadcasting increased this trend toward professionalism. *See also* Press Council.

Jouvet, Louis (1887–1951) French actor and theater director. As a director of the Comédie Française from 1936, he directed the first productions of most of the plays of Jean *Giraudoux and gave notable performances in productions of Molière. He published *Réflexions du comédien* in 1939.

Jovian, Flavius (c. 331–64 AD) Roman emperor (363–64). He served with the emperor *Julian the Apostate in Persia. After Julian's death (363), Jovian was named emperor by the army. He made an unpopular peace with the Persians and died before his return to Constantinople.

Joyce, James (1882–1941) Irish novelist and poet. After a distinguished student career at a Jesuit college, Joyce graduated from University College, Dublin, in 1902, having decided to devote himself to writing. Accompanied by Nora Barnacle (whom he did not marry until 1931), he left Ireland in 1904, living first in Trieste (until 1915) and later in Zurich during World War I and Paris (1920–40). *Dubliners* (1914), a volume of short stories, was followed by the semiautobiographical novel *Portrait of the Artist as a Young Man* (1916). In 1922 he published *Ulysses,* a stream-of-consciousness epic portraying a single day in the lives of several Dubliners. He carried linguistic experiment to further extremes in *Finnegans Wake* (1939), a dream recounted in puns and wordplay.

JP. *See* justice of the peace.

Juan Carlos (1938–　) King of Spain (1975–　). The grandson of Alfonso XIII, he was designated heir to the throne by Francisco *Franco and became king when he died, presiding over Spain's peaceful transition to democracy. In 1962 he married Sophia (1938–　), daughter of King Paul of Greece.

Juan de Fuca, Strait of A strait between *Vancouver Island (SW Canada) and the Olympic Peninsula (US), linking the Pacific Ocean to Puget Sound and Georgia Strait.

Juan Fernández Islands A Chilean group of three volcanic islands, in the S Pacific Ocean. Alexander Selkirk, who inspired Daniel Defoe's *Robinson Crusoe* (1719), lived on the largest island Más-a-Tierra (1704–09). Area: about 70 sq mi (180 sq km).

Juárez. *See* Ciudad Juárez.

Juárez, Benito (Pablo) (1806–72) Mexican statesman, who was the first Indian president of Mexico (1861–65, 1867–72). He became acting president in 1857 but was forced by conservative opposition to flee from Mexico City. In 1861 he returned and was elected president, winning popularity by nationalizing ecclesiastical property. He led the successful opposition (1864–67) to the French invasion (*see* Maximilian) and was reelected president in 1867 and 1871, dying in office.

Juba River A river in East Africa. Rising in S central Ethiopia, it flows S across Somalia to enter the Indian Ocean near Kismayu. Length: 1030 mi (1660 km).

Jubbulpore. *See* Jabalpur.

Juchen Nomadic tribes that originated in the area N of Korea and around the Liaodong peninsula. The Juchen became especially powerful in *Song times, when they founded their own dynasty (1122–1234) modeled on the Chinese system of government.

Judah ha-Levi (*or* Halevy; c. 1075–1141) Jewish poet and philosopher. He was born and spent most of his life in Spain, living in both Christian (Toledo) and Muslim (Cordoba) centers, where he practiced as a physician. Some 1100 of his poems, on religious and secular subjects, are extant and he is considered one of the greatest of Jewish poets and the most important one to emerge from medieval Arabic culture. His major prose work, *Sefer ha-Kuzari,* is a philosophical dialogue on Judaism and the nature of religious truth. According to tradition, he left Spain in the last year of his life on a pilgrimage to Jerusalem; he was enthusiastically received by the Jews of Alexandria and Cairo but died before reaching the Holy Land.

Judah, tribe of One of the 12 *tribes of Israel. It claimed descent from Judah, the son of Jacob and Leah, and occupied territory W of the Dead Sea, which included Jerusalem and Bethlehem. It became the royal house of David in fulfillment of Jacob's dying prophecy. After the division of Israel (*see* Ten Lost Tribes of Israel), it formed with the tribe of *Benjamin the southern kingdom of Judah.

Judaism The religion of the *Jews. Its fundamental tenet is trust in a single, eternal, invisible God, who created the world and desires its welfare. Man's duty is to serve God with all his being. Judaism's most sacred text is the *Torah, which, according to tradition, contains not only a record of history and revealed law but a complete guide to human life and the mysteries of the universe. Judaism has no official creed and no central authority; it lays stress on right behavior (*see* halakhah) rather than on doctrine.

There is no agreement as to when Judaism began. Tradition attaches importance to the early figures of *Abraham and *Moses, but many of the characteristic ideas and institutions emerged during the *Babylonian exile and the period of the Second *Temple. After the destruction of the temple the *rabbis codified and elaborated the traditional teachings (*see* Midrash; Mishnah; Talmud), and in the Middle Ages philosophy and the *kabbalah exerted a great influence. The modern enlightenment (*see* Haskalah) undermined traditional values and gave rise to several conflicting movements. Orthodox Judaism asserts the supernatural authority of Torah and halakhah, which is challenged by *Reform Judaism. Conservative Judaism and Reconstructionism, which are strongest in the US, attempt to reach a compromise between these extreme views.

Judas tree A shrub or small tree of the genus *Cercis* (7 species), also called redbud, native to S Europe, Asia, and North America, and cultivated for ornament. The pinkish-red clusters of flowers appear before the heart-shaped leaves have opened. The name is used particularly for *C. siliquastrum,* from which Judas Iscariot is said to have hanged himself. Family: *Leguminosae.*

Jude, St In the New Testament, one of the 12 Apostles. He is generally identified with Thaddeus and also known as Judas Thaddeus. Referred to as "Judas of James," he was probably the brother of *James ("the Lord's brother") and therefore a half-brother of Jesus. According to tradition he was martyred in Persia with St *Simon, whose feast is held on the same day. Feast day: Oct 28.

The Epistle of Jude in the New Testament is ascribed to him. Of uncertain date, it is a brief warning against certain immoral teachers who were currently infiltrating the Church.

Judea The southern division of ancient Palestine. The Old Testament kingdom of Judah survived Syrian, Assyrian, and Philistine attacks following Solomon's death but came to an end after conquest by *Nebuchadnezzar II of Babylon, when its capital, Jerusalem, was destroyed (586 BC) and the Jews were exiled. Judea came next under Persian domination, when the Jews were allowed to return and rebuild Jerusalem, but under the Seleucids Antiochus IV Epiphanes' desecration of the temple in 167 BC instigated the *Maccabees' revolt. Judea achieved a shortlived independence until the Roman conquest in 63 BC. After years of unrest the Roman province of Syria absorbed it in 135 AD.

Judges An Old Testament book of unknown authorship, but ascribed by Jewish tradition to Samuel. It covers the history of the Israelites from the death of Joshua to shortly before the commencement of the monarchy under Saul (11th century BC). The book introduces a philosophy of history in which God repeatedly causes nations to oppress Israel, as punishment for its apostasy, and then delivers it through the "judges" or virtuous leaders, such as Gideon and Samson, each time it repents.

Judiciary Acts A series of laws enacted by the US Congress that provided for a structured judicial system. An act of 1789 established the Supreme Court, with a chief justice and five associate justices, 13 district courts, 3 circuit courts, and the attorney general's office. Subsequent legislation reduced the number of Supreme Court justices (1801) and then added them back (1802), but it was not until 1869 that the number of justices was fixed at nine.

Judith A Jewish widow who deceived and assassinated a general of Nebuchadnezzar's invading army and thus caused the Assyrian army to flee from her home city. The incident is recorded in the **Book of Judith**, a book of the *Apocrypha. Its purpose was probably to inspire Jewish resistance to the policy of *Antiochus IV Epiphanes.

judo An international form of wrestling developed from *jujitsu in Japan by Jigoro Kano (1860–1938). It was included in the Olympic Games for the first time in 1964. Contestants wear kimonos and colored belts to indicate their proficiency. The five *kyu* (pupil) grades wear white, orange, green, blue, or brown belts in order of increasing skill, the 12 *dan* (master) grades all wear black belts. Contests take place on a mat 30 ft (9 m) square and usually last 2 to 10 minutes. The contestants score points by executing prescribed throws, ground holds, and locks. Balance, speed, surprise, and the ability to use an opponent's strength characterize the skillful judoka. *See also* martial arts.

Jugendstil The German equivalent of the *Art Nouveau style. Named for the magazine *Jugend* (*Youth*), which was first published in 1896, Jugendstil originated in about 1894 in the embroideries of curving plant forms by Hermann Obrist (1863–1927). Other leading exponents were the architects Peter *Behrens and Henry *van der Velde.

Jugoslavia. *See* Yugoslavia.

jugular vein A vein that drains blood from the head and neck regions to the larger veins passing to the heart. There are two jugular veins on each side of the neck: a large internal and a smaller external jugular, the latter lying just beneath the skin.

Jugurtha (c. 160–104 BC) King of Numidia (118–105). He was the illegitimate grandson of Masinissa (d. 148) and initially ruled with Masinissa's legitimate grandsons Hiempsal and Adherbal. He assassinated Hiempsal and the Romans divided Numidia, a Roman dependency, between Jugurtha and Adherbal. Jugurtha's attack (112) on Adherbal caused Rome to declare war (the Jugurthine War), which continued intermittently until 105, when Jugurtha was captured. He was taken to Rome and executed.

JUDO *Competitors in the 1976 Judo Championships at Ruislip (England).*

Juiz de Fora 21 47S 43 23W An industrial city in SE Brazil, in Minas Gerais state on the Rio Paraibuna. It specializes in the manufacture of textiles, especially of knitted goods, and has a university (1960). Population (1980): 299,728.

jujitsu (Japanese name: *yawara*) The form of self-defense, usually unarmed, used by the Japanese *samurai. The object was to disable, cripple, or kill an opponent by using his own momentum and strength against him. It evolved in about the 16th century and was taught in many forms in different schools. It was misused and fell into disrepute in the late 19th century, when the activities of the samurai were curtailed, but *judo, *aikido, and *karate developed from it.

jujube A small thorny tree of the genus *Zizyphus* that produces sweet edible fruit. *Z. jujuba*, native to China, has been widely introduced to other hot dry regions. It grows up to a height of 30 ft (9 m) and has small yellow flowers; blood-red berries are collected and eaten fresh or made into glacé fruits. Family: *Rhamnaceae. See also* crown of thorns.

Juliana (1909–) Queen of the Netherlands (1948–80) following the abdication of her mother Wilhelmina. In 1937 she married Prince Bernhard von Lippe-Biesterfeld. In 1980 Queen Juliana abdicated in favor of her eldest daughter *Beatrix.

Julian calendar. *See* calendar.

Julian the Apostate (Flavius Claudius Julianus; 332–63 AD) Roman emperor (360–63). Julian was the only non-Christian emperor after Constantine. The army proclaimed Julian emperor (360) and he attained power after the death in 361 of Constantius II. In spite of a Christian upbringing, Julian embraced paganism and as emperor restored pagan temples and deprived Christian churches of subsidy. He was killed fighting the Persians.

Julius II (Giuliano della Rovere; 1443–1513) Pope (1503–13). The protégé of his uncle, *Sixtus IV, Julius became a cardinal in 1471 but lived in exile during the pontificate of his rival Alexander VI. Following his election he restored and extended the papal states in Italy. In 1511 he formed a Holy League against the invading Louis XII of France, who, after trying to depose Julius, was forced to withdraw. Julius is best known as a patron of artists, especially Michelangelo and Raphael; he began the building of St Peter's, Rome.

Jullundur 31 18N 75 40E A city in India, in Punjab. An important communications and agricultural center, it manufactures sporting goods. Population (1991): 519,530.

July Seventh month of the year. It is named in honor of Julius Caesar and has 31 days. The zodiac signs for July are Cancer and Leo; the flowers are water lily and larkspur, and the birthstone is the ruby. US Independence Day is celebrated on July 4.

July Revolution Three days of rioting in Paris in July 1830, which brought *Louis Philippe to the French throne. Rebelling against *Charles X's reactionary ordinances, bourgeoisie and workers alike barricaded the streets. Charles abdicated, and the Chamber of Deputies elected Louis Philippe as king.

Jumna River (Jamuna R *or* Yamuna R) A river in N India. Rising in Uttar Pradesh, it flows S and SE past Delhi to join the Ganges River near Allahabad. This confluence is sacred to the Hindus. Length: 860 mi (1385 km).

jumping bean A Mexican shrub, *Sebastiana pringlei,* the seeds of which may contain the caterpillars of a moth, *Carpocapsa saltitans.* When warmed (for example, when held in the hand) the caterpillars wriggle, causing the seed to jump. The seeds of some species of *Colliguaja* of South America may also contain these caterpillars. Family: *Euphorbiaceae.*

jumping mouse A small long-legged rodent belonging to the subfamily *Zapodinae* (5 species), of North America and Asia; 3.1–4 in (8–10 cm) long, jumping mice have long tails (4–6 in; 10–15 cm) and are gray, golden, or yellow-brown in color. Living either in nests on the ground or in very shallow burrows, they feed at night on fruit, seeds, and insects. They hibernate in winter. Family: *Zapodidae.*

Junagadh 21 32N 70 32E A city in India, in Gujarat. An agricultural trading center, it is famous for its Buddhist caves (3rd century BC) and temples. Population (1991): 130,132.

junction transistor. *See* transistor.

June Sixth month of the year. The derivation of the name varies; it is probably named for the Roman goddess Juno, but could come from the Latin *juniores,* which means "youths." It has 30 days. The zodiac signs for June are Gemini and Cancer; the flower is the rose, and the birthstones are the pearl, the moonstone, or the alexandrite.

Juneau 58 20N 134 20W The capital city of Alaska, in the S part of the state, on the Gastineau Channel. A supply center for a fur-trading and mining region, it is also an ice-free port. Industries include salmon fishing and sawmills. Willow South is planned to replace Juneau as the state capital. Population (1990): 26,751.

June beetle A brown beetle, also called May beetle or June bug, belonging to a genus (*Phyllophaga*) of *chafers; 0.47–1 in (12–25 mm) long, June beetles are commonly seen during early summer evenings, being attracted to lights. They can sometimes be serious pests, destroying crops of corn, potato, and strawberry. The adults feed on the foliage and flowers, while the larvae (white grubs) attack the roots.

Jung, Carl Gustav (1875–1961) Swiss psychiatrist and pioneer psychoanalyst. Jung worked in Zurich and collaborated with Sigmund *Freud until, in 1912, their differences became irreconcilable. Jung originated the concept of introvert and extrovert personalities and made valuable studies of mental disorders, including schizophrenia. In his major work, *Psychology of the Unconscious* (1912), Jung regarded the unconscious part of the mind as containing both the personal experiences of the individual and the common inherited cultural experiences (*see* collective unconscious) of the particular social group to which he belongs. Jung later applied his theories to historical studies of religion and to the way in which the layers of the unconscious become manifest in dreams. He also developed psychiatric methods for the treatment of the elderly.

Jungfrau 46 33N 7 58E A mountain peak in S central Switzerland, in the Bernese Oberland. It forms a massif with the Eiger and the Mönch. A railroad climbs to 11,333 ft (3454 m) at the **Jungfraujoch**, the pass between the Jungfrau and the Mönch. Height: 13,632 ft (4158 m).

Junggar Pendi (Dzungarian Basin) A region in NW China, in Xinjiang Uygur Autonomous Region. A semidesert plateau among mountains, it is inhabited chiefly by nomadic herdsmen. There are some state farms and oil and coal are produced.

jungle fowl An Asian forest bird belonging to the genus *Gallus* (4 species). The males have a large fleshy comb and wattles at the sides of the bill and, in the breeding season, fight fiercely using their sharp leg spurs. The red jungle fowl (*Gallus gallus*) is the ancestor of domestic *poultry. Family: *Phasianidae* (fowl and pheasants).

juniper A coniferous tree or shrub of the genus *Juniperus* (60 species), widely distributed in the N hemisphere. Junipers have two kinds of leaves: needlelike and scalelike. All species have needles when young and some have both needles and scales when mature. Male and female flowers grow on separate trees and the cone is a fleshy "berry." The common juniper (*J. communis*) is native to N Europe, North America, and SW Asia; it rarely exceeds 13 ft (4 m) in height and is often planted for ornament. It has needlelike leaves and blue-black cones, 0.24–0.35 in (6–9 mm) in diameter, used for flavoring gin and foods, as a source of oil, and as a diuretic. Family: *Cupressaceae*. *See also* cade; pencil cedar; savin.

Junius, Letters of A series of letters, written by a still unidentified author, criticizing the government of Britain's King George III. They appeared in the *Public Advertiser* between Jan 21, 1769, and Jan 21, 1772. Sir Philip Francis is thought to be the most likely author, although the names of Edmund Burke and Tom Paine, among others, have also been suggested.

Junkers A class of Prussian aristocrats. From small landowners the Junkers rose from the 15th century to control land, industry, and trade. Encouraged by Frederick the Great and Bismarck, they became notorious for arrogance and privilege, enjoying a monopoly of power in the army and civil service that remained unbroken until the 1930s.

Juno (astronomy) A *minor planet (153 mi [247 km] diameter), the orbit of which lies between those of Mars and Jupiter.

Juno (mythology) A principal Roman goddess, the wife of Jupiter. She was concerned with all aspects of women's life, especially marriage and childbirth, and is usually portrayed as a matronly figure. In 390 BC the warning given by her sacred geese on the Capitoline hill saved Rome from an attack by the Gauls. She was identified with the Greek *Hera.

Jupiter (astronomy) The largest and most massive planet, orbiting the sun every 11.86 years at a mean distance of 483 million mi (778.3 million km). Its rapid axial rotation (in less than 10 hours) has produced a nonspherical shape: equatorial diameter 88,675 mi (142,800 km), polar diameter 84,150 mi (135,500 km). In a telescope, light and dark bands of clouds are visible, running parallel to the equator, together with spots and streaks.

Jupiter is composed mainly (99%) of hydrogen and helium (in the ratio 88:12). Ammonia, methane, and other compounds are present in the cloud layers. The gaseous atmosphere is 620 mi (1000 km) thick. The planetary interior is liquid hydrogen with possibly a small rocky core. Jupiter radiates, as heat, about twice as much energy as it receives from the sun, suggesting an internal energy reservoir. It is also a source of radio waves. It has a magnetic field and radiation belts of great intensity.

The planet has at least 16 *satellites, 4 of major size, and a satellite ring of rocks, discovered in 1979. *See also* planetary probe.

Jupiter (mythology) The principal Roman god, identified with the Greek *Zeus. Originally a sky god, he controlled the weather and used the thunderbolt as his weapon. His temple on the Capitoline hill was the principal Roman religious structure. He was a protective god and the guardian of honor, being concerned with oaths, treaties, and marriages.

Jura An island in NW Scotland, in the Inner Hebrides, separated from the mainland by the Sound of Jura. It is mountainous and sparsely populated. Area: 147 sq mi (381 sq km).

Jura Mountains A mountain range in E France and NW Switzerland. It extends along the border in a NE–SW arc between the Rhine and Rhône rivers, rising to 5653 ft (1723 m) at Crêt de la Neige. The area is chiefly agricultural.

Jurassic period A geological period of the Mesozoic era, between about 200 and 135 million years ago, following the Triassic and preceding the Cretaceous periods. The dinosaurs and other reptiles flourished and diversified in this period. Fossils of the earliest birds and mammals have also been found in Jurassic rocks.

Juruá, Rio A river in South America, rising in E central Peru and flowing NE through NW Brazil to join the Amazon River. Length: 1200 mi (1900 km).

jury A body of people, usually 12. They are selected according to law to evaluate the truthfulness of the evidence before them and decide questions of fact arising in a court case.

Jussieu A French family of botanists. **Antoine de Jussieu** (1686–1758) was a physician, who wrote many papers on natural history and made a collection of European plants. He became director of the Jardin des Plantes, Paris. His brother **Bernard de Jussieu** (1699–1777) originated a method of classifying plants that was developed by his nephew **Antoine-Laurent de Jussieu** (1748–1836). The youngest brother of Antoine, **Joseph de Jussieu** (1704–79), spent many years in South America and introduced the garden heliotrope to Europe.

Justice, Department of US cabinet-level executive branch department that represents citizens in enforcing the law in the public interest. It plays a key role in protection against criminals and subversion; in ensuring healthy competition of business; in safeguarding the consumer; and in enforcing drug, immigration, and naturalization laws. Headed by the attorney general, the department conducts all suits concerning the government in the Supreme Court. It was established in 1870.

Justinian I (482–565 AD) Byzantine emperor (527–65). His reign saw chiefly defensive wars on the eastern frontier but in the west his general *Belisarius crushed the Vandals in Africa (533) and the Ostrogoths in Italy (535–53). Justinian, who was greatly influenced by his wife *Theodora, reformed provincial administration and codified *Roman law, which he issued in the *Corpus Juris Civilis* (Body of Civil Law), informally known as the Justinian Code. An orthodox Christian, he attempted to wipe out paganism and built the great church of St Sophia at Constantinople.

Justinian II (c. 669–711 AD) Byzantine emperor (685–95, 705–11), the last of the Heraclian dynasty. He was a notoriously harsh ruler and after a revolt in 695 his nose was cut off (hence his nickname Rhinotmetus) and he was banished to the Crimea. With Bulgar support he returned to Constantinople as emperor, instigating savage reprisals. He was killed in a second revolt.

Justinian Code. *See* Roman law.

Justin Martyr, St (c. 100–c. 165 AD) Christian apologist and martyr, born in Samaria. After his conversion (c. 130) he taught in Ephesus and founded a school of Christian philosophy at Rome, where he was later beheaded. His only certain works are two *Apologies* addressed to the emperor Marcus Aurelius and the Roman Senate and the *Dialogue*, defending Christianity against Judaism. Feast day: Apr 14.

jute Either of two Indian annual plants, *Corchorus capsularis* or *C. olitorius*, cultivated in India, Pakistan, and Thailand for their fibers. Growing to a height of 10 ft (3 m), they have straight spearlike stems and small yellow flowers. The stems are cut, soaked in water, and beaten to remove the fibers, which are processed into burlap, etc. There are many grades, used for ropes, sacks, carpet backings, hessian, and tarpaulin. Blending jute with man-made fibers has increased its uses. Family: *Tiliaceae*.

Jutes A Germanic people, probably from Jutland, who invaded Britain together with the *Angles and Saxons in the 5th century AD. Archeological evidence supports *Bede's statement that the Jutes settled in what are now Kent, the Isle of Wight, and Hampshire.

Jutland (Danish name: Jylland) A peninsula in N Europe, between the North Sea, the Skagerrak, the Kattegat, and the Little Belt. It is occupied by the continental part of Denmark and part of the *Land* of Schleswig-Holstein in Germany.

Juvenal (Decimus Junius Juvenalis; c. 60–c. 130 AD) Roman satirist. The biographical records are unreliable, but it is probable that he was born in Aquinum, SE of Rome, and that he was exiled to Egypt under the emperor Domitian but later became relatively prosperous under the emperor Hadrian. His 16 *Satires*, probably written in the period 98–128 AD, are savage indictments of the corruption and immorality of contemporary Roman society and of the absurd follies of mankind in general.

juvenile delinquency The commission of offenses against the law by a person under a specified age, whatever the age of majority is in a particular state. Most such cases are tried by special Juvenile Courts, to which the press and public are not admitted and in which the terms "sentence" and "conviction" may not be used. The juvenile offender may be bound over to his parents, put under supervision, or committed to a child care officer.

Jylland. *See* Jutland.

K

K2 (*or* Mt Godwin Austen) 35 53N 76 32E The second highest mountain in the world (after Mount Everest), in N Pakistan in the Karakoram Range. As it was the second peak to be measured in the range it was given the symbol K2. The summit was first reached on July 31, 1954, by an Italian team. Height: 28,250 ft (8611 m).

Kaaba The cube-shaped building at the center of the great mosque at Mecca. Muslims believe that it was built by Abraham and Ishmael for the worship of God, was corrupted by Arab paganism, but was then purified and adopted for Islam by Mohammed. In the annual pilgrimage the Muslims circumambulate it and kiss the Black Stone, supposedly brought to Abraham by Gabriel, which is fixed in the interior in the SE corner.

Kabardino-Balkar Republic An administrative division of Russia, on the N side of the Caucasus Mountains. A large part of this mountainous region is unsettled and without roads. The population is 45% Kabardinian, 10% Balkar, and 40% Russian. The Kabardinians, most of whom are Muslims, speak a Northwest Caucasian language, while the Balkars are Turkic-speaking. The principal industries of the region are mining, timber, engineering, and food processing. The main crops are cereals, and livestock, poultry, and dairy farming are also important. *History*: the Kabardinians were associated with the Russians from 1557 and, although the Balkars resisted Russian rule, the region was annexed by Russia in 1827. It became an autonomous republic in 1936. In 1943 the Balkars, accused of collaborating with the Germans, were deported; they were returned in 1956. Area: 4825 sq mi (12,500 sq km). Population (1991 est): 778,000. Capital: Nalchik.

kabbalah (Hebrew: tradition) An esoteric Jewish theosophical system. The classical kabbalistic text is the **Zohar* (*Book of Splendor*), written in Aramaic in 13th-century Spain, but kabbalah has much older roots. It has strong connections with *gnosticism and also with magical practices. An important 16th-century kabbalistic school flourished at Safed, in Galilee, around Isaac *Luria, and Christian interpretations of the kabbalah blended with *Neoplatonism in the 16th and 17th centuries. In modern times a thirst for occult teachings has revived considerable amateur interest in the kabbalah.

Kabinda. *See* Cabinda.

Kabuki A form of Japanese popular theater that developed from the aristocratic *No theater during the 17th century. The earliest notable dramatist was Chikamatsu Monzaemon (1653–1724). The plays are performed with musical accompaniment on a wide revolving stage and emphasize visual effects and acting skills. The conventional scenery, costumes, and the actors' makeup are elaborate. Female roles are played by male actors. A traditional program consists of both historical and domestic dramas separated by dance plays.

Kabul 34 30N 69 10E The capital of Afghanistan, situated in the NE of the country at an altitude of 6000 ft (1830 m) on the Kabul River. It is over 3000 years old, with a strategic position commanding high mountain passes. It has been destroyed and rebuilt many times, being in the path of the great invasions of India by Alexander the Great, Genghis Khan, and others. It was capital of the Mogul Empire (1504–1738), becoming capital of Afghanistan in 1773. The city

KABUKI *The interior of a theater, from a print by Utagawa Toyokuni. The performers enter and leave the stage from the back of the theater along the "flower path," a section of which extends from the stage at the bottom left. Music and sound effects are produced by the group behind the lattice at the right of the stage.*

was badly damaged by the civil war of the 1980s and 1990s. Population (1988 est): 1,424,000.

Kabwe (former name: Broken Hill) 14 29S 28 25E A city in central Zambia. The first Rhodesian (Zambia was formerly Northern Rhodesia) railroad was built here to serve the mines that now produce some of the world's highest grades of lead, zinc, and vanadium. In 1921 prehistoric hominid fossils were discovered here (*see* Homo). Population (1990 est): 166,500.

Kabyle A *Berber people of NE Algeria. They are Muslims and speak the Sanhajah dialect of the Berber language. The Kabyle are mainly settled cultivators living in autonomous villages (firquahs) occupied by patrilineal clans and governed by assemblies of adult males. There are also several castelike groups of inferior status, such as smiths and butchers.

Kádár, János (1912–89) Hungarian leader. Head of the Hungarian secret police (1948–50), in 1956 Kádár led the opposition in the *Hungarian Revolution to Imre *Nagy's government and after the Soviet invasion became first secretary of the Hungarian Socialist Workers' Party. He was also prime minister (1956–58, 1961–65).

Kaduna 10 28N 7 25E A city in Nigeria. Formerly a colonial administrative center, it developed as a railroad junction and is a major textile and local trade center. Population (1990 est): 295,000.

Kaesŏng 37 59N 126 30E A city in SW North Korea, a former Korean capital (938–1392). Many historic buildings here were destroyed during the Korean War (1950–53). Population (1987 est): 120,000.

Kaffirs The former collective name for the Pondo and Xhosa peoples of the E Cape Province of South Africa, with whom the advancing white settlers fought a series of wars (the *Cape Frontier Wars) in the late 18th and 19th centuries.

Kafirs A people of the Hindu Kush mountains of Afghanistan and Pakistan, who speak a Dardic language (*see* Dards). Their name (Arabic *kafir*: infidel) was acquired from their Muslim neighbors on account of their traditional religion, which is polytheistic and involves sacrifice and divination by shamans.

Kafka, Franz (1883–1924) Czech writer. Born in Prague (then in Bohemia), the son of German Jewish parents, he studied law and worked in an insurance company until tuberculosis forced him to leave. His own inner conflicts are reflected in fantasies and parables that portray the individual isolated in an incomprehensible and uneasy environment. Most of his work was published posthumously, against his instructions, by his friend Max Brod. Among his best-known writings are the stories *Metamorphosis* (1912) and *In the Penal Settlement* (1919) and the novels *The Trial* (1925) and *The Castle* (1926).

Kafue River A river in Zambia, rising on the Zaïre frontier and flowing generally S and E to join the Zambezi River. Length: 600 mi (966 km). The **Kafue Dam** (1972) provides about two-thirds of Zambia's hydroelectric power.

Kagoshima 31 37N 130 32E A port in Japan, in S Kyushu on Kagoshima Bay. It was the site of *Francis Xavier's landing in Japan (1549). Its university was established in 1949. It has porcelain and textile industries, a naval yard, and a rocket base. Population (1990): 536,752.

Kagu A rare virtually flightless bird, *Rhynochetus jubatus,* occurring on remote forested mountains of New Caledonia; 22 in (55 cm) long, it has a dark-barred gray plumage, an erectile crest, and reddish eyes, legs, and downcurved bill. It lives on the ground, feeding at night on insects and snails. It is the only member of its family (*Rhynochetidae*). Order: *Gruiformes* (cranes, rails, etc.).

Kahn, Louis I(sadore) (1901–74) US architect. Kahn's first major building was the Yale University Art Gallery (1951–53), which he designed while he was a professor there. He developed a striking and individual form of *functionalism, for example at the Medical Research Building, University of Pennsylvania (1957–60). Other designs include the Kimbell Art Museum in Fort Worth, Tex. (1966–72), and the Yale Center for British Art, New Haven, Conn. (1969–74).

Kaikoura Ranges Twin mountain ranges in New Zealand, comprising the Inland and the Seaward Kaikouras. They extend SW–NE in NE South Island, reaching 9465 ft (2885 m) at Tapuaenuku in the Inland Kaikouras, and are separated by the Clarence River.

Kairouan (*or* Qairouan; Arabic name: al Qayrawan) 35 42N 10 01E A city in N central Tunisia. An ancient town and holy city of Islam, its importance has declined and today it is a local trade center producing carpets and other craft goods. Population (1984): 72,200.

kaiser The title (derived from the Latin: Caesar) adopted by the German kings as Holy Roman Emperors (800–1806). It was assumed by William I of Prussia in 1871 and borne by the German emperors until 1917.

kakapo A rare nocturnal New Zealand *parrot, *Strigops habroptilus,* also called owl parrot. It is the largest and only flightless parrot, having disks of stiff feathers around the eyes resembling an owl. Its green plumage is barred with yellow and brown and it has a heavy bill for grinding plant material.

Kakinomoto Hitomaro (c. 680–710) Japanese poet. He is considered the greatest of the poets whose works appear in the Man'yo-shu, an 8th-century anthology of lyric poetry. He was poet to the court of Empress Jito and Emperor Mommu and many of his poems describe court life.

Kalahari Desert A semiarid area in S Africa, chiefly in Botswana. It is sparsely inhabited by nomadic Bushmen, and although its few rivers are generally dry there is some vegetation. Wildlife is concentrated in the game reserves in the S. Area: about 96,505 sq mi (250,000 sq km).

Kalamazoo 42 17N 85 36W A city in Michigan, on the Kalamazoo River. It produces paper, fishing tackle, and stoves. Population (1990): 80,277.

Kalanchoe A genus of small tropical shrubs (over 100 species) having fleshy leaves and clusters of colorful flowers on tallish stems. They are popular house plants, requiring good draining and water supply and warm temperatures. Most flower in winter, having white, red, yellow, or pink flowers. Family: *Crassulaceae.*

kale A variety of *cabbage, also called borecole, or collards, grown for its large edible leaves, which are used as a winter vegetable and as livestock food. Curly kales, which have curled crimped leaves, are the most popular as vegetables. Some produce tender spring shoots. They are more hardy than most other brassicas.

Kali In Hindu mythology, the goddess of death. The wife of *Shiva in her destructive aspect, she is represented as a hideous four-armed black woman, adorned with skulls, and is propitiated by nocturnal sacrifices of animals.

Kalidasa (5th century AD) Indian poet, considered to be the greatest writer in classical Sanskrit. Almost nothing is known of his life, but he is traditionally associated with the court of Chandra Gupta II. The seven works attributed to him include two epics, two shorter poems, and three dramas, of which the most famous is the *Sakuntala,* concerning the love of King Dusyanta for a semidivine nymph.

Kalimantan The Indonesian part of *Borneo, comprising the SE two-thirds of the island. It is little developed, but its dense forests provide valuable timber. Small-scale agriculture includes the growing of rice, tobacco, sugar cane, coffee, and rubber. It is a longstanding source of gold and also produces oil and coal. Since Indonesian independence in 1949 separatism against the Java-based government has remained strong with active guerrilla activity. Area: 212,388 sq mi (550,203 sq km). Chief cities: Banjarmasin and Pontianak.

Kalinin (name until 1931: Tver) 56 49N 35 57E A port in Russia, on the Volga River. The city was renamed Kalinin in 1931 in honor of the revolutionary M. I. *Kalinin. It is a major industrial and administrative center, with industries that include engineering and textiles. Population (1987): 447,000.

Kalinin, Mikhail Ivanovich (1875–1946) Soviet statesman. A loyal supporter of Stalin, he was formally head of state (1919–46) as chairman of what came to be called the presidium of the Supreme Soviet.

Kaliningrad (name until 1946: Königsberg) 54 40N 20 30E A Russian port on the Pregolya River near its mouth at the Baltic Sea. Founded in 1255 as a fortress for the Teutonic Knights, it passed to Prussia in the 16th century and became a major German naval base. It was ceded to the Soviet Union in 1945. Its industries include ship building, timber, paper, textiles, and food processing. Population (1987): 394,000.

Kalmyk Autonomous Republic An administrative division in Russia, on the Caspian Sea. The Kalmyk people, who speak a Mongolian language, are traditionally Buddhists. Industries include fish processing, canning, and manufacture of building materials, but the economy is predominantly agricultural and cattle breeding and fodder crops are particularly important. The Kalmyks were deported to Siberia for collaborating with the Germans in World War II but some were returned in 1957. Area: 29,300 sq mi (75,900 sq km). Population (1990 est): 329,000. Capital: Elista.

Kaluga 54 31N 36 16E A port in Russia on the Oka River. It produces railroad equipment, electrical equipment, textiles, and consumer goods. Population (1990 est): 366,000.

Kama In Hindu mythology, the god of love. He is the son of *Shiva and his popular epithet of Ananga (bodyless) derives from his having been reduced to ashes by a glance from his father's eye when Kama playfully shot his arrows at him.

Kama River A river in E Russia, rising in the Ural Mountains and flowing mainly SW to the Volga River. It is a main waterway. Length: 1260 mi (2030 km).

Kamakura 35 19N 139 33E A city in Japan, in SE Honshu on an inlet of the Pacific Ocean. A former Japanese capital (1192–1333), it is now a religious center, noted for its shrines and temples and for its bronze Buddha, 43 ft (13 m) high. Population (1990): 174,307.

Kamchatka A peninsula in the extreme E of Russia. It is about 746 mi (1200 km) long and separates the Sea of Okhotsk from the Bering Sea. There are many lakes, rivers, and forests, two mountain chains, and about 20 active volcanoes. Area: about 104,225 sq mi (270,000 sq km).

Kamehameha I (c. 1758–1819) King of Hawaii (1810–19), who founded the Kamehameha dynasty. Ruler of part of Hawaii from 1782, by 1810 he had united all the Hawaiian islands. He maintained Hawaiian independence despite the arrival of European explorers following James Cook's discovery of Hawaii in 1779. His encouragement of foreign trade established Hawaiian prosperity.

Kamehameha IV (1834–63) King of Hawaii (1854–63). He instituted social reforms, including free medical care, and encouraged greater commercial activity. He successfully opposed annexation by the US in 1853–54 and curbed the political influence of US missionaries by inviting representatives of the Church of England to share their educational work.

Kamenev, Lev Borisovich (1883–1936) Soviet politician. Kamenev failed to win a favorable position in the power struggle after Lenin's death and he was arrested for participating in *Kirov's assassination (1934). He was tried in the first public purge trial and executed.

Kamikaze A Japanese aircraft crashed deliberately by its pilot into its target. Such suicide missions were first flown at the battle of Leyte Gulf (1944) in World War II; at Okinawa (1945) some 3000 sorties sunk 21 US ships. Kamikaze means divine wind and refers to the typhoon that scattered Kublai Khan's invasion fleet in 1281.

Kampala 0 20N 32 30E The capital of Uganda, N of Lake Victoria. Founded by the British in the late 19th century, it became the capital in 1962. In 1979 its fall to the combined forces of Tanzanians and exiled Ugandans effected the end of President Idi Amin's regime. It has two cathedrals and Makerere University (1970). It is chiefly an administrative center with some small industries. Population (1991): 773,463.

Kampuchea, Democratic. *See* Cambodia.

Kananga (name until 1966: Luluabourg) 5 53S 22 26E A city in central Zaïre, on the Lulua River. A major commercial center, it serves an agricultural and diamond-producing area. Population (1991 est): 372,000.

Kanarese A *Dravidian language of SW India, also called Kannada. It is the official language of Mysore. Texts written in the Kanarese alphabet date from the 6th century.

Kanazawa 36 35N 136 38E A city in Japan, in central Honshu. It is renowned for its landscape garden. Its university was established in 1949. Industries include textiles, porcelain, and lacquerware. Population (1990): (442,868).

Kanchenjunga, Mount. *See* Kangchenjunga, Mount.

Kanchipuram (*or* Conjeeveram) 12 50N 79 44E A city in India, in Tamil Nadu. It is one of the oldest cities in S India and is sacred to the Hindus. It is noted for its silk and cotton fabrics. Population (1991): 145,028.

Kandahar (*or* Qandahar) 31 36N 65 47E A city in S Afghanistan. Situated on main routes to central Asia and India, it is built on the site of several ancient cities. It was the first capital (1747) of a unified Afghanistan. Kandahar is a major commercial center. Population (1988 est): 226,000.

Kandinsky, Wassily (1866–1944) Russian expressionist painter and art theorist, born in Moscow, where he graduated in law. In 1896 he moved to Munich to study. There he painted the first purely abstract pictures in European art (c. 1911). These are characterized by freely applied paint and dazzling colors, from which he drew analogies to music in his book *Concerning the Spiritual in Art* (1911). He was a founder of the *Neue Kunstlervereinigung (1909) and Der *Blaue Reiter (1911); following a stay in Russia (1914–21), he taught at the *Bauhaus school of design, where his style became more geometrical. He settled in France in 1933.

Kandy 7 17N 80 40E A city in central Sri Lanka. Capital of the kingdom of Kandy (1480–1815), when it was occupied by the British, it has a famous Buddhist temple, Dalada Malagawa. Kandy is the commercial center for Sri Lanka's major tea-producing region. Population (1990 est): 129,000.

Kanem Bornu An African empire that controlled the area around Lake Chad. Kanem, situated on the eastern trade routes, became a center of Muslim civilization in the 11th century. The king was expelled in 1389 and founded a new dynasty in Bornu, which in the 16th century conquered Kanem and expanded the empire. Torn by internal strife, the empire collapsed in about 1800.

kangaroo The largest *marsupial mammal. There are two species, the red kangaroo (*Macropus rufus*) of Australia and the gray kangaroo (*M. kanguru*) of Australia and Tasmania. Red kangaroos can reach a height of 7 ft (2 m) and a weight of 198 lb (90 kg). Kangaroos have short front legs and long hind legs and feet: they travel by a succession of leaps. When moving slowly, they use their long heavy tail as a prop. The red kangaroos graze across the plains while gray kangaroos live in open woodland. Family: *Macropodidae. See also* wallaby; wallaroo; tree kangaroo. □mammal.

kangaroo paw A stiff hairy plant of the Australian genus *Anigozanthos* (10 species), also known as Australian sword lilies and sometimes planted in gardens in warm regions. The flowers, borne in short branched terminal clusters, are long, tubular, and hairy, with six pointed flaring lobes, usually yellow, green, or red. Unopened flowers resemble kangaroos' paws. Family: *Hemodoraceae*.

kangaroo rat A North American desert rodent of the genus *Dipodomys* (22 species). Up to 8 in (20 cm) long, kangaroo rats have long back legs and very long hairy tails. they do not need to drink as they obtain water from their food (seeds, tubers, and other vegetation). They spend the day in relatively cool humid burrows, in which they also store food during droughts. □mammal.

Kangchenjunga, Mount (*or* Mt Kanchenjunga) 27 44N 88 11E The third highest mountain in the world (after Mount Everest and K2), on the Sikkim (India)–Nepal border in the Himalayas. It was first climbed in 1955 by a British expedition that stopped just short of the actual summit in deference to the religious wishes of the Sikkimese. Height: 28,208 ft (8598 m).

KaNgwane. *See* Bantu Homelands.

Kang Xi (*or* K'ang-hsi; 1654–1722) Chinese emperor (1661–1722) of the Qing dynasty, who completed the Qing conquest of China started by *Nurhachi. He was a powerful ruler, who led his armies in person against the Mongols and carried out tours of inspection of his vast empire. He built the imperial summer palace at Jehol (now Chengde) and sponsored engineering works to prevent the Yellow River from flooding and to improve communications. His greatest achievement was probably in his sponsorship of the arts.

Kang You Wei (1858–1927) Chinese reformer. A major influence on the *Hundred Days of Reform (1898), he was subsequently forced to flee China and in 1907, in British Columbia, founded the China Reform Association. He returned to China in 1914 and became an opponent of Sun Yat-sen.

Kano 12 00N 8 31E A city in N Nigeria. It was an important trade center for caravans crossing the Sahara. It was captured by the British (1903) and trade developed with the S. It is now an important trade center, particularly for groundnuts and cattle, with some local industries. Population (1992 est): 700,000.

Kanpur (former name: Cawnpore) 26 27N 80 14E A city in India, in Uttar Pradesh on the Ganges River. Ceded to the British East India Company (1801), it became an important British frontier station and during the Indian Mutiny was the scene (1857) of a massacre of British soldiers. Today Kanpur is one of India's largest cities and major communications and industrial center; the chief manufactures are wool, cotton, jute, leather goods, plastics, and chemicals. Several educational institutions are located here, including a university (1966) and an Institute of Technology (1960). Population (1991 est): 1,958,282.

Kansas A midwestern state in the central US. Missouri lies to the E, Oklahoma to the S, Colorado to the W, and Nebraska to the N. It consists mainly of the Great Plains and is crossed by the Kansas and Arkansas rivers. Famous for its wheat fields, which stretch over the vast, seemingly endless terrain, Kansas is the country's main wheat growing area. Located in the US heartland, it has a continental climate typical of inland regions, with extreme temperatures and dramatic storms, blizzards, and tornadoes. Manufacturing is significant with aircraft production, food and meat processing, and a range of different processing industries. Beef production is especially important, and cattle raising constitutes the leading agricultural revenue producer of the state. Its large mineral resources yield oil, natural gas, coal, sand and gravel, cement, stone, chalk, zinc, and lead. Kansas is also an important agricultural state, being the US's main wheat-growing area; other crops include sorghum grains and hay. Beef production is especially important. *History*: first explored by the Spanish in the 16th century, it was claimed by the French (1682) and formed part of the Louisiana Purchase (1803) by the US. The establishment of Kansas as a territory came late as a result of controversy over the slavery issue. Attempts had been made to organize Kansas and Nebraska as a single territory. but proslavery interests opposed the *Missouri Compromise (which sought to settle the slavery issue in the territories, and would have designated Kansas-Nebraska a nonslavery territory). Thus, attempts to organize the territory were continually defeated. As a concession to the South, Kansas and Nebraska were given free choice, or "squatter sovereignty," on the slavery question. Opposing forces, each seeking to win support for its side, inflamed the sentiments of the settlers to the point of pitched battle. The territory became known as Bleeding Kansas. It was in Kansas that the abolitionist John *Brown formulated a plan to liberate the slaves that culminated in his raid on Harpers Ferry, Va. Kansas fought with the Union in the Civil War. The arrival of the railroad in the late 1860s and 1870s brought many cattlemen. Area: 82,264 sq mi (213,063 sq km). Population (1990): 2,477,574. Capital: Topeka.

Kansas City 39 07N 94 39W A city in NE Kansas, across the Kansas River from Kansas City, Mo. Settled in 1843 as Wyandot City by the Wyandot Indians, it became Kansas City in 1886. It is known as a meat-packing center, but also has extensive automobile, petroleum, railroad, food processing, paper, metal, and chemical industries. Population (1990): 149,767.

Kansas-Nebraska Act (1854) US law that gave territories the freedom to decide by popular vote (or popular sovereignty) the question of slavery. Sponsored by Sen. Stephen A. *Douglas, it was intended to quell the growing acrimony between anti- and pro slavery factions; instead, it brought the nation closer to war. The act also repealed the *Missouri Compromise, changed existing laws concerning territorial slavery, and created Kansas and Nebraska territories.

Kansu. *See* Gansu.

Kant, Immanuel (1724–1804) German philosopher, who made many original and influential contributions to thought. He spent much of his life (1755–97) teaching at the university in his native Königsberg (now Kaliningrad in Russia). His early works, notably *Theory of the Heavens* (1755), sought to examine metaphysics in the light of the work of *Newton and *Leibniz. Acquaintance with Hume's *empiricism, however, initiated his so-called "critical period" in which he evolved his doctrine of transcendental idealism. In the famous *Critique of Pure Reason* (1781) he explored the limitations of reason by which mankind interprets experience. The *Critique of Practical Reason* (1788) and the *Critique of Judgment* (1790) deal respectively with *ethics and aesthetic and teleological judgments. Reason makes experience possible by imposing upon the raw data supplied by the senses the forms of understanding. Kant identified 12 of these basic forms (which he called "categories"), such as causality; they were transcendental in as much as they were not derived from experience but were found in pure reason independently of experience. But reason is also practical and as such he identified it with morality. He maintained that there was an absolute moral law, which can never be modified by expediency (it can never be right to tell a lie), and called the obligation to obey this moral law the "categorical imperative," binding upon every rational human being.

Kao-hsiung. *See* Gaoxiong.

kaolin A group of clay minerals consisting of hydrous aluminum silicates. It includes kaolinite (the most important), nacrite, and dickite. Kaolin is the main constituent of *china clay. It has many industrial uses apart from the ceramic industry, particularly as a mineral filler in the manufacture of paper, paint, textiles, rubber, plastics, and cosmetics. It is also used in medicine.

Kapitza, Peter Leonidovich (1894–1984) Soviet physicist, who went to England's Cambridge University in 1921 and worked with *Rutherford on high transient magnetic fields. Returning to the Soviet Union in 1934 he transferred his attention to low-temperature physics, which led him to the discovery of superfluid helium (1941). For this work he was awarded the Nobel Prize (1978).

kapok The fine silky hairs covering the seeds of the silk-cotton tree (*Ceiba pentandra*), which are extracted and used for stuffing mattresses, etc. Impervious to water, kapok can also be used to fill life jackets and oil pressed from the seeds is used in soap making and is edible. The tree is native to tropical America and widely cultivated in the tropics. Growing to 1378 ft (35 m), it has huge horizontal branches, large buttresses at the base of the trunk, and clusters of white or red flowers. Family: *Bombacaceae*.

KAPOK *The fruit pods of the silk-cotton tree ripen in about two months. They split open to release masses of white kapok, which surrounds the black seeds.*

Kara-Bogaz-Gol A shallow gulf of the E Caspian Sea. Its water evaporates fast, drawing more in from the Caspian and creating the richest natural deposits of marine salts in the world. Area: about 5018 sq mi (13,000 sq km).

Karachai-Cherkes An autonomous republic in W Russia. It was formed in 1922 for the Muslim Karachai and Cherkes peoples. Mining, engineering, and chemical industries are important, and the chief agricultural activities are live-stock raising and cereal production. Area: 5440 sq mi (14,100 sq km). Population (1990 est): 427,000. Capital: Cherkessk.

Karachi 24 51N 67 02E The largest city and chief seaport in Pakistan, situated on the Arabian Sea just NW of the Indus delta. A modern city, it developed rapidly from the mid-19th century as a port. It became the capital of Pakistan (1947) following partition, which brought a further influx of refugees to an al-ready overcrowded city. The subsequent removal of the capital to Islamab (1959) and the building of new satellite towns has to some extent eased the housing situation. The University of Karachi was established here in 1957. The city is Pakistan's principal naval base and its port is a major outlet for the agri-cultural produce of the Sind and Punjab provinces. Industries include jute, silk, wool and cotton textiles, chemicals and plastics, and engineering. Population (1981 est): 5,103,000.

Karaganda 49 53N 73 07E A city in central Kazakhstan. Founded in 1857, Karaganda grew rapidly in the 1920s and 1930s as the Karaganda coal basin was exploited. Today it is one of the largest producers of bituminous coal in the country. Although coal mining and the production of coal mining equipment dominate the city's industries, it also produces building materials and has light industries. Population (1987): 633,000.

Karageorge (George Petrović Karadordević; c. 1762–1817) Serbian revolu-tionary leader. In 1804 he led a successful revolt against Turkey and in 1808 be-came the "Supreme Serbian hereditary leader." Turkey regained control of Serbia in 1813 and after a five-year exile in Austria Karageorge was murdered, proba-bly by his rivals, the *Obrenovic family.

Karajan, Herbert von (1908–89) Austrian conductor. Educated at Vienna and the Salzburg Mozarteum, he was musical director of the Vienna State Opera (1957–1964). He founded the Salzburg Easter Festival in 1967 and conducted the Berlin Philharmonic Orchestra from 1955 until his death.

Kara-Kalpak Autonomous Republic An administrative division in Uzbek-istan, on the Aral Sea; formerly part of the Soviet Union. The population con-sists mainly of Kara-Kalpaks, a Turkic-speaking people closely related to the Kazakhs. Kara-Kalpakia's main industries are the manufacture of bricks, leather goods, and furniture and canning and wine making. It is a major producer of al-falfa; other crops grown include cotton, rice, corn, and jute. Cattle and karakul sheep are raised. *History*: the Kara-Kalpaks were under the rule of the *Kaza-khs, passing under Russian rule in the late 19th and early 20th centuries. Kara-Kalpakia was within the Kazakh SSR (1925–30) before being incorporated into the Russian Republic. It became an autonomous republic in 1932 and became part of independent Uzbekistan in 1991. Area: 63,900 sq mi (165,600 sq km). Population (1991 est): 1,274,000. Capital: Nukus.

Karakoram Range A mountain range mainly in SW China, NE Pakistan, and NW India. It extends about 280 mi (450 km) between the Pamirs and the Hi-malayas and includes *K2, the second highest mountain in the world. In 1978 the **Karakoram Highway** was opened connecting China with Pakistan over the Khunjerab Pass, 16,188 ft (4933 m) high.

Karakorum The former Mongol capital founded (c. 1220) by *Genghis Khan in the upper valley of the Orhon Gol River (Outer Mongolia). It replaced the nearby Uighur capital of the same name. After *Kublai Khan moved the capital from Karakorum (1267) the city declined and was eventually destroyed (1388).

karakul A breed of sheep originating in central Asia. The young lambs bear a coat of fine tightly curled black wool, known as Persian lamb.

Kara Kum A desert between the Caspian Sea to the W and the Amu Darya River to the E, comprising most of Turkmenistan. Area: about 115,806 sq mi (300,000 sq km).

Karamanlis, Constantine (1907–) Greek statesman; prime minister (1955–63, 1974–80), president (1980–85). Karamanlis resigned in 1963 and went into exile, returning in 1974, after the fall of the military dictatorship, to form a civilian government.

Kara Sea A section of the Arctic Ocean off the N coast of Russia, between Novaya Zemlya and Severnaya Zemlya. It is frozen for much of the year but is used to reach the port of Novy Port some 373 mi (600 km) inland on the Gulf of Ob.

karate An oriental form of unarmed combat that was systematized in Okinawa, one of the Ryukyu Islands, in the 17th century and spread to Japan in the 1920s, where it absorbed elements of *jujitsu. Breath-control techniques as well as philosophical attitudes, such as the necessity of mental calm, were taken from Zen Buddhism. The aim is to focus the body's total muscular power in one instant. Hands, feet, elbows, etc., are toughened in stylized training sequences against padded or wooden blocks, and karate fighters also perform feats of strength, such as wood breaking. In actual fights, however, which last two or three minutes, blows are stopped short before impact. As in *judo, grades are distinguished by colored belts and points are awarded in combat. *See also* martial arts.

KARATE *A championship bout in one of the most popular of the martial arts.*

Karatepe A fortified hilltop site near Adana (S Turkey), founded (c. 740 BC) by Asitawandas, King of the Danuna (possibly the same people as the Danaoi, mentioned by Homer). King Sanduarri of Karatepe was beheaded by *Esarhaddon (676 BC). A palace with sculptured reliefs and an important bilingual Phoenician and Hittite hieroglyphic inscription have been found.

Karbala (*or* Kerbela) 32 37N 44 03E A city in central Iraq, S of Baghdad. Muslim pilgrims are attracted to the tomb of Husan (the son of *Ali), who was martyred here. It is a trading center for dates and other agricultural produce. Population (1985): 185,000.

Karelian Autonomous Republic (*or* Karelia) An administrative division in Russia. Comprising largely forest, it also possesses thousands of lakes and rivers. The Karelians speak a Finno-Ugric language, and W Karelia has formed part of Finland for much of its history, but was finally ceded to Russia in 1940. Industries include mining, timber, and chemicals. Some cereals, potatoes, and fodder crops are grown and fishing is important. Area: 66,560 sq mi (172,400 sq km). Population (1991 est): 800,000. Capital: Petrozavodsk.

Karelian Isthmus A land bridge between the Gulf of Finland in the W and Lake Ladoga in the E. It connects Finland with Russia, to which it was ceded in 1944. It is 25–70 mi (40–113 km) wide and 90 mi (145 km) long and its principal cities are Leningrad and Vyborg.

Karen A group of peoples of S Myanmar (formerly Burma) who speak tonal languages distantly related to those of the Tibeto-Burman branch of the *Sino-Tibetan family. There are many different and distinct groups and languages broadly divided into the White Karens (including Sgaw and Pwo) and the Red Karens (including Bre, Padaung, Yinbaw, and Zayein). Only Sgaw and Pwo have written forms and all are much influenced by surrounding languages. Their religion is animistic.

Kariba, Lake A reservoir in Zambia and Zimbabwe. It is formed by the Zambezi River above the **Kariba Dam** (completed 1959) and is used for generating hydroelectric power. Length: 175 mi (282 km).

Karl-Marx-Stadt (name 1953–89; German name, Chemnitz) 50 49N 12 50E A city in S Germany, on the Chemnitz River. A textile center since the 14th century, it became famous for machine construction in the 19th century, when the first German machine tools and the first German locomotive were made here. Population (1991 est): 294,000.

Karloff, Boris (William Pratt; 1887–1969) British character actor, who worked mostly in US films. Following his great success as the monster in *Frankenstein* (1931), he was typecast in a number of sinister and gruesome roles in horror films.

Karlovy Vary (German name: Karlsbad) 50 14N 12 53E A spa city in the Czech Republic, in W Bohemia. It has many hot sodium sulfate springs, including the Vřídlo (Sprudel) at a temperature of 162°F (72°C). Population (1989 est): 58,200.

Karlskrona 56 10N 15 35E A seaport in S Sweden, on the Baltic coast. It has been the main naval station of Sweden since 1680. Its industries include the manufacture of naval equipment, granite quarrying, and sawmilling. Population (1988 est): 58,700.

Karlsruhe 49 00N 8 24E A city in SW Germany, in Baden-Württemberg. The capital of the former *Land* of Baden, it is the site of the federal court of justice and a university (1825). It has a harbor on the Rhine and varied industries, including oil refining and machinery manufacturing. It is a center for nuclear research and development. Population (1991 est): 275,000.

Karlstad 59 24N 13 32E A port in SW Sweden, on the N shore of Lake Vänern, at the outlet of the Klar River. Its industries are based on timber and heavy machinery and it has a university (1967). Population (1988 est): 75,000.

karma (Sanskrit: action) The sum of all human actions, which according to Hinduism and Jainism are passed from one individual existence to the next and determine the nature of the individual's rebirth. In *Buddhism, karma is associated with mental and physical elements passed on in the cycle of rebirth until the personal self is annihilated in attaining *nirvana.

Karnak 25 44N 32 39E A village near *Thebes (Upper Egypt), the site of the huge temple of *Amon, built (c. 1320–1237 BC) mainly by the pharaohs Seti I (reigned 1313–1292) and *Ramses II. *See also* Luxor.

Karnataka (name until 1973: Mysore) A state in SW India, on the Arabian Sea, stretching E over the Western Ghats onto the Deccan plateau. Rice, sugar cane, coffee, tea, cotton, and fruit are grown. Hill forests provide teak and sandalwood. Iron ore, gold, manganese, and bauxite are mined. Industries include iron and steel, engineering, food products, and silk. Most of the population are Kanarese-speaking Hindus. *History*: long ruled by Hindu dynasties, Karnataka was conquered (1761) by a Muslim, Hyder Ali, whose son Britain dispossessed (1799). Area: 74,024 sq mi (191,773 sq km). Population (1990): 44,806,468. Capital: Bangalore.

Károlyi, Mihály, Count (1875–1955) Hungarian statesman. Károlyi led the campaign for Hungarian independence during World War I and became (January 1919) the provisional president of the new Hungarian Democratic Republic. In a confrontation between conservatives and communists, he was forced in March to resign and was succeeded by Béla Kun.

Karpov, Anatoly (1951–   ) Soviet chess player, who became an International Grandmaster at 19 and subsequently world champion (1975). In 1978 he beat *Korchnoi in a much publicized match at Manila but lost his title in 1985 to fellow Soviet Gary Kasparov, who also defeated him in a 1990 rematch.

karri A tree, *Eucalyptus diversicolor*, native to SW Australia and cultivated elsewhere. It grows to a height of over 115 ft (35 m) in moist areas and produces excellent timber. The attractive leaves are dark green above and lighter below. Family: *Myrtaceae*.

Karroo A plateau in S South Africa, divided by the Groot-Swartberge range into the **Great Karroo** and, to the S, the **Little Karroo**. Seasonal rains turn them into rich pasture for sheep.

karst region An area of the earth's surface typified by sink holes, uvalas (depressions), and underground drainage, produced by the solution of limestone or dolomite. Such features are notable in the Karst region of Slovenia, Croatia, and E Italy.

karting (*or* go-karting) A form of *automobile racing that originated in the US in the 1950s. A kart usually has a tubular chassis, no body or suspension system, and a single driving seat. It has a maximum wheelbase of 50 in (1.27 m) and is usually powered by a single-cylinder two-stroke engine; 100 cc, 200 cc, and 270 cc are among the more common engine capacities. Most karts are capable of about 100 mph (160 km per hour).

Kasai River A river in central Africa. Rising in Angola, it flows N into Zaïre to join the Zaïre River as its main tributary. It forms part of the Angola–Zaïre border and is rich in alluvial diamonds. Length: 1300 mi (2100 km).

Kasavubu, Joseph (c. 1917–69) Congolese statesman; president (1960–65). A teacher, Kasavubu joined with *Lumumba to lead the Congo (now Zaïre) to independence. In 1961 he deposed Lumumba, until then prime minister, with the help of *Mobutu but was himself deposed in Mobutu's second coup in 1965. He retired to his farm, where he died.

Kashmir The northernmost region of the Indian subcontinent, bordered by China to the NE and Afghanistan to the NW. The S Jammu lowlands rise into the Himalaya and Karakoram Mountains. Except for the Indus Valley and the beautiful Vale of Kashmir, the valleys are small. Rice, other grains, silk, cotton, fruits, and sheep are farmed. Embroidery and other crafts help tourism to thrive. *History*: most Kashmiris became Muslims in the 14th century but in the 19th century Hindu princes won power under British control. Britain's withdrawal (1947) was followed by a Muslim revolt; the Hindu maharajah acceded to India but Pakistan intervened and fighting between the two sides resulted in the partition of the region. Pakistan rules 30,468 sq mi (78,932 sq km) of the W and barren N. China occupies 16,496 sq mi (42,735 sq km) in the E. The remainder forms the Indian state of *Jammu and Kashmir. Area: 85,783 sq mi (222,236 sq km).

Kassel 51 18N 9 30E A city in Germany, in Hessen. Notable buildings include the Orangery Palace (1701–11). Bombed for its aircraft and tank industries during World War II, its manufactures now include railroad engines and textiles. Population (1988): 185,000.

Kassites A people of mysterious racial origins who moved SW from the Zagros Mountains to overrun *Babylonia in the 16th century BC. Although Indo-European gods were apparently worshiped, the Kassite language is neither Indo-European nor Semitic. The Kassites ruled Babylon for about 400 years until overthrown by *Assyria.

Katanga. *See* Shaba.

Kathmandu (*or* Katmandu) 27 42N 85 19E The capital of Nepal, near the confluence of the Baghmati and Vishnumati Rivers. Founded in the 8th century AD, it possesses numerous historical buildings and a university (1959) and is the site of several religious festivals. Its development as the country's main commercial center has been assisted by a program of road building. Population (1981): 235,200.

Katmai, Mount An active volcano in S Alaska, in the Aleutian Range. Following its violent eruption in 1912, the *Valley of Ten Thousand Smokes was formed. Height: 7000 ft (2100 m). Depth of crater: 3700 ft (1130 m). Width of crater: about 2.5 mi (4 km).

Katowice (former name [1953–56]: Stalinogrod) 50 15N 18 59E A city in S central Poland. It is an important industrial center within the Upper Silesia coalfield; manufactures include iron and steel. The Silesian University was established here in 1968. Population (1985 est): 363,500.

Katsura Taro (1847–1913) Japanese soldier and statesman who was instrumental in introducing into the Japanese army a general-staff system on German lines. He was prime minister three times (1901–06, 1908–11, 1912–13) and presided over the victorious *Russo-Japanese War (1904–05) and the annexation of Korea (1910).

Kattegat A strait between Denmark and Sweden linking the Skagerrak with the Baltic Sea. Length: about 149 mi (240 km).

katydid A *bush cricket of the subfamily *Pseudophyllinae*, common in the tropics and E North America. It takes its name from the repetitive song—"katydid, katy-didn't"—of male katydids of the genus *Pterophylla*. Katydids are generally green and have long wings but never fly. They are mainly herbivorous, although some species eat insects.

Katyn Massacre The execution during World War II of 4250 Polish officers in the Katyn forest, near Smolensk in the Soviet Union. The bodies of the Poles, who had been interned by the Russians following the Soviet occupation of Polish territory in 1939, were discovered by the Germans in 1943. The Russians denied responsibility, countercharging the Germans with the massacre. The Soviet Union forbade the Red Cross investigation requested by the Polish Government in exile, with which it broke diplomatic relations. The weight of evidence points to Soviet accountability.

Kauai Island An island in NW Hawaii. It was the first Hawaiian island visited by Capt. James Cook in 1778. Volcanic mountains rise above fertile valleys where extensive pineapples, sugar cane, and rice are cultivated. The highest point is at Mt Waialeale (5148 ft; 1570 m) deep. The island has the rainiest location in the world—an average of 460 in (1169 mm) of rain falls annually near Mt Waialeale. The seat of island government and largest town is Lihue. Area: 555 sq mi (1438 sq km).

Kaufman, George S(imon) (1889–1961) US dramatist. He worked as a newspaper columnist while collaborating, especially with Moss *Hart, on an enormous number of Broadway comedy hits. With Hart he wrote *You Can't Take it With You* (1936), which won a Pulitzer Prize, and *The Man Who Came to Dinner* (1939). With Marc Connelly he wrote *Beggar on Horseback* (1925), with Edna Ferber *Royal Family* (1927), *Dinner at Eight* (1932), and *Stage Door* (1936), and with Howard Dietz and Arthur Schwartz, *Bandwagon* (1931). With George *Gershwin he wrote *Of Thee I Sing* (1932), and he also wrote the scripts of two *Marx brothers films.

Kaunas (Russian name: Kovno) 54 52N 23 55E A port in Lithuania, at the confluence of the Neman and Viliya rivers. It was held successively by Lithuania, Poland, and Russia before becoming (1918) the capital of independent Lithuania; it was occupied by German forces during World War II. It is a major educational, cultural, and industrial center, with industries that include chemicals, plastics, textiles, and iron and steel production. Population (1991 est): 433,000.

Kaunda, Kenneth (David) (1924–   ) Zambian statesman; president (1964–91). He trained as a teacher and joined the African National Congress in 1949. In 1958 he founded the more militant Zambia African National Congress and was imprisoned for subversion. On his release in 1960 he became president of the United National Independence Party, which took Northern Rhodesia to independence as Zambia in 1964. He remained as president until defeated in the 1991 elections, the first since 1972.

Kaunitz, Wenzel Anton, Count von (1711–94) Austrian statesman. As chancellor (1753–92) he controlled Habsburg foreign policy under Empress Maria Theresa and her son Emperor Joseph and was also influential in the reform of internal administration. His most striking achievement was to reverse (1756–57) the European alliances of the War of the *Austrian Succession, making France and Russia Austria's allies in the *Seven Years' War against Prussia.

kauri pine A coniferous tree, *Agathis australis*, from New Zealand. Growing to a height of 151 ft (46 m), it has oblong leaves, 2 in (5 cm) long and 0.8 in (2 cm) wide, and spherical cones, 2–3.1 in (5–8 cm) in diameter. It yields a resin (kauri copal or gum) used in making varnishes; the best resin is fossilized, derived from extinct trees and dug out of the ground. Its timber is used for general building purposes. Family: *Araucariaceae. See also* dammar.

kava A shrub, *Piper methysticum*, of the Pacific Islands and Australia, the ground and fermented roots of which are made into a narcotic drink. The roots are also chewed, and continued use produces inflammation and ulcers of the mouth. It has been used medicinally and as a local anesthetic. Family: *Piperaceae.*

KENNETH KAUNDA *Here he is about to lay the foundation of the Chinese-built Tanzam Railway (1975), which connected two countries (Tanzania and Zambia) that were already close political partners.*

Kawabata Yasunari (1899–1972) Japanese novelist. He was one of a group known as the Neo-Impressionists, which opposed the preceding realist movement in Japanese literature. His novels, which include *Snow Country* (1935–47) and *The Sound of the Mountain* (1949–54), are characterized by melancholy and loneliness, probably related to his being orphaned at an early age. He was awarded the Nobel Prize (1968).

Kawasaki 35 32N 139 41E A city in Japan, in SE Honshu. Part of the Tokyo-Yokohama industrial complex, it has shipbuilding, iron and steel, and chemical industries. Population (1990): 1,173,603.

kayak A native Eskimo canoe consisting of waterproofed animal skins stretched over a light framework and having one or two openings in the top with flexible watertight closures for one or two occupants.

Kayseri 38 42N 35 28E A city in central Turkey on the site of ancient Caesarea Mazaca. Kayseri has remains of the Seljuq civilization, notably the Great Mosque build in 1136. Population (1990): 421,362.

Kazakh A Turkic people of Kazakhstan and Xinjiang Uygur AR in China. With the Kirgiz, *Bashkir, and *Tatars they form the Kipchak division of the Turkic peoples. They were traditionally nomadic herders of horses, sheep, and goats who lived on milk products and mutton. Their movable dome-shaped dwellings (yurts) were constructed of wooden frames across which skins were stretched. Except in Xinjiang Uygur AR they are now settled stock breeders. Clan units, comprising extended-family groups and headed by chiefs, were the main social organization. *See* Turkic languages.

Kazakhstan, Republic of (*or* Kazakhstan) A country in central Asia, a constituent republic of the Soviet Union until 1991. The *Kazakhs comprise some

30% of the population, which includes Russians (43%) and Ukrainians (7%). The area is rich in mineral resources, especially coal, oil, copper, and iron ore. The atomic power station on the Mangyshlak peninsula has the world's first industrial fast-breeder reactor. An important agricultural area, it produces cereals, cotton, rice, and fruit. Kazakhstan is also noted for its sheep, from which excellent quality wool is obtained. *History*: conquered by Mongols in the 13th century, the region came under Russian rule in the 18th and 19th centuries. It became a constituent republic in 1936 and, with the disintegration of the USSR, an independent country in 1991. It became a member of the Commonwealth of Independent States in 1991 and the United Nations in 1992. Area: 1,048,030 sq mi (2,715,100 sq km). Population (1992 est): 16,800,000. Capital: Alma Ata.

Kazan (*or* Kasan) 53 45N 49 10E The capital city of Tatar Republic in Russia on the Volga River. It is a major historic, cultural, educational, commercial, and industrial center and supports a wide range of industries including oil refining, electrical engineering, chemical production, and food processing. *History*: founded in the 14th century by the *Tatars, it became the capital of an independent khanate and was captured (1552) by Ivan the Terrible. Its trade and industry developed during the 19th century and by 1900 it was one of the chief manufacturing cities in Russia. It became the capital of the Tatar ASSR in 1920. Lenin and Tolstoi studied at Kazan's university (1804). Population (1991 est): 1,107,000.

Kazan, Elia (E. Kazanjoglous; 1909–   ) US stage and film director and novelist, born in Turkey of Greek parentage. He first achieved success as a stage actor and helped to found the *Actors' Studio in 1947. For the stage he directed *The Skin of Our Teeth* (1942), *A Streetcar Named Desire* (1947), *Death of a Salesman* (1949), and other outstanding plays. His films include *Viva Zapata* (1952), *On the Waterfront* (1954), *East of Eden* (1955), and *The Arrangement* (1969), which is based on his own novel. Other novels include *America, America* (1963) and *The Anatolian* (1982).

Kazantzakis, Nikos (1885–1957) Greek novelist and poet, who also wrote plays, travel books, and essays. His epic poem *I Odysseia* (1938), a continuation of Homer's *Odyssey*, embodies many of his religious and philosophical ideas. He is best known for the novels *Zorba the Greek* (1946) and *Christ Recrucified* (1954).

Kean, Edmund (c. 1787–1833) British actor, especially famous for his Shakespearean roles. He was particularly successful as Shylock in *The Merchant of Venice*, his first London success in 1814, Richard III, Macbeth, Iago in *Othello*, and Barabas in Marlowe's *The Jew of Malta*, all roles suited to his forceful and passionate style of acting.

Kearny, Stephen Watts (1794–1848) US soldier. He fought in the War of 1812 and then was assigned to frontier duty. By 1846 he commanded, as a general, the Army of the West and during the *Mexican War was responsible for taking New Mexico (1846). He then advanced toward California with a small force, joined those of John C. *Fremont and Robert F. Stockton (1795–1866), and captured San Diego (1846), San Gabriel (1847), and Los Angeles (1847). Kearny finally won the fight over who would administer California. He later served as governor of Veracruz and Mexico City (1848).

Keating, Paul John (1944–   ), Australian political leader; prime minister (1991–   ). A labor union official before entering Parliament in 1969 as an Australian Labor party representative, he held cabinet-level offices as treasurer (1983–91) and deputy prime minister (1990–91). Known for his forthright statements, Keating succeeded *Robert Hawke as prime minister and focused on reviving the economy.

Keaton, Buster (Joseph Francis K.; 1895–1966) US comedian of silent films. He worked with his parents in vaudeville before starting his film career in 1917. He developed his character of the unsmiling and resilient clown in a series of classic silent comedies, including *The Navigator* (1924), *The General* (1926), and *The Cameraman* (1928). He was awarded a special Academy Award for his screen comedies in 1959. His autobiography is *My Wonderful World of Slapstick* (1962).

Keats, John (1795–1821) British poet. Despite the failure of his first volume, *Poems* (1817), which contained the sonnet "On First Looking into Chapman's Homer," and the savage criticism directed at his second, *Endymion* (1818), Keats persisted and between 1819 and 1820 wrote most of his best-known poems. His short life was dogged by tragedies, especially the death of his brother in 1818 and his unrequited love for Fanny Brawne. Such poems as *La Belle Dame Sans Merci, The Eve of Saint Agnes*, and the great odes ("To a Nightingale," "On a Grecian Urn," etc.), all published in 1820, eventually established his reputation. He died in Rome of tuberculosis.

Keble, John (1792–1866) British churchman and a leader of the *Oxford Movement. While professor of poetry at Oxford (1831–41) he preached a famous sermon, entitled "National Apostasy," which effectively began the Oxford Movement. Keble College, Oxford, was founded in his memory (1870).

Kebnekaise A mountain range in N Sweden. It rises to 6965 ft (2123 m) at Kebnekaise Sydtopp, the highest mountain in Sweden.

Kecskemét 46 56N 19 43E A city in central Hungary. It lies on a wide fertile plain that is Hungary's most important agricultural area, notably for such fruit as apricots. Population (1991 est): 104,000.

Kedah A state in NW Peninsular Malaysia, bordering on Thailand. Rice is grown on the W coastal plain; other products include rubber, tin, tungsten, and iron. Area: 3639 sq mi (9425 sq km). Population (1990): 1,412,800. Capital: Alor Star.

Keeling Islands. *See* Cocos Islands.

Keelung. *See* Jilong.

Keeshond A breed of dog traditionally used by the Dutch as barge dogs. It has a compact body with a foxlike face and a long thick gray coat with black-tipped hairs. The tail is carried over the back and a dense ruff surrounds the neck. Height: 17–18 in (43–45 cm).

Keewatin A district of N Canada, in the *Northwest Territories. It consists of the mainland E of 102°W and N of 60°N plus most islands in Hudson Bay. Part of the Canadian Shield, it is mostly tundra. Some fur trapping takes place. Area: 228,160 sq mi (590,934 sq km). *See also* Barren Grounds.

Kefallinía. *See* Cephalonia.

Kefauver, (Carey) Estes (1903–63) US politician. He practiced law in Tennessee before serving in the US House of Representatives (1939–48) and Senate (1949–63). He achieved national recognition through his televised Senate Crime Investigation Committee hearing in 1951–52. He ran unsuccessfully for vice president in 1956.

Keflavík 64 01N 22 35W A town and fishing port in SW Iceland. It has a NATO air base. Population (1980): 6622.

Keighley 53 52N 1 54W A city in N England, in West Yorkshire on the River Aire. The main products are woolens and worsteds, textile machinery, and machine tools. Population (1981 est): 57,451.

Keitel, Wilhelm (1882–1946) German field marshal, who was Hitler's chief military adviser throughout World War II. In 1945 in Berlin he confirmed the German surrender. He was hanged for war crimes.

Kekulé von Stradonitz, (Friedrich) August (1829–96) German chemist, whose main interest was in valence. He was the first chemist to establish the valence of the elements and to introduce the notion of single, double, and triple bonds. He went on to deduce the structural formulae of many organic molecules, including that of benzene (**Kekulé formula**), which he claimed to have thought of in 1865 while dozing on a bus. *See also* aromatic compound.

Kelantan A state in central Peninsular Malaysia, bordering on Thailand. It was ruled by Siam (now Thailand) from the early 19th century until 1909. Rice is grown on the NE coastal plain, and rubber, copra, and minerals are produced. Area: 5765 sq mi (14,931 sq km). Population (1990): 1,220,100. Capital: Kota Baharu.

Keller, Gottfried (1819–90) German-Swiss poet and novelist. His early poetry (1846) won him a scholarship to study in Germany. His works include the novel *Der grüne Heinrich* (1854–55) and short stories, including *Die Leute von Seldwyla* (1856–74), describing life in a small town.

Keller, Helen Adams (1880–1968) US social worker and writer. At the age of 19 months she lost her sight and hearing through an illness. Despite these handicaps she learned to speak, read, and write with the dedication of her teacher, Anne Sullivan, and finally graduated from Radcliffe College in 1904. She lectured in many countries and raised money for the education of handicapped people. Her books include *The Story of My Life* (1903), *The World I Live In* (1908), and *The Open Door* (1957). A play about her early life, William Gibson's *The Miracle Worker*, received the Pulitzer Prize (1960).

Kellogg, Frank Billings (1856–1937) US statesman, diplomat, and politician. A lawyer, he was a special prosecutor in Pres. Theodore Roosevelt's administration and fought monopolies successfully, including the Standard Oil Company (1906) and the Union Pacific Railroad (1907). He served in the US Senate (1917–23) and then was US ambassador to Britain (1924–25). Returning in 1925 to serve as secretary of state under Pres. Calvin *Coolidge, he formulated the *Kellogg-Briand Pact. Awarded the Nobel Peace Prize (1929), he was a member (1930–35) of the International Court of Justice.

Kellogg-Briand Pact (1928) An international agreement that condemned war as a means of settling disputes. The pact of perpetual friendship, negotiated by the US secretary of state, Frank B. Kellogg (1856–1937) and French foreign minister, *Briand, was signed in Paris in 1928 by representatives of 15 nations, and later by 48 others. Some success in South American disputes was achieved by invoking the treaty, but it proved ineffective against the Japanese invasion of Manchuria (1931), the Italian invasion of Ethiopia (1938), and against Hitler's aggression.

Kells (Irish name: Ceanannus Mór) 54 48N 6 14W A market town in the Republic of Ireland, in Co Meath. A monastery was founded here in the 6th century AD by St Columba in which *The Book of Kells*, an 8th-century illuminated manuscript of the Gospels, is reputed to have been written. Population: 2391.

Kelly, Grace (1929–82) US film actress. Her films include *High Noon* (1952), *Dial M for Murder* (1954), *Rear Window* (1954), *The Country Girl* (1955), for which she received an Academy Award, *To Catch a Thief* (1955), and *High Society* (1956). She retired from acting when she married Prince Rainier III of Monaco in 1956. She died following an automobile accident.

Kelly, Ned (1855–80) Australian outlaw. He and his brother Dan formed a gang in 1878 that became notorious for its daring robberies in Victoria and New South Wales. He was captured and hanged in 1880 after a gunfight with the police in which the other gang members were killed.

NED KELLY *A contemporary engraving of the famous bushranger during his final battle (1880). All members of the gang wore heavy homemade armor.*

kelp A large brown *seaweed belonging to the order *Laminariales* (about 30 genera), found in cold seas, usually below the level of low tide, and often covering large areas. The giant kelp *Macrocystis*, of the E Pacific coast, reaches a length of 213 ft (65 m). Its branching fronds are kept afloat by air bladders. The name kelp is also used for the ashes of seaweed, from which potassium and sodium salts and iodine were once obtained. *See also* Laminaria.

kelpie A breed of short-haired dog developed in Australia from the Border Collie and used for herding sheep and cattle. Named for a champion sheepdog of the 1870s, the kelpie has a long muzzle and pricked ears. The coat may be black or red (with or without tan), fawn, chocolate, or smoke-blue. Height: 17–20 in (43–50 cm).

kelvin (K) The *SI unit of *thermodynamic temperature equal to 1/273.16 of the thermodynamic temperature of the triple point of water. Named for Lord *Kelvin.

Kelvin, William Thomson, 1st Baron (1824–1907) Scottish physicist, who was professor at Glasgow University (1846–99). Kelvin was the first physicist to take notice of *Joule's work on heat and to press for its recognition. The two physicists then worked together, discovering the *Joule-Kelvin effect; both also made great contributions to the new science of thermodynamics. In 1848 Kelvin postulated that there is a temperature at which the motions of particles cease and their energies become zero. He called this temperature *absolute zero and suggested a scale of temperature, now known as the Kelvin scale, in which the zero point is absolute zero. In 1852 he suggested that a *heat pump was a feasible device. Kelvin was also active in the study of electricity; during the 1860s he worked on the electrical properties of cables in conjunction with the laying of the first transatlantic cable in 1866. Kelvin was knighted for his contribution to this work in the same year and was created baron in 1896. The unit of temperature (*see* kelvin) is named for him.

Kemal, (Mehmed) Namik (1840–88) Turkish poet, novelist, and dramatist. He was strongly influenced by European Romanticism and became one of the founders of modern Turkish literature. He was a member of a literary group known as the "Young Ottomans" and was imprisoned for the liberal and patriotic ideas he expressed in his most famous play, *Vatan yahnut Silistre (Fatherland or Silistria*; 1871).

Kemerovo 55 25N 86 05E A city in Russia, on the Tom River. It is the center of the *Kuznetsk Basin coalfield and is one of the country's major chemical-producing cities. Population (1991 est): 521,000.

Kempis, Thomas à. *See* Thomas à Kempis.

Kendall, Edward Calvin (1886–1972) US biochemist, who shared the Nobel Prize in medicine and physiology (1950) with Phillip Hench and Tadeus Reichstein for their work on hormones. In 1916 he isolated the hormone thyroxine produced by the thyroid gland and later isolated several hormones from the adrenal cortex. This work laid the basis for the modern study of endocrinology.

kendo A Japanese *martial art deriving from *samurai sword fighting. Combatants using bamboo staffs or wooden swords try to deliver blows on specified target areas of each other's bodies. Two hits constitute a win.

Kendrew, John Cowdery (1917–   ) British biochemist, who shared the Nobel Prize in chemistry (1962) with Max *Perutz for his discovery of the structure of the myoglobin molecule. Kendrew, working at Cambridge University, used the technique of *X-ray diffraction, analyzing his results with a computer.

Kenilworth 52 21N 1 34W A city in central England. Its castle was presented to Robert Dudley, Earl of Leicester, by Elizabeth I in 1563 and described in Sir Walter Scott's novel *Kenilworth*. Population (1981): 19,315.

Kennedy, Anthony M. (1936–   ) US jurist; associate justice of the Supreme Court (1988–   ). Considered a moderate conservative, he was named to the Supreme Court in 1987 by Pres. Ronald Reagan and confirmed by the Senate in 1988. He had previously served in the Ninth Circuit Court of Appeals (1975–87) in California.

Kennedy, Cape. *See* Canaveral, Cape.

Kennedy, John Fitzgerald (1917–63) US statesman; 35th President of the United States (1961–63). Son of Joseph Patrick *Kennedy, he was educated at Harvard and served as a PT boat commander in the Pacific during World War II. As the grandson of former Boston mayor John F. Fitzgerald, Kennedy became active in the *Democratic party and began his political career as a member of the US House of Representatives (1947–53). In 1952, Kennedy was elected to the US Senate and quickly rose to national prominence in an attempt to gain the 1956 Democratic vice-presidential nomination. He actively campaigned for the presidency in 1960 and after a bitter primary campaign became the Democratic candidate. Choosing Sen. Lyndon *Johnson as his running mate, he defeated Republican Richard *Nixon by a slim plurality. His election marked the first time that a Roman Catholic was elected president and did much to allay opposition to Catholics in public office.

Kennedy's administration was marked by innovation and an ambitious social program that he called the New Frontier. In addition to his active support for the cause of civil rights at home, he worked for cooperation with the nations of Latin America through the *Alliance for Progress and established the *Peace Corps. In 1961 the ill-fated Bay of Pigs invasion of Cuba chilled US-Soviet relations, and the Cuban Missile Crisis of 1962 brought the two superpowers into direct confrontation. A lasting achievement of the Kennedy administration was the ratification of the Nuclear Test Ban Treaty in 1963. While beginning his 1964 reelection campaign, he was assassinated in Dallas, Tex., on Nov 22, 1963.

JOHN F. KENNEDY *President (1961–63) whose assassination in Dallas on Nov 22, 1963, shocked the world.*

Kennedy, Joseph Patrick (1888–1969) US businessman and diplomat. Son of Irish immigrants, Kennedy earned a fortune in the stock market and pursued various business interests. Active in the *Democratic party, he was appointed chairman of the Securities and Exchange Commission in 1934 by Pres. Franklin Roosevelt. He later served as US Ambassador to Great Britain (1937–40). He had five daughters and four sons, three of whom entered public life. The eldest, **Joseph Patrick Kennedy, Jr.** (1915–44), a naval pilot, was killed in World War II. John Fitzgerald *Kennedy (1917–63), president of the US (1961–63), was assassinated. **Robert Francis Kennedy** (1925–68), who served as US attorney general (1961–64) and US senator (1965–68), was assassinated in 1968. The youngest son of the family, **Edward Moore Kennedy** (1932–   ), has served as US Senator and one of the leaders of the *Democratic party since 1962.

Kennelly, Arthur Edwin (1861–1939) US electrical engineer. On learning that *Marconi had succeeded in transmitting radio waves across the Atlantic, despite the earth's curvature, Kennelly guessed that the waves were being reflected by an electrically charged layer in the upper atmosphere. The existence of this layer was confirmed independently by Oliver *Heaviside and was known as the Kennelly-Heaviside layer (now known as the E-layer of the *ionosphere).

Kenneth I MacAlpine (died c. 858) King of the Scots of Dalriada (c. 844–c. 858). He formed the kingdom of Alba, the foundation of modern Scotland.

Kent A county of SE England, bordering on the English Channel and Greater London. It consists chiefly of undulating lowlands, crossed by the North Downs from W to E, and rising to the The Weald in the SW. The chief rivers are the Thames, Medway, and Stour. There are impressive chalk cliffs, notably at Dover. Often called the Garden of England, it is the country's leading fruit and hop-growing area. Other important agricultural activities include market gardening and arable, cattle, and sheep farming. The main industries are paper manufacture, shipbuilding, and oil refining. Area: 1440 sq mi (3730 sq km). Population (1987): 1,510,000. Major cities: Maidstone, Dover, Canterbury.

Kent 41 09N 81 22W A city in NE Ohio, on the Cuyahoga River, NE of Akron. Kent State University (1910), the site of anti-Vietnam War rallies and the shooting of four students by National Guardsmen in 1970, is there. Industries include the manufacture of rubber, plastic, sports and hardware products and of motor vehicles. Population (1990): 28,835.

Kent, William (1685–1748) English architect, landscape gardener, and interior designer. Kent is possibly the most famous exponent of English *Palladianism. His most notable buildings were Holkham Hall, Norfolk (1734), the Horse Guards, London (built after his death), but his greatest contribution to English art was his development of *landscape gardening, later continued by such designers as Capability *Brown.

Kentucky A state in the central US, lying to the E of the Mississippi River. The meandering Ohio River forms the N boundary with Ohio, Indiana, and Illinois. The Mississippi River, which joins the Ohio near Covington, forms the W border with Missouri. (The SW tip of Kentucky is cut off entirely from the rest of the state by a sharp turn in the Mississippi.) The S border with Tennessee forms a straight E–W line across the bottom of the state. In the SE, Kentucky borders Virginia, and in the NE the Big Sandy River forms the boundary with West Virginia. It consists of the Appalachian Mountains in the E, the Bluegrass region in the center, an undulating plain in the W, and the basins of the Tennessee and Ohio Rivers in the SW. Manufacturing in the state includes machinery, iron and steel products, paints, varnishes, textiles, whiskey, and food products. It is an important coal mining state and also produces petroleum and natural gas. Local timber is used in the furniture and wood industries. The principal agricultural products are tobacco, corn, hay, soybeans, cattle, sheep, and pigs. It is also an important region for the breeding of thoroughbred horses. Kentucky is a rural state with a strong rural tradition and folk culture. *History*: Daniel Boone explored the area (1769), blazing the Wilderness Road westward through the Cumberland Gap in Kentucky's Appalachian Mountains and onward to the Ohio River. After rapid settlement Kentucky achieved statehood (1792). As a so-called border state, Kentucky was torn on the slavery issue, but eventually joined the Union side in the Civil War. However, Kentucky soldiers fought on both Union and Confederate sides. In the late 19th century coal mining was begun and has since played a large role in Kentucky's economic life and history. The industry was well established by the 20th century; Kentucky is now the leading US producer of bituminous and lignite coal. As the labor movement gained ground in the 1930s and the United Mine Workers attempted to unionize in Kentucky, violent strife erupted, particularly in Harlan County. Mining subsequently declined but the energy crisis of the 1970s brought new life to the industry. Area: 40,395 sq mi (104,623 sq km). Population (1990): 3,685,296. Capital: Frankfort.

Kentucky and Virginia Resolutions Three resolutions, two (Kentucky) written by Thomas *Jefferson (1798, 1799) and one (Virginia) by James Madison (1798) that recommended repeal of the *Alien and Sedition Acts, which had had strong support from the Federalists. It was felt by the Jeffersonians that states should have the right to decide such matters and that the federal government had far exceeded its powers.

Kenya, Mount 0 10S 37 30E An extinct volcano in Kenya, the second highest mountain in Africa. It has 12 small glaciers radiating from its summit. Height: 17,058 ft (5200 m).

Kenya, Republic of A country in East Africa, on the Indian Ocean. The land rises gradually from the coast to the highlands of the interior reaching heights of over 17,000 ft (5000 m). In the W the Great Rift Valley runs N–S. Most of the inhabitants are Africans, including *Kikuyu, *Luo, *Masai, and Kamba. *Economy*: agricultural production and processing forms the basis of the economy. A variety of subtropical and temperate crops are grown. The chief cash crops are coffee, tea (of which Kenya is Africa's leading producer), sisal, and pineapples; livestock rearing and dairy farming are also important. Forestry is being developed and mineral resources include soda ash, gold, limestone, and salt. Hydroelectricity is a valuable source of power and industries include food processing, with oil refining at Mombasa. Tourism is an important source of income with Kenya's abundant big game; wildlife reserves include the huge Tsavo National Park. *History*: some of the earliest known fossil *hominid remains have been found in the region by the *Leakey family. The coastal area was settled by the Arabs from the 7th century AD and was controlled by the Portuguese during the 16th and 17th centuries. It became a British protectorate (East Africa Protectorate) in 1895 and a colony (Kenya) in 1920. In the 1950s independence movements, especially among the Kikuyu, led to the *Mau Mau revolt. Kenya gained independence in 1963 and in 1964 became a republic within the British Commonwealth, with Jomo *Kenyatta as its first president. Following independence, Kenya gained a reputation for its stable government, democratic policies, and steady economic growth. An abortive coup in 1982, reflecting frustration with a declining economy and with the policies of Pres. Daniel arap Moi, tarnished this image and generated concern among western nations. Moi responded with repressive measures that continued sporadically into the 1990s. The nation's first multiparty elections were held in 1992. President: Daniel arap Moi. Official languages: Swahili and English. Official currency: Kenya shilling of 100 cents. Area: 224,960 mi (582,600 sq km). Population (1990 est): 25,393,000. Capital: Nairobi. Main port: Mombasa.

Kenyatta, Jomo (c. 1891–1978) Kenyan statesman; president (1964–78). Son of a poor farmer of the Kikuyu tribe, Kenyatta studied anthropology in London, where his doctoral thesis on the Kikuyu was published in 1938 as *Facing Mount Kenya*. On his return to Kenya he became (1947) president of the Kenya African Union and in 1953 was imprisoned for seven years by the colonial government for his part in the *Mau Mau rebellion. While in jail he was elected leader of the Kenya African National Union (1960), which achieved Kenya's independence in 1963. Kenyatta was prime minister before becoming president of a one-party state.

Kepler, Johannes (1571–1630) German astronomer, who was one of the first supporters of *Copernicus's heliocentric theory of the solar system. In 1597 he went to Prague to study under Tycho *Brahe; on Brahe's death, Kepler inherited his astronomical observations. Kepler used this data to deduce the shape of planetary orbits, discovering that they were elliptical. He published this discovery, the first of *Kepler's laws, together with his second law in *Astronomia Nova* (1609). In 1619 he published his third law relating a planet's year to its distance from the sun. In 1610 he received a telescope built by *Galileo, which he used to observe Jupiter. In 1611 he constructed an improved version, now known as a Keplerian *telescope.

JOMO KENYATTA *Known as Mzee (Grand Old Man), he was invariably seen with a fly whisk, a traditional symbol of power.*

Kepler's laws Three laws of planetary motion proposed by Johannes Kepler in 1609 and (third law) 1619. They state that: (1) each planet moves round the sun in an elliptical orbit with the sun at one focus of the ellipse; (2) the line joining a planet to the sun sweeps out equal areas in equal times, i.e. orbital velocity decreases as distance from the sun increases; (3) the square of the *sidereal period (P) of a planet is directly proportional to the cube of its mean distance (a) from the sun. For P in years and a in *astronomical units, $P^2 = a^3$.

Kerala A state in SW India, extending along the W coastal plain and Western Ghats to India's S tip. Tropical, beautiful, and poor, it is India's most densely populated state, with little industry or mining. Rice, tea, coffee, pepper, rubber, nuts, and fruit are farmed. Fishing is also important. *History*: a civilization separate from Aryan N India, Malayalam-speaking Kerala has traded with the Near and Far East since ancient times, flourishing in the 9th and 10th centuries. Area: 14,998 sq mi (38,855 sq km). Population (1991): 29,032,828. Capital: Trivandrum.

keratin An insoluble fibrous protein that is the major constituent of hair, nails, feathers, beaks, horns, and scales. Keratin is also found in the outer protective layers of the skin.

Kerch 45 22N 36 27E A port in Ukraine, on the Black Sea on the Strait of Kerch. Founded in the 6th century BC by Greek colonists, it was captured from the Tatars by Russia in 1771. Fishing is important, and related activities, together with iron and steel production, form the basis of its industry. Population (1991 est): 178,000.

Kerenski, Aleksandr Feodorovich (1881–1970) Russian revolutionary. A member of the Socialist Revolutionary Party, after the outbreak of the Russian Revolution in February 1917, Kerenski became minister of justice and then minister of war in *Lvov's provisional government. In July, after Lvov's fall, he became prime minister. His insistence that Russia remain in World War I, and his mismanagement of internal economic affairs, led to the Bolshevik coup d'état in October. Kerenski fled to Paris and in 1940 to the US.

Kerguelen Islands 49 30S 69 30E An archipelago in the S Indian Ocean, in the French Southern and Antarctic Territories. Kerguelen Island, the largest, is mountainous and glacial and the site of several scientific bases. Area: 2786 sq mi (7215 sq km).

Kérkira (*or* Kérkyra). *See* Corfu.

Kerman 30 18N 57 05E A city in E Iran. It is an agricultural trading center and carpet-making town. Kerman University was founded in 1974. Population (1986): 257,300.

Kermanshah 34 19N 47 04E A city in W Iran, with a largely Kurdish population. It has a university (1974) and an oil refinery that is connected by pipeline to oil fields near the Iraqi border. Population (1986): 560,500.

kermes A scale insect of the genus *Kermes*, especially *K. ilices* of Europe and W Asia, the dried bodies of which were formerly used to produce a red dye. They feed on the small evergreen kermes oak (*Quercus coccifera*), which is native to S Europe, N Africa, and W Asia and grows to a height of 23 ft (7 m).

Kern, Jerome (David) (1885–1945) US composer of musical comedies, the most famous of which was *Show Boat* (1927), written in collaboration with Oscar *Hammerstein II. After 1939 he devoted himself to film music. Two of his best-known songs are "Ol' Man River" and "Smoke Gets in Your Eyes."

kerosene A mixture of hydrocarbons that boil in the range 302–572°F (150–300°C) and have a relative density of 0.78–0.83. It is obtained from crude *oil by distillation and is used as a fuel for domestic heating and for aircraft.

Kerouac, Jack (1922–69) US novelist. He was a leading figure of the *Beat movement, of which his novel *On the Road* (1957) was a seminal work. Other works including *The Dharma Bums* (1958), *Big Sur* (1962), and *Desolation Angels* (1965) were largely autobiographical.

Kerr effects Two effects concerned with optical changes produced by magnetic or electric fields. In the magneto-optical effect, plane-polarized light is slightly elliptically polarized when reflected by the pole of an electromagnet. In the electro-optical effect, the plane of polarization of a beam of light is rotated when passed through certain liquids or solids across which a potential difference

1401 Key, Francis Scott

is applied. This effect is utilized in the **Kerr cell**, which consists of a transparent cell containing a liquid, such as nitrobenzene; two parallel plates immersed in the liquid enable a field to be applied so that the passage of a beam of polarized light can be interrupted. The cell is used as a high-speed shutter and to modulate *laser beams. Named for the discoverer John Kerr (1824–1907).

Kerry (Irish name: Chiarraighe) A county in the SW Republic of Ireland, in Munster bordering on the Atlantic Ocean. Chiefly mountainous with a deeply indented coastline, it rises in the S to *Macgillycuddy's Reeks and contains the famous Lakes of Killarney, noted for their beauty. The chief occupations are fishing, farming, and tourism. Area: 1815 sq mi (4701 sq km). Population (1986): 124,200. County town: Tralee.

Kertanagara (d. 1292) King of Java (1268–92). Honored as Java's greatest leader, he took advantage of the disunited Malay world in the 13th century to unite Java and became the most powerful ruler in SE Asia. He protected Indonesia from Kublai Khan's efforts to exact tribute and upheld Buddhism and Javanese culture.

Kesey, Ken (1935–) US novelist. His best-known novel, *One Flew Over the Cuckoo's Nest* (1962), a satire based on his own experience in a mental hospital, was made into a successful film by Miloš *Forman. Later works include *Sometimes a Great Notion* (1964) and *Kesey's Garage Sale* (1973).

Kesselring, Albert (1885–1960) German general, who commanded the Luftwaffe in World War II. He held the air command in the invasions of Poland (1939) and France (1940) and in the battle of Britain (1940). In 1943 he became commander of land and air forces in Italy and in 1945 on the Western Front. His death sentence as a war criminal was commuted to life imprisonment and he was released in 1952.

Kesteven, Parts of. *See* Lincolnshire.

kestrel A small *falcon characterized by a long tail and the ability to hover, with the tail fanned out, before diving on its prey. The common kestrel (*Falco tinnunculus*), 13 in (32 cm) long, is widespread in Eurasia and Africa, and hunts small rodents, birds, and insects. The female has a brown streaked plumage; the male is blue-gray with black-streaked pale-brown underparts, a black-tipped tail, and a black eye stripe.

ketch A fore-and-aft-rigged □sailing vessel with two masts, a taller one set approximately one-third of the boat's length from the bows, a shorter one just forward of the rudder post. Ketches are a favored rig for yachts, for the split rig reduces the area of each sail, making handling easier. Ketches do not sail as well toward the wind as *sloops do. *See also* yawl.

ketone A class of organic chemicals having the general formula RCOR″, where R and R″ are hydrocarbon groups. Ketones are prepared by the oxidation of secondary alcohols. *Acetone (dimethyl ketone) is a common example.

Kettering, Charles Franklin (1876–1958) US engineer, whose inventions, notably the electric starter (1912), greatly improved automobiles. He also pioneered the use of leaded gasoline and antiknock compounds; in 1951 he developed a high-compression car engine.

kettledrums. *See* timpani.

Key, Francis Scott (1779–1843) US lawyer and poet; author of "The *Star-Spangled Banner." He practiced law in Washington, D.C. and in 1814, during the War of 1812, negotiated the release of a friend who was held prisoner on a British ship in Chesapeake Bay. Because of the British bombardment of Fort McHenry, near Baltimore, Key was forced to spend the night aboard ship. In the morning, relieved to see the American flag still flying over the fort, he was inspired to write a poem; the words, set to the tune of a British drinking song, officially became the US national anthem in 1931.

key. *See* tonality.

Keynes, John Maynard, 1st Baron (1883–1946) British economist, whose ideas continue to exert influence on modern government economic policies (*see* Keynesianism). After attending the Versailles peace conference as a British Treasury representative, Keynes published *The Economic Consequences of the Peace* (1919), which attacked the war reparations imposed on Germany. In his greatest work, *General Theory of Employment, Interest and Money* (1936), written during the Depression years, he argued that unemployment can only be alleviated by increased public spending. During World War II he worked for the British government on war finance and in 1944 was the chief British representative at the Bretton Woods conference, at which the *International Monetary Fund was established.

Keynesianism The economic theories of the British economist J. M. *Keynes, whose *General Theory of Employment, Interest and Money* (1936) has had a pervasive influence. Keynes's central departure from established theory was the premise that what is rational for the individual and the firm is not necessarily rational for the government, and that rather than reinforcing the *trade cycle the government should counter it by public spending with money raised by *deficit financing. This has been developed by later thinkers, not all of whose ideas Keynes himself would have agreed with, into a doctrine of expansive *fiscal policy and government interventionism.

Keystone Kops A zealous but incompetent police force that featured in the silent film comedies produced by Mack *Sennett for the Keystone Film Company between 1912 and 1917. They were the butt of much irreverent slapstick comedy, preserving their imperturbable masks of dignity even during the absurd accelerated chase sequences.

Key West 24 34N 81 48W A city in the US, in Florida, situated at the tip of the Florida Keys. A naval, air, and coastguard base, Key West is a popular tourist center and was the home of Ernest Hemingway. Population (1990): 24,832.

KGB (Committee of State Security) The Soviet secret police concerned with internal security and intelligence. It was founded in 1954, after the fall of *Beria, and replaced the more brutal MGB (Ministry of State Security; 1946–53).

Khabarovsk 48 32N 135 08E A port in Russia, on the Amur River. Situated on the Trans-Siberian Railroad, it is an important transport center. Industries include engineering, machine building, and oil refining. Population (1991 est): 613,000.

Khachaturian, Aram Ilich (1903–78) Soviet composer of Armenian birth. He studied composition at the Moscow conservatory. His music was deeply influenced by the scales and rhythms of Caucasian folk music. His compositions include concertos for piano (1936) and violin (1940) and the famous ballets *Gayaneh* (1942) and *Spartacus* (1954).

Khafre (Greek name: Chephren) King of Egypt (c. 2550 BC) of the 4th dynasty. He emerged victorious from the dynastic strife that followed the death of his father *Khufu. Khafre built the second pyramid and (probably) the Sphinx at *Giza.

Khakass An autonomous region (*oblast*) in Russia. It was formed in 1930 for the Turkic-speaking Khakass people, who are Orthodox Christians. Khakass is rich in minerals, including gold, coal, iron ore, and copper, and timber and wood-working industries are also important. Livestock is raised. Area: 23,855 sq mi (61,900 sq km). Population (1991 est): 577,000. Capital: Abakan.

khaki (Hindi-Urdu: dust-colored) A yellowish-brown fabric of cotton, wool, or synthetic fiber used chiefly for military uniforms. Khaki was first worn by British troops in India as a form of camouflage. From about 1900 it became the regular British uniform for battle and has since been adopted by most other nations.

Khalid Ibn Abdul Aziz (1913–82) King of Saudi Arabia (1975–82). Son of *Ibn Saud, the founder of Saudi Arabia, Khalid had a traditional Muslim educa- tion. He became king on the death of his brother *Faisal Ibn Abdul Aziz.

Khalifa. *See* Abd Allah.

Khama, Sir Seretse (1921–80) Botswana statesman; president (1966–80). Trained as a lawyer in England, Seretse Khama married an Englishwoman, as a result of which he had to renounce the chieftaincy of the Bamangwato tribe be- fore returning to what was then Bechuanaland in 1956. In 1961 he founded the Bechuanaland Democratic Party, which gained independence for Botswana in 1966.

khamsin A hot dry southerly wind that blows across Egypt from the Sahara Desert. Most common in April and June, it precedes *depressions moving E along the N African coast. According to Arab tradition it blows for 50 days.

Kharga, El (*or* al-Wahat al-Kharijah) A large oasis in Egypt, in the Libyan Desert. It produces dates, figs, olives, and vegetables; efforts have been made to increase irrigation by sinking deep wells. Chief town: El Kharga.

Kharkov 50 00N 36 15E A city in Ukraine. It was almost destroyed in World War II, when its importance as a road and railroad junction led to bitter fighting. Today, it is the third (after Moscow and Leningrad) largest railroad junction in the country. The nearby Donets Basin coalfield supports a major engineering in- dustry. Population (1991 est): 1,623,000.

Khartoum (*or* al-Khurtum) 15 40N 32 52E The capital of the Sudan, at the confluence of the Blue and the White Nile Rivers. An Egyptian army camp in the early 19th century, it later became a garrison town. In 1885 *Gordon was be- sieged and killed here and the town destroyed by the forces of the Mahdi (*see* Mahdi, al-) but was recaptured by Anglo-British forces in 1898 and rebuilt. It has several cathedrals and two mosques; its university was founded in 1956 and it also houses part of Cairo University (1955). An important trading center, it produces textiles and glass. Population (1983): 476,300.

Khazars A Turkic people who inhabited the lower Volga basin from the 7th to 13th centuries. Noted for their laws, tolerance, and cosmopolitanism, the Kha- zars were the main commercial link between the Baltic and the Muslim empire. In the 8th century the Khazars embraced Judaism. Slavonic and nomadic Turkic invaders brought the downfall of the Khazars in the 11th century. Itil, near mod- ern Astrakhan, was their capital.

khedive The title bestowed in 1867 by the sultan of the Ottoman Empire on the hereditary viceroy of Egypt. It was used until 1914, when Egypt became a British protectorate.

Kherson 46 39N 32 38E A port in Ukraine on the Dnepr River. It is 15 mi (25 km) from the Black Sea and, founded in 1778, was Russia's first naval base on the Sea. Shipbuilding remains the chief industry. Population (1991 est): 365,000.

Khiva 41 25N 60 49E A town in Uzbekistan on the Amu Darya River. It may have existed in the 6th century AD and was the center of the khanate of Khiva from the 16th century until 1873, when it was captured by Russia. Its architectural remains attract many tourists. Cotton spinning is also important.

Khlebnikov, Velimir (Victor K.; 1885–1922) Russian poet, who founded the Russian futurist movement (*see* futurism) with *Mayakovskii. His poetry was characterized by verbal experimentation and technical virtuosity; much of it was written on scraps of paper during his many travels. He died of typhus and starvation while returning from Persia.

Khmer A people of Cambodia, Thailand, and Vietnam who speak the Khmer language, belonging to the Mon-Khmer Division of the *Austro-Asiatic languages, which includes Vietnamese, *Mon, and Palaung. They are rice cultivators and fishers, living in village communities headed by an elected chief. Their religion is Theravada Buddhism, but magical beliefs and practices survive from pre-Buddhist times. The Khmer empire was founded in 616 AD and between the 9th and 13th centuries Khmer kings presided over the advanced civilization that was responsible for the great stone buildings of *Angkor. The name Khmer was adopted by the anti-French nationalist movement of *Cambodia (which was called the Khmer Republic from 1971–1975) and the name continued in the communist Khmer Rouge movement.

Khoisan The racial grouping comprising the Hottentot and Bushmen people of S Africa. The Khoisan languages, of which the Hottentot Nama and the Bushman Kung have been most studied, are noted for their click sounds. Formerly widespread S of the Zambezi River, the Khoisan tribes have been decimated by Bantu and European encroachments since 1700 and their traditional culture and racial integrity almost exterminated. The Hottentots were nomads, herding sheep and cattle. They were divided into clans, each with its own territory and chief, but with no overall political coherence. The Bushmen were traditionally hunters and gatherers, but most are now farm workers. Some groups in the desert regions of W Botswana still roam in small bands, with the women collecting roots and berries and the men hunting with bows and poisoned arrows. Bushman rock paintings survive in many areas of South Africa.

Khomeini, Ayatollah Ruholla (1900–89) Iranian Shiite Muslim leader (ayatollah). Following the overthrow of the shah (1979) he returned from 16 years of exile to lead the so-called Islamic Revolution. Subsequently, he ruthlessly suppressed opposition to his rule and instituted a government based on fundamental Islamic principles that continued after his death.

Khorana, Har Gobind (1922–) US biochemist, born in India, who was responsible for deciphering the *genetic code, i.e. the hereditary information carried by DNA molecules. Khorana shared a Nobel Prize (1968) with R.W. Holley and M. Nirenberg. In 1976 Khorana and his team were responsible for constructing the first entirely synthetic yet biologically active gene.

Khosrow I King of Persia (531–79 AD), who came to the throne after prolonged social disturbance and took measures to restore prosperity and to reform the state. He reorganized the army, strengthened his frontiers, and expanded his territory. His only serious rival, the Byzantine empire, was forced to concede tribute and territory but remained hostile. Khosrow's firm yet benevolent rule over an empire stretching from the Oxus River (now Amu Darya) to the Yemen marked the summit of *Sasanian power.

Khosrow II (d. 628 AD) King of Persia (590–628) of the Sasanian dynasty, who accepted Byzantine aid to secure his throne, conceding territory in return. Its subsequent recovery and the conquest of Anatolia, Syria, and Egypt over-

taxed Persian resources. The Byzantine counterattack reached his capital, Cte-
siphon, and Khosrow was assassinated; the Sasanian empire disintegrated and
was soon overrun by the Arabs.

Khrushchev, Nikita S(ergeevich) (1894–1971) Soviet statesman; first secretary of the Soviet Communist party (1953–64) and prime minister (1958–64).
Khrushchev was a close associate of Stalin and emerged victorious from the
power struggle that followed his death. In 1956 Khrushchev began a program of
destalinization and the degree of liberalization that ensued within the Soviet
Union gave rise to revolts in other communist countries, such as the *Poznan
Riots in Poland and the *Hungarian Revolution. Owing to the failure of his economic policies and his unsuccessful foreign policy, notably his attempt to install
missiles in Cuba (1962) and his antagonism toward China, he was ousted by
*Brezhnev and *Kosygin.

Khudzhand (name until 1936: Khodzhent; name 1936–91: Leninabad)
59 55N 30 25E A city in W Tajikistan, on the Syr Darya River. Located on the
ancient *Silk Road, it supports a major silk industry. Consumer goods are also
produced. Population (1991 est): 164,000.

Khufu (*or* Cheops) King of Egypt (c. 2600 BC) of the 4th dynasty; the father of
*Khafre. He built the Great Pyramid at *Giza, which was said to have taken 20
years to construct. Khufu's funeral barge has been discovered in good condition.

Khulna 22 49N 89 34E A city in S Bangladesh, on the Ganges delta. An agricultural trading center, its industries include shipbuilding and the manufacture
of cotton cloth. Population (1991): 545,849.

Khyber Pass (Khaybar Pass *or* Khaibar Pass) 34 06N 71 05E A mountain
pass in the Safid Kuh range of the Hindu Kush, connecting Kabul in
Afghanistan with Peshawar in Pakistan. Rising to 3518 ft (1072 m) in barren
country, it is of strategic importance, having been used many times over the centuries by invading armies, the progress of which has often been impeded by hostile Afridi tribesmen.

kiang A wild *ass, *Equus hemionus kiang,* of the Himalayas. It is the tallest
wild ass, 5 ft (1.4 m) at the shoulder, and has a chestnut-colored coat. *See also*
onager.

kibbutz An Israeli collective settlement in which land and property are owned
or leased by all its members and work and meals are organized collectively.
Adults generally have private quarters but children are housed together. About
3% of the population live in *kibbutzim*. A **moshav** is a smallholders' cooperative
in which machinery is shared but land and property is generally privately
owned. About 5% of the Israeli population live in *moshavim*.

Kicking Horse Pass A pass through the Canadian Rocky Mountains, NW of
Banff. It is the highest point on the Canadian Pacific Railroad. Height: 5339 ft
(1627 m).

Kidd, William (c. 1645–1701) Scottish sailor. He spent his youth privateering
for the English against the French off the North American coast and in 1695 he
was given a royal commission to suppress pirates in the Indian Ocean. He
reached Madagascar, a pirates' center, where he seems to have joined them. He
was arrested on his return to Boston, sent to England, and executed (possibly un-
justly).

Kidinnu (4th century BC) Babylonian mathematician and astronomer, who discovered the precession of the equinoxes, an effect that causes the position of the
sun at equinox to move slowly backward through the zodiac. He also calculated
the interval of time between successive new moons to within a second.

kidneys The two organs of excretion in vertebrate animals and man, which also regulate the amount of salt and water in the blood. The human kidneys are bean-shaped, each about 5 in (12 cm) long and weighing about 5 oz (150 g), and situated on either side of the spine below the diaphragm. They contain millions of tubules, the outer parts of which filter water and dissolved substances from blood supplied by the renal artery. Most of the water and some substances are reabsorbed back into the blood further down the tubules: the remaining fluid (*see* urine) contains waste products of protein metabolism and passes on to the pelvis of the kidneys and out through the ureters to the *bladder. The reabsorption of water is controlled by a hormone (vasopressin) from the pituitary gland. The kidneys also secrete a hormone (*see* renin) that assists in controlling blood pressure.

If one kidney ceases to function or is removed the other will enlarge and take over its function. Removal of both kidneys requires the use of an artificial kidney machine (*see* dialysis) unless a suitable donor kidney is available for *transplantation.

Kiel 54 20N 10 08E A city in N Germany, the capital of Schleswig-Holstein. A Baltic port, famed for its annual regatta, it was the chief naval port of Germany by the late 19th century. The naval mutiny here in 1918 sparked off revolutions throughout Germany. It has a university (1665) and a 13th-century palace, restored after World War II. Its chief industries are shipbuilding and engineering. Population (1988): 244,000.

Kiel Canal (German name: Nord-Ostsee Kanal; former name: Kaiser Wilhelm Canal) A canal in Germany, Schleswig-Holstein *Land*, linking Kiel on the Baltic Sea with the Elbe estuary on the North Sea.

Kielce 50 51N 20 39E A city in S central Poland. During World War II it contained four German concentration camps. Notable buildings include its cathedral (12th century). It is a major industrial center. Population (1985 est): 203,500.

Kierkegaard, Søren (1813–55) Danish philosopher. Although critical of *Hegel, particularly in *The Concept of Irony* (1841), he remained under his influence. Kierkegaard was a prolific writer; much of his work is poetic and paradoxical even in its titles, for example *Either-Or* (1843) and *Concluding Unscientific Postscript* (1846). Suspicious of both science and the established Church, he saw man as existing in isolation and relating only to God. Among his specifically religious books is *Works of Love* (1847). His journal reveals him as a deeply religious, if unorthodox, thinker. He greatly influenced 20th-century *existentialism.

Kiev 50 28N 30 29E The capital and largest city of Ukraine, on the Dnepr River. It is a major economic and cultural center. Industries include metallurgy, the manufacture of machinery and instruments, chemicals, and textiles. Among its many educational institutions is the Kiev State University (1833), and its opera and ballet companies have a worldwide reputation. Outstanding buildings include the 11th-century St Sophia cathedral, now a museum, and the Golden Gate of Kiev. *History*: Kiev, "the mother of cities," was probably founded in the 6th or 7th century AD and from the 9th to the 13th centuries was the center of a feudal state ruled by the Rurik dynasty—Kiev-Rus, the historical nucleus of the Soviet Union. Recurrent Tatar attacks virtually destroyed the city, which subsequently passed to Lithuania. Russian rule was established in the 17th century. After the Russian Revolution Kiev became the capital of the short-lived Ukrainian republic and in 1934, the capital of the Ukrainian SSR. In World War II the city was occupied after a long siege by the Germans and thousands of its inhabitants were massacred. Its postwar reconstruction has been spectacular, and it remains one of Europe's most beautiful cities. Population (1987): 2,554,000.

Kigali 1 58S 30 00E The capital of Rwanda (since 1962). It is the center of the country's mining industry and has a trade in coffee. Population (1991): 232,733.

Kikuyu A Bantu-speaking tribe of Kenya. They cultivate cereals and sweet potatoes and keep considerable numbers of livestock, particularly cattle. Small groups of patrilineal kin occupy scattered homesteads of conical-shaped huts. These kin groups are organized into clans but there is little hierarchical organization or centralization of authority. Age grades are an important basis of social organization, boys being initiated by circumcision. Political authority is held by a council of members of the senior age grade. The largest tribe in Kenya, the Kikuyu were deeply involved in the anticolonial *Mau Mau movement during the 1950s and have had a dominant voice in postindependence government.

Kilauea A volcanic crater in Hawaii, on the E side of Mauna Loa. It is one of the largest active craters in the world. Height: 4090 ft (1247 m). Width: 2 mi (3 km).

Kildare (Irish name: Contae Cill Dara) A county in the E Republic of Ireland, in Leinster. It consists chiefly of a low-lying fertile plain containing part of the Bog of Allen in the N and the Curragh, an area noted for its racehorse breeding and race track. Cattle rearing and arable farming are also important. Area: 654 sq mi (1694 sq km). Population (1986): 116,300. County town: Naas.

Kilimanjaro, Mount 3 02S 37 20E A volcanic mountain in Tanzania on the Kenyan border, the highest mountain in Africa. It has two volcanic peaks: Kibo at 19,340 ft (5895 m), and Mawenzi at 17,300 ft (5273 m).

Kilkenny (Irish name: Contae Cill Choinnigh) A county in the SE Republic of Ireland, in Leinster. Chiefly hilly, it is drained by the Rivers Suir, Barrow, and Nore. Agriculture is the chief occupation with cattle rearing and dairy farming. Area: 796 sq mi (2062 sq km). Population (1986): 73,200. County town: Kilkenny.

Kilkenny (Irish name: Cill Choinnigh) 52 09N 7 15W A city in the Republic of Ireland, the county town of Co Kilkenny. One of Ireland's oldest towns, it has two cathedrals and a 12th-century castle. Population (1981): 7700.

Killarney (Irish name: Cill Airne) 52 03N 9 30W A town in the Republic of Ireland in Co Kerry. A tourist center near the three Lakes of Killarney, it is famous for its lake, mountain, and forest scenery.

killer whale A large toothed whale, *Orcinus orca,* common in Pacific and Antarctic waters but found in all other oceans. Up to 30 ft (9 m) long, killer whales are black above and pure white beneath, with an erect dorsal fin as tall as a man. They are notorious for their voracious appetites, hunting in packs and tackling even sharks and other whales. Like other dolphins, they are intelligent and trainable in captivity. Family: *Delphinidae* (dolphins).

killifish One of several small elongated fish, also called egg-laying top minnows, belonging to the family *Cyprinodontidae,* especially the genus *Fundulus.* Killifish occur chiefly in tropical America, Africa, and Asia in fresh, brackish, or salt water and feed at the surface on plant or animal material. Up to 6 in (15 cm) long, many are brightly colored and kept as aquarium fish. Similar related fish are the live-bearing top minnows of the family *Poeciliidae.* Order: *Atheriniformes.*

Kilmarnock 55 37N 4 30W An industrial city in SW Scotland. Industries include engineering, carpets, woolens, lace, whisky, footwear, and earthenware. The Burns museum contains many of his manuscripts. Population (1981): 52,080.

KILLER WHALE *A specimen living in captivity. Killer whales are known for their spectacular jumps, during which they may cover a distance of 40–45 ft (12–13.5 m).*

kilogram (kg) The *SI unit of mass equal to the mass of the platinum-iridium prototype kept at the International Bureau of Weights and Measures near Paris.

kiloton A measure of the explosive power of a nuclear weapon. It is equivalent to an explosion of 1000 tons of trinitrotoluene (TNT).

kilowatt-hour (kW-hr) A unit of energy used in charging for electricity. It is equal to the work done by a power of 1000 watts (1 kw) in 1 hour.

kilt. *See* Highland dress.

Kimberley 28 45S 24 46E A city in South Africa, in N Cape Province. It was founded (1871) following the discovery of diamonds and is today the world's largest diamond center. The famous Kimberley Open Mine, 1 mi (1.6 km) in circumference, was closed in 1915. Industries include engineering, clothing, and diamond cutting. Population (1980): 144,923.

Kimberleys. *See* Western Australia.

Kim Il Sung (Kim Song Ju; 1912–) North Korean statesman; prime minister (1948–72) and then president (1972–). He became leader of the Soviet-dominated N in 1945 and with the establishment there of the Democratic People's Republic of Korea in 1948, its first prime minister and chairman of the Korean Workers' party. In 1950 he ordered the invasion of South Korea in an unsuccessful attempt to reunite Korea (*see* Korean War).

kimono The traditional costume of Japan for men and women from the 7th century AD, now worn mainly by women for formal occasions. It is an ankle-length wide-sleeved robe, often silk, wrapped over at the front and tied with an *obi* (sash) in a large bow at the back of the waist.

Kincardine (*or* Kincardineshire) A former county of NE Scotland. Under local government reorganization in 1975 it became part of Grampian Region.

kindergarten A school for young children, usually aged five to six years, preceding first grade. The term kindergarten, a German word meaning "children's garden," was originated by the German educator Friedrich *Froebel for children aged three to five, but the education of young children is now generally referred to as nursery school.

kinematics. *See* mechanics.

kinetic energy Energy possessed by a body by virtue of its motion. If the body, mass m, is moving in a straight line with velocity v, its kinetic energy is $^1/_2mv^2$. If it is rotating its rotational kinetic energy is $^1/_2I\omega^2$, where I is its moment of inertia and ω its angular velocity.

kinetics. *See* mechanics.

kinetic theory A theory developed in the 19th century, largely by *Joule and *Maxwell, in which the behavior of gases is explained by regarding them as consisting of tiny dimensionless particles in constant random motion. Collisions, either between the particles or between the particles and the walls of the container, are assumed to be perfectly elastic. The theory explains the pressure of a gas as being due to collisions between the particles and the walls, its temperature as a measure of the *average* *kinetic energy of the particles, and the heat of the gas as the *total* kinetic energy of the particles. The kinetic theory is based on the concept of an *ideal gas obeying ideal *gas laws; real gases consist of molecules having a finite volume (*see* Van der Waals). The kinetic theory is extended to all matter and regards the heat of a body as the total of the translational, rotational, or vibrational energy of its constituent particles.

King, Billie Jean (*born* Moffitt; 1943–) US tennis player, who was Wimbledon singles champion in 1966, 1967, 1968, 1972, 1973, and 1975. She was champion in the US Open in 1967 (as an amateur), and again in 1971, 1972, and 1974. She won many other titles and took a record 20th Wimbledon title in 1979.

King, Larry (Lawrence Harvey Zeiger, 1933–) US television talk-show host, who achieved prominence in the 1992 US elections through his interviews of the presidential candidates. He first achieved success in Florida as a radio disc jockey, television show host, and newspaper columnist, but his career collapsed amid financial and emotional difficulties. He came back with the immensely successful *The Larry King Show* on radio and *Larry King Live* on television, both shows featuring his trademark nonintrusive interviewing style.

King, Jr, Martin Luther (1929–68) US civil-rights leader. The son of a minister, he became one himself. He achieved national recognition in 1955–56 by leading a boycott of buses in Montgomery, Ala., in order to end segregation on them. He then helped found the Southern Christian Leadership Conference to work for African-Americans' civil rights and became its president. An outstanding orator, he followed principles of nonviolent resistance in organizing demonstrations against racial inequality and was one of the leaders of the great March on Washington (1963), joined by over 250,000 people. At the Washington rally he delivered his famous "I Have a Dream" speech. The same year he organized civil rights demonstrations in Birmingham, Ala. His campaigns contributed to the passing of the Civil Rights Act (1964) and the Voting Rights Act (1965) and earned him the Nobel Peace Prize (1964). He was assassinated in Memphis, Tenn., where he was supporting striking garbage collectors, by James Earl Ray. His birthday, Jan 15, is a legal holiday in most states.

King, William Lyon Mackenzie (1874–1950) Canadian statesman; Liberal prime minister (1921–26, 1926–30, 1935–48). His administration enacted moderate welfare legislation and increased Canadian trade with the US and UK. His chief political aim was national unity, achieved by enlisting the support of Progressives and French Canadians.

MARTIN LUTHER KING *Holding the gold medal of the Nobel Peace Prize (Oslo, 1964).*

King Charles spaniel A breed of *spaniel having a compact body, short legs, a short neck, and a large head with a short upturned nose. There are four color varieties: Blenheim, ruby, tricolor, and black and tan, the last being associated with King Charles II. Weight: 7.7–13.2 lb (3.5–6 kg); height: about 10 in (25 cm). The Cavalier King Charles spaniel has a similar coloration but is lighter bodied, with relatively longer legs and a longer muzzle. Weight: 13–18 lb (5–8 kg); height: about 12 in (30 cm).

kingcup. *See* marsh marigold.

kingfisher A bird belonging to a family (*Alcedinidae*; 85 species) divided into two subfamilies: the *Alcedininae* are narrow-billed and live near water, feeding on small fish; the *Dacetoninae* are broad-billed insectivorous birds not closely associated with water. Kingfishers are 5–18 in (12–45 cm) long, mostly compact with a bright plumage of blues, greens, purples, and reds, and are often crested; they have large heads with often brightly colored bills and usually nest in burrows in banks. Order: *Coraciiformes* (hornbills, etc.).

King George's War (1744–48) An indecisive conflict between Britain and France for control of North America. Governor William Shirley of Massachusetts blocked French efforts to take Nova Scotia in 1744, and in 1745 led a colonial force that captured the French fortress of Louisbourg, returned to the French at the end of the war. It was an aspect of the War of the *Austrian Succession.

King James Version The Authorized Version of the English *Bible that appeared in 1611 under the patronage of James I. A scholarly translation from the original languages, it preserved the best from previous versions. It was based on the earlier Bishops' Bible (1568), but the translators also consulted and made use of the *Geneva Bible and the *Douai Bible. It was much indebted to the translations of William *Tyndale. Its rich and vigorous language has had a unique influence on English prose style.

King Philip's War (1675–76) A war of resistance on the part of the Indians, led by King Philip of the Wampanoags, to the westward expansion of English settlers in Massachusetts, Connecticut, and Rhode Island. War broke out after a Wampanoag attack on a settlement in Plymouth colony. The fighting was savage, particularly in the Great Swamp Fight in Rhode Island (1675), in which 300 Indians were killed, lasting until Indian resistance collapsed after the death of King Philip in August 1676. The war toll was enormous on both sides.

Kings, Books of Two Old Testament books of unknown authorship. They are the major source for the history of the Hebrew kings after David, continuing the narrative from the point where the Books of Samuel end. The first book traces the reign of Solomon (c. 970–933 BC) and his building of the Temple at Jerusalem. After his death, the kingdom was divided into Judah and Israel, the histories of which are continued alternately in the second book. The work of the prophets Elisha and Elijah is treated in detail. After the fall of Israel to Assyria in 722 BC the narrative is devoted to the history of Judah alone up to the *Babylonian exile (586 BC).

Kings Canyon National Park A national park in E central California, in SE Sierra Nevada. Established in 1940, it adjoins Sequoia National Park to the S. The middle and S forks of the Kings River cut through the mountains; the highest peak in the park is North Palisade (14,242 ft; 4,341 m). Scattered throughout the park are groves of giant sequoia trees; in the General Grant Grove stands the General Grant tree, 267 ft (82 m) high and almost 108 ft (33 m) around, which is over 3500 years old. Area: 719 sq mi (1862 sq km).

king's evil. *See* scrofula.

Kingston 17 58N 76 48W The capital and main port of Jamaica, in the SE. Founded in 1692, it became the capital in 1872. In the early 20th century it suffered much damage from hurricanes and an earthquake. The University of the West Indies was founded nearby in 1962. Most industry is associated with agriculture. Population (1991): 103,771.

Kingston 44 14N 76 30W A city and port in central Canada, in SE Ontario at the point where Lake Ontario becomes the St Lawrence River. Founded as a fort (1673), it has Canada's Royal Military College, as well as numerous prisons and Queen's University (1841). Kingston's industry includes ship repairing, aluminum, chemicals, and food processing. Population (1991): 56,597.

Kingston-upon-Hull. *See* Hull.

kinkajou A nocturnal arboreal mammal, *Potos flavus,* of Central and South American forests. Up to 43 in (110 cm) long including the tail (16–22 in [40–55 cm]), it has a soft woolly golden-brown coat, small ears, and a prehen-

Kinnock, Neil 1412

sile tail. An agile climber, it feeds mainly on fruit and honey. Family: *Procyonidae* (*see* raccoon).

Kinnock, Neil (Gordon) (1942–) British Labour politician. He became a member of the National Executive Committee of the Labour party in 1978 and Labour leader (1983–) following Michael Foot's resignation.

kinnor A musical instrument, the ancient Jewish form of the *kithara. A type of *lyre, it is the biblical instrument traditionally reputed to have been played by David.

Kinsey, Alfred (1894–1956) US zoologist and sociologist, who initiated surveys of human sexual behavior. His reports *Sexual Behavior in the Human Male* (1948) and *Sexual Behavior in the Human Female* (1953) aroused great publicity and helped create more open attitudes to sex.

Kinshasa (name until 1966: Léopoldville) 4 18S 15 18E The capital of Zaïre, on the Zaïre River on the S shore of Malebo Pool. It has a long history of human settlement and was occupied by the Humbu when *Stanley discovered it in the late 19th century. A campus of the National University was founded in 1954. One of Africa's largest cities, it is an important industrial and commercial center with food-processing, woodworking, and textile industries. Population (1991 est): 3,805,000.

kinship The social recognition of real or ascribed blood relationship. It is usually distinguished from affinity (relationship by marriage). Kinship implies genetic relationship but this is defined very differently in different societies. Many people deny the genetic contribution of either the father or the mother to the child and count the kin of only one parent as their own. These are known respectively as matrilineal and patrilineal systems. Different societies recognize relationships of very different degrees of distance, some counting as kin those descended from common ancestors many generations back. In primitive societies kinship systems are the fundamental basis of social organization.

Kioga, Lake. *See* Kyoga, Lake.

Kiowa A North American Indian people of Oklahoma. With the *Comanche, they were among the most warlike tribes, raiding settlers in Texas during the 19th century. They also fought against the US Government and were one of the last tribes to be subdued. Their culture was typical of the Plains region. Their language forms part of the *Aztec-Tanoan family.

Kipling, (Joseph) Rudyard (1865–1936) British writer and poet. Born in Bombay, he was educated in England, returning to India in 1882 to work as a journalist. When Kipling returned to London in 1889, he was already famous for his satirical verses and for stories, such as those in *Plain Tales from the Hills* (1882). His popularity was confirmed with *Barrack Room Ballads and Other Verses* (1892), a volume that includes such well-known poems as "The Road to Mandalay," "If," and "Gunga Din." From 1892 to 1896 he lived with his American wife in New England, where he wrote *The Jungle Books* (1894, 1895). *Kim* (1901) is his best novel and the last he wrote with an Indian setting. Among his many other works is *Just So Stories* (1902), for children. He won the Nobel Prize in literature (1907).

kipper. *See* herring.

Kipp's apparatus A laboratory apparatus for producing a gas as a result of a reaction between a liquid and a solid. It is often used to produce hydrogen sulfide by reacting hydrochloric acid with sticks of ferrous sulfide ($2HCl + FeS = FeCl_2 + H_2S$). The device is named for its Dutch inventor, Petrus Jacobus Kipp (1808–64).

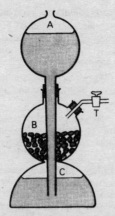

KIPP'S APPARATUS *When the tap* T *is opened the liquid in* C *rises until it reaches the solid in* B, *with which it reacts to produce a gas. When* T *is closed, gas production continues until the liquid has been forced back into* C *against the head produced by the liquid in the reservoir* A.

Kirchhoff, Gustav Robert (1824–87) German physicist, who was appointed professor at Heidelberg University in 1854. There, working with Robert *Bunsen, he invented the technique of spectroscopy. Using this technique, Kirchhoff and Bunsen discovered the elements cesium and rubidium in 1861. Kirchhoff, working alone, also discovered several elements in the sun, by investigating the solar spectrum. He is also known for his work on thermal radiation and on networks of electrical wires (*see* Kirchhoff's laws).

Kirchhoff's laws Two laws applying to electrical networks, discovered by G. R. *Kirchhoff. The first states that the net current flowing into and out of any point in the network is zero. The second states that the algebraic sum of the voltages in any closed loop of the network is equal to the algebraic sum of the products of the currents and the resistances through which they flow.

Kirchner, Ernst Ludwig (1880–1938) German expressionist painter and printmaker, who helped found the art movement called Die *Brücke (The Bridge) in 1905 (*see also* expressionism). His diverse influences ranged from *Grünewald to *Munch and African art in paintings notable for their eroticism, vibrant colors, and angular outlines. He painted many satirical street scenes in Berlin (1911–17) before moving to Switzerland, where he concentrated mainly on landscapes. After Nazi condemnation of his work he committed suicide.

Kirgiz Soviet Socialist Republic (*or* Kirgizia). *See* Kyrgyzstan.

Kiribati, Republic of (name until 1979: Gilbert Islands) A country in the S Pacific Ocean comprising the Gilbert Islands, the Phoenix Islands, and some of the Line Islands together with Ocean Island. The majority of the inhabitants are Micronesians. *Economy*: chiefly fishing and subsistence agriculture, including crops such as coconuts, pandanus palm, and breadfruit. Ocean Island is rich in phosphates, which, with copra, are the chief exports. *History*: first sighted by the Spanish in the 16th century, the islands became a center for sperm whale hunting in the 19th century. Part of the British protectorate of the Gilbert and Ellice Islands from 1892, they became a colony in 1915. Links with Ellice Islands (*see* Tuvalu, State of) were severed in 1975 and they became independent in 1979 as

the Republic of Kiribati. The Banabans of Ocean Island are seeking independence from Kiribati to become an associate state of Fiji. Chief minister: Teatao
Teannaki. Official languages: English and Gilbertese. Official currency: Australian dollar of 100 cents. Area: 332 sq mi (861 sq km). Population (1990):
65,600. Capital and main port: Tarawa.

Kirk, Norman (Eric) (1923–74) New Zealand statesman; Labour prime minister (1972–74). He implemented social-welfare and housing measures and recognized the People's Republic of China.

Kirkcaldy 56 07N 3 10W A city in E central Scotland, in Fife Region on the
Firth of Forth. It is a port, mainly for coastal trade, and manufactures linoleum
and coarse textiles, such as canvas. It is the birthplace of Adam Smith. Population (1981): 46,300.

Kirkland, (Joseph) Lane (1922–   ) US labor leader; head of the *AFL-CIO
(1979–   ). In the merchant marines during World War II, he graduated from
Georgetown School of Foreign Service (1948) and worked for George Meany,
head of the American Federation of Labor. After being named secretary-treasurer
of the merged AFL-CIO in 1969, he succeeded Meany as president in 1979.

Kirkuk 35 28N 44 26E A city in NE Iraq, in a rich oil field. It is the origin of
pipelines to Syria, Lebanon, and, until it was cut in the war of 1948, Haifa (Israel). Population (1985): 208,000.

Kirov (name from 1780 until 1934: Vyatka) 58 38N 49 38E A port in NW Russia on the Vyatka River. Founded in 1181, it fell to the Russians in the 15th century and became important as a stopping place on the Moscow–Siberia route. It
was renamed in honor of S. M. Kirov. Population (1991 est): 491,000.

Kirov, Sergei Mironovich (1888–1934) Soviet politician. As one of Stalin's
closest associates Kirov quickly rose to power and became first secretary of the
Leningrad branch of the Communist Party. His assassination, which Stalin
claimed to be part of a plot against the entire Soviet leadership and led to the
Great Purge trials (1934–38), was probably instigated by Stalin himself.

Kirovobad. *See* Gyandzha.

Kirov Ballet A Soviet ballet company based at the Kirov State Theater of
Opera and Ballet (formerly the Maryinsky Theater) in St Petersburg. The theater
was renamed in honor of S. M. *Kirov in 1935. The company's style of dancing
owes much to the Imperial Russian Ballet, founded in 1935, of which *Nijinsky
was a product. Some of the Kirov's leading dancers, including Rudolf
*Nureyev, Natalia Makarova, and Mikhail *Baryshnikov, defected to the West
and earned international reputations.

Kirovograd (name until 1924: Yelisavetgrad; name from 1924 until 1936: Zi-
noviyevsk) 48 31N 32 15E A city in S central Ukraine. It is a major agricultural
trading center. Population (1991 est): 278,000.

kirsch (*or* kirschwasser) A *spirit distilled from fermented liquor of wild cherries (German *Kirsch*, cherry). It is drunk neat, or used in cooking, especially in
cheese fondue or poured over pineapple.

Kisangani (name until 1966: Stanleyville) 0 33S 25 14E A riverport in NE
Zaïre, on the Zaïre River. It is an agricultural center and industries include furniture, brewing, and clothing. Zaïre University was founded here in 1963. Population (1991): 371,862.

Kish A city of ancient *Sumer, near Babylon. Built on Mesopotamia's fertile
alluvial plains, Kish was one of the oldest centers of civilization, retaining its
preeminence until eclipsed by *Ur (c. 2600 BC). Under the Babylonian empire

Kish became obscure but remained inhabited until the 2nd century AD. Excavated between 1923 and 1933, its site has produced valuable evidence of Sumerian civilization, including the earliest known example of writing—pictograms on a limestone tablet dating to soon after 3500 BC.

Kishinev (Romanian name: Chişinău) 47 00N 28 50E A city in and capital of Moldova. Founded in the 15th century, it passed from the Turks to the Russians (1812), becoming the capital of Bessarabia; it was under Romanian rule (1918–40). It is an important food-processing center. Population (1991 est): 677,000.

Kissinger, Henry (Alfred) (1923–) US diplomat and political scientist, born in Germany; secretary of state (1973–76). Appointed adviser to President Nixon on national security (1969), Kissinger and *Le Duc Tho were jointly awarded the Nobel Peace Prize (1973) for helping to negotiate an end to the Vietnam War. Under President Ford he became well known for his flying-shuttle style of diplomacy while negotiating a truce between Syria and Israel (1974). His publications include *Nuclear Weapons and Foreign Policy* (1956), *The White House Years* (1979), and *Years of Upheaval* (1982). He headed a bipartisan committee on Central America in 1983.

Kisumu 0 03S 34 47E A city in W Kenya, on the NE shore of Lake Victoria. It is an important commercial and industrial center with trade links with Mombasa. Population (1984 est): 167,000.

kit A tiny high-pitched violin used by dancing masters in the 18th century. Its neck, to accommodate the fingers, is disproportionately large.

Kitagawa Utamaro (1753–1806) Japanese artist of the *Ukiyo-e movement, whose color woodblock prints were the first to be popularized in Europe. His book of *Insects* (1788) introduced naturalistic observation into the art of color print. However, he specialized chiefly in scenes of women engaged in everyday tasks or pastimes and half-length portraits of women, such as the series of *Ten Physiognomies of Women* and *Beauties of the Gay Quarters*. In 1804 his prints of the military ruler's wife and mistresses so offended the government that he was handcuffed for 50 days.

Kitakyushu 33 52N 130 49E A city in Japan, in N Kyushu on the Shimonoseki Strait. Formed in 1963 from the cities of Wakamatsu, Yawata, Tobata, Kokura, and Moji, it is one of Japan's leading trade and deepsea fishing ports as well as an important center of heavy industry. Population (1990): 1,026,455.

Kitasato, Shibasaburo (1852–1931) Japanese bacteriologist, who, during an epidemic of bubonic plague in Hong Kong, identified the bacillus responsible. In Berlin Kitasato worked with *Behring on tetanus and diphtheria, demonstrating the value of antitoxin in conferring passive immunity. Kitasato founded a laboratory near Tokyo that was incorporated with the university in 1899. In 1914 he founded the Kitasato Institute.

Kitchener 43 27N 80 30W A city in central Canada, in SW Ontario. Established by German-speaking settlers after 1800, it was called Berlin until 1916. Kitchener is a financial, distribution, and manufacturing center, producing furniture, foods, and leather and rubber goods. Population (1981): 139,734.

Kitchener of Khartoum, Horatio Herbert, 1st Earl (1850–1916) British field marshal. After service with the Royal Engineers, he was appointed to the Egyptian army (1883), becoming commander in chief in 1892. By 1898, with the battle of Omdurman, he had reconquered the Sudan, becoming its governor general (1899). In the second *Boer War he suppressed the guerrillas by a scorched-earth policy and the internment of civilians in concentration camps. In

1914, as war secretary, his recruitment campaign was successful but he lost power in the direction of strategy.

kite A *hawk belonging to the subfamily *Milvinae*, which occurs throughout the world, most commonly in warm regions. Typically reddish brown and 21–23 in (52–57 cm) long, kites have long narrow wings, a long often forked tail, and a narrow bill and feed on insects, small mammals, and reptiles; some are scavengers.

kithara An ancient Greek plucked instrument, traditionally believed to have been invented by Apollo. It was a large wooden-framed *lyre; Greek vases show it held against the player's body. It was used to accompany epic song and declamation.

kittiwake A North Atlantic *gull, *Rissa tridactyla*, that is adapted for nesting on narrow cliff ledges. It is 16 in (40 cm) long and has a white plumage with black-tipped gray wings, short black legs, dark eyes, and a yellow bill. It feeds at sea on fish and offal, going ashore only to breed. Kittiwakes nest in dense colonies, anchoring their seaweed nests with mud.

Kitwe 12 48S 28 14E A city in N central Zambia. It is the chief commercial, industrial, and communications center of the *Copperbelt. Population (1990): 338,207.

Kitzbühel 47 27N 12 23E A town in W Austria, in the Tirol in the Kitzbühel Alps. A famous winter sports center, it is also a health and tourist resort. Population: 8000.

Kivi, Alexis (A. Stenvall; 1834–72) Finnish poet, dramatist, and novelist, who was chiefly responsible for establishing the western dialect as the modern literary language of Finland. His greatest work was the novel *Seitsemän veljestä* (*Seven Brothers*; 1870), a naturalistic portrayal of rural life.

Kivu, Lake 1 50S 29 10E A lake between Zaïre and Rwanda. It is 60 mi (96 km) long and drained by the Ruzizi River S into Lake Tanganyika.

kiwi (bird) A secretive flightless bird belonging to a family (*Apterygidae*; 3 species) occurring in forested regions of New Zealand; 10–16 in (25–40 cm) long, kiwis have tiny wings hidden in coarse gray-brown plumage and strong legs with large claws. Kiwis are nocturnal and have weak eyes but well-developed hearing; the long bill is used to probe the soil for worms, insect larvae, etc. The kiwi is the national emblem of New Zealand. Order: *Apterygiformes*.

kiwi (plant) A Chinese climbing shrub, *Actinidia chinensis*, also called Chinese gooseberry. It has hairy leaves, white or yellow flowers, and an edible rough-skinned fruit, up to 2 in (5 cm) long, which has a gooseberry-like flavor. Family: *Actinidiaceae*.

Klaipeda (German name: Memel) 55 43N 21 07E A port in Lithuania, on the Baltic Sea. It has shipyards and other industries include fish canning, textiles, and fertilizers. *History*: dating from the 7th century AD, it was conquered by the Teutonic Knights in 1252, subsequently passing under Prussian rule. In 1919, after World War I, the Allies imposed a French administration over the region, which was seized by Lithuania in 1923. The Memel Statute (1924) recognized Lithuanian possession. It was occupied by the Germans in World War II. Population (1991 est): 208,000.

Klaproth, Martin Heinrich (1743–1817) German chemist, who pioneered the techniques of analytical chemistry. He isolated the oxides of uranium, zirconium, and titanium from minerals and investigated the chemistry of the rare-earth metals.